CHURCH
Socials

782 Delicious Recipes
from Our Church Communities for All
Your Special Celebrations

Edited by

BARBARA GREENMAN

Illustrations by

HIROKO SANDERS

BLACK DOG
& LEVENTHAL
PUBLISHERS
NEW YORK

CHURCH SOCIALS

Text copyright © 2008 by Black Dog & Leventhal Publishers, Inc.
Illustrations copyright © 2008 by Hiroko Sanders

Published by
Black Dog & Leventhal Publishers, Inc.
151 West 19th Street
New York, NY 10011

Designed by Susi Oberhelman
Lace border by Karen Stimson, www.woolsweaterstreet.com

Manufactured in China

ISBN 978-1-57912-430-4

Contents

Introduction

The inspiration for this book came more than a year ago when wonderful feedback poured in for the recipes in its predecessor, *Church Suppers*. The churchgoing community sent us many comments such as, "Perfect for potlucks or big crowds," and "This is a winner at every bake sale." One note, "Great when made 24 hours before the event," made me ask, "What event?" The answer was a community Thanksgiving dinner at a church in the Midwest, where, they told me, hardly a month goes by without a gala church social featuring delicious food from all the parishioners.

"Church social"—does the term have an old-fashioned ring? It did to me, until I realized how varied and new its meaning is today. We asked churches across the country to tell us about their events, and contribute favorite recipes. From the very first replies it was clear that in America today—winter, spring, summer, or fall, for any occasion and at any hour on any day—there is a church social, or maybe hundreds, in full swing.

A church social can be any event where members and friends—and often the entire community—gather for good fellowship, support for the needy, entertainment, and delicious food. In warm weather, it might be an Easter pancake breakfast, a picnic on the grounds, a strawberry social, a watermelon-eating contest, a graduation party, a hayride, a bake sale, or a harvest celebration. Winter days are busy with coffee hours, potluck suppers, community Thanksgiving dinners, chili cook-offs, Valentine's Day banquets, and formal Christmas dinners and caroling concerts. In any season, a brunch or supper may be celebrating a baptism or a confirmation, a wedding, a birthday, or a house blessing.

The term "dinner on the grounds" was new to me, although a quick Internet search leads to thousands of links to this popular phrase. We decided dinner on the grounds deserved a chapter of its own, where we could include many recipes for quick and delicious (mostly warm-weather) dishes, brimming with fresh summer fruits and vegetables. The Southern tradition of dinner on the grounds began at a time when inadequate transportation prevented churchgoers from traveling home after morning services. Each family packed food for the day, spread a cloth on the ground, and stayed for the evening service before returning home. A dinner on the grounds, it seems, can be any informal feast consumed either *on* the ground on a blanket or at a picnic table, or inside the church hall. And today, dinners on the grounds often accompany a day of sacred harp, or shape-note, singing, which is another uniquely American tradition enjoying renewed popularity in churches across the country.

While many of these traditions remain, what's new today is the scope of the church social. In the 1960s, churches responded to changes in urban America and began shifting events away from feeding their own members to feeding the community at large. Today, a church's community concerns appear in its social events. Parties with a purpose raise money to help the elderly, the sick, and the homeless, like Feeding the 5,000 (page 76) and the Annual Community Thanksgiving Dinner (page 196).

What hasn't changed is the central role food plays at church gatherings. And it is the members, in their own church cookbooks, who have provided treasured, home-tested recipes often handed down from one generation to the next. The men and women who know their recipes will be set down in black and white type and bound in between book covers make sure they contribute their very best. And so, from the more than 12,000 recipes submitted to us, we selected the best of the best—arranged in chapters devoted to after-the-service breakfasts, dinners on the grounds, potluck suppers, holidays and special celebrations, bake sale treats, and kids' favorites. Several churches contributed special-event menus with accompanying recipes that have been perennial favorites, and we have highlighted these in each chapter.

The majority of the recipes in *Church Socials* are family size. But if you are planning to feed a crowd at a church event, a family reunion, a neighborhood barbeque, or any gathering of 12 to 100 guests, you will find helpful tips for multiplying recipes and food quantity charts in Cooking for a Crowd (page 390). These helpful tips will ensure your crowd doesn't leave hungry!

Special thanks, again, to my publisher, J. P. Leventhal, for his support and encouragement, to my editor, Judy Pray, who is always the first to know what I'm trying to do and makes it better, to Candie Frankel, copyeditor extraordinaire, Hiroko Sanders, illustrator, and Susi Oberhelman, designer.

True to the spirit of church socials, this book relies on a network of members who shared with us the menus and recipes from the special annual events in their churches. Thanks to Kristine Walden for the Easter Pancake Breakfast at Harrison Community Baptist Church, Harrison, Idaho; to Holly Day for the Annual Community Thanksgiving Dinner at Cumming First United Methodist Church, Cumming, Georgia; to Carrolyn Schmidt for the Mariners' Christmas Party at First Presbyterian Church, Berkeley, California; and to Gary Cook for the Valentine Dinner and Dance at Crescent Hill Presbyterian Church, Louisville, Kentucky. Many other contributors and contributing churches are listed on the next page. You all made this book possible.

BARBARA GREENMAN

CONTRIBUTORS AND CONTRIBUTING CHURCHES

Karen Betler
Ruby Carr
Gus Clouse
Gary Cook
Catherine Cutter
Holly Day
Patsy Ferebee
Judith Gaines,
    The Good News Shop
Elizabeth Green
Karen Hanna
Susan Hindle
Kathy Hoagland
Darrell Huckaby, author
    Dinner on the Grounds
Louise Kirkland
Nancy Litteral
Carl Molesworth,
    Welcome Press
Cindy Morris,
    Cookbook Publishers, Inc.
Ruby Olson
Janese Passow
Julie Peak
Melanie Petru
Reta Romans
Michael Scharff
Carrolyn Schmidt
June Spielman
Carol Stevens
Linda Thompson
Judy Tonseth
Kristine Walden
Barbara White

Ascension Lutheran Church, Minocqua, Wisconsin
Christ Church, Frederica, St. Simons Island, Georgia
Christ Episcopal Church, Charlotte, North Carolina
Church of the Canyons Women's Ministries, Canyon Country,
    California
Crescent Hill Presbyterian Church, Louisville, Kentucky
Cumming First United Methodist Church, Cumming, Georgia
First Baptist Church, Russell, Kentucky
First Moravian Church, Greensboro, North Carolina
First Presbyterian Church, Berkeley, California
First Presbyterian Church, Du Quoin, Illinois
Grace on the Hill United Methodist Church, Corbin, Kentucky
Harrison Community Baptist Church, Harrison, Idaho
Memorial Baptist Church, Tulsa, Oklahoma
Messiah United Methodist Church, York, Pennsylvania
Methow Valley United Methodist Church, Twisp, Washington
Miracle Deliverance Holiness Church, Columbia, South Carolina
Northbrook United Methodist Church, Roswell, Georgia
Oakwood Church of God in Christ, Godfrey, Illinois
Pinemount Baptist Church, McAlpin, Florida
Pittsboro Baptist Church, Pittsboro, North Carolina
Presbyterian Church of Gonzales, Gonzales, Texas
Sorento Assembly of God Church, Sorento, Illinois
St. Andrew's Episcopal Church, Rocky Mount, North Carolina
St John's Guild, St. John's Church, West Bend, Wisconsin
St. Mark's Lutheran Church, Conshohocken, Pennsylvania
Terrace Acres Baptist Church, Fort Worth, Texas
Trinity Evangelical Lutheran Church, Lansdale, Pennsylvania
Trinity Presbyterian Church, Little Rock, Arkansas
United Methodist Church, Estancia, New Mexico
Unity Baptist Church, Morgantown, Indiana
Vincent Memorial United Methodist Church, Nutter Fort,
    West Virginia
Westside Baptist Church, Antlers, Oklahoma
Women's Missionary Auxiliary, Bay Springs, Mississippi

After the Service

ANNUAL EASTER BREAKFAST— AND THE MEN DO THE COOKING!

For many years, the men of the Harrison Community Baptist Church in Harrison, Idaho, have hosted an annual Easter breakfast for the community. We asked one of the gentlemen of the church, Paul Anderson, how long the church had been doing the breakfast. He remembered attending in the early 1960s, when he returned home from a tour in the military and came to Harrison with his parents. No, there's no family recipe involved. Even back then, the chefs relied on Krusteaz pancake mix, but they always added huckleberries—Idaho's state fruit—picked the previous summer (the location is top secret) and frozen for almost a year. Come Easter, the berries are generously stirred into the batter for a truly mouthwatering treat and a harbinger of summer days to come.

Over time, parishioners at Our Lady of Perpetual Help made it a tradition to come down the hill and join in the fun, and now their men are helping prepare and serve the food—platters of ham, eggs, pancakes, and pitchers of coffee and juice. Ours is one church basement you'll never leave hungry.

HARRISON COMMUNITY BAPTIST CHURCH
Harrison, Idaho

Huckleberry Pancakes

1 cup Krusteaz pancake mix
¾ cup cold water
Handful of huckleberries

1. Lightly grease an electric griddle and preheat to 375°F.
2. Place pancake mix in a gallon pitcher, add water, and whisk just until moistened, so that the batter remains slightly lumpy. Fold in huckleberries.
3. Pour about ¼ cup of batter onto griddle and pray. Cook for 1 to 1½ minutes, just until the underside is golden brown. Flip once and cook 1 minute more. Serve hot. Makes 8 small pancakes.

❖ **HARRISON COMMUNITY BAPTIST CHURCH** | Harrison, Idaho

Morning Orange Drink

1 can (6 oz.) frozen orange juice concentrate
1 cup cold water
1 cup milk

⅓ cup sugar
1 teaspoon vanilla
10 ice cubes

1. Combine orange juice, water, milk, sugar, and vanilla in a blender at high speed.
2. Add ice cubes a few at a time and blend until smooth. Serve immediately. Makes 4 to 6 servings.

❖ **SARA GOTTLIEB** | Trinity Evangelical Lutheran Church, Lansdale, Pennsylvania

Orange Mist Drink

3 cups unsweetened orange juice, divided
1 tablespoon lemon juice
1 cup lemon-lime sparkling water, chilled

1. Pour 1½ cups of the orange juice into an ice cube tray. Freeze until firm, about 4 hours.
2. Release frozen orange juice cubes into the container of an electric blender. Add the remaining 1½ cups orange juice and lemon juice. Cover and blend until slushy.
3. Combine juice mixture and sparkling water in a serving pitcher, stirring well. Makes 1 quart.

❖ **JANE VAUGHT** | First Moravian Church, Greensboro, North Carolina

Coffee Lovers' Freeze

¾ cup sugar
1½ cups milk
1½ cups coffee, chilled

1 teaspoon vanilla
2 cups whipping cream, divided

1. Combine sugar and milk in a large saucepan over medium heat. Bring to a boil and stir until sugar is dissolved. Remove from heat. Allow to cool.

2. Add coffee, vanilla, and 1 cup of the whipping cream to milk mixture, stirring until well blended. Pour mixture into a loaf pan. Freeze until slushy, 1 to 2 hours.

3. Just before serving, beat remaining cup of whipping cream until stiff peaks begin to form. Stir slush mixture, spoon it into dessert dishes, and top with a dollop of whipped cream. Makes 12 servings.

FREDA GANTT | Methow Valley United Methodist Church, Twisp, Washington

Kerah's Tea Scones

½ cup milk
3 tea bags
1 egg, lightly beaten
2 cups flour

2 teaspoons baking powder
½ cup sugar
¼ teaspoon salt
¼ cup butter, chilled, cut into pieces

1. Heat milk in small saucepan until boiling. Add tea bags, cover, and remove from heat. Let steep for 5 minutes. Remove tea bags and allow to cool. Add egg and beat well.

2. Preheat oven to 400°F. Lightly coat a baking sheet with nonstick cooking spray and dust with flour.

3. Combine flour, baking powder, sugar, and salt in the bowl of a food processor. Add butter and process for 25 seconds. Gradually add tea mixture, pulsing just to combine.

4. Turn dough onto baking sheet and pat into an 8-inch circle. Score with a knife into 8 wedges but do not separate. Bake for 20 to 25 minutes or until golden brown. Cool on a wire rack. Makes 8 servings.

JEAN SPRATT | Christ Episcopal Church, Charlotte, North Carolina

Curried Fruits

1 can (16 oz.) pineapple chunks, drained
1 can (16 oz.) peach halves, drained
1 can (16 oz.) pear halves, drained
1 can (16 oz.) apricots, drained
1 jar (6 oz.) Maraschinos, drained

5⅓ tablespoons butter, melted
¾ cup brown sugar
2 teaspoons curry powder
⅔ cup blanched slivered almonds or
    ½ cup chopped pecans (optional)

1. Preheat oven to 325°F.

2. Arrange pineapple, peaches, pears, apricots, and Maraschinos in a 2-quart casserole.

3. Combine melted butter, brown sugar, and curry powder. Pour over fruit. Sprinkle with almonds or pecans. Bake until fruits are cooked and top is bubbling and caramelized, about 1 hour. Allow to cool at least 10 minutes before serving. Makes 8 servings.

 **MARY REDDING** | Christ Episcopal Church, Charlotte, North Carolina

Fruit Soup

2 cups sliced strawberries	2 to 3 tablespoons sugar
3 or 4 bananas, sliced	4 tablespoons tapioca
1 cup sliced seedless grapes	2½ cups water, divided
3 or 4 fresh peaches, sliced	1 can (6 oz.) frozen orange juice concentrate

1. Place strawberries, bananas, grapes, and peaches in a large serving bowl.

2. Combine sugar, tapioca, and 1 cup of the water in a saucepan over medium heat. Cook until sugar dissolves and mixture turns thick and clear. Add orange juice concentrate and stir until melted. Stir in remaining 1½ cups water.

3. Pour mixture over fruit and allow to cool. Serve chilled. Makes 6 to 8 servings.

DOT HEASLIP | Christ Episcopal Church, Charlotte, North Carolina

Cranberry Fruit Dip

1 container (8 oz.) vanilla-flavored yogurt
½ cup cranberry-orange relish
¼ teaspoon nutmeg
¼ teaspoon ginger
Orange peel twist (for garnish)
Assorted fresh or canned fruit

1. Combine yogurt, cranberry-orange relish, nutmeg, and ginger in a small bowl. Stir with a fork until well blended. Cover and chill.

2. Spoon dip into a small bowl and garnish with an orange peel twist. Serve with assorted fruits for dipping. Makes about 1¼ cups.

These fruits are good for dipping:
- apple slices
- banana chunks
- mandarin orange slices
- pineapple chunks
- whole strawberries
- kiwifruit slices
- pear slices
- peach slices

 **JOAN HOLOHAN** | St. Mark's Lutheran Church, Conshohocken, Pennsylvania

Fruit Dip

1 package (8 oz.) cream cheese,
   room temperature
½ cup sour cream
1 cup whipped cream

¼ cup sugar
¼ cup brown sugar
1 tablespoon maple syrup
1 teaspoon vanilla

1. Combine cream cheese, sour cream, and whipped cream in a medium bowl.
2. Add sugar, brown sugar, maple syrup, and vanilla. Mix until well blended and smooth. Chill until ready to serve. Makes 2 cups.

❖ LAYLA BURNEY | Methow Valley United Methodist Church, Twisp, Washington

Sour Cream Dip for Strawberries

1 cup sour cream
1 teaspoon grated lemon zest
1 teaspoon lemon juice

½ cup confectioners' sugar
Whole fresh strawberries

1. Combine sour cream, lemon zest, lemon juice, and confectioners' sugar in a medium bowl.
2. Beat with a handheld electric or rotary beater until light and fluffy. Serve with fresh strawberries for dipping. Makes 1¼ cups.

❖ MEMORIAL BAPTIST CHURCH | Tulsa, Oklahoma

Minted Lime Dressing

1 container (8 oz.) plain yogurt
½ to 1 teaspoon grated lime zest
1 tablespoon lime juice
2 teaspoons sugar

2 teaspoons finely snipped mint or
   ½ teaspoon crushed dried mint
¼ teaspoon salt

1. Combine yogurt, lime zest, lime juice, sugar, mint, and salt in a small bowl.
2. Stir until well blended. Cover and chill. Serve over cut-up fresh fruit. Makes 1 cup.

❖ SUSAN SEGRAVES | Trinity Evangelical Lutheran Church, Lansdale, Pennsylvania

Hot Spiced Fruit

3 pears, peeled, cored, and sliced
3 Golden Delicious, Granny Smith,
   or Rome Beauty apples, peeled,
   cored, and sliced
1 can (11 oz.) mandarin oranges, drained
1 cup fresh cranberries, rinsed and
   coarsely chopped

¼ cup brown sugar
2 tablespoons cornstarch
¼ teaspoon cinnamon
¼ teaspoon ginger
⅛ teaspoon cloves
1 cup apple, white grape, or
   cranberry juice

1. Preheat oven to 375°F. Grease a 2½-quart shallow baking dish.

2. Place pears, apples, mandarin oranges, and cranberries in baking dish.

3. Combine brown sugar, cornstarch, cinnamon, ginger, and cloves in a small bowl. Add apple, white grape, or cranberry juice and stir. Pour mixture over fruit. Bake uncovered for 30 to 35 minutes or until fruit is tender. Allow to cool at least 10 minutes before serving. Serve warm or chilled. Makes 12 servings.

✧ SUSAN SEGRAVES | Trinity Evangelical Lutheran Church, Lansdale, Pennsylvania

Apple Cinnamon French Toast

5 tablespoons butter
2 or 3 large baking apples, peeled, cored,
   and sliced; prepare more if needed
1 cup brown sugar
2 tablespoons dark corn syrup

1 teaspoon cinnamon
8 thick slices of French bread
3 large eggs
1 cup milk
1 teaspoon vanilla

1. Melt butter in a large heavy skillet over medium heat. Add apple slices and cook, stirring occasionally, until tender, 4 to 6 minutes. Add brown sugar, corn syrup, and cinnamon, stirring until brown sugar dissolves.

2. Transfer apple mixture to a 13 x 9 x 2-inch baking dish and spread evenly. Arrange bread slices in a single layer on top.

3. Whisk together eggs, milk, and vanilla. Pour egg mixture over egg slices. Cover with plastic wrap, place in refrigerator, and let set overnight.

4. Preheat oven to 375°F. Remove plastic wrap. Bake for 30 to 35 minutes or until firm and golden. Allow to cool in pan 5 minutes. To serve, invert onto a large platter so that apple layer is on the top. Makes 8 servings.

✧ JANICE KELLER | Trinity Evangelical Lutheran Church, Lansdale, Pennsylvania

French Toast Casserole

1 large loaf French bread, cut into 1-inch cubes
8 eggs, beaten
3 cups milk
4 tablespoons sugar
2 teaspoons vanilla
Dash of salt
Cinnamon
Butter

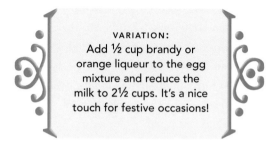

VARIATION:
Add ½ cup brandy or orange liqueur to the egg mixture and reduce the milk to 2½ cups. It's a nice touch for festive occasions!

1. Grease a 13 x 9 x 2-inch baking dish. Add bread cubes and spread evenly.

2. Whisk together eggs, milk, sugar, vanilla, and salt. Pour over bread cubes. Cover with plastic wrap, place in refrigerator, and let set at least 8 hours or overnight.

3. Preheat oven to 350°F. Remove plastic wrap from baking dish. Sprinkle cinnamon over the top and dot with butter. Bake for 45 minutes or until lightly browned. Makes 8 servings.

❖ **LINDA BRENNAN** | Trinity Evangelical Lutheran Church, Lansdale, Pennsylvania

French Toast Soufflé

16 slices of hearty white bread,
   cut into cubes (about 10 cups)
Cooking spray
1 package (8 oz.) Neufchâtel,
   room temperature
8 eggs

1½ cups 2% milk
⅔ cup half-and-half
1¼ cups maple syrup, divided
½ teaspoon vanilla
2 tablespoons confectioners' sugar

1. Lightly coat a 13 x 9 x 2-inch baking dish with cooking spray. Layer bread cubes evenly in dish.

2. Beat Neufchâtel in a large mixer bowl at medium speed until soft and fluffy. Add eggs one at a time, beating well after each addition. Add milk, half-and-half, ½ cup of the maple syrup, and vanilla. Beat until smooth.

3. Pour mixture over bread cubes, cover with plastic wrap, and refrigerate overnight.

4. Preheat oven to 375°F. Remove baking dish from refrigerator and let stand 30 minutes. Bake for 50 minutes or until set. Sprinkle confectioners' sugar over the top. Pass remaining ¾ cup maple syrup on the side. Makes 8 servings.

❖ **PATSY FEREBEE** | St. Andrew's Episcopal Church, Rocky Mount, North Carolina

Jane's Puffy Apple Pancakes

2 tablespoons butter
½ cup plus 2 tablespoons sugar, divided
1 cup water
6 Granny Smith apples, peeled, cored,
    and cut into wedges

3 eggs
¾ cup milk
¾ cup flour
¼ teaspoon salt

1. Preheat oven to 425°F.
2. Heat butter, ½ cup of the sugar, and water in 12-inch oven-safe skillet over medium heat. Bring to a boil, add apples, and cook, stirring occasionally, until apples begin to caramelize, about 15 minutes.
3. Combine eggs, milk, flour, salt, and remaining 2 tablespoons sugar in a blender or food processor fitted with a dough blade. Blend until smooth.
4. Pour batter over apples. Transfer skillet to oven and bake for 15 to 20 minutes or until lightly browned. Serve warm. Makes 6 servings.

LOUISE BEACH | Trinity Presbyterian Church, Little Rock, Arkansas

Sourdough Pancakes

3 cups water
3 cups flour
1 envelope (.25 oz.) active dry yeast
3 eggs

1 tablespoon salt
1 tablespoon sugar
1 teaspoon baking soda
3 tablespoons oil, plus more for griddle

1. Combine water, flour, and yeast in a large bowl. Allow to stand overnight at room temperature.
2. Add eggs, salt, sugar, baking soda, and oil to batter. Mix until well combined.
3. Heat griddle and add a small amount of oil. Pour or ladle batter onto hot griddle. Cook until small bubbles form on the surface and burst, 3 to 5 minutes. Flip the pancakes and cook until the underside is browned, 2 to 4 minutes more. Makes 4 to 6 servings.

SHIRLENE HEPLER | Messiah United Methodist Church, York, Pennsylvania

For perfectly cooked pancakes, the griddle and oil must be hot. Let a few drops of batter fall onto the surface to test if it's ready. If the batter sizzles, the griddle is ready to cook!

Autumn Apple Pancakes

1 cup chunky applesauce

2 cups pancake mix

2 eggs, beaten

1 cup milk

1 teaspoon cinnamon

¾ cup brown sugar

1. Apply nonstick cooking spray to an electric skillet. Preheat to 375°F.

2. Combine applesauce, pancake mix, eggs, milk, cinnamon, and brown sugar in a medium bowl. Mix with a spatula or wooden spoon until smooth.

3. Drop 2 tablespoons of batter onto skillet for each apple pancake. Cook, flipping once, until lightly browned on each side, about 4 minutes total. Serve with applesauce or syrup. Makes 4 servings.

❖ **SHIRLENE HEPLER** | Messiah United Methodist Church, York, Pennsylvania

Oatmeal Pancakes with Orange Sauce

1½ cups rolled oats

2 cups milk

1 cup flour

2½ teaspoons baking powder

1 teaspoon salt

2 tablespoons sugar

2 eggs, beaten

¼ cup wheat germ

⅓ cup oil

1. Place oats in a medium bowl. Pour milk over oats, cover, and let stand.

2. Sift together flour, baking powder, salt, and sugar.

3. Stir eggs into oats mixture. Add flour mixture and wheat germ and stir to combine. Stir in oil.

4. Pour or ladle batter onto a hot greased griddle and cook, flipping once, until golden brown on both sides, about 4 minutes total. Serve immediately with warm orange sauce passed on the side (recipe follows). Makes 4 to 6 servings.

ORANGE SAUCE

1 cup sugar

2 tablespoons cornstarch

2 cups orange juice

2 tablespoons lemon juice

½ cup butter

1. Whisk together sugar and cornstarch in a medium saucepan.

2. Stir in orange juice and lemon juice and set over medium heat. Cook, stirring continuously, until mixture thickens and turns clear.

3. Bring to a boil and cook for 1 minute, stirring constantly. Remove from heat. Blend in butter. Transfer to a small pitcher and keep warm until ready to serve. Makes 2 cups.

Cook the orange sauce while the oats for the pancakes are soaking.

❖ **JUDI LEMAY** | Church of the Canyons Women's Ministries, Canyon Country, California

Zucchini Pancakes

2 cups shredded zucchini
½ cup Bisquick baking mix
¼ cup Parmesan
2 eggs

Salt and pepper
Oil for frying
Sour cream

1. Toss zucchini, baking mix, and Parmesan in a large bowl. Add eggs and mix until well combined. Season with salt and pepper.

2. Heat oil in a heavy skillet over medium heat. Drop zucchini mixture by the heaping tablespoonful into hot oil and flatten with a spatula. Fry, flipping once, until golden brown on both sides, 8 to 10 minutes. Continue cooking in batches until all mixture is used. Serve topped with sour cream. Makes 12 pancakes.

JUDI LEMAY | Church of the Canyons Women's Ministries, Canyon Country, California

Happy Pancake Day

Most people love to eat warm pancakes covered with butter and syrup in the morning. But do you know that the pancake has a holiday all its own? Pancake Day (or Pancake Tuesday) is a tradition that started many years ago in England. It occurs annually the day before Ash Wednesday, a day known in different countries as Shrove Tuesday, Fat Tuesday, Mardi Gras, Carnival, Fastnacht, and Fetter Dienstag. But for those who routinely celebrate breakfast, it is better known as Pancake Day.

Large or small, fat or wafer thin, and made with a wide range of flours, pancakes are given different names by different peoples. There are American hotcakes, griddlecakes, or flapjacks, French crêpes, Hungarian palacsinta, Scottish drop-scones, Chinese egg rolls, Jewish blintzes, Russian blini, Italian cannelloni, Swedish plättar, Mexican tortillas, Indian dosas, German pfannkuchen, Norwegian lefser, Australian pikelets, Austrian palatschinken, and Welsh crempogs.

Bacon Quiche

8 to 10 slices of bacon

½ cup coarsely chopped onion

1 unbaked 9- or 10-inch pie shell

1 egg white, lightly beaten

1 cup grated Swiss cheese

2 cups evaporated milk

4 eggs, beaten

¾ teaspoon salt

½ teaspoon pepper

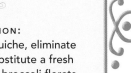

A custard filling is set when a knife inserted 2 inches from the edge of the crust comes out dry.

VARIATION:
For a vegetable quiche, eliminate the bacon and substitute a fresh vegetable, such as broccoli florets. Steam the florets for 6 minutes before adding them to the quiche.

1. Preheat oven to 450°F.

2. Fry bacon in a skillet over high heat until crisp. Drain on paper towels. Crumble.

3. Pour off all but 1 tablespoon of the bacon drippings from skillet. Return skillet to medium heat, add onion, and sauté until browned, 6 to 8 minutes.

4. Brush pie shell with egg white. Layer bacon, onion, and cheese into pie shell. Whisk together evaporated milk and eggs and pour into pie shell. Sprinkle with salt and pepper. Place in oven, immediately reduce heat to 400°F, and bake for 12 minutes. Reduce heat to 325°F and bake 30 minutes more, or until custard is set and lightly browned. Serve hot. Makes 4 to 6 servings.

KATHY JOHANNESSON | Trinity Evangelical Lutheran Church, Lansdale, Pennsylvania

Brunch in a Dish

1 lb. hot or sweet sausage
1 package (16 oz.) frozen hash
   browns, thawed
6 eggs, beaten

1½ cups milk
Salt and pepper
1 cup grated cheddar cheese

1. Preheat oven to 350°F. Lightly grease a 13 x 9 x 2-inch baking dish.
2. Brown sausage in a skillet over medium heat. Drain on paper towels.
3. Layer sausage and potatoes in baking dish. Whisk together eggs, milk, and salt and pepper. Pour egg mixture evenly over sausage and potatoes. Add cheddar cheese on top. Cover with foil and bake for 45 minutes. Remove foil and bake 15 minutes more, or until eggs are set. Makes 8 servings.

SARA LOWE | Christ Episcopal Church, Charlotte, North Carolina

Tomato Pie

2 or 3 tomatoes
Seasoned salt
1 Vidalia onion, sliced
Dried basil flakes

1 prebaked 9-inch pie shell
Mayonnaise
Grated cheese
Crumbled cooked bacon

1. Preheat oven to 350°F.
2. Core and slice tomatoes, sprinkle with seasoned salt, and set on paper towels to drain.
3. Layer tomatoes, onion, and dried basil in pie shell. Spread mayonnaise over the top. Top with grated cheese and bacon bits. Bake for 30 to 40 minutes or until topping is golden brown. Makes 4 to 6 servings.

PATSY FEREBEE | St. Andrew's Episcopal Church, Rocky Mount, North Carolina

Gouda Grits

1 cup quick grits
½ cup butter
1 round (8 oz.) Gouda, shredded

1 can (12 oz.) evaporated milk
Paprika

1. Preheat oven to 350°F. Lightly butter a 1½-quart casserole.
2. Cook grits according to package directions.
3. Combine grits, butter, Gouda, and evaporated milk, stirring until well blended. Pour mixture into casserole. Bake for 45 to 60 minutes. Serve hot, garnished with paprika. Makes 6 servings.

JUDY GAINES | Christ Episcopal Church, Charlotte, North Carolina

Grits Casserole

1 cup quick-cooking grits
1 teaspoon seasoned salt (such as Lawry's)
1 roll (4 oz.) garlic-flavored cheese
½ cup butter
2 eggs

Milk
3 slices of bacon, cooked and crumbled
1 cup cornflakes, crushed
½ cup grated sharp cheddar cheese

1. Preheat oven to 350°F. Lightly grease a 1½-quart casserole.

2. Combine grits and seasoned salt. Cook grits following package directions.

3. Add garlic cheese and butter to hot cooked grits, stirring to blend as butter melts.

4. Beat eggs until frothy. Transfer eggs to a measuring cup and add milk until liquid measures 1 cup. Add egg mixture to grits and stir to combine. Transfer grits to casserole. Sprinkle crumbled bacon, crushed cornflakes, and grated cheddar cheese over the top. Bake for 45 minutes or until cheese is bubbling. Makes 6 to 8 servings.

PATSY FEREBEE | St. Andrew's Episcopal Church, Rocky Mount, North Carolina

Delicious Potatoes

2 packages (1 lb. each) frozen hash browns
1 teaspoon salt
½ cup chopped onions
2 cups grated cheese

2 cups sour cream or low-fat sour cream
2 cans (10.75 oz. each) cream of chicken soup
1½ cups cornflakes, crushed
½ cup butter, melted

1. Preheat oven to 350°F. Break up potatoes and put in a 13 x 9 x 2-inch baking dish. Sprinkle with salt.

2. Combine onions, grated cheese, sour cream, and cream of chicken soup. Stir until well blended. Spread mixture evenly over potatoes.

3. Combine crushed cornflakes and melted butter. Layer evenly over top of casserole. Bake for 45 minutes. Serve hot. Makes 12 servings.

JAN CLARK, JUDY FERLA, BEV MCGUIRE, and **FAY S. MILLER** | Trinity Evangelical Lutheran Church, Lansdale, Pennsylvania

Sausage and Cheese Casserole

12 slices of bread, crusts removed, divided
1 lb. sausage
1½ cups grated cheddar cheese
5 eggs

2 cups milk
1 teaspoon mustard
1 teaspoon salt

1. Lightly butter 13 x 9 x 2-inch baking dish. Line bottom of dish with 6 slices of the bread.

2. Brown sausage in a skillet over medium heat. Drain on paper towels.

3. Combine sausage and cheddar cheese in a medium bowl. Spread over bread in baking dish. Top with remaining 6 slices of bread.

4. Whisk together eggs, milk, mustard, and salt. Pour over bread layers. Cover with plastic wrap and refrigerate several hours or overnight.

5. Preheat oven to 350°F. Remove plastic wrap and bake casserole for 30 to 40 minutes. Serve hot. Makes 6 servings.

PATSY FEREBEE | St. Andrew's Episcopal Church, Rock Mount, North Carolina

Prayer of Thanks

For each new morning with its light,
For rest and shelter of the night,
For health and food,
For love and friends,
For everything Thy goodness sends.
Father in heaven,
We thank Thee.

RALPH WALDO EMERSON

Bacon and Cheese Oven Omelet

6 slices American cheese

12 slices of bacon

8 eggs, beaten

1 cup milk

1. Preheat oven to 350°F. Lightly butter a 9-inch pie plate. Cut cheese slices in half and layer into bottom of pie plate.

2. Cook bacon in a skillet over high heat until almost crisp. Drain on paper towels. Roll one slice into a curl and finely chop four slices.

3. Whisk together eggs and milk. Add chopped bacon. Pour egg mixture into pie plate. Bake for 30 minutes.

4. Set bacon curl on top of omelet at center and arrange remaining 7 slices of bacon around it. Return omelet to oven and bake 10 minutes more, or until bacon curl and slices turn crisp. Let stand 5 minutes before cutting. Makes 5 to 6 servings.

FAY S. MILLER | Trinity Evangelical Lutheran Church, Lansdale, Pennsylvania

Blueberry Buckle Coffee Cake

½ cup butter
¾ cup sugar
1 egg
2 cups flour
2 teaspoons baking powder
½ teaspoon salt
½ cup milk
1½ to 2 cups blueberries

TOPPING:
⅔ cup sugar
2 tablespoons flour
1 teaspoon cinnamon
½ cup butter

1. Preheat oven to 350°F. Lightly grease a 13 x 9 x 2-inch baking pan.

2. Cream butter and sugar in the large bowl of an electric mixer. Add egg and beat well. With mixer running, gradually add flour, baking powder, salt, and milk. Fold in blueberries. Spread batter evenly in baking pan.

3. To make topping: Combine sugar, flour, and cinnamon. Sprinkle topping evenly over batter in pan. Dot with butter. Bake for 30 minutes or until topping is browned. Cool in pan. To serve, cut into squares. Makes 1 coffee cake.

❖ **KATE BUCKFELDER** | Christ Episcopal Church, Charlotte, North Carolina

Banana Brunch Bundt Coffee Cake

2 ripe bananas, mashed
1 package (18.25 oz.) yellow cake mix
1 package (3.4 oz.) instant vanilla
    pudding mix
½ cup vegetable oil
4 eggs

1 teaspoon vanilla
½ cup chopped pecans or walnuts
⅓ cup brown sugar
½ teaspoon nutmeg
1 teaspoon cinnamon

1. Preheat oven to 300°F. Lightly grease and flour a 12-cup Bundt pan.

2. Combine bananas, cake mix, pudding mix, oil, eggs, and vanilla in a large mixer bowl. Mix on low speed until moistened; then beat for 8 minutes.

3. Toss pecans or walnuts, brown sugar, nutmeg, and cinnamon until combined.

4. Pour half of batter into pan. Spread nut mixture evenly over batter. Add remaining batter. Swirl a knife through the batter in a figure eight motion to mix the layers. Be careful not to overmix. Bake for 55 to 60 minutes or until a tester inserted near center comes out clean. Cool in pan 20 minutes before turning out onto a wire rack. Makes 12 to 14 servings.

❖ **MARY LOUISE WILSON** | Trinity Presbyterian Church, Little Rock, Arkansas

Coffee Kuchen

2 eggs
¾ cup sugar, plus more for topping
1¼ teaspoons salt
1 large cake (2 oz.) compressed wet yeast
   (such as Red Star), crumbled
1 can (12 oz.) evaporated milk

1¾ cups cold water
About 9 cups flour, divided
⅜ to ½ cup shortening, melted
¼ cup butter, melted
Cinnamon

1. Place eggs, sugar, salt, and yeast in a large mixer bowl and beat to combine. Add milk and water. With mixer running on low, gradually add half of the flour, the melted shortening, and the remaining flour. Continue mixing until well blended. Remove bowl from mixer and let stand overnight.

2. Divide batter among five 10 x 4-inch greased tube pans or five 11 x 7 x 2-inch greased baking pans. Let rise for 1 to 1½ hours.

3. Preheat oven to 375°F. Place pans in oven and bake for 25 minutes or until a tester inserted near center comes out clean. Cool in pans 10 minutes before turning out onto wire racks. Brush tops with melted butter and sprinkle with sugar and cinnamon. Makes 5 coffee cakes.

❖ MRS. CLARENCE WILKENS | St. John's Guild, St. John's Church, West Bend, Wisconsin

Cinnamon-Laced Swirl Coffee Cake

½ cup chopped pecans
2 cups plus 2 tablespoons sugar, divided
1 teaspoon cinnamon
1 cup butter, room temperature
2 eggs

2 cups sifted cake flour
1 teaspoon baking powder
⅛ teaspoon salt
1 teaspoon vanilla
1 container (8 oz.) sour cream

1. Preheat oven to 350°F. Lightly grease and flour a 10-cup Bundt pan or a 10 x 4-inch tube pan.

2. Combine pecans, 2 tablespoons of the sugar, and cinnamon.

3. Cream butter in a large mixer bowl. Add remaining 2 cups sugar and beat at medium speed until well blended. Beat in eggs one at a time.

4. Sift together cake flour, baking powder, and salt. Add gradually to butter mixture, mixing until well blended. Stir in vanilla. Fold in sour cream.

5. Transfer half of batter to pan and spread evenly. Sprinkle half of pecan mixture over batter. Transfer remaining batter to pan and top with remaining pecan mixture. Bake for 55 to 65 minutes or until a tester inserted in center comes out clean. Cool in pan. Invert onto a cake plate to serve. Makes 10 to 12 servings.

❖ LOUISE BONNER, JANE BRUCE, and MURIEL WILLIAMS | Christ Episcopal Church, Charlotte, North Carolina

Quick Coffee Cake

2½ cups flour
¾ cup sugar
1¼ to 1½ cups brown sugar, divided
¾ cup vegetable oil
½ teaspoon nutmeg
1½ teaspoons cinnamon, divided
1 egg

1 cup sour milk (scant cup of milk +
    1 tablespoon vinegar)
1 teaspoon baking powder
¾ teaspoon baking soda
½ teaspoon salt
⅔ cup pecans, chopped
3 or 4 tablespoons butter, melted

1. Preheat oven to 350°F. Lightly grease a 13 x 9 x 2-inch baking pan.
2. Combine flour, sugar, 1 cup of the brown sugar, oil, nutmeg, and ½ teaspoon of the cinnamon in a large bowl. Set aside ¾ cup of this mixture for the topping. Make a well in the remaining mixture.
3. Whisk together egg, sour milk, baking powder, baking soda, and salt. Pour the egg mixture into the well and stir to combine. Spread batter evenly in baking pan.
4. Combine the reserved flour mixture, remaining ¼ to ½ cup brown sugar, remaining teaspoon cinnamon, and pecans in a bowl. Add melted butter and stir to combine. Sprinkle evenly over batter. Bake for 30 to 35 minutes or until browned. Cut into squares and serve warm. This cake freezes well. Makes 12 servings.

SUSAN CALHOON | Trinity Presbyterian Church, Little Rock, Arkansas

Low-fat Apple Coffee Cake

4 cups chopped Granny Smith apples
½ cup unsweetened orange juice, divided
1½ teaspoons cinnamon
3 cups sifted cake flour
2 teaspoons baking powder
¼ teaspoon salt

½ cup skim milk
½ cup butter, room temperature
1 cup sugar
1 carton (8 oz.) egg substitute, thawed
2½ teaspoons vanilla
2 tablespoons brown sugar, divided

1. Preheat oven to 350°F. Lightly grease and flour a 9 x 9 x 2-inch baking pan.
2. Combine apples, ¼ cup of the orange juice, and cinnamon. Set aside.
3. Sift together flour, baking powder, and salt.
4. Combine remaining ¼ cup orange juice and skim milk.
5. Cream butter and sugar in a large mixer bowl. Beat in egg substitute and vanilla. With mixer running, add flour and milk mixtures alternately to batter.
6. Layer half of apple mixture in baking pan. Add half of batter and sprinkle with 1 tablespoon of the brown sugar. Layer remaining apples and batter and sprinkle with remaining tablespoon brown sugar. Bake for 1 hour or until lightly browned. Cut into squares and serve warm. Makes 16 servings.

SUE HARDWICK | Christ Episcopal Church, Charlotte, North Carolina

Overnight Coffee Cake

¾ cup butter

1 cup sugar

1 cup brown sugar, divided

2 eggs, lightly beaten

2 cups flour

1 teaspoon baking powder

2 teaspoons baking soda

½ teaspoon salt

2 teaspoons cinnamon, divided

1 teaspoon nutmeg

1 cup sour cream

1. Lightly grease a 13 x 9 x 2-inch baking pan.

2. Cream butter, sugar, and ½ cup of the brown sugar until well blended. Beat in eggs one at a time.

3. Sift together flour, baking powder, baking soda, salt, 1 teaspoon of the cinnamon, and nutmeg. With mixer running, gradually add flour mixture to batter. Stir in sour cream by hand. Transfer batter to pan.

4. Combine remaining ½ cup brown sugar and remaining teaspoon cinnamon in a small bowl. Sprinkle evenly over top of batter. Cover pan with plastic wrap and refrigerate overnight.

5. Preheat oven to 350°F. Remove plastic wrap from pan. Bake, uncovered, for 30 to 35 minutes or until lightly browned. Cut into squares and serve warm. Makes 16 to 20 servings.

MARY JENKINS | Women's Missionary Auxiliary, Bay Springs, Mississippi

Coffee Cake from Aunt Nancy

1 cup butter

1⅓ cups sugar

2 eggs

3 cups flour

1 teaspoon baking powder

1 teaspoon salt (optional)

1 cup milk

½ teaspoon vanilla

CRUMB TOPPING:

2¼ cups flour

2 cups sugar

2 teaspoons baking powder

5 teaspoons cinnamon

2 teaspoons vanilla

1 cup butter, melted

Confectioners' sugar

1. Preheat oven to 400°F. Lightly grease a 15 x 10½ x 2-inch baking pan.

2. Cream butter and sugar in the large bowl of an electric mixer. Beat in eggs one at a time.

3. Sift together flour, baking powder, and salt. Add flour mixture and milk alternately to batter, mixing well after each addition. Stir in vanilla. Transfer batter to pan.

4. To make crumb topping: Combine flour, sugar, baking powder, and cinnamon in a bowl. Add vanilla and melted butter and stir with a fork until moistened. Sprinkle topping over batter.

5. Bake for 25 to 30 minutes or until topping is browned. Cool in pan and cut into serving pieces. Sprinkle with confectioners' sugar when ready to serve. Makes 20 servings.

BETH HERTZ | Trinity Evangelical Lutheran Church, Lansdale, Pennsylvania

A Baptismal Brunch

CHRIST EPISCOPAL CHURCH
Charlotte, North Carolina

Carolina Apple Cake with Glaze

2 cups sugar
1½ cups canola oil
3 eggs
3 cups flour
1 teaspoon baking soda
1 teaspoon salt
1 teaspoon cinnamon
1 teaspoon vanilla

1 teaspoon lemon extract
4 to 6 apples, peeled, cored, and
    chopped (about 3 cups)
1 cup chopped pecans

GLAZE:
1½ to 2 cups confectioners' sugar
⅓ to ½ cup fresh lemon juice

1. Preheat oven to 300°F. Lightly grease a 13 x 9 x 2-inch baking pan.

2. Combine sugar and oil in a large mixer bowl. Beat in eggs.

3. Sift flour, baking soda, salt, and cinnamon. Add to oil mixture and mix on low speed to make a thick batter. Stir in vanilla and lemon extract. Fold in apples and pecans. Transfer batter to pan and spread evenly. Bake for 80 minutes or until a tester inserted in center comes out clean.

4. To make glaze: Combine confectioners' sugar and lemon juice, stirring until smooth. Drizzle over cake while it is still hot. Cool in pan 10 minutes before cutting into squares. Serve warm or at room temperature. Makes 12 servings.

❖ **SUE HEAD** | Christ Episcopal Church, Charlotte, North Carolina

Crumb Cake

3 cups flour
2 cups sugar
½ cup butter
3 teaspoons baking powder
½ teaspoon salt

½ cup milk
2 eggs, separated
1 teaspoon vanilla
Cinnamon (optional)
Nutmeg (optional)

1. Preheat oven to 350°F. Lightly grease a 13 x 9 x 2-inch baking pan.

2. Whisk together flour and sugar. Cut in butter with a pastry blender or two knives until mixture resembles coarse crumbs. Set aside 1 cup of crumb mixture for topping.

3. To remaining crumb mixture, add baking powder, salt, milk, egg yolks, and vanilla. Mix until well blended.

4. Beat egg whites until soft peaks form. Fold into batter. Gently transfer batter to pan. Sprinkle reserved crumb mixture evenly on top. Sprinkle with cinnamon and nutmeg if desired. Bake for 30 to 35 minutes or until topping is browned. Cut into squares and serve while still warm. Makes 10 to 12 servings.

BARBARA PISTON | Trinity Evangelical Lutheran Church, Lansdale, Pennsylvania

Heart-Healthy Coffee Cake

⅔ cup flour
½ cup whole wheat flour
1 teaspoon baking soda
1 teaspoon cinnamon
¼ teaspoon salt
2 large Granny Smith apples, peeled, cored, and finely chopped (about 1½ cups)
¼ cup frozen egg substitute, thawed
¾ cup sugar
¼ cup chopped pecans
¼ cup applesauce

TOPPING:

¼ cup brown sugar
1 tablespoon flour
1 tablespoon whole wheat flour
½ teaspoon cinnamon
1 tablespoon butter
¼ cup chopped pecans

1. Preheat oven to 350°F. Lightly grease and flour a 9 x 2-inch round cake pan.

2. Sift together flour, whole wheat flour, baking soda, cinnamon, and salt.

3. Combine apples and egg substitute in a large bowl. Add sugar, pecans, and applesauce and stir to combine. Add flour mixture and stir just until moistened. Pour batter into pan.

4. To make topping: Combine brown sugar, all-purpose flour, whole wheat flour, and cinnamon in a small bowl. Cut in butter with a pastry blender or two knives until crumbly. Stir in pecans.

5. Sprinkle topping over batter. Bake for 30 to 35 minutes or until a tester inserted in the center comes out clean. Cool in pan 10 minutes. Cut into wedges and serve warm. Makes 8 to 10 servings.

PRESBYTERIAN CHURCH OF GONZALES | Gonzales, Texas

Our Favorite Apple Kuchen

PASTRY:

1 cup flour

2 tablespoons sugar

¼ teaspoon salt

½ cup butter, room temperature

APPLE FILLING:

4 cups peeled, sliced apples

½ cup sugar

1 tablespoon flour

STREUSEL:

½ cup flour

¼ cup sugar

¼ cup brown sugar

¼ teaspoon salt

4 tablespoons butter

Cinnamon

> Add sugar to an apple filling according to the sweetness or tartness of the apples and the overall desired sweetness.

1. Preheat oven to 350°F. Lightly grease an 11 x 7 x 2-inch baking pan.

2. To make pastry: Whisk together flour, sugar, and salt. Cut in butter with a pastry blender or your fingers until crumbly. Pat mixture into bottom and partway up sides of pan (½ to ¾ inch).

3. To make apple filling: Toss apples with sugar and flour until evenly coated. Spread apples evenly into pastry shell.

4. To make streusel: Combine flour, sugar, brown sugar, and salt. Cut in butter with a pastry blender or your fingers until crumbly. Layer streusel evenly over apples. Sprinkle with cinnamon. Bake for 45 to 50 minutes or until apples are tender and streusel is lightly browned. Makes 12 servings.

❖ **MRS. WILBERT JAEGER** | St. John's Guild, St. John's Church, West Bend, Wisconsin

Apricot Fritters

1 tablespoon oil plus more for deep-frying

1 egg, lightly beaten

⅔ cup milk

1 cup flour

2 tablespoons sugar

1 teaspoon baking powder

¼ teaspoon salt

1 can (16 oz.) unpeeled apricot halves, drained and patted dry

Confectioners' sugar

1. Pour oil 2 to 3 inches deep into a deep fryer or saucepan. Heat to 365°F.

2. Combine egg and milk in a large bowl. Stir in 1 tablespoon oil. Whisk together flour, sugar, baking powder, and salt. Add to egg mixture and stir just until moistened.

3. Using tongs, dip apricots in batter, drain off excess, and gently place in hot oil. Fry in batches, turning as needed, until evenly browned, about 4 minutes. Remove with a slotted spoon and set on paper towels to drain. Let cool slightly and roll in confectioners' sugar. Serve immediately. Makes 4 servings.

❖ **LINDA S. THOMPSON** | Oakwood Church of God in Christ, Godfrey, Illinois

Cranberry Cake with Vanilla Sauce

¼ cup butter

1⅓ cups sugar

2⅔ cups flour

4 teaspoons baking powder

¼ teaspoon salt

1¼ cups milk

4 cups cranberries

1. Preheat oven to 350°F. Lightly grease a 13 x 9 x 2-inch baking pan.

2. Cream butter and sugar in a large mixer bowl. With mixer running, add flour, baking powder, and salt. Gradually add milk, mixing to combine. Stir in cranberries. Transfer batter to pan. Bake for 45 minutes or until cake springs back when gently pressed. Cool in pan 10 minutes. Cut into squares and serve warm with vanilla sauce (recipe follows). Makes 12 servings.

VANILLA SAUCE

½ cup butter

1 cup sugar

¾ cup whipping cream

1 tablespoon cornstarch

1 to 2 teaspoons vanilla

1. Combine butter, sugar, whipping cream, and cornstarch in a small saucepan over medium heat. Bring to a boil and cook, stirring continuously, until thickened, 3 to 5 minutes.

2. Remove from heat and stir in vanilla. Makes 1¼ cups.

ANNE T. NEAL | Christ Episcopal Church, Charlotte, North Carolina

Cranberry Swirl Coffee Cake

1½ cups butter

1 cup sugar

2 eggs

2 cups flour

1 teaspoon baking powder

1 teaspoon baking soda

½ teaspoon salt

1 cup sour cream

1 teaspoon almond extract

1 can (16 oz.) whole cranberry sauce

½ cup chopped nuts

1. Preheat oven to 350°F. Coat a 10-cup Bundt pan with cooking spray.

2. Cream butter and sugar in a large mixer bowl. Beat in eggs one at a time.

3. Whisk together flour, baking powder, baking soda, and salt. With mixer running, add flour mixture and sour cream alternately to batter. Stir in almond extract.

4. Transfer half of batter to pan. Layer half of cranberry sauce on batter. Add remaining batter, remaining cranberry sauce, and nuts. Bake for 50 to 55 minutes or until top is golden brown and a tester inserted in center comes out clean. Cool in pan. Invert onto a cake plate to serve. Makes 10 servings.

MARY E. KENNEY | Methow Valley United Methodist Church, Twisp, Washington

Blueberry Tea Cake

2 cups flour
2 teaspoons baking powder
½ teaspoon salt
¼ cup butter
¾ cup sugar
1 egg
½ cup milk
2 cups fresh or frozen blueberries

CRUMB TOPPING:

½ cup sugar
¼ cup flour
½ teaspoon cinnamon
2 tablespoons butter

1. Preheat oven to 375°F. Lightly grease a 9 x 9 x 2-inch baking pan.

2. Sift together flour, baking powder, and salt.

3. Cream butter and sugar. Add egg and beat until fluffy. Add flour mixture and milk alternately, mixing just until blended. Fold in blueberries. Transfer batter to pan.

4. To make crumb topping: Combine sugar, flour, and cinnamon. Cut in butter with a pastry blender or your fingers until crumbly. Sprinkle topping over batter. Bake for 45 minutes or until topping is lightly browned. Set pan on a wire rack to cool. Cut into squares. Serve warm or at room temperature. Makes 9 servings.

❖ **FAY S. MILLER** | Trinity Evangelical Lutheran Church, Lansdale, Pennsylvania

Brazil Nut Coffee Cake Bars

2 cups flour
1 teaspoon baking powder
1 cup sugar
3 teaspoons cinnamon
½ cup vegetable shortening
½ cup butter, room temperature
1 egg plus 1 egg yolk

TOPPING:

1 egg white
⅓ cup sugar
1 teaspoon cinnamon
1 cup chopped Brazil nuts

1. Preheat oven to 350°F. Lightly grease a 15½ x 10½ x 1-inch sheet pan.

2. Whisk together flour, baking powder, sugar, and cinnamon. Cut in shortening and butter with a pastry blender or two knives. Add egg and egg yolk and mix until moistened. Turn dough into pan and spread evenly.

3. To make topping: Whisk egg white and brush it onto dough. Combine sugar, cinnamon, and nuts. Sprinkle over top of dough. Bake for 25 minutes or until golden brown. Cool in pan and cut into bars. Makes 15 bars.

❖ **ROSE JUSTMAN** | St. John's Guild, St. John's Church, West Bend, Wisconsin

Fruit Kuchen

1¼ cups flour
¼ cup sugar
1 teaspoon baking powder
½ teaspoon salt
2 tablespoons butter
1 egg, beaten, plus milk to measure ½ cup

FRUIT FILLING:
3 cups raspberries, sliced apples,
   or sliced peaches
1 cup sugar

STREUSEL:
⅔ cup flour
½ cup light brown sugar
⅓ cup butter
Cinnamon

To make a kuchen with cherries or plums in the filling, increase the sugar from 1 cup to 1½ cups.

1. Preheat oven to 350°F. Lightly grease an 11 x 7 x 2-inch baking pan.

2. Whisk together flour, sugar, baking powder, and salt. Cut in butter with a pastry blender until crumbly. Make a well in center, add egg mixture, and stir with a fork to make a dough. Roll or pat dough to a ¼-inch thickness and place in pan.

3. To make fruit filling: Arrange raspberries or sliced fruit in rows on pastry. Sprinkle sugar over the top.

4. To make streusel: Combine flour, light brown sugar, and butter with your fingers until crumbly. Sprinkle over the fruit filling. Sprinkle with cinnamon. Bake for 15 minutes, reduce heat to 325°F, and bake 15 to 20 minutes more or until streusel is golden brown. Cut into squares and serve while still warm. Makes 12 servings.

❖ **ESTHER KLEIN** | St. John's Guild, St. John's Church, West Bend, Wisconsin

Sour Cream Coffee Cake

½ cup butter

1 cup sugar

2 eggs

2 cups flour

1½ teaspoons baking powder

1 teaspoon baking soda

1 cup sour cream

1 teaspoon vanilla

FILLING/TOPPING:

½ cup sugar

1 tablespoon cinnamon

¼ cup chopped nuts

1. Preheat oven to 350°F. Grease a 10 x 4-inch tube pan.

2. Cream butter and sugar in a large mixer bowl. Add eggs and beat until fluffy.

3. Sift together flour, baking powder, and baking soda. With mixer running, gradually add flour mixture to batter. Fold in sour cream and vanilla.

4. To make filling/topping: Combine sugar, cinnamon, and nuts.

5. Spread half of batter in pan. Sprinkle with half of filling/topping. Add remaining batter and remaining filling/topping. Bake for 35 minutes or until a cake tester inserted near center comes out clean. Serve warm. Makes 10 servings.

❖ **VIOLET CROUSE** | Trinity Evangelical Lutheran Church, Lansdale, Pennsylvania

French Breakfast Puffs

5 tablespoons vegetable shortening

½ cup sugar

1 egg

1½ cups flour

1½ teaspoons baking powder

½ teaspoon salt

½ teaspoon nutmeg

½ cup milk

COATING:

3 tablespoons vegetable shortening

3 tablespoons butter, melted

½ cup sugar

1 teaspoon cinnamon

1. Preheat oven to 350°F. Grease a 12-cup muffin pan.

2. Combine shortening, sugar, and egg in a large mixer bowl. Sift together flour, baking powder, salt, and nutmeg. With mixer running, add flour mixture and milk alternately to batter. Stir just until combined. Fill muffin cups two-thirds full. Bake for 20 to 25 minutes or until golden brown.

3. To make coating: Combine shortening and melted butter in a shallow bowl. In a separate bowl, whisk together sugar and cinnamon. Dip warm roll puffs in melted butter mixture and then roll in sugar mixture. Set on wire racks. Serve warm. Makes 12 puffs.

❖ **GAIL CARR** | Christ Episcopal Church, Charlotte, North Carolina

Kringles

4½ cups flour

1 tablespoon brown sugar

1 envelope (.25 oz.) active dry yeast

¼ teaspoon salt

2 cups butter

4 egg yolks, beaten

1 cup sour cream

Fruit pie filling, jam, or jelly

Confectioners' sugar

Water

1. Whisk together flour, brown sugar, yeast, and salt. Cut in butter with a pastry blender. Add egg yolks and sour cream and mix by hand to make a smooth dough. Shape dough into 3 balls, wrap in plastic wrap, and chill at least 4 hours or overnight.

Kringles may be made up to the point of baking and frozen. To bake frozen kringles, increase baking time to 40 minutes.

2. Preheat oven to 375°F. Lightly grease two baking sheets.

3. Cut each ball of dough in half. Roll out very thin to a 9 x 15-inch rectangle. Spread filling in center third of dough. Fold one end of dough (about one-third) over filling. Spread more filling over folded area. Fold remaining third of dough over new filling. Press edges together to seal. Repeat with remaining dough.

4. Transfer pastries to baking sheets. Bake for 30 minutes or until golden brown. Cool on baking sheet. Stir together confectioners' sugar and water to make a thin glaze and drizzle over top. Makes 6 or 12 servings.

SUE SCHACHEL | St. John's Guild, St. John's Church, West Bend, Wisconsin

Morning Glory Muffins

2 cups flour

1 cup sugar

2 teaspoons baking soda

2 teaspoons cinnamon

½ teaspoon salt

1 apple, cored and shredded

2 carrots, shredded

½ cup raisins

½ cup shredded coconut

½ cup chopped pecans

3 eggs, beaten

1 cup vegetable oil

2 teaspoons vanilla

1. Preheat oven to 350°F. Lightly grease two 10-cup muffin pans.

2. Sift together flour, sugar, baking soda, cinnamon, and salt. Add apples, carrots, raisins, coconut, and pecans and toss to combine. Stir in eggs, oil, and vanilla until well blended.

3. Pour batter into muffin pans. Bake for 25 minutes or until golden and a tester inserted in center comes out clean. Cool in pans 5 minutes before turning out onto wire racks. Serve warm. Makes 18 to 20 muffins.

JUDY VAN NAMEN | Christ Episcopal Church, Charlotte, North Carolina

Healthy Apple-Walnut Muffins

2 large eggs

1 cup plus 2 tablespoons frozen apple juice
concentrate, thawed

⅔ cup buttermilk

2 cups flour

1 teaspoon baking soda

¼ teaspoon cinnamon

¼ teaspoon ginger

¼ teaspoon allspice

¼ teaspoon nutmeg

¼ rounded teaspoon salt

2 tablespoons oat bran

2 small Granny Smith apples, peeled,
cored, and chopped

⅓ cup chopped walnuts

1 small apple, peeled, cored, and cut into 12 slices

1. Preheat oven to 375°F. Grease a 12-cup muffin pan or insert paper liners.

2. Combine eggs, apple juice, and buttermilk in a large bowl. Whisk together flour, baking soda, cinnamon, ginger, allspice, nutmeg, and salt. Add flour mixture and oat bran to egg mixture, stirring just until moistened. Fold in chopped apples and walnuts.

3. Spoon batter into muffin cups until two-thirds full. Top each with an apple slice. Bake for 25 minutes or until tops are lightly golden and spring back when pressed. Cool in pan 5 minutes before turning out onto a wire rack. Makes 12 muffins.

JENNIFER FREY | Sorento Assembly of God Church, Sorento, Illinois

Breakfast Bran Muffins

2 cups flour

¾ cup bran cereal (such as All-Bran)

½ cup shredded coconut

2 teaspoons baking powder

1 teaspoon cinnamon

1 jar (3.5 oz.) macadamia nuts, chopped

½ cup butter

1 cup sugar

¼ cup brown sugar

3 eggs

2 ripe bananas, mashed (about ¾ cup)

1 can (8 oz.) crushed pineapple, drained

2 teaspoons vanilla

1. Preheat oven to 350°F. Grease two 12-cup muffin pans or insert paper liners.

2. Whisk together flour, bran cereal, coconut, baking powder, cinnamon, and macadamia nuts in a large bowl.

3. Cream butter, sugar, and brown sugar. Add eggs and blend well. Stir in bananas, pineapple, and vanilla. Add fruit mixture to flour mixture. Stir just until moistened.

4. Spoon batter into muffin cups until two-thirds full.

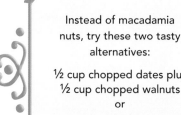

Instead of macadamia nuts, try these two tasty alternatives:

½ cup chopped dates plus
½ cup chopped walnuts
or
1 cup raisins

Bake for 20 to 30 minutes or until golden brown and a toothpick inserted in center comes out clean. Cool in pan 2 minutes before turning out onto a wire rack. Makes 24 muffins.

DAVI LANGSTON | Christ Church, Frederica, St. Simons Island, Georgia

Refrigerator Bran Muffins

1 box (20 oz.) raisin bran flakes
5 cups flour
3 cups sugar
5 teaspoons baking soda
2 teaspoons salt

4 eggs (or equivalent egg substitute), beaten
1 quart low-fat buttermilk
1 cup skim milk
1 cup vegetable oil

1. Whisk together bran flakes, flour, sugar, baking soda, and salt in a large bowl. Make a well in center and add eggs, buttermilk, milk, and oil. Stir just until moistened. Cover and chill at least 4 hours.

2. Preheat oven to 350°F. Grease a 12-cup muffin pan or insert paper liners. Spoon batter into muffin cups until two-thirds full. Bake for 20 minutes or until golden brown. Cool in pan 5 minutes before turning out onto a wire rack. Store remaining batter, covered, in refrigerator until needed, up to 5 weeks. Makes 48 muffins.

A bran muffin served with half a grapefruit makes a satisfying breakfast.

PHYLLIS GOULDEY | Trinity Evangelical Lutheran Church, Lansdale, Pennsylvania

Raspberry Streusel Muffins

½ cup butter, room temperature
½ cup sugar
1 egg
2 cups flour
½ teaspoon baking powder
½ teaspoon baking soda
½ teaspoon cinnamon
¼ teaspoon salt
½ cup sour cream
½ cup milk
1 teaspoon vanilla
1 cup fresh or frozen raspberries

STREUSEL:
¼ cup flour
¼ cup quick-cooking rolled oats
3 tablespoons sugar
¼ teaspoon cinnamon
⅛ teaspoon salt
3 tablespoons cold butter
Confectioners' sugar

1. Preheat oven to 400°F. Grease one 12-cup and one 6-cup muffin pan or insert paper liners.

2. Cream butter and sugar until light and fluffy. Beat in egg.

3. Whisk together flour, baking powder, baking soda, cinnamon, and salt. In a separate bowl, combine sour cream, milk, and vanilla. Add flour mixture and sour cream mixture alternately to batter, stirring just until moistened after each addition. Gently fold in raspberries. Spoon batter into muffin cups until two-thirds full.

4. To make streusel: Whisk together flour, oats, sugar, cinnamon, and salt. Cut in butter until crumbly. Sprinkle over muffins. Bake for 18 to 22 minutes or until a tester inserted in center comes out clean. Cool in pan 10 minutes before turning out onto a wire rack. Dust with confectioners' sugar. Makes 18 muffins.

FREDA GANTT | Methow Valley United Methodist Church, Twisp, Washington

Peach Muffins

1½ cups flour
½ teaspoon baking soda
¾ teaspoon salt
1 cup sugar
2 eggs, beaten
½ cup oil

½ teaspoon vanilla
⅛ teaspoon almond extract
¼ cup chopped almonds
2 large or 3 small peaches, fresh or canned,
   coarsely chopped (1¼ cups)

1. Preheat oven to 350°F. Grease a 12-cup muffin pan or insert paper liners.
2. Whisk together flour, baking soda, salt, and sugar. Make a well in the center, add eggs and oil, and stir until moistened. Stir in vanilla, almond extract, almonds, and peaches.
3. Spoon ⅓ cup batter into each muffin cup. Bake for 20 to 25 minutes or until a tester inserted in center comes out clean. Cool in pan 5 minutes before turning out onto a wire rack. Makes 12 muffins.

MICHAEL PETERS | Methow Valley United Methodist Church, Twisp, Washington

The peach muffin batter also makes a delicious quick bread. Spoon the batter into a greased and floured 9 x 5 x 3-inch loaf pan and bake at 350°F for 1 hour.

Carrot Muffins

2 cups flour
1¼ cups sugar
2 teaspoons baking soda
2 teaspoons cinnamon
½ teaspoon salt
2 cups grated carrots
½ cup nuts

½ cup raisins
½ cup shredded coconut
1 apple, peeled, cored, and grated
3 eggs
1 cup oil
2 teaspoons vanilla

1. Preheat oven to 350°F. Grease three 6-cup muffin pans or insert paper liners.
2. Whisk together flour, sugar, baking soda, cinnamon, and salt in a large bowl. Stir in carrots, nuts, raisins, coconut, and apple.
3. In a separate bowl, beat eggs, oil, and vanilla until well combined. Add to batter and stir until blended.
4. Spoon batter into muffin cups, filling almost to the top. Bake for 20 minutes or until puffed up and browned. Cool in pan 5 minutes before turning out onto a wire rack. Makes 14 to 18 muffins.

DAVI LANGSTON | Christ Church, Frederica, St. Simons Island, Georgia

Butterscotch Muffins

2 cups flour

1 cup sugar

1 package (3.4 oz) instant butterscotch
    pudding mix

1 package (3.4 oz.) instant vanilla
    pudding mix

2 teaspoons baking powder

1 teaspoon salt

1 cup water

4 eggs

¾ cup oil

1 teaspoon vanilla

TOPPING:

⅔ cup brown sugar

½ cup chopped pecans

2 teaspoons cinnamon

1. Preheat over to 350°F. Grease one 12-cup and one 6-cup muffin pan or insert paper liners.

2. Whisk together flour, sugar, butterscotch pudding mix, vanilla pudding mix, baking powder, and salt in a large mixing bowl. In a separate bowl, whisk together water, eggs, oil, and vanilla. Stir egg mixture into flour mixture just until moistened.

3. Spoon batter into muffin cups until two-thirds full. Combine brown sugar, pecans, and cinnamon. Sprinkle over batter. Bake for 15 to 20 minutes or until a tester inserted in center comes out clean. Cool in pan 5 minutes before turning out onto a wire rack. Makes 18 muffins.

✦ FRANCES MISHLER | Methow Valley United Methodist Church, Twisp, Washington

Bagels

1 envelope (.25 oz.) active dry yeast

⅔ cup water, boiled and cooled to
    lukewarm, divided

2 tablespoons sugar, plus more for cooking

1½ teaspoons salt

3 tablespoons oil

1 egg, beaten

3 cups flour

1. Dissolve yeast in ⅓ cup of the water. Let stand 10 minutes.

2. Place remaining ⅓ cup water in a large mixer bowl. Add sugar, salt, and oil and stir to combine. Stir in yeast, egg, and half of the flour using a dough hook attachment. Gradually add remaining flour. Knead for 8 to 10 minutes or until dough is smooth and elastic and springs back when pressed with a finger.

3. Transfer dough to a large oiled bowl, cover, and set aside in a warm place until doubled in size, 2 to 3 hours.

4. Punch down dough, divide into 12 pieces, and form into rings. Allow enough time so that dough begins to rise, up to 1 hour.

5. Preheat oven to 400°F. Grease a baking sheet. Bring a stockpot of water to a boil over high heat. Sprinkle sugar into the water. Place dough rings into boiling water in batches, cooking until they rise to the surface. Remove with a large slotted utensil and place on baking sheet. Bake for 20 minutes or until lightly browned. Makes 12 bagels.

✦ RACHEL MCLEAN DABRITZ | Methow Valley United Methodist Church, Twisp, Washington

Sesame Corn Muffins

1 cup cornmeal

½ cup wheat germ

¼ cup flour

¼ cup sesame seeds

3 tablespoons sugar

¾ teaspoon baking soda

½ teaspoon salt

1 egg, beaten

1 cup buttermilk

⅓ cup salad oil

1. Preheat oven to 350°F. Grease a 12-cup muffin pan.

2. Whisk together cornmeal, wheat germ, flour, sesame seeds, sugar, baking soda, and salt in a mixing bowl.

3. In a separate bowl, combine egg, buttermilk, and oil. Add to flour mixture and stir until moistened.

4. Spoon batter into muffin cups until two-thirds full. Bake for 20 minutes or until golden brown. Turn out onto a wire rack to cool. Makes 12 muffins.

❖ KATHY PALMER | Christ Church, Frederica, St. Simons Island, Georgia

Blueberry Muffins

1½ cups flour

2 teaspoons baking powder

½ teaspoon salt

½ cup sugar

1 egg

½ cup milk

¼ cup butter, melted

2 cups fresh blueberries

1. Preheat oven to 375°F. Grease a 12-cup muffin pan.

2. Whisk together flour, baking powder, salt, and sugar.

3. In a separate bowl, beat egg and milk until blended. Add egg mixture and melted butter to flour mixture and stir just until moistened. Batter should be lumpy. Fold in blueberries.

4. Spoon batter into muffin cups until three-fourths full. Bake for 20 to 25 minutes or until a cake tester inserted in the center comes out clean. Turn out onto a wire rack to cool. Makes 12 muffins.

❖ JENNIFER MILLS | First Baptist Church, Russell, Kentucky

Cranberry Muffins

4 cups flour

2 cups sugar

3 teaspoons baking powder

1 teaspoon baking soda

2 teaspoons salt

½ cup shortening

2 eggs

1½ cups orange juice

2 teaspoons grated orange zest

1 cup pecans or walnuts

2 cups chopped cranberries

1. Preheat oven to 350°F. Grease and flour two 6-cup muffin pans.

2. Sift together flour, sugar, baking powder, baking soda, and salt. Cut in shortening with a pastry blender.

3. In a separate bowl, whisk together eggs, orange juice, and zest. Add to flour mixture and stir just until moist. Fold in pecans or walnuts and cranberries.

4. Spoon batter into muffin cups. Bake for 20 to 25 minutes or until a toothpick inserted in center comes out clean. Turn out onto wire racks to cool. Serve warm with butter or cream cheese. Makes 12 muffins.

✦ **MRS. ROBERT ALLEN** | Christ Church, Frederica, St. Simons Island, Georgia

Lemon Raspberry Muffins

2 cups flour

1 cup sugar

1 tablespoon baking powder

½ teaspoon salt

2 eggs

1 cup half-and-half

½ cup vegetable oil

1 teaspoon lemon extract

1 cup fresh or frozen unsweetened raspberries
    (if frozen, do not thaw)

1. Preheat oven to 375°F. Grease one 12-cup and one 6-cup muffin pan or insert paper liners.

2. Whisk together flour, sugar, baking powder, and salt in a large bowl.

3. In a separate bowl, combine eggs, half-and-half, oil, and lemon extract. Make a well in flour mixture, add egg mixture, and stir just until moistened. Fold in raspberries.

4. Spoon batter into muffin cups until two-thirds full. Bake for 18 to 20 minutes or until golden brown. Cool 5 minutes in pan before turning out onto a wire rack. Makes 16 to 18 muffins.

✦ **FAYE HOGGATT** | Memorial Baptist Church, Tulsa, Oklahoma

Blueberry Scones

2¼ cups flour

½ cup butter

½ cup sugar

2 teaspoons baking powder

½ teaspoon salt

2 eggs

¼ cup milk

1 teaspoon vanilla

¼ teaspoon grated lemon zest

½ cup blueberries

1. Preheat oven to 375°F. Grease a baking sheet.

2. Place flour in a mixing bowl. Cut in butter with a pastry blender. Add sugar, baking powder, and salt. Stir just until combined.

3. In a separate bowl, combine eggs, milk, vanilla, and lemon zest. Add to flour mixture and stir to combine. With lightly floured hands, knead in blueberries.

4. Gather up dough, pat into a 9-inch circle, and set on baking sheet. Score with a knife into 8 pieces. Bake for 30 to 35 minutes or until lightly browned. Serve warm with butter. Makes 8 scones.

✦ **SALLY CROSS** | Methow Valley United Methodist Church, Twisp, Washington

Sausage Biscuits

1 envelope (.25 oz.) active dry yeast
¼ cup warm water
¾ lb. hot bulk pork sausage
2⅔ cups flour
2 tablespoons sugar
1 teaspoon baking powder

½ teaspoon baking soda
½ teaspoon salt
½ cup shortening
1 cup buttermilk
Melted butter

1. Preheat oven to 425°F. Grease a baking sheet.

2. Dissolve yeast in warm water (105°F to 115°F). Let stand 5 minutes.

3. Cook sausage in a skillet, crumbling it with long-handled spoon, until browned. Drain on paper towels.

4. Whisk together flour, sugar, baking powder, baking soda, and salt. Cut in shortening until it resembles coarse meal.

5. Add yeast to buttermilk and stir to combine. Pour buttermilk over flour mixture and stir until moistened. Knead in sausage.

6. Turn out dough onto a floured surface. Knead lightly. Roll out dough to a ½- to ¾-inch thickness. Cut into 2½-inch rounds and place on baking sheet. Bake for 10 minutes or until golden brown. Cool 5 minutes on wire racks. Serve warm. Makes 8 to 12 biscuits.

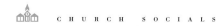 **LYNDA McKEE** | Presbyterian Church of Gonzales, Gonzales, Texas

Blue Cheese and Ham Cornmeal Biscuits

1⅔ cups flour
⅓ cup yellow cornmeal
1 tablespoon baking powder
1 tablespoon sugar
⅛ teaspoon cayenne pepper

3 tablespoons butter, cut into small pieces
½ cup crumbed blue cheese
½ cup baked ham, chopped
1 tablespoon chopped scallion
⅔ cup skim milk or 1% milk

1. Preheat oven to 425°F. Lightly coat a baking sheet with cooking spray.

2. Whisk together flour, cornmeal, baking powder, sugar, and cayenne pepper in a large bowl. Cut in butter and blue cheese with a pastry blender until crumbly. Stir in ham and scallion.

3. Make a well in center of flour mixture, pour in milk, and stir until well moistened and firm. With floured hands, knead dough once or twice in the bowl.

4. Turn out dough onto a floured surface and roll or pat to a ¾-inch thickness. Cut out biscuits with a 2½-inch cutter. Transfer to baking sheet. Bake for 12 to 14 minutes or until browned and crusty. Serve hot. Makes 12 biscuits.

DEBRA O'STEEN | Oakwood Church of God in Christ, Godfrey, Illinois

Brunch after Church

TRINITY EVANGELICAL LUTHERAN CHURCH
Lansdale, Pennsylvania

Bacon-Cheese Corn Muffins

8 strips bacon
1 egg
1 cup milk
¼ cup butter, melted
1 can (8.75 oz.) creamed corn
1 cup yellow cornmeal

1 cup flour
3 tablespoons sugar
3 tablespoons baking powder
½ teaspoon salt
1 tablespoon hot sauce
1½ cups (6 oz.) grated cheddar cheese

1. Preheat oven to 400°F. Grease a 12-cup muffin pan.

2. Cut bacon into small pieces and cook until crisp. Drain on paper towels.

3. Whisk together egg, milk, and melted butter in a medium bowl. Add creamed corn, cornmeal, flour, sugar, baking powder, and salt and stir to combine. Fold in hot pepper sauce, cheese, and bacon bits.

4. Spoon batter into muffin cups until three-fourths full. Bake for 20 to 25 minutes or until tops are lightly browned and a toothpick inserted in center comes out clean. Cool in pan 10 minutes before turning out onto a wire rack. Serve warm or cool completely, seal in zip-close bags, and freeze for later use. Makes 12 muffins.

DAVI LANGSTON | Christ Church, Frederica, St. Simons Island, Georgia

Mississippi Spice Muffins

1 cup butter
2 eggs
1 cup chopped nuts
2 cups hot applesauce
4 cups flour
3 teaspoons cinnamon

2 teaspoons allspice
2 cups sugar
1 teaspoon cloves
2 teaspoons baking soda
½ teaspoon salt
Confectioners' sugar

1. Preheat oven to 350ºF. Grease two 12-cup muffin pans.

2. Cream butter in a mixer bowl. Beat in eggs, nuts, and applesauce.

3. Whisk together flour, cinnamon, allspice, sugar, cloves, baking soda, and salt. Add to applesauce mixture and stir just until moistened.

4. Spoon batter into muffin cups until half full. Bake for 15 minutes or until a tester inserted in center comes out clean. Cool in pan 5 minutes before turning out onto a wire rack. Roll warm muffins in confectioners' sugar. Bake muffins in batches or store unused batter, covered, in refrigerator for up to 3 weeks for baking at a later date. Makes 48 muffins.

DORIS MASON | Memorial Baptist Church, Tulsa, Oklahoma

Christiana Campbell's Tavern Sweet Potato Muffins

½ cup butter
1¼ cups sugar
2 eggs
1¼ cups canned sweet potatoes, mashed
1½ cups all-purpose flour
2 teaspoons baking powder

¼ teaspoon salt
1 teaspoon cinnamon
¼ teaspoon nutmeg
1 cup milk
¼ cup pecans or walnuts, chopped
½ cup raisins, chopped

1. Preheat oven to 400ºF. Grease three 24-cup (1½-inch) mini muffin pans.

2. Cream butter and sugar in a mixer bowl. Add eggs and mix well. Blend in sweet potatoes.

3. Sift together flour, baking powder, salt, cinnamon, and nutmeg. Add flour mixture and milk alternately to sweet potato batter, stirring just until combined. Fold in pecans or walnuts and raisins.

4. Spoon batter into muffin pans until two-thirds full. Bake for 25 minutes or until lightly browned. Turn out onto a wire rack to cool. Serve warm. Leftover muffins may be frozen in a zip-close bag and reheated. Make 72 mini muffins.

MAXINE HARRIS | First Baptist Church, Russell, Kentucky

Baking Powder Biscuits

2 cups flour
1 tablespoon baking powder
½ teaspoon salt

⅓ cup shortening
¾ to ⅞ cup milk

1. Preheat oven to 450°F. Grease a baking sheet.
2. Sift together flour, baking powder, and salt. Cut in shortening with a pastry blender until particles are the size of rice grains.
3. Add milk all at once and stir quickly until dough stiffens up. The dough should be rather soft. The larger amount of milk will probably be required in cold weather.
4. Turn out dough onto a floured surface. Knead 12 to 15 times. Roll or pat out to a ⅜- to ¾-inch thickness. Cut dough with a biscuit cutter dipped in flour. Set on baking sheet. Bake for 10 to 15 minutes or until lightly browned. Cool on a wire rack. Serve warm. Makes 12 to 15 biscuits.

❖ **WOMEN'S MISSIONARY AUXILIARY** | Bay Springs, Mississippi

To save time in the kitchen, mix up a triple batch of baking powder biscuits (everything except the milk) and store in an airtight container at room temperature. When you want to make a batch of biscuits, simply measure out a cup or two of the dry ingredients and add enough milk to make a dough of the right consistency.

Grilled Biscuits

2 cups self-rising flour
1 teaspoon salt
⅓ cup shortening

⅔ cup milk
4 tablespoons butter, melted

1. Prepare outdoor charcoal grill.
2. Whisk together flour and salt. Cut in shortening with a pastry blender until mixture resembles coarse meal. Add milk and stir just until flour is moistened and dough starts to come together.
3. Turn out dough onto a lightly floured board. Roll out to a ½-inch thickness. Cut out rounds with a biscuit cutter. Brush tops with melted butter.
4. Arrange coals and/or adjust grill height for low heat. Place biscuit rounds directly on grill and cover with foil. Bake, turning once for even browning on both sides, about 10 minutes. Makes 16 biscuits.

❖ **MIRACLE DELIVERANCE HOLINESS CHURCH** | Columbia, South Carolina

Cheese Biscuits

½ cup butter, room temperature

2 cups grated sharp cheddar cheese

1½ cups flour, sifted

½ teaspoon salt

¼ teaspoon cayenne pepper

1 tablespoon caraway seeds

VARIATION:
Omit the caraway seeds from the dough. Just before baking, top each round of dough with a pecan.

1. Cream butter and cheddar cheese in a mixer bowl. Whisk together flour, salt, cayenne pepper, and caraway seeds. Add flour mixture to cheese mixture and mix until well combined.

2. Gather dough into a ball, divide in half, and shape into two logs, each 1½ inches in diameter. Wrap in waxed paper and chill for 2 hours, or until firm.

3. Preheat oven to 350°F. Grease a baking sheet. Cut thin slices from logs and place on baking sheet. Bake for 10 minutes or until lightly browned. Transfer onto wire racks and allow to cool. Store in a covered tin. Makes 80 to 100 thin biscuits.

JO RANKIN | Christ Episcopal Church, Charlotte, North Carolina

No-Knead Butterhorns

4 cups flour

¼ cup plus 3 tablespoons sugar, divided

1 teaspoon salt

1 tablespoon grated lemon zest

1 cup butter

¼ cup warm water (105°F to 115°F)

1 envelope (.25 oz.) active dry yeast

1 cup warm milk (105°F to 115°F)

3 egg yolks, well beaten

3 tablespoons butter, melted

1½ teaspoons cinnamon

Confectioners' sugar

1. Whisk together flour, ¼ cup of the sugar, salt, and lemon zest in a large bowl. Cut in butter until particles are fine.

2. Pour water into a small bowl, add yeast, and stir until dissolved. Pour yeast mixture, milk, and egg yolks into flour mixture. Stir just until blended. Cover tightly with foil. Refrigerate at least 2 hours or overnight.

3. Divide dough into 3 equal pieces. Roll out one piece into a 12-inch circle. Brush lightly with 1 tablespoon of melted butter. Combine remaining 3 tablespoons sugar and cinnamon; sprinkle one-third of mixture onto dough circle.

4. Cut dough into 12 wedges. Roll up each wedge, beginning at wide end, and press to seal the point. Place 2 inches apart on greased baking sheets with points on the underside. Repeat with remaining dough. Cover and set aside in a warm, draft-free place until doubled in size, about 1 hour.

5. Preheat oven to 400°F. Bake for 10 to 15 minutes or until lightly browned. Cool on wire racks. Drizzle with confectioners' sugar. Makes 36 butterhorns.

MRS. GABRIELE RIGGSBEE | Pittsboro Baptist Church, Pittsboro, North Carolina

Philadelphia Sticky Buns

1¼ cups milk

1 envelope (.25 oz.) active dry yeast

¼ cup warm water

5 cups flour, divided

1½ teaspoons salt

¾ cup sugar plus 1 tablespoon, divided

½ cup shortening

2 eggs

1 cup light or dark corn syrup, plus more for drizzling

¼ cup butter, room temperature

½ cup brown sugar

2 teaspoons cinnamon

½ cup walnuts, chopped

½ cup raisins

1. Pour milk into a large saucepan, heat to scalding, and cool to lukewarm.

2. Dissolve yeast in warm water and let stand 10 minutes.

3. To make sponge, combine milk and yeast in a large bowl. Add 2 cups of the flour, salt, and 1 tablespoon sugar. Beat until smooth. Set aside in a warm place.

4. Beat shortening in a mixer bowl until light. Whip in remaining ¾ cup sugar and eggs, one at a time. When sponge is bubbly, add shortening mixture and beat until blended. Stir in remaining 3 cups flour. Cover and let rise until double in size, 1 to 1½ hours.

5. Butter bottom and sides of two 9 x 9 x 2-inch baking pans. Pour corn syrup into pans to a depth of ¼ inch.

6. Divide dough in half. Roll each half into a ¼-inch-thick rectangle. Spread with butter. Mix brown sugar with cinnamon and sprinkle over dough. Add walnuts and raisins. Drizzle with remaining corn syrup. Roll up dough jelly-roll style and cut into 1½-inch lengths. Stand buns, cut side up, in pans. Cover and let rise until double in size, 30 minutes to 1 hour.

7. Preheat oven to 350°F. Bake for 45 minutes or until golden brown. Turn out of pans onto wire racks. Serve warm. Makes 24 buns.

CHRISTINE RITCHIE | Trinity Evangelical Lutheran Church, Lansdale, Pennsylvania

Quaker Muffins

1 cup milk

1 cup rolled oats

1 cup flour

3 tablespoons sugar

4 teaspoons baking powder

½ teaspoon salt

1 egg, beaten

1 tablespoon butter, melted

1. Scald milk, pour over rolled oats, and let stand for 30 minutes.

2. Preheat oven to 350°F. Grease a 12-cup muffin pan.

3. Sift together flour, sugar, baking powder, and salt. Add to oats mixture and stir to combine. Stir in egg and melted butter.

4. Pour batter into muffin cups. Bake for 30 minutes or until a tester inserted in center comes out clean. Turn out onto a wire rack to cool. Makes 12 muffins.

Adapted from *The Best of the Old Church Cookbooks* by Florence Ekstrand, courtesy of Welcome Press

Hush Puppies

Oil for frying
½ cup flour
2 teaspoons baking powder
1 tablespoon sugar
½ teaspoon salt

1½ cups white cornmeal
1 small onion, finely chopped
1 egg, beaten
¾ cup milk

1. Pour oil 2 to 3 inches deep into a deep fryer and heat to 360°F.

2. Whisk together flour, baking powder, sugar, salt, and cornmeal. Add onion and toss to coat. Add egg and milk and mix thoroughly.

3. Drop batter by the teaspoonful into hot oil. Fry in batches until golden brown, 2 to 3 minutes. Drain on paper towels. Serve hot. Makes 8 servings.

MRS. SARA ROBERTS | Pittsboro Baptist Church, Pittsboro, North Carolina

For crisp fried foods, don't crowd a deep fryer.
Foods should be free to bob about. Overcrowding causes the oil temperature to drop,
which in turn causes foods to absorb the oil and become soggy.

Crullers or Tanglebritches

Oil for frying
1 cup butter, room temperature
2 cups sugar
4 eggs
10½ cups flour, divided

½ teaspoon baking soda
2 teaspoons baking powder
1 teaspoon nutmeg
1 cup buttermilk
½ teaspoon vinegar

1. Pour oil 2 to 3 inches deep into a deep fryer and heat to 360°F.

2. Cream butter and sugar in a mixer bowl. Beat in eggs one at a time. With mixer running on low speed, add 5 cups of the flour, baking soda, baking powder, and nutmeg. Add buttermilk and vinegar. Gradually add remaining 5½ cups flour, mixing just until combined.

3. Turn out dough onto a floured board. Roll to a ¼-inch thickness. Use a pastry wheel to cut dough into 2½ x 4-inch strips. Slit the middle and pull one end through the opening to twist the sides. Fry in batches, four or five at a time, until golden brown, 2 to 3 minutes. Remove with slotted spoon and set on brown kraft paper to drain. Sprinkle with confectioners' sugar. Makes 40 to 50 pieces.

MARGARET TURNER | First Moravian Church, Greensboro, North Carolina

Cottage Cheese Butterhorns

1¼ cups butter
1 container (16 oz.) small curd cottage cheese
2¼ cups flour
¼ teaspoon salt

ICING:

1½ cups confectioners' sugar
1½ tablespoons butter, room temperature
1½ tablespoons milk
¼ teaspoon vanilla

1. Cream butter and cottage cheese in a large mixer bowl. Add flour and salt and mix until well combined. Divide dough into thirds and roll into three balls. Flatten each ball slightly, wrap in plastic wrap, and refrigerate overnight.

2. Preheat oven to 350°F. Lightly grease two baking sheets.

3. Roll out one dough disk to a ⅛-inch thickness. Cut into 16 wedges. Roll each wedge, starting at the wide end. Place on baking sheet with pointed end on the bottom. Repeat for remaining two disks. Bake for 30 to 40 minutes or until golden brown. Cool on wire racks.

4. To make icing: Combine confectioners' sugar, butter, milk, and vanilla in a small mixing bowl. Beat until smooth. Drizzle icing over pastry. Makes 48 pastries.

WOMEN'S MISSIONARY AUXILIARY | Bay Springs, Mississippi

Popovers

1 cup flour
¼ teaspoon salt
2 eggs

1 cup milk
1 tablespoon butter, melted,
    plus more for pan

1. Preheat oven to 450°F. Warm an 8-cup popover or muffin pan in oven.

2. Combine flour and salt in a large mixer bowl.

3. Whisk eggs until frothy, add milk, and whisk to combine. Slowly add egg mixture to flour mixture, beating constantly to prevent lumps. Blend in melted butter.

4. Remove muffin pan from oven. Brush muffin cups generously with melted butter. Add batter, filling cups one-third full. Bake for 25 minutes at 450°F. Reduce heat to 350°F and bake 15 minutes more. Turn out muffins onto a wire rack. Serve hot with butter and jam. Makes 8 popovers.

❖ **JUNE SPIELMAN** | St. John's Guild, St. John's Church, West Bend, Wisconsin

Orange Muffins

1 cup sugar
½ cup orange juice
½ cup butter
1 cup sugar
2 cups sifted flour

1 teaspoon baking soda
1 teaspoon salt
¼ cup sour cream
1 teaspoon grated orange zest

1. Preheat oven to 375°F. Grease one 12-cup and one 6-cup muffin pan.

2. Combine sugar and orange juice in a small bowl. Set aside.

3. Cream butter and sugar in a mixer bowl. Sift together flour, baking soda, and salt. Add flour mixture and sour cream alternately to batter. Stir in zest.

4. Spoon batter into muffin cups until two-thirds full. Bake for 12 to 15 minutes or until lightly browned. Turn out onto a wire rack. Dip warm muffins in juice mixture and allow to cool. Makes 18 muffins.

❖ **PAM SOUTHERLAND** | First Moravian Church, Greensboro, North Carolina

Ham and Cheese Muffins

1 tablespoon butter
⅓ cup diced green and red bell peppers
⅓ cup finely chopped onion
1 egg
½ cup milk

3 tablespoons vegetable oil
1 tablespoon sour cream
1½ cups biscuit mix
¾ cup shredded cheddar cheese
½ cup diced cooked ham

1. Preheat oven to 400°F. Coat a 12-cup muffin pan with cooking spray.

2. Heat butter in a nonstick skillet over medium heat until melted. Add pepper and onion and sauté until onion is limp and translucent, 4 to 6 minutes.

3. Whisk together egg, milk, oil, and sour cream in a large bowl. Stir in biscuit mix, cheddar cheese, and ham. Do not overmix.

4. Spoon batter into muffin cups until three-fourths full. Bake for 15 minutes or until golden brown. Cool in pan 5 minutes before turning out onto a wire rack. Serve warm. Makes 12 muffins.

✧ **GAIL GLASGOW** | Trinity Presbyterian Church, Little Rock, Arkansas

Breadsticks

24 hot dog buns
2 cups butter, melted
½ teaspoon Tabasco sauce
¼ teaspoon garlic powder

1 tablespoon dried parsley
1 tablespoon dried onion flakes
Grated Parmesan

1. Preheat oven to 250°F. Lightly coat a baking sheet with cooking spray.

2. Open each bun and slice it lengthwise into six pieces. Lay pieces side by side on baking sheet.

3. Combine melted butter, Tabasco sauce, garlic powder, parsley, and onion flakes. Spoon or brush mixture over bun slices. Sprinkle liberally with Parmesan. Bake for 1½ hours, or until crusty and golden brown. Cool on a wire rack. Store in an airtight container. Makes 12 dozen breadsticks.

✧ **LYNDA MCKEE** | Presbyterian Church of Gonzales, Gonzales, Texas

English Scones

2 cups self-rising flour
¼ cup sugar
⅓ cup butter, plus more for serving
⅔ cup buttermilk
1 egg

½ cup raisins
Strawberry jam
Clotted cream

1. Preheat oven to 450°F. Lightly grease a baking sheet.

2. Combine flour, sugar, and butter in a mixer bowl.

3. Whisk together buttermilk and egg. Add to flour mixture and stir to combine. Stir in raisins.

4. Turn out dough onto a floured surface and knead gently. Roll out to a ½-inch thickness. Cut into 12 pieces with a floured knife or pastry blade. Transfer to baking sheet. Bake for 10 to 12 minutes or until lightly browned. To serve, split warm scones in half, spread both halves with butter, and top with strawberry jam and clotted cream. Refrigerate leftover scones in a zip-close bag and microwave 10 to 15 seconds to reheat. Makes 12 scones.

✧ **JEAN BONNER** | Terrace Acres Baptist Church, Fort Worth, Texas

Drop Doughnuts

1 egg	1 tablespoon baking powder
½ cup sugar	1 teaspoon nutmeg
2 tablespoons oil	Oil for frying
½ cup milk	Confectioners' sugar
1½ cups flour	Cinnamon

1. Whisk egg in a large bowl. Add sugar, oil, and milk and whisk to combine.

2. Sift together flour, baking powder, and nutmeg. Add to egg mixture and stir to make a stiff dough. Chill for 15 minutes.

3. Pour oil 2 to 3 inches deep into a deep fryer and heat to 350°F. Drop dough by the teaspoonful into hot oil. Fry, turning once, until golden brown and cooked all the way through, about 3 minutes. Drain on paper towels.

4. Combine confectioners' sugar and cinnamon in a paper lunch bag. Gently shake warm doughnuts in bag, a few at a time, until coated. Makes 20 doughnuts.

 **LINDA S. THOMPSON** | Oakwood Church of God in Christ, Godfrey, Illinois

Raised Doughnuts

½ of a large cake (1 oz.) compressed wet yeast (such as Red Star)	1 cup hot mashed potatoes
1½ cups warm water	1 teaspoon salt
⅔ cup shortening	2 eggs
⅔ cup sugar	6½ cups sifted flour
	Oil for frying

1. Dissolve yeast in warm water. Let stand 10 minutes.

2. Cream shortening and sugar in a mixer bowl. Add hot mashed potatoes, mix gently, and allow to cool.

3. Stir yeast mixture into potatoes. Add salt, eggs, and flour and knead with a dough hook until no longer sticky. Cover and let rise in a warm place until doubled in bulk, 1 to 2 hours.

4. Roll out dough to a ½-inch thickness. Cut with a floured 3-inch doughnut cutter. Transfer to parchment paper and let rise until doubled in size, 30 minutes to 1 hour.

5. Pour oil 2 to 3 inches deep into a deep fryer and heat to 360°F. Gently drop doughnuts, three or four at a time, into hot oil. Fry in batches, turning once as they rise to the surface, until golden brown, 3 to 4 minutes. Remove with a slotted spoon and drain on paper towels. Makes 48 doughnuts.

MRS. L. A. WESTPHAL | St. John's Guild, St. John's Church, West Bend, Wisconsin

Easy-Drop Fastnacht Doughnuts

Oil for frying
⅓ cup sugar
½ cup milk
1 egg
2 tablespoons vegetable shortening, melted, plus more for spoon
1½ cups flour
2 teaspoons baking powder

COATINGS:
Sugar
Confectioners' sugar
Honey
Molasses
Nutmeg

The batter for doughnut holes loves to stick to your spoon. For a smoother release, dip the spoon into hot melted shortening just before scooping up the batter.

1. Pour oil 2 to 3 inches deep into a deep fryer and heat to 360°F.

2. Combine sugar, milk, egg, and melted shortening until well blended. Add flour and baking powder and stir to moisten.

3. Drop batter by the teaspoonful into hot oil. Fry in batches of three or four, turning once, until golden brown, 2 to 3 minutes. Drain on paper towels.

4. To add toppings: Add sugar or confectioners' sugar to a brown paper lunch bag, add a few doughnut holes, and shake gently to coat. Or place doughnut holes on waxed paper or parchment and drizzle with honey or molasses. Grate nutmeg over the top. Serve warm. Makes 24 doughnuts.

❖ **DOROTHY R. MYERS** | Trinity Evangelical Lutheran Church, Lansdale, Pennsylvania

Doughnuts

4 cups flour
2 to 3 teaspoons baking powder
2 eggs
2 cups sugar

1 cup milk
Nutmeg
Lard for frying

1. Sift together flour and baking powder.

2. Beat eggs and sugar. Add flour mixture (reserving a little for rolling out), milk, and nutmeg. Mix to make a firm dough.

3. Roll out dough on a lightly floured surface. Cut into shapes with cookie cutters or biscuit cutters. Fry in hot lard. Makes 24 doughnuts.

❖ **MRS. J. P. RANDLE** | *Presbyterian Cookbook*, 2nd Edition, 1924 | Presbyterian Church of Gonzales, Gonzales, Texas

Corn Sticks

2 tablespoons shortening
½ cup cornmeal
½ cup flour
1 teaspoon baking powder
¼ to ½ teaspoon baking soda

½ teaspoon salt
½ cup buttermilk
½ cup water
1 egg

1. Preheat oven to 450°F. Divide shortening among corn stick pans and melt in oven.

2. Whisk together cornmeal, flour, baking powder, baking soda, and salt. Make a well in center, add buttermilk, water, and egg, and beat until smooth.

3. Pour batter into stick pans. Bake for 25 minutes or until tops are golden brown. Serve hot. Makes 12 corn sticks.

JANE NOOE | Pittsboro Baptist Church, Pittsboro, North Carolina

Scottish Scones

2 cups self-rising flour
1 tablespoon baking powder
Salt
2 tablespoons cold butter, cut into
    small pieces

1 to 1⅓ cups milk plus more for tops
Strawberry jam
Unsweetened whipped cream

1. Preheat oven to 350°F. Lightly grease a baking sheet.

2. Sift together flour, baking powder, and salt. Cut in butter with your fingers until crumbly. Make a well in center of mixture, add milk, and mix with a fork to make a dough that barely holds together.

3. Turn out dough onto a floured board and knead gently. Roll out with a floured rolling pin to a ¾-inch thickness. Cut with a 2-inch fluted or plain cookie cutter. Set rounds on baking sheet, 1 to 1½ inches apart. Brush tops with milk. Bake for 8 to 10 minutes or until dough rises and turns golden brown. Transfer to a wire rack and allow to cool for 5 minutes. Serve warm with strawberry jam and unsweetened whipped cream. Makes 12 scones.

LINDA BROWN | Messiah United Methodist Church, York, Pennsylvania

Dinner on the Grounds

SUMMERTIME ON THE CHURCH GROUNDS

Dinner on the grounds! What precious memories those words bring back. Memories of a slower, simpler lifestyle . . . The smells that came through the open window of our little mill village church could tempt a bishop. We always drew extra large crowds on days that dinner on the grounds would be served, and no preacher could resist the opportunity to preach an extremely eloquent (translation: long) sermon when a large crowd was gathered.

Of course, that made the wait almost intolerable, but the meal was always worth the wait. So much good food! Casseroles, made from scratch; fried chicken and roast beef and ham; pickles and relish of every description; every garden fresh vegetable known to man; huge washtubs of sweet ice tea and lemonade; a black kettle of Brunswick stew, slow-cooked all night over an open fire; desserts galore—cakes, pies, cookies, brownies—the list is endless and the memories are precious.

From *Dinner on the Grounds* by Darrell Huckaby © 2000

Red Beans over Rice

1 ham hock
2 packages (16 oz. each) red kidney beans,
    sorted and rinsed
Salt and pepper
2 bay leaves
1 can (14.5 oz.) beef broth or bouillon
¼ cup bacon drippings
2 large onions, chopped
5 stalks celery, chopped

1 tablespoon flour
1 pepper, chopped
1 can (4 oz.) tomato purée
1 tablespoon prepared horseradish
1 teaspoon thyme
1 teaspoon sage
1 teaspoon ground cumin
2 packages (14 oz. each) Polish sausage, sliced
8 to 10 cups cooked rice

1. Place ham hock and beans in a large stockpot. Add water to cover. Sprinkle with salt and pepper. Add bay leaves and beef broth. Cook over low heat, stirring frequently, until beans are softened, 5 hours.
2. Heat bacon drippings in a large skillet over medium heat. Add onion and celery and sauté until limp, 4 to 5 minutes.
3. Stir in flour, pepper, tomato purée, horseradish, thyme, sage, and cumin until well combined. Add to beans and cook until sauce is thick, 1 hour more. Add sausage during last 30 minutes of cooking. Serve over rice. Makes 16 servings.

SUZIE LOWE | Christ Episcopal Church, Charlotte, North Carolina

Horseradish Cheese Ball with Crackers

1 package (4 oz.) dried beef
2 tablespoons dried parsley
2 packages (8 oz. each) cream cheese,
    room temperature
1 to 2 tablespoons horseradish
⅛ teaspoon celery salt
¼ teaspoon garlic powder

This cheese ball makes a festive hostess gift. Wrap it in clear plastic and tie with a pretty bow. Don't forget the crackers.

1. Working in small batches, coarsely chop dried beef in a blender or food processor. Combine 2 tablespoons of the chopped beef with dried parsley.
2. Combine cream cheese, remaining dried beef, horseradish, celery salt, and garlic powder until well blended.
3. Roll cheese mixture by hand into a ball. Roll in chopped beef–parsley mixture to coat. Chill until firm. Serve with crackers. Makes 10 to 12 servings.

MAUREEN LYONS | Trinity Evangelical Lutheran Church, Lansdale, Pennsylvania

Spinach Bread

¾ cup butter, divided
1 small onion, chopped
1 package (10 oz.) frozen chopped spinach,
    thawed and squeezed dry

1 cup grated mozzarella
1 cup grated cheddar cheese
One 1-lb. loaf or 2 mini loaves of French bread
Parmesan

1. Preheat oven to 350°F.

2. Heat ½ cup of the butter in a skillet over medium heat until melted. Add onion and sauté until golden and limp, 4 to 5 minutes. Remove from heat and stir in spinach, mozzarella, and cheddar cheese.

3. Slice bread lengthwise. Butter both sides with remaining ¼ cup butter. Spread spinach mixture on each side of bread. Sprinkle with Parmesan.

4. Place loaf halves back together. Using a serrated knife, cut crosswise or at an angle to make 1½- to 2-inch-wide slices. Wrap tightly in foil. Heat in oven for 20 minutes. Makes 6 to 8 servings.

LYNN ARMSTRONG | Christ Episcopal Church, Charlotte, North Carolina

Deviled Eggs

12 eggs
1 teaspoon honey mustard
1 teaspoon red wine vinegar
2 teaspoons sugar
¼ to ⅜ cup mayonnaise
Salt and pepper
Sliced olives
Paprika

Have you ever had difficulty peeling a hard-boiled egg? The fresher the egg, the more difficult it is to peel. For easier peeling, choose eggs with an expiration date that is less than 2 weeks away. Cook two or three more eggs than you need to allow for peeling mistakes and to give you some extra yolks.

1. Place eggs in a large saucepan, add cold salted water to cover, and bring to a boil over medium heat. Boil for 15 to 20 minutes.

2. Drain off cooking water and immediately fill saucepan with cold tap water. Crack the shells as soon as eggs are cool enough to handle. Return eggs to cold water in pan and allow to cool 5 minutes more. Peel eggs under cold running water. Set on paper towels to drain.

3. Cut each egg in half lengthwise. Scoop out yolks into a mixer bowl. Place whites, cavity side up, on a platter.

4. Add honey mustard, vinegar, sugar, and ¼ cup of the mayonnaise to yolks. Beat on medium to high speed until very smooth and the consistency of cake frosting. Add additional mayonnaise, 1 teaspoon at a time, to achieve desired consistency. Sprinkle with salt and pepper.

5. Transfer yolk mixture to a pastry bag fitted with a large tip. Pipe the mixture into the egg white cavities. Top with an olive slice or sprinkle with paprika. Makes 20 deviled eggs.

REGINA ROBINSON | First Baptist Church, Russell, Kentucky

Cheese Ball

2 packages (8 oz. each) cream cheese,
   room temperature
10 oz. grated sharp cheddar cheese
1 tablespoon chopped pimiento
1 tablespoon chopped green pepper
1 tablespoon minced onion

1 teaspoon lemon juice
Dash of cayenne pepper
Dash of salt
2 tablespoons Worcestershire sauce
1 cup chopped pecans

1. Combine cream cheese, cheddar cheese, pimiento, green pepper, onion, lemon juice, cayenne pepper, salt, and Worcestershire sauce in a mixer bowl. Mix on low speed until well combined. Chill.
2. Roll cheese mixture into a ball. Roll ball in chopped pecans until fully coated. Chill until ready to serve. Makes 10 to 12 servings.

NITA HARTER | Trinity Presbyterian Church, Little Rock, Arkansas

Summer Picnic on the Grounds

SUGGESTED MENU

Horseradish Cheese Ball with Crackers
PAGE 55

Summer Main Dish Party Salad
PAGE 70

Zucchini-Potato Salad
PAGE 97

Tomato Salad from Great Grammy Beatty
PAGE 98

Marinated Green Beans with Horseradish Dressing
PAGE 82

Chocolate-Orange Muffins
PAGE 104

Peaches and Cream Cheese Pie
PAGE 98

Iced Tea

TRINITY EVANGELICAL LUTHERAN CHURCH
Lansdale, Pennsylvania

Bacon Cheese Logs

1 lb. sliced bacon

1½ packages (12 oz.) cream cheese,
    room temperature

4 drops Tabasco sauce

½ cup pecans, chopped

½ teaspoon garlic salt

½ teaspoon Worcestershire sauce

1 tablespoon chili powder

1. Cook bacon in batches until crisp, drain on paper towels, and crumble into a mixing bowl.

2. Add cream cheese, Tabasco sauce, pecans, garlic salt, and Worcestershire sauce to bacon. Stir until well blended.

3. Divide mixture in half and roll into two logs. Sprinkle chili powder onto waxed paper and roll the logs in it. Wrap in plastic wrap and refrigerate until ready to serve. Makes 2 cheese logs.

TOMELA KEENAN | Trinity Presbyterian Church, Little Rock, Arkansas

Nacho Mountain

1 package (8 oz.) cream cheese

1 container (12 oz.) cottage cheese

1 package (1 oz.) taco seasoning mix

2 cups shredded lettuce

8 chopped green onions

1 cup chopped tomatoes

8 oz. shredded cheese

1 jar (16 oz.) taco sauce

1. Combine cream cheese, cottage cheese, and taco seasoning mix until well blended. Spread on a large round serving platter.

2. Layer shredded lettuce, green onions, tomatoes, and shredded cheese over cheese base on platter. Chill in refrigerator.

3. Just before serving, pour taco sauce over the top. Serve nacho chips on the side. Makes 1 party dip platter.

GERRI HOLSINGER | First Baptist Church, Russell, Kentucky

Minted Melon

1 medium cantaloupe

1 medium honeydew

½ cup sugar

1 cup water

6 to 8 fresh mint leaves plus more
    for garnish

1. Cut cantaloupe and honeydew in half. Scoop out and discard seeds and pulp. Scoop out flesh with a melon baller and place in a large bowl.

2. Combine sugar, water, and mint leaves in a saucepan over medium heat. Bring to a boil and simmer, stirring occasionally, until slightly thickened, about 10 minutes. Strain and cool.

3. To serve, spoon melon balls into dessert dishes, pour mint sauce over the top, and garnish with fresh mint leaves. Makes 6 to 8 servings.

❖ NANCY PAHEL | First Moravian Church, Greensboro, North Carolina

Uncle Charlie's Cukes

8 cucumbers
3 green peppers
3 medium brown or white onions
2 tablespoons celery seed
2 tablespoons salt
2 cups sugar
1½ cups red wine vinegar

 Enjoy these fresh, not-too-sweet pickles piled high on sandwiches.

1. Cut cucumbers, green peppers, and onions into thin slices. Place in a large bowl, add celery seed and salt, and toss to combine.

2. Dissolve sugar in vinegar. Pour over cucumbers and stir until evenly coated.

3. Transfer cucumbers to a pickle crock or resealable plastic container (such as Tupperware). Let marinate in the refrigerator at least 3 hours and up to 3 months. You can add more sliced cucumbers, peppers, or onions to the brine throughout the summer. Makes 1 quart.

❖ CAROL MURPHY | Church of the Canyons Women's Ministries, Canyon Country, California

Black-Eyed Pea Hummus

3 garlic cloves, peeled and minced
Juice of 2 lemons (about ½ cup)
⅓ cup tahini (sesame seed paste)
1 teaspoon ground cumin
½ teaspoon salt

½ teaspoon paprika
2 cans (15.5 oz. each) black-eyed peas, drained
Fresh chives
14 pitas, 6-inch diameter, quartered

1. Combine garlic, lemon juice, tahini, cumin, salt, paprika, and peas in a food processor. Blend together, scraping down sides of bowl occasionally, until smooth.

2. Cover and chill until ready to serve, up to 2 days in advance. Garnish with chives. Serve with pita slices. Makes 3½ cups.

❖ LINDA S. THOMPSON | Oakwood Church of God in Christ, Godfrey, Illinois

Apple Dip

1 package (8 oz.) cream cheese,
   room temperature
1 teaspoon vanilla
¼ cup sugar

¾ cup brown sugar
½ cup unsalted dry roasted peanuts
7 Granny Smith apples

1. Combine cream cheese, vanilla, sugar, and brown sugar in a mixer bowl. Mix until well blended.
2. Chop peanuts in a blender or food processor until finely ground. Add to cheese mixture and stir to combine. Refrigerate until ready to serve.
3. Just before serving, core apples and cut into wedges. Arrange apples on a serving platter with bowl of dip. Makes 6 to 8 servings.

❖ JEAN HUBER | Trinity Evangelical Lutheran Church, Lansdale, Pennsylvania

Avocado Salsa

⅓ cup white wine vinegar
1 tablespoon honey
¾ teaspoon salt
½ teaspoon ground cumin
¼ teaspoon pepper

1 small onion, chopped
1 can (4 oz.) chopped green chilies, undrained
1 large garlic clove, minced
2 avocados, peeled and diced

1. Combine vinegar, honey, salt, cumin, pepper, onion, chilies, and garlic.
2. Add avocados and toss gently to combine. Serve with tortilla chips, chicken, or seafood. Makes 1½ cups.

❖ JEAN BARNETT | Presbyterian Church of Gonzales, Gonzales, Texas

Cucumber Cream Cheese Spread

2 packages (8 oz. each) cream cheese,
   room temperature
2 teaspoons lemon juice
¼ teaspoon prepared horseradish

¼ teaspoon salt
⅛ teaspoon hot sauce
2 teaspoons minced onion
½ medium cucumber, peeled and finely chopped

1. Beat cream cheese until smooth.
2. Add lemon juice, horseradish, salt, and hot sauce. Mix until well combined.
3. Stir in onion and cucumber. Cover and chill at least 1 hour before serving. Makes 2¼ cups.

❖ FREDA GANTT | Methow Valley United Methodist Church, Twisp, Washington

Virginia's Salsa Fresco

8 plum tomatoes (about 1 lb.),
  cut into ¼-inch pieces
2 tablespoons finely chopped yellow onion
2 garlic cloves, finely minced
1 can (4 oz.) chopped mild green chilies

2 tablespoons finely chopped cilantro
1 tablespoon lime juice
1 teaspoon salt
1 teaspoon sugar
½ teaspoon ground cumin

1. Combine tomatoes, onion, garlic, chilies, cilantro, lime juice, salt, sugar, and cumin in a large bowl. Toss until well blended.

2. Chill for 30 minutes, just to allow flavors to combine. Serve fresh with taco chips. Makes 2 cups.

For a hot salsa, add chopped jalapeños or serranos. A little goes a long way, so add a little at a time and taste as you go.

✦ **VIRGINIA NEILL** | Unity Baptist Church, Morgantown, Indiana

Lime Fresh Fruit Dip

1 cup plain low-fat yogurt
2 tablespoons honey
2 tablespoons lime juice

1 teaspoon grated lime zest
¼ teaspoon ginger
Fresh fruit, cut in chunks, with toothpicks inserted

Combine yogurt, honey, lime juice, lime zest, and ginger in a bowl. Stir until well combined. Serve with fresh fruit for dipping. Makes 1¼ cups dip.

✦ **KIM WHITE** | Methow Valley United Methodist Church, Twisp, Washington

Stuffed Cherry Tomatoes

24 large cherry tomatoes
1 small package (3 oz.) cream cheese,
  room temperature
1 tablespoon chopped parsley

½ teaspoon dry mustard
2 tablespoons shredded cheddar cheese
1 or 2 drops hot pepper sauce

1. Slice off tops of tomatoes. Scoop out seeds with a melon baller.

2. Combine cream cheese, parsley, mustard, cheddar cheese, and hot pepper sauce in a bowl. Stir until well blended.

3. Fill each tomato with a heaping scoop of cheese mixture. Makes 24 appetizers.

✦ **MR. TRAPP** | Miracle Deliverance Holiness Church, Columbia, South Carolina

Zesty Avocado Dip

1 avocado, peeled, pit removed, and sliced
1 cup sour cream
1 package (1 oz.) green onion dip mix
1 tablespoon lemon juice

1. Combine avocado, sour cream, green onion dip mix, and lemon juice in a blender until smooth.
2. Transfer dip to a serving bowl, cover with plastic wrap, and chill until ready to serve. Serve with fresh raw vegetables. Makes 2 cups.

Here are some fresh raw vegetables that are good for dipping:
• Baby carrots
• Sliced cucumber rounds
• Broccoli florets
• Red and yellow peppers, cut into strips
• Green beans
• Radishes

🔹 **RENAE DURHAM** | Miracle Deliverance Holiness Church, Columbia, South Carolina

Fresh Fruit Compote

3 medium peaches, peeled and sliced
2 cups sliced strawberries
2 cups blueberries

2 cups melon balls
3 medium bananas
1 bottle (25 oz.) sparkling grape juice, chilled

1. Layer peaches in a large glasss bowl or trifle dish. Add strawberries, blueberries, and melon balls in layers. Cover tightly and chill.
2. Just before serving, peel and slice bananas. Arrange bananas over fruit layers. Pour juice over compote. Makes 8 to 10 servings.

🔹 **T.T.** | Miracle Deliverance Holiness Church, Columbia, South Carolina

Summertime Picnic Relish

2 tablespoons salad oil
1 cup chopped onion
1 cup chopped green pepper
2 tablespoons vinegar

1½ teaspoons salt
½ teaspoon sugar
¼ teaspoon dry mustard
⅛ teaspoon pepper

1. Heat oil in a large skillet over medium heat. Add onion and green pepper and cook until tender, 6 to 8 minutes.
2. Stir in vinegar, salt, sugar, mustard, and pepper. Bring to a boil, remove from heat, and allow to cool. Transfer to a container, cover, and refrigerate at least 3 days before serving, to allow flavors to blend. Makes 3 cups.

🔹 **TIM** | Miracle Deliverance Holiness Church, Columbia, South Carolina

Hearty Shrimp Gazpacho

1 lb. tomatoes, seeded and chopped (2 cups)
1 can (15 oz.) garbanzo beans, drained
1 can (7 oz.) whole kernel shoepeg corn,
　　drained
1 green pepper, chopped
1 small cucumber, peeled and diced
1 green onion, chopped
2 garlic cloves, minced
1 tablespoon fresh lime juice

2¼ cups vegetable juice (such as V-8)
1 cup water
¼ cup hot salsa
½ teaspoon sugar
Salt and pepper
½ lb. cooked medium shrimp,
　　peeled and deveined
Lime wedges
Hot pepper sauce or cayenne pepper

1. Combine tomatoes, garbanzo beans, corn, green pepper, cucumber, onion, and garlic in a large bowl. Sprinkle with lime juice.
2. Combine vegetable juice, water, hot salsa, and sugar in a medium bowl. Sprinkle with salt and pepper. Cover both mixtures with plastic wrap and chill for 1 hour.
3. Just before serving, stir salsa mixture into tomato mixture. Add shrimp and toss to combine. Ladle soup into bowls. Garnish with lime wedges. Add a few dashes of hot pepper sauce or cayenne pepper as desired. Makes 6 servings.

CHRIST CHURCH | Frederica, St. Simons Island, Georgia

Four-Tomato Salsa

7 plum tomatoes, chopped
7 medium red tomatoes, chopped
3 medium yellow tomatoes, chopped
3 medium orange tomatoes, chopped
1 teaspoon salt
2 tablespoons lime juice
2 tablespoons olive oil or vegetable oil
1 medium white onion, chopped
1 small red onion, chopped
2 green onions, chopped

1 small sweet red pepper, chopped
1 small yellow pepper, chopped
1 small orange pepper, chopped
1 small green pepper, chopped
3 pickled sweet banana wax peppers,
　　chopped
½ cup minced parsley
2 tablespoons minced cilantro or
　　additional parsley

1. Layer plum tomatoes, red tomatoes, yellow tomatoes, and orange tomatoes in a colandar, sprinkling with salt as you go. Let drain for 10 minutes.
2. Transfer tomatoes to a large bowl. Add lime juice, oil, white onion, red onion, green onion, red pepper, yellow pepper, orange pepper, green pepper, banana peppers, parsley, and cilantro. Toss to combine. Serve with tortilla chips. Refrigerate or freeze leftovers. Makes 14 cups.

MARIETTA HENDERSON | Unity Baptist Church, Morgantown, Indiana

Cream of Carrot Soup

2 tablespoons butter
2 cups sliced onions
5 cups coarsely chopped carrots
½ cup white rice, uncooked

8 cups chicken broth, divided
Salt and pepper
½ cup sour cream

1. Heat butter in a large skillet over medium heat until melted. Add onions and carrots and sauté until tender, 7 to 8 minutes.
2. Add rice and 4 cups of the chicken broth. Cover and simmer until rice is tender, 20 to 25 minutes.
3. Add remaining 4 cups broth. Sprinkle with salt and pepper. Allow to cool slightly. Transfer mixture to a food processor and purée until smooth. Serve chilled or hot, garnished with sour cream. Makes 6 servings.

JANE BRUCE | Christ Episcopal Church, Charlotte, North Carolina

Cold Cucumber Soup

1 cucumber, peeled and seeded
1 medium or small onion, cut in half
1 cup chicken broth
1 can (10.75 oz.) cream of chicken
   condensed soup

¾ cup sour cream, yogurt, or buttermilk
Dash of Tabasco sauce
Dash of Worcestershire sauce
½ teaspoon curry powder

1. Combine cucumber, onion, chicken broth, cream of chicken soup, sour cream (or yogurt or buttermilk), Tabasco sauce, Worcestershire sauce, and curry powder in a blender. Mix until smooth. Taste soup and adjust seasonings.
2. Transfer soup to a covered container. Chill at least 1 hour before serving. Store, covered, in refrigerator up to 3 days. Makes 4 or 5 servings.

LINDSAY LOWE OWENS | Christ Church, Frederica, St. Simons Island, Georgia

Summer Crab Soup

1 package (7.5 oz.) frozen crabmeat, thawed
1 pint sour cream
1 cup chicken bouillon
½ cup white wine
½ teaspoon dillweed

½ teaspoon salt
⅛ teaspoon white pepper
2 cups diced cucumber
½ cup chopped green onions
½ cup parsley

1. Slice crabmeat, reserving leg meat for garnish. Drain well.
2. Combine sour cream, chicken bouillon, and wine until well blended. Stir in dillweed, salt, and pepper.
3. Add sliced crabmeat, cucumber, green onions, and parlsey to sour cream mixture. Stir gently to combine. Chill for 2 to 3 hours. Serve icy cold, garnished with reserved crab. Makes 4 to 6 servings.

MARIAN CARTER | First Moravian Church, Greensboro, North Carolina

Cream of Peanut Soup

¼ cup butter	2 quarts chicken stock
1 medium onion, chopped	2 cups smooth peanut butter
2 ribs of celery, chopped	1¾ cups light cream
3 tablespoons flour	Chopped peanuts

1. Heat butter in a large skillet over medium heat until melted. Add onion and celery and sauté until soft, but not browned, 3 to 4 minutes.
2. Stir in flour until well blended. Add chicken stock, stirring constantly, and bring to a boil. Remove from heat.
3. Pass mixture through a sieve into a large bowl. Add peanut butter and light cream. Stir until thoroughly blended.
4. Return mixture to skillet. Cook over low heat until warmed through, 3 to 4 minutes. Serve garnished with chopped peanuts. Soup can also be served chilled. Makes 10 to 12 servings.

LIZ NICHOLAS | Trinity Evangelical Lutheran Church, Lansdale, Pennsylvania

Savory Party Bread

1 whole round loaf sourdough bread	1 teaspoon garlic powder
½ lb. Swiss cheese, sliced	½ cup chopped green onions
½ lb. cheddar cheese, sliced	2 to 3 teaspoons poppy seeds
½ cup butter, melted	½ cup grated Parmesan

1. Preheat oven to 350°F.
2. Cut bread loaf lengthwise and crosswise without cutting through the bottom crust.
3. Insert Swiss cheese and cheddar cheese slices between the cuts.
4. Combine melted butter, garlic powder, and green onions. Drizzle over top of loaf. Sprinkle with poppy seeds and Parmesan.
5. Wrap loaf in foil and place on baking sheet. Bake for 15 minutes. Peel back foil to expose top of loaf, and bake until cheese is melted, 10 minutes more. Makes 6 to 8 servings.

KATHY HOAGLAND | Terrace Acres Baptist Church, Fort Worth, Texas

Pepperoni Cheese Bites

1 package (10 oz.) sliced pepperoni
1 package (10 oz.) frozen chopped spinach,
    thawed and well drained
2 cups ricotta
1½ cups Parmesan
1¼ cups chopped mushrooms

½ cup chopped onion
1 teaspoon oregano
½ teaspoon salt
2 eggs
¼ cup sour cream

1. Preheat oven to 375°F. Lightly grease two 24-cup mini muffin pans with nonstick cooking spray.
2. Place one pepperoni slice in the bottom of each muffin cup. Cut remaining slices into 48 wedges for garnish.
3. Combine spinach, ricotta, Parmesan, mushrooms, onion, oregano, salt, and eggs. Stir until well blended. Spoon mixture into muffin cups. Bake for 20 to 25 minutes or until eggs are cooked and tops are lightly browned. Cool 10 minutes in pan before transferring to a serving platter. Top each with sour cream and a pepperoni wedge. Serve warm. Freeze leftovers in a resealable bag; to use, thaw in refrigerator and bake at 350°F for 10 minutes. Makes 48 bites.

ANNE SCOTT | Christ Episcopal Church, Charlotte, North Carolina

Softshell Crab Sandwiches

8 live softshell crabs (2 to 3 oz. each)
⅓ cup vegetable oil
2 garlic cloves, sliced
1 teaspoon Old Bay Seasoning
Salt and pepper
8 English muffins, split and flattened
    with a rolling pin

HERB BUTTER:
½ cup butter
2 tablespoons lemon juice
2 tablespoons minced parsley
1 tablespoon minced shallot
Salt and pepper

1. Rinse crabs under cold running water. With scissors, cut off the heads about ¼ inch behind the eyes. Cut off the white gills. Peel back the aprons and cut them off. Rinse again and pat dry with paper towels.
2. Combine oil, garlic, and Old Bay Seasoning in a large bowl. Sprinkle with salt and pepper. Add crabs, turning until evenly coated. Cover and set in refrigerator to marinate, at least 2 hours.
3. To make herb butter: Combine butter, lemon juice, parsley, and shallot in a small saucepan over moderately low heat. Stir until butter is melted. Remove from heat. Sprinkle with salt and pepper.
4. Prepare charcoal grill. Remove crabs from marinade and drain. Place crabs in a grill basket or directly on the grill over hot coals. Cook, turning once, until red on both sides, 3 to 5 minutes per side. Transfer to a platter.
5. Brush English muffins with herb butter. Grill, turning once, until lightly toasted, 1 to 2 minutes per side. Assemble sandwiches and serve. Makes 8 servings.

BETTY LINK | Christ Church, Frederica, St. Simons Island, Georgia

Fruited Wild Rice and Chicken Salad

5 boneless, skinless chicken breast halves

1 cup wild rice

2 Golden Delicious apples (do not substitute), peeled, sliced, and chopped into 1-inch pieces

Juice of 1 lemon

1 cup golden raisins

1 cup halved seedless red grapes

2 tablespoons minced mint

2 tablespoons minced parsley

2 tablespoons minced chives

Salt and pepper

1 cup pecan halves

DRESSING:

1 cup olive oil or vegetable oil

⅓ cup fresh orange juice, strained

2 tablespoons honey

Be sure to use fresh herbs, not dried, for this hearty salad. Increase each herb amount by 1 tablespoon when doubling or tripling the recipe. If the salad seems to soak up dressing, add a little orange juice and oil.

1. Roast or poach chicken breasts until tender and juices run clear. Do not overcook. Allow to cool. Cut into bite-size pieces.

2. Cook wild rice according to package directions. Do not overcook. Drain off water when rice begins to pop or salad will be mushy. Allow to cool.

3. Combine chopped apples and lemon juice in a large bowl. Add raisins, grapes, mint, parsley, and chives. Toss to combine. Add wild rice and chicken. Toss to combine.

4. To make dressing: Combine oil, orange juice, and honey. Pour over salad and toss until well combined. Sprinkle with salt and pepper. Cover and chill several hours or overnight. Add pecans and toss gently just before serving. Makes 8 to 10 servings.

LAURAINE SCHNEIDER | Ascension Lutheran Church, Minocqua, Wisconsin | Adapted from *A Taste of Heaven*, winner of a church cookbook contest sponsored by the *Milwaukee Journal Sentinel*

Fried Chicken

6 cups nonfat buttermilk

**¼ cup plus 5 teaspoons coarse
 kosher salt, divided**

⅓ cup Tabasco sauce

**2 whole chickens (2 to 3 lbs. each),
 washed and cut into 8 pieces each
 for frying (16 pieces total)**

3 cups flour

1 teaspoon pepper

1½ teaspoons cayenne pepper

2 teaspoons baking powder

2 lbs. vegetable shortening (for frying)

2 tablespoons bacon drippings (for frying)

 Fry dark meat and white meat separately to ensure doneness. Dark meat takes longer to cook.

1. Combine buttermilk, ¼ cup of the kosher salt, and Tabasco sauce in a large, airtight container. Add chicken pieces, turning to coat. Cover and refrigerate at least 2 hours or overnight.

2. Preheat oven to 200°F. Combine flour, remaining 5 teaspoons kosher salt, black pepper, cayenne pepper, and baking powder in a brown paper bag. Shake vigorously to combine. Add chicken pieces to bag, one at a time, and shake to coat. Place coated pieces on a clean plate or tray.

3. Preheat oven to 180°F (or use a warming oven). Divide shortening and bacon drippings between two 10-inch cast iron skillets. Heat over medium-low heat until oil comes to a medium (not rolling) boil and temperature on a frying thermometer registers 375°F.

4. Use tongs to place drumsticks and thighs in hot oil. Fry, turning once, until coating is dark and golden and an instant-read thermometer inserted in thighs registers 170°F, 10 to 14 minutes per side. Remove cooked pieces from skillet and drain on paper towels. Transfer to baking sheets and place in oven to keep warm. Use a slotted spoon to remove and discard any coating left in skillets.

5. Place breasts and wings in skillets and fry in same way, turning once, until dark and golden, 10 to 14 minutes per side. Drain on paper towels. Arrange dark and light meat on a serving platter. Makes 16 pieces.

MARTHA STEWART | Miracle Deliverance Holiness Church, Columbia, South Carolina

Spicy Fried Chicken Wings

**10 chicken wings, cut into
 3 pieces each**

Vegetable oil for frying

MARINADE:

⅓ cup light soy sauce

⅓ cup Worcestershire sauce

2 tablespoons blackened seasoning

2 tablespoons garlic salt

2 tablespoons onion salt

2 tablespoons seasoned salt

2 tablespoons brown sugar

1. To make marinade: Combine soy sauce, Worcestershire sauce, blackened seasoning, garlic salt, onion salt, seasoned salt, and brown sugar in a 1-gallon resealable plastic food storage bag. Seal tightly and shake vigorously until sugar is dissolved.

2. Add chicken to marinade and shake. Refrigerate from 1 to 24 hours, turning chicken several times.

3. Pour oil into a deep-fry pot or electric skillet until half full. Heat oil to 325°F. Fry chicken wings in batches until juices rung clear, about 7 minutes each. Drain on paper towels. Makes 30 pieces.

LINDA S. THOMPSON | Oakwood Church of God in Christ, Godfrey, Illinois

Chicken Salad for 25

2 large chickens (3 to 4 lbs. each),
    cooked until tender
4 tablespoons salad oil
4 tablespoons orange juice
4 tablespoons vinegar
2 teaspoons salt
2½ cups rice

2 cups mandarin orange sections
3 cups pineapple tidbits
3 cups chopped green onions
2 cups slivered almonds, toasted
3 cups diced celery
1 quart mayonnaise

1. Remove chicken meat from bones and cube.

2. Combine oil, orange juice, vinegar, and salt in a large bowl. Add chicken cubes, toss to combine, and set in refrigerator to marinate at least 4 hours or overnight.

3. Cook rice in boiling salted water following package directions. Rinse in cold water and drain.

4. Add mandarin oranges, pineapple, green onions, almonds, and celery to salad. Toss to combine. Add rice and toss. Stir in mayonnaise just before serving. Makes 25 servings.

Adapted from *The Best of the Old Church Cookbooks* by Florence Ekstrand, courtesy of Welcome Press

Peppered Shrimp

5 lbs. shrimp (shells on)
2 cups butter, melted
Juice of 4 lemons
1 bottle (16 oz.) Italian salad dressing
1 box (2 oz.) pepper

VARIATION:
Instead of Italian dressing, use
½ cup Worcestershire sauce,
2 teaspoons hot sauce, 2 teaspoons
salt, and 4 cloves of garlic, minced.

1. Preheat oven to 350°F. Lightly grease a 4-quart casserole.

2. Layer shrimp in casserole. Combine melted butter, lemon juice, Italian dressing, and pepper. Cover and bake, stirring occasionally, until shrimp turn pink, 30 minutes. Serve hot. Makes 8 to 10 servings.

MARGARET TABB | Christ Episcopal Church, Charlotte, North Carolina

Summer Main Dish Party Salad

3 cups cooked chicken or turkey,
   cut into 1-inch cubes
1½ cups chopped celery
1 can (6 oz.) sliced water chestnuts, drained
2 cups seedless grapes
1 can (15 oz.) pineapple chunks, drained
¼ cup butter
1 package (5.5 oz.) slivered almonds
Salt
8 artichoke hearts, cooked and chilled

DRESSING:

2 cups mayonnaise
2 tablespoons lemon juice
2½ tablespoons soy sauce
1 tablespoon curry powder
1 tablespoon onion juice or
   finely grated onion
1 tablespoon chutney

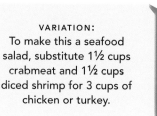

VARIATION:
To make this a seafood salad, substitute 1½ cups crabmeat and 1½ cups diced shrimp for 3 cups of chicken or turkey.

1. To make dressing: Combine mayonnaise, lemon juice, soy sauce, curry powder, onion juice, and chutney in a large bowl. Mix well.

2. Add cooked chicken or turkey, celery, water chestnuts, grapes, and pineapple chunks to dressing. Toss until chicken or turkey is evenly coated. Cover and refrigerate. Allow time for flavors to blend, at least 8 hours or overnight.

3. Heat butter in a small skillet over medium heat until melted. Add almonds and stir to coat. Increase heat and cook, stirring frequently, until lightly toasted, 5 to 6 minutes. Sprinkle with salt. Toss warm almonds into salad. Place an artichoke heart on each serving plate. Spoon salad on top. Makes 8 servings.

JOYCE BITNER | Trinity Evangelical Lutheran Church, Lansdale, Pennsylvania

Shrimp Addie

6 slices bacon
1 can (16 oz.) whole tomatoes
2 large green peppers, chopped
1 garlic clove, minced

½ teaspoon salt
Pepper
1 lb. peeled shrimp
2 cups cooked rice

1. Cook bacon in a large skillet, drain on paper towels, and crumble.

2. Add tomatoes, green peppers, and garlic to skillet. Sprinkle with salt and pepper. Cook on low heat, stirring occasionally, until slightly thickened, 20 to 30 minutes.

3. Add shrimp and bacon to skillet. Cook just until shrimp turn pink and are warmed through, 4 minutes. Serve over rice. Makes 4 servings.

LAURA WHEDON | Christ Episcopal Church, Charlotte, North Carolina

Soy Barbecued Shrimp

2 lbs. large shrimp, fresh or frozen
   (thaw if frozen)

MARINADE:

2 garlic cloves
½ teaspoon salt
½ cup olive oil or vegetable oil
¼ cup soy sauce
3 tablespoons finely chopped parsley
2 tablespoons finely chopped onion
½ teaspoon pepper

1. Peel and devein shrimp. Leave tails intact. Arrange in a shallow dish.

2. To make marinade: Mash garlic with salt in a small bowl. Blend in oil, soy sauce, parsley, onion, and pepper. Pour marinade over shrimp, cover, and marinate in refrigerator 2 to 3 hours.

3. Soak 12 bamboo skewers in water for 30 minutes.

4. Prepare charcoal grill. Thread shrimp on skewers. Set on grill rack and cook over hot coals, basting with marinade and turning once until shrimp turn pink, 2 to 3 minutes per side. Heat leftover marinade to boiling, allow to cool, and use as a dip for grilled shrimp. Makes 6 servings.

JUDITH THOMAS | Christ Episcopal Church, Charlotte, North Carolina

Shrimp Florentine

4 packages (10 oz. each) frozen chopped
   spinach, thawed and drained
2 lbs. medium shrimp, cooked and peeled
½ cup butter
1 medium onion, chopped
½ cup flour

3 cups half-and-half
1 cup dry white wine
Salt and pepper
2 teaspoons paprika
2 cups grated cheddar cheese

1. Preheat oven to 325°F. Lightly coat 13 x 9 x 2-inch baking dish with nonstick cooking spray.

2. Layer spinach on bottom of casserole. Layer shrimp on top of spinach.

3. Heat butter in a large skillet over medium heat until melted. Add onion and sauté until soft, 3 to 5 minutes. Stir in flour. Gradually blend in half-and-half, stirring continuously, until thickened, 5 to 7 minutes more. Slowly stir in wine. Sprinkle with salt, pepper, and paprika.

4. Pour sauce over shrimp. Top with grated cheese. Bake uncovered until spinach is cooked and cheese is bubbly, 30 minutes. Let cool 5 to 10 minutes before serving. Makes 12 servings.

JANE DOWD | Christ Episcopal Church, Charlotte, North Carolina

Fresh Tuna Escabeche

6 lbs. fresh tuna

¼ cup salt

1 quart water

6 to 8 tablespoons olive oil, divided

2 large garlic cloves, minced

2 medium red peppers, minced

1 large bay leaf

Juice of 1 lime

1 small red chili pepper, thinly sliced

1 large red onion, thinly sliced

½ cup white wine vinegar

2 teaspoons minced oregano or
    ¾ teaspoon dried oregano

2 teaspoons minced sweet marjoram or
    ¾ teaspoon dried marjoram

¼ teaspoon ground cumin

3 drops Tabasco sauce

1 can (10.5 oz.) chicken broth

Lettuce or watercress

Black olives

Cherry tomatoes

Hard-boiled eggs, sliced

1. Cut tuna into bite-size chunks. Dissolve salt in water, add tuna, and let stand for 30 minutes. Remove tuna from brine, drain, and pat dry.

2. Heat 6 tablespoons of the olive oil in a large heavy skillet over medium heat. Add garlic and sauté just until soft, 1 minute or less. Stir in red pepper and drop in bay leaf.

3. Add tuna to skillet and sauté in batches, stirring occasionally, until cooked through, 10 to 12 minutes per batch. Use a large slotted spoon to transfer tuna to a bowl. Sprinkle with lime juice and set aside.

4. Add 1 or 2 tablespoons oil to skillet, add chili pepper and red onion, and sauté until onion is translucent, 3 to 5 minutes. Add vinegar, oregano, marjoram, cumin, and Tabasco sauce. Reduce to a simmer and cook 15 minutes more, adding chicken broth 1 tablespoon at a time as liquid cooks off. Remove from heat. Allow to cool.

5. Pour sauce over tuna. Mix gently with a wooden spoon. Refrigerate or set in a cool place. To serve, arrange lettuce or watercress on platter, spoon escabeche on top, and garnish with black olives, tomatoes, and slices of hard-boiled egg. Can also be arranged on individual serving plates. Makes 6 to 8 servings.

◆ **BETH CRIMMINS** | Trinity Evangelical Lutheran Church, Lansdale, Pennsylvania

Bolgogie: Korean Shish Kebab

2 to 3 lbs. boneless sirloin steak

Red or green pepper, cut into
    1-inch squares

White onions, cut into chunks

Cherry tomatoes

Mushrooms, cut in half

MARINADE:

1 garlic clove, minced

1 scallion, green and white parts, minced

3 tablespoons sugar

6 oz. soy sauce

1 teaspoon sesame seeds

Pinch of salt

Pinch of red pepper

2 pinches of black pepper

1. To make marinade: Combine garlic, scallion, sugar, soy sauce, sesame seeds, salt, red pepper, and black pepper in a large bowl.

2. Cut steak into 1-inch cubes. Add steak to marinade and toss to coat. Let marinate in refrigerator at least 4 hours or overnight.

3. Prepare charcoal grill. Thread steak cubes, peppers, onions, cherry tomatoes, and mushrooms on skewers. Grill kabobs over hot coals, rotating until all sides are cooked, 10 to 15 minutes. Makes 15 to 20 servings.

RUTH GUMPER | Presbyterian Church of Gonzales, Gonzales, Texas

Grilled Lamb with Herb and Shallot Sauce

Leg of lamb (4 to 4½ lbs.), boned, fat and membrane removed	2 bay leaves
	6 sprigs of parsley
	2 teaspoons salt
MARINADE:	½ teaspoon pepper
1 cup olive oil	½ tablespoon sage
⅔ cup lemon juice	½ tablespoon rosemary
5 garlic cloves	1 tablespoon thyme

1. To make marinade: Combine oil, lemon juice, garlic, bay leaves, parsley, salt, pepper, sage, rosemary, and thyme in a large bowl.

2. Add lamb to marinade and turn to coat. Marinate in refrigerator for 24 hours, turning occasionally.

3. Prepare gas grill. Drain off and reserve marinade. Place lamb on grill and cook, turning until all sides are seared. Lower heat and continue cooking, basting frequently with reserved marinade, 45 to 60 minutes. Do not overcook; inside should remain pink. Cut off slices, arrange on serving platter, and dress with herb and shallot sauce. Makes 4 to 6 servings.

HERB AND SHALLOT SAUCE

½ cup beef stock	½ tablespoon rosemary
¼ cup red wine	½ tablespoon thyme
2 tablespoons chopped shallots	3 tablespoons butter, room temperature
½ tablespoon sage	3 tablespoons minced fresh parsley

1. Combine beef stock, wine, shallots, sage, rosemary, and thyme in a saucepan over medium heat. Bring to a boil and cook, stirring occasionally, until sauce reduces to ½ cup.

2. Remove from heat. Stir in butter and parsley.

JOE BRADFORD | Christ Church, Frederica, St. Simons Island, Georgia

Blue Cheese Burgers

3 lbs. ground chuck
¼ lb. crumbled blue cheese
1 or 2 green onions, chopped
¼ teaspoon Tabasco sauce

1 teaspoon Worcestershire sauce
2 tablespoons mustard
Salt and pepper
12 toasted hamburger buns

1. Combine ground chuck and blue cheese in a large bowl.
2. Add green onions, Tabasco sauce, Worcestershire sauce, and mustard. Sprinkle with salt and pepper. Toss lightly to combine. Cover and chill for at least 2 hours to blend flavors.
3. Prepare charcoal grill. Shape ground chuck mixture into 12 patties, handling as little as possible. Grill, turning once, at least 5 minutes on each side or until done to your liking.
5. Serve on buns. Makes 12 servings.

BOB ALLEN | Christ Church, Frederica, St. Simons Island, Georgia

New England Maple Ribs

2 lbs. spareribs, precooked
¾ cup pure maple syrup
¼ cup chili sauce
¼ cup chopped onion

1 tablespoon vinegar
1 tablespoon Worcestershire sauce
1 teaspoon dry mustard
1 garlic clove, finely chopped

1. Place ribs in a large bowl.
2. In a separate bowl, combine maple syrup, chili sauce, onion, vinegar, Worcestershire sauce, mustard, and garlic. Pour over ribs. Cover and marinate in refrigerator, turning occasionally, for at least 4 hours.
3. Grill or broil ribs as desired, basting frequently with marinade. Makes 4 servings.

KATHY HOAGLAND | Terrace Acres Baptist Church, Fort Worth, Texas

Pineapple Beef Teriyaki

2 lbs. sirloin steak, cut in
    1-inch pieces
1 pineapple, cored and cut into
    1-inch chunks
2 to 3 cups cooked rice

MARINADE:
¼ cup brown sugar
¼ cup soy sauce
2 tablespoons lemon juice
1 tablespoon oil
¼ teaspoon ginger
1 garlic clove, minced

1. To make marinade: Combine brown sugar, soy sauce, lemon juice, oil, ginger, and garlic in a bowl.

2. Add steak to marinade and toss to coat. Cover and set in refrigerator to marinate, at least 1½ hours.

3. Soak 12 bamboo skewers in water for 30 minutes.

4. Prepare charcoal grill. Thread steak and pineapple chunks on skewers. Grill kabobs over hot coals, rotating until all sides are cooked, 10 to 15 minutes. Serve over rice. Makes 4 to 6 servings.

❖ **KATHY HOAGLAND** | Terrace Acres Baptist Church, Fort Worth, Texas

VARIATION: To prepare this dish indoors, cook steak and marinade in a skillet over low heat, simmering until steak is cooked through, 20 to 30 minutes. Stir in canned pineapple chunks that have been drained of their juice.

Parker's Eastern North Carolina Barbecue with Barbecue Sauce

1 boneless pork roast (3 to 4 lbs.)

1 teaspoon cayenne pepper or
   red pepper flakes

1 tablespoon pepper

2 teaspoons salt

½ cup barbecue sauce plus more
   for serving (recipe follows)

4 slices of bacon

8 large sandwich buns, sliced

1. Preheat oven to 250°F.

2. Combine cayenne pepper or red pepper flakes, pepper, and salt. Rub pepper mixture into roast. Rub ½ cup barbecue sauce into roast.

3. Lay bacon strips on roast. Place in covered roasting pan and bake, frequently basting with sauce, until tender and cooked through, 8 hours.

4. Allow to cool. Remove bacon and any fat. Chop meat into small pieces. Season with barbecue sauce. Serve on buns. Makes 8 sandwiches.

BARBECUE SAUCE

½ cup butter

1 cup cider vinegar

1 large or 4 small sour pickles, minced

1 tablespoon minced or grated onion

2 tablespoons Worcestershire sauce

1 tablespoon lemon juice

1 tablespoon molasses

1. Combine butter, cider vinegar, pickles, onion, Worcestershire sauce, lemon juice, and molasses in a saucepan over low heat.

2. Cook, stirring frequently, until butter is melted and sauce is well blended. Makes 2 cups.

❖ **SIS CRANZ** | Christ Episcopal Church, Charlotte, North Carolina

Hobos

2 lbs. ground beef or chuck

1 large onion, coarsely chopped

2 peppers, coarsely chopped

3 medium potatoes, cut into ½-inch cubes

2 or 3 carrots, sliced crosswise

1. Prepare charcoal grill.

2. Shape ground beef into 8 to 12 patties. Set each patty on a piece of foil.

3. Pile onions, peppers, potatoes, and carrots on each patty. Tightly wrap each foil packet so that juices won't leak out.

4. Set packets on grill over hot coals. Cook, turning every 10 minutes, until patties are cooked through and vegetables are soft, 35 to 40 minutes. Serve hot in the packets. Makes 8 to 12 servings.

PEBBLES BAILEY | Unity Baptist Church, Morgantown, Indiana

Feeding the 5,000

Since its founding in 1943, Christ Church has had many mouths to feed:

- Banquets for hundreds commemorating parish anniversaries or program initiatives
- New member dinners
- Casual on-the-grounds picnics for parish day celebrations
- Midweek luncheons for commissions and committees
- Receptions to honor people and occasions

We also feed those who come to Christ Church from the greater church and community. Many of our members work in the soup kitchen or provide casseroles and sandwiches for citizens of God's kingdom who do not have the means to provide for themselves.

SUGGESTED MENU

Crowd Pleaser, page 365

Red Beans over Rice, page 55

Company Green Salad with Dijon Vinaigrette, page 218

Spinach Bread, page 56

Pumpkin Spice Bars, page 358

ANNE B. TOMLINSON
Christ Episcopal Church, Charlotte, North Carolina

Margarita Pork Kebabs

1 lb. pork tenderloin, cut into 1-inch cubes
1 cup margarita drink mix
1 teaspoon coriander
1 garlic clove, minced
2 tablespoons butter, room temperature
2 teaspoons lime juice
1 tablespoon minced parsley
⅛ teaspoon sugar
1 large green or red pepper, cut into 1-inch squares
2 ears of corn, cut into 8 pieces

To make margarita drink mix from scratch, blend together:

1 cup lime juice
4 teaspoons sugar
½ teaspoon salt

1. Place pork cubes in large resealable plastic food storage bag. Combine margarita mix, coriander, and garlic and pour into bag. Seal bag and turn it until pork cubes are coated. Set aside to marinate at least 30 minutes.

2. Combine butter, lime juice, parsley, and sugar in small bowl. Set aside.

3. Prepare charcoal grill. Soak 4 bamboo skewers in water for 30 minutes.

4. Thread pork cubes, peppers, and corn onto skewers. Grill over hot coals, turning frequently and basting with butter mixture, 15 to 20 minutes. Makes 4 servings.

LINDA S. THOMPSON | Oakwood Church of God in Christ, Godfrey, Illinois

BBQ Sauce for Beef and Pork

2 tablespoons butter
1 medium onion
½ cup chopped sweet pepper
1 garlic clove, chopped
½ cup chopped celery
3 tablespoons molasses
1 can (1 lb.) tomatoes
1 can (8 oz.) tomato sauce

2 teaspoons dry mustard
1 cup red wine vinegar
¼ teaspoon cloves
¼ teaspoon allspice
1 lemon, cut in wedges, seeds removed
1½ teaspoons salt
2 teaspoons Tabasco sauce
1 bay leaf

1. Heat butter in a large skillet over medium heat until melted. Add onion and sauté until limp and golden, 3 to 4 minutes. Stir in sweet pepper, garlic, and celery. Cook until celery is tender and soft, 3 to 4 minutes more.

2. Add molasses, tomatoes, tomato sauce, mustard, vinegar, cloves, allspice, lemon, salt, Tabasco sauce, and bay leaf. Stir to combine. Cover and simmer, stirring often, for 2 hours.

3. Transfer sauce to a food processor and puree. Makes about 4 cups.

JAMES D. GOULD IV | Christ Church, Frederica, St. Simons Island, Georgia

Spareribs Hawaiian

2 lbs. meaty pork spareribs,
    cut into serving pieces
4 fresh or canned pineapple slices
4 tomato wedges

MARINADE:
2 tablespoons ketchup
½ teaspoon ginger or 1 tablespoon
    minced fresh ginger root
1½ tablespoons brown sugar
3 tablespoons unsweetened pineapple juice
1 garlic clove, minced or pressed
¼ cup teriyaki sauce

1. Arrange ribs in a single layer in a shallow baking pan.

2. To make marinade: Combine ketchup, ginger, brown sugar, pineapple juice, garlic, and teriyaki sauce. Pour over ribs. Marinate in refrigerator, turning meat several times, at least 1 hour.

3. Prepare charcoal grill. Grill ribs over medium-hot coals, basting occasionally with marinade from pan, until well browned and fork-tender, about 45 minutes.

4. Brush pineapple slices with marinade. Grill pineapple, turning once, until heated through, 5 to 7 minutes per side. To serve, arrange ribs and pineapple on a platter and top with tomato wedges. Makes 4 to 6 servings.

SIS. JACKIE THOMAS | Miracle Deliverance Holiness Church, Columbia, South Carolina

Southwest Lasagna

1 lb. ground beef
1 medium onion, chopped
1 can (15 oz.) enchilada sauce
1 can (14.5 oz.) diced tomatoes, undrained
1 can (2.25 oz.) sliced ripe olives, drained
1 teaspoon salt
¼ teaspoon garlic powder

¼ teaspoon pepper
1 cup small-curd cottage cheese
1 egg
½ lb. Monterey Jack, thinly sliced
Eight 8-inch corn tortillas, cut in half
½ cup shredded cheddar cheese

1. Preheat oven to 350°F. Grease a 13 x 9 x 2-inch baking dish.

2. Brown ground beef and onion in a large skillet over medium to high heat. Drain off fat.

3. Stir in enchilada sauce, tomatoes, olives, salt, garlic powder, and pepper. Bring to a boil. Reduce heat and simmer, uncovered, for 20 minutes.

4. Combine cottage cheese and egg in a small bowl. Spread one-third of the meat sauce in baking dish. Top with half of the Monterey Jack, half of the cottage cheese mixture, and half of the tortillas. Repeat layers, ending with meat sauce. Sprinkle with cheddar cheese. Cover and bake for 20 minutes. Uncover and bake 10 minutes more. Makes 6 to 8 servings.

MARGARET DEMEO | Methow Valley United Methodist Church, Twisp, Washington

Dr. Bill's Venison Chili

¼ cup oil

1 onion, chopped

1½ tablespoons garlic, chopped

3 lbs. ground venison

1 can (14 oz.) whole tomatoes

1 can (14 oz.) diced tomatoes with chilis

½ can (6 oz.) beer

1 package (1.25 oz.) chili seasoning mix

1½ tablespoons chili powder

1 teaspoon oregano

½ teaspoon ground cumin

½ teaspoon paprika

¼ cup soy sauce

2 celery ribs, sliced

1 can (4.5 oz.) sliced black olives

1 can (15 oz.) black beans

1 can (15 oz.) red kidney beans

1. Heat oil in a large stockpot over medium heat. Add onion and garlic and sauté until onions are limp and translucent, 3 to 5 minutes.

2. Add ground venison to skillet. Cook, stirring to break up lumps, until lightly browned, 8 to 10 minutes. Drain off fat.

3. Add whole tomatoes, diced tomatoes, beer, chili seasoning mix, chili powder, oregano, cumin, paprika, soy sauce, celery, and black olives to pot. Reduce heat to a simmer, cover, and cook for hours (or transfer to a slow cooker and cook on high for 4 hours).

4. Stir in black beans and red kidney beans. Cook 1½ hours more. Makes 12 to 16 servings.

❖ **DR. BILL ORMSBEE** | Trinity Presbyterian Church, Little Rock, Arkansas

Bert's Superb Barbecue Sauce

¼ cup vinegar

½ cup water

2 tablespoons sugar

1 tablespoon prepared mustard

½ teaspoon salt

½ teaspoon pepper

½ teaspoon cayenne pepper

Thick slice of lemon

1 onion, sliced

¼ cup butter

⅓ cup ketchup

2 tablespoons Worcestershire sauce

1½ teaspoons liquid or powdered smoke

1. Combine vinegar, water, sugar, mustard, salt, pepper, cayenne pepper, lemon, onion, and butter in a large saucepan over medium heat. Simmer, uncovered, for 20 minutes.

2. Stir in ketchup, Worcestershire sauce, and liquid or powdered smoke. Bring to a boil. Remove from heat. Serve hot on spareribs, boiled chicken, short ribs, or lamb chops. Can also be used as a basting sauce when broiling chicken, roasting lamb or spareribs, or braising short ribs. Makes about 2 cups.

❖ **LILLA GARNETT** | Pittsboro Baptist Church, Pittsboro, North Carolina

Apple-Pork Kebabs

2 lbs. boneless pork roast (loin or shoulder)
¼ cup apple juice
¼ cup sugar

¼ cup soy sauce
1½ teaspoons allspice
1½ teaspoons pepper

1. Trim fat and gristle from pork roast. Cut pork into 1½- to 2-inch chunks. Place in a stainless steel or glass bowl.
2. Combine apple juice, sugar, soy sauce, allspice, and pepper. Pour over pork and mix until coated. Marinate at room temperature for 1 hour or cover and refrigerate overnight.
3. Soak 4 wooden skewers in water for 30 minutes.
4. Thread pork onto skewers. Grill or broil 6 to 8 inches from source of heat, turning often and brushing with marinade, until meat is no longer pink, 20 to 25 minutes. Remove from skewers and serve hot. Makes 6 to 8 servings.

TONYA MINOR | Oakwood Church of God in Christ, Godfrey, Illinois

Bobby's Barbecue Sauce

½ cup butter
1 cup ketchup
2 tablespoons brown sugar
2 tablespoons Worcestershire sauce

20 dashes of Tabasco sauce
3 tablespoons vinegar
Juice and zest of 1 lemon
Salt and pepper

1. Combine butter, ketchup, brown sugar, Worcestershire sauce, Tabasco sauce, vinegar, and lemon juice and zest in a large saucepan over low heat. Sprinkle with salt and pepper.
2. Cook, stirring occasionally, until butter melts and sauce is well blended and heated through. Keep refrigerated until ready to use. Use with beef, pork, chicken, and shellfish. Makes 1½ cups.

BOB AMME | Christ Church, Frederica, St. Simons Island, Georgia

Asparagus Mimosa

2 hard-boiled eggs
1 tablespoon minced fresh chervil or
    1 teaspoon dried
1 tablespoon minced fresh parsley or
    1 teaspoon dried
1 tablespoon minced fresh chives or
    1 teaspoon dried

¼ cup wine vinegar
¼ cup Dijon mustard
¾ cup olive oil
Salt and pepper
40 to 48 spears fresh asparagus,
    cooked and chilled

1. Peel eggs and press through a sieve.
2. Whisk together chervil, parsley, chives, vinegar, mustard, oil, and salt and pepper. Pour ¼ to ½ cup of the vinaigrette over the asparagus and toss lightly to coat. Arrange asparagus on a platter and sprinkle with egg. Pass remaining dressing in a small pitcher. Makes 8 to 10 servings.

✤ **CHRIS PURYEAR** | First Moravian Church, Greensboro, North Carolina

Hot Spiced Chili

2 lbs. ground beef
2 medium onions, chopped
3 garlic cloves, minced
1 jalapeño, chopped
1 can (6 oz.) tomato paste
1 jar (2 oz.) picante sauce
3 tablespoons chili powder
1 tablespoon dry mustard
1 tablespoon red wine vinegar
1 tablespoon Worcestershire sauce

1½ teaspoons ground cumin
1 teaspoon salt
1 teaspoon pepper
¾ teaspoon allspice
½ teaspoon cinnamon
6 bay leaves
Several dashes of hot sauce
¼ teaspoon red pepper flakes
2 cans (12 oz. each) chili sauce

1. Combine ground beef, onion, garlic, and jalapeño in a large Dutch oven. Cook over medium heat, crumbling beef with a wooden spoon, until beef is browned. Drain off fat.
2. Add tomato paste, picante sauce, chili powder, mustard, vinegar, Worcestershire sauce, cumin, salt, pepper, allspice, cinnamon, bay leaves, hot sauce, and red pepper flakes. Mix until well combined. Reduce heat to low and cook, uncovered and stirring occasionally, for 1½ hours. Add chili sauce during last 10 minutes of cooking. Remove bay leaves before serving. Makes 8 to 10 servings.

✤ **TISH MILLER** | Trinity Presbyterian Church, Little Rock, Arkansas

Tomatoes with Parsley Pesto

1 cup packed fresh parsley
¼ cup snipped fresh chives
1 garlic clove
¼ teaspoon salt

Dash of pepper
3 tablespoons olive oil or vegetable oil
2 tablespoons cider or red wine vinegar
3 medium tomatoes, cut into wedges

1. Combine parsley, chives, garlic, salt, and pepper in a food processor until finely chopped.
2. Add oil and vinegar and mix well. Transfer pesto to a bowl, cover, and refrigerate. To serve, toss pesto with tomatoes. Makes 4 to 6 servings.

✤ **LORI NORTHCOTT** | Methow Valley United Methodist Church, Twisp, Washington

Marinated Green Beans with Horseradish Dressing

2 lbs. fresh whole green beans
2 tablespoons vegetable oil
1 tablespoon cider vinegar
1 small onion, minced
½ teaspoon salt
¼ teaspoon pepper
Romaine lettuce
Tomatoes

DRESSING:
½ cup sour cream
½ cup mayonnaise
1 tablespoon fresh lemon juice
1 tablespoon horseradish
2 teaspoons minced onion
1 teaspoon dry mustard

1. Wash and drain green beans, snap off ends, and place in large bowl.

2. Whisk together oil, vinegar, onion, salt, and pepper. Pour over beans, cover, and let marinate in the refrigerator overnight.

3. To make dressing: Mix sour cream, mayonnaise, lemon juice, horseradish, onion, and mustard until well combined.

4. Drain beans and place in a serving bowl. Pour dressing over the beans and stir to coat. Serve on a bed of romaine lettuce leaves garnished with tomatoes. Makes 6 to 8 servings.

SUE MILLER | Trinity Evangelical Lutheran Church, Lansdale, Pennsylvania

Copper Pennies

2 lbs. carrots, cut into ¼-inch-thick
   rounds (4½ cups)
2 onions, thinly sliced
1 green pepper, cut into thin strips

MARINADE:
1 can (10.5 oz.) condensed tomato soup
¾ cup vinegar
⅔ cup sugar
½ cup cooking oil
1 teaspoon Worcestershire sauce
1 teaspoon prepared mustard
½ teaspoon salt

1. Pour just enough lightly salted water into a large saucepan to cover the bottom. Bring to a boil, add carrots, and cook until tender, 8 to 10 minutes. Drain.

2. Combine carrots, onions, and green peppers in a large bowl.

3. To make marinade: Whisk together tomato soup, vinegar, sugar, oil, Worcestershire sauce, mustard, and salt.

4. Pour marinade over carrots and toss to coat. Cover and marinate in refrigerator at least 3 hours or overnight. Drain, reserving marinade. Return leftover vegetables to marinade and refrigerate. Makes 6 to 8 servings.

MRS. GABRIELE RIGGSBEE | Pittsboro Baptist Church, Pittsboro, North Carolina

Asparagus and Pine Nuts

1 lb. fresh asparagus
3 tablespoons pine nuts
¼ cup olive oil
1 tablespoon fresh lemon juice
1 or 2 garlic cloves, mashed to a paste

½ teaspoon dried oregano
½ teaspoon dried basil
½ teaspoon salt
Pepper

1. Soak asparagus in water and rinse thoroughly to remove sand. Break off ends of asparagus stems. Steam asparagus until tender but still crisp, 5 to 7 minutes. Plunge into cold water to stop cooking. Drain.
2. Toast pine nuts in a small skillet over medium heat, stirring continuously, until golden brown. Transfer to a small bowl.
3. Whisk together olive oil, lemon juice, garlic, oregano, basil, salt, and pepper. Add to skillet and heat just until hot, 3 minutes. Toss hot dressing with asparagus and arrange on a platter. Serve at room temperature, sprinkled with pine nuts. Makes 4 to 6 servings.

❖ **MONICA HESEMAN** | Trinity Presbyterian Church, Little Rock, Arkansas

Martha's Layered Salad

1 package (10 oz.) prewashed fresh spinach
1 lb. bacon, cooked and crumbled
6 hard-boiled eggs, sliced
1 large head or 2 small heads of lettuce, broken up
1 package (10 oz.) frozen petite peas, thawed and drained
Salt and pepper
Sugar
2 or 3 small Vidalia onions, sliced
2 cups mayonnaise
Lemon juice
Grated Swiss cheese

Layer this salad one day ahead. Add the dressing and toss on the day of the picnic.

1. Layer the spinach, bacon, eggs, and lettuce in a large salad bowl.
2. Place peas in a separate bowl. Sprinkle with salt, pepper, and sugar and toss to combine. Add peas to salad bowl. Top with sliced onions. Cover with plastic wrap and refrigerate overnight.
3. Place mayonnaise in a bowl. Whisk in just enough lemon juice to make it runny. Just before serving, pour mayonnaise over salad and toss to combine. Makes 6 to 8 servings.

❖ **MARTHA FITZGERALD** | Christ Church, Frederica, St. Simons Island, Georgia

Sesame Cucumbers

8 cups thinly sliced cucumbers
1 tablespoon salt
2 green onions, sliced
1 garlic clove, minced
2 to 3 tablespoons soy sauce

2 tablespoons vinegar
1 tablespoon vegetable oil
1 tablespoon sesame seeds, toasted
⅛ teaspoon cayenne pepper

1. Put cucumbers in a colander, sprinkle with salt, and toss gently. Drain for 30 minutes. Rinse and drain.
2. Combine onions, garlic, soy sauce, vinegar, oil, sesame seeds, and cayenne in a large bowl. Add cucumbers and toss to coat. Cover and refrigerate until ready to serve. Makes 16 servings.

DENISE PETERS | Methow Valley United Methodist Church, Twisp, Washington

Fried Green Tomatoes "The Southern Way"

2 firm medium green tomatoes
½ teaspoon salt
½ teaspoon pepper

½ cup white cornmeal
½ cup bacon drippings

1. Cut tomatoes into ½-inch slices. Sprinkle with salt and pepper. Dredge in cornmeal.
2. Heat bacon drippings in a heavy skillet over medium heat. Add tomatoes and cook, turning once, until browned. Drain on paper towels. Makes 2 to 3 servings.

BETTY LEWIS MCCARTNEY | Christ Church, Frederica, St. Simons Island, Georgia

Tomato Refresher

6 medium tomatoes, sliced about ½-inch thick
2 small green peppers, diced
⅔ cup diced celery
2 small onions, diced
1 tablespoon salt

¼ teaspoon pepper
¼ cup vinegar
¼ cup sugar
1 cup cold water

1. Layer tomato slices in a serving bowl.
2. Combine peppers, celery, onion, salt, pepper, vinegar, sugar, and cold water. Pour over tomatoes. Cover and chill at least 3 to 4 hours or overnight. Makes 8 to 10 servings.

AUDREY MONROE | Memorial Baptist Church, Tulsa, Oklahoma

Avocado Salad

1 large ripe avocado
2 teaspoons lime juice
¼ cabbage or 1 whole Chinese leaf
   cabbage, finely shredded

3 medium tomatoes, sliced
1 medium onion, sliced into rings

1. Cut avocado lengthwise, remove the stone, and cut into thick slices. Remove the skin. Sprinkle slices with lime juice.

2. Arrange shredded cabbage on a serving plate. Top with avocado slices, tomatoes, and onions. Serve immediately. Makes 4 servings.

❖ **U.D.** | Miracle Deliverance Holiness Church, Columbia, South Carolina

Oven-Roasted Herbed Tomatoes

18 large plum tomatoes (3½ lbs.),
   halved lengthwise
½ cup olive oil
2 tablespoons chopped fresh parsley

2 tablespoons chopped fresh basil
1 tablespoon chopped fresh rosemary
1 tablespoon chopped fresh thyme
Salt and pepper

1. Preheat oven to 350°F.

2. Place tomatoes, cut side up, on a rimmed baking sheet. Brush with oil.

3. Combine parsley, basil, rosemary, and thyme. Sprinkle half of herb mixture over tomatoes. Season with salt and pepper. Roast until tomatoes are tender and slightly brown around edges, 1 hour and 15 minutes. Cool 5 minutes and sprinkle with remaining herbs. Makes 16 to 20 servings.

❖ **PEARL TALBERT** | Christ Church, Frederica, St. Simons Island, Georgia

Fresh Mushroom Salad

6 tablespoons salad oil
¼ cup fresh lemon juice
1 tablespoon sugar
½ to 1 teaspoon tarragon

1 lb. mushrooms, thinly sliced
¼ cup chopped green onions
Lettuce leaves

1. Whisk together oil, lemon juice, sugar, and tarragon.

2. Pour dressing over mushrooms and green onions. Toss gently. Chill 1 hour. To serve, arrange lettuce on salad plates and place mushrooms in center. Makes 5 servings.

❖ **LOUISE DUNLAP** | First Presbyterian Church, Du Quoin, Illinois

Springtime Salad

4 cups torn lettuce leaves

2 cups broccoli florets

1 cup fresh strawberries, sliced or fresh,
    or canned pineapple chunks

2 oranges, peeled and sectioned

DRESSING:

¼ cup honey

¼ cup vinegar

1 tablespoon poppy seeds

1 tablespoon sunflower seeds

3 tablespoons fresh lemon juice

1 tablespoon Dijon mustard

1 tablespoon finely minced onion

⅛ teaspoon salt

⅔ cup vegetable oil

1. To make dressing: Combine honey, vinegar, poppy seeds, sunflower seeds, lemon juice, mustard, onion, and salt in a small bowl. Gradually add oil, whisking until well combined.

2. Toss lettuce, broccoli, strawberries, and oranges in a salad bowl. Pour dressing over salad and toss lightly. Makes 8 servings.

❖ **ANN M. SHADE** | Trinity Evangelical Lutheran Church, Lansdale, Pennsylvania

Summer Squash Squares

¼ cup salad oil

1 small onion, finely chopped

1 garlic clove, minced

2½ cups grated zucchini or
    crookneck squash

6 eggs, lightly beaten

⅓ cup fine dry bread crumbs

½ teaspoon salt

½ teaspoon dried basil

½ teaspoon dried oregano

½ teaspoon pepper

3 cups (12 oz.) shredded cheddar cheese

½ cup grated Parmesan

¼ cup sesame seeds

1. Preheat oven to 325°F. Grease a 13 x 9 x 2-inch baking dish.

2. Heat oil in a large skillet over medium heat. Add onion and cook, stirring until soft, 5 minutes. Add garlic and squash and cook, stirring, until squash is tender, 3 minutes.

3. Combine eggs, bread crumbs, salt, basil, oregano, pepper, and cheddar cheese. Stir into squash mixture. Spread in baking dish. Sprinkle with Parmesan and sesame seeds. Bake until eggs are set, about 30 minutes. Cool in pan at least 15 minutes. Cut into 1-inch squares. Makes 10 dozen appetizers.

❖ **LINDA DU LAC** | Methow Valley United Methodist Church, Twisp, Washington

Coleslaw from Smokey's

3 small heads cabbage, chopped
    (about 18 cups)
1½ cups shredded carrots
1 large onion, minced
⅓ cup chopped parsley

DRESSING:

1 cup plus 2 tablespoons sugar
1 tablespoon celery seed
1 teaspoon salt
¼ teaspoon pepper
3 cups mayonnaise
1½ cups fresh lemon juice

1. Combine cabbage, carrots, onion, and parsley in a large bowl.
2. To make dressing: Combine sugar, celery seed, salt, pepper, and mayonnaise. Gradually whisk in lemon juice. Pour dressing over slaw and toss until well coated. Cover and refrigerate at least 4 hours and up to 24 hours before serving. Makes 24 cups.

◆ CAROL NASE | Trinity Evangelical Lutheran Church, Lansdale, Pennsylvania

Citrus-Apple Tossed Salad with Honey Lemon Dressing

8 cups torn salad greens
3 medium navel oranges,
    peeled and sectioned
2 medium red apples, thinly sliced
1 medium pink grapefruit,
    peeled and sectioned
1 medium cucumber, thinly sliced
1 celery rib, chopped
½ cup cubed cream cheese
Seasoned salad croutons

DRESSING:

⅓ to ½ cup canola oil
⅓ cup lemon juice
¼ cup snipped chives
1 tablespoon honey
½ teaspoon paprika
¼ teaspoon salt

1. Combine salad greens, oranges, apples, grapefruit, cucumber, and celery in a salad bowl.
2. To make dressing: Combine oil, lemon juice, chives, honey, paprika, and salt in a jar with a tight-fitting lid. Cover and shake well.
3. Pour dressing over salad and toss to coat. Top with cream cheese and croutons. Makes 10 to 12 servings.

◆ CAROL GASTON | Methow Valley United Methodist Church, Twisp, Washington

Three-Bean Salad

1 can (16 oz.) green beans
1 can (16 oz.) wax beans
1 can (19 oz.) kidney beans
1 cup chopped green pepper
½ cup chopped onion

½ cup sugar
⅔ cup vinegar
⅓ cup salad oil
Salt and pepper

1. Rinse and drain green beans, wax beans, and kidney beans.

2. Place beans in a large bowl. Add green pepper and onion.

3. Whisk together sugar, vinegar, and oil. Pour over beans. Sprinkle with salt and pepper. Toss to combine. Chill before serving. Makes 6 to 8 servings.

❖ **MARY THOMPSON** | Christ Church, Frederica, St. Simons Island, Georgia

Black Bean and Corn Salad

1 can (15 oz.) black beans, drained
1 can (11 oz.) sweet corn
   (such as Green Giant Niblets)
2 tomatoes, peeled, seeded, and diced
1 red or green pepper, diced
4 green onions, sliced

3 tablespoons minced cilantro or parsley
Salt and pepper
2 tablespoons red wine vinegar
½ teaspoon ground cumin
⅛ teaspoon red pepper flakes
3 tablespoons olive oil

1. Combine black beans, corn, tomatoes, pepper, green onions, and cilantro or parsley in a large bowl. Sprinkle with salt and pepper.

2. Whisk together vinegar, cumin, red pepper flakes, and olive oil. Pour over bean and corn mixture and toss to coat. Chill at least 4 hours or overnight. Makes 6 servings.

❖ **BECKY ROWELL** | Christ Church, Frederica, St. Simons Island, Georgia

Parsleyed Potatoes

1½ lbs. small new red potatoes, scrubbed
1 teaspoon vegetable oil
1 medium onion, chopped
1 garlic clove, crushed

1 cup chicken broth
1 cup chopped fresh parsley, divided
Salt and pepper

1. Peel a strip of skin from around the middle of each potato. Place potatoes in cold water.

2. Heat a large skillet over medium-high heat. Add oil. Add onion and garlic and sauté for 5 minutes.

3. Stir broth and ½ cup of the parsley into skillet and bring to a boil. Add potatoes to skillet in a single layer. Return to a boil, reduce heat, and simmer, covered, until potatoes are tender, 10 minutes. Transfer potatoes to a serving platter with a slotted spoon.

4. Add salt and pepper to sauce. Pour sauce over potatoes and sprinkle with remaining parsley. Makes 6 to 8 servings.

✦ LINDA S. THOMPSON | Christ Church, Frederica, St. Simons Island, Georgia

Broccoli Salad

1 bunch fresh broccoli	DRESSING:
1 cup grated mozzarella	**¼ cup sugar**
½ red onion, coarsely chopped	**1 tablespoon red wine vinegar**
8 slices of bacon, fried and crumbled	**½ cup mayonnaise**

1. Wash broccoli and break into pieces. Peel off thick skins and cut tender parts of stalks into slices.

2. Toss broccoli, mozzarella, red onion, and bacon in a bowl.

3. To make dressing: Combine sugar and vinegar in a small saucepan over low heat. Cooking, stirring continuously, until sugar is dissolved. Remove from heat. Cool 5 minutes and whisk in mayonnaise.

4. Pour dressing over salad and toss to coat. Refrigerate any leftover dressing. Makes 6 to 8 servings

✦ MARTHA PATE | Christ Church, Frederica, St. Simons Island, Georgia

Cole Slaw

1 head of cabbage, grated
1 onion, chopped
1 green pepper, chopped
1 cup sugar
¾ cup cider vinegar

1 teaspoon mustard
1 teaspoon celery seed
1 tablespoon salt
½ cup salad oil

1. Combine cabbage, onion, and green pepper in a bowl. Sprinkle with sugar.
2. Combine vinegar, mustard, celery seed, salt, and olive oil in a small saucepan over medium-high heat. Bring to a boil. Pour liquid over cabbage but do not stir. Let marinate in refrigerator for 8 hours. Stir just before serving. Store covered in refrigerator up to 2 weeks. Makes 10 to 12 servings.

❖ JEANNE ALAIMO | Christ Church, Frederica, St. Simons Island, Georgia

Cucumber Mint Salad with Dressing

3 large cucumbers, peeled, halved,
   and sliced crosswise
½ cup chopped fresh mint or
   ¼ cup dried mint

Zest of 1 orange
½ cup olive oil
½ to 1 cup red wine vinegar or balsamic vinegar
¼ cup sugar

1. Combine cucumbers, mint, and orange zest in a bowl.
2. Whisk together oil, vinegar, and sugar. Pour over cucumbers. Cover and chill 4 hours. Makes 6 to 8 servings.

❖ MARSHA RICH | Christ Episcopal Church, Charlotte, North Carolina

Summer Corn and Cabbage Salad

3 fresh medium ears of corn,
   or 1 package (10 oz.) frozen
   whole kernel corn
1½ cups shredded green cabbage
1 medium sweet red pepper, chopped
1 celery rib, thinly sliced
1 medium onion, thinly sliced

¼ cup olive oil or vegetable oil
¼ cup lemon juice
1 to 2 tablespoons honey
1 teaspoon dry mustard
¼ teaspoons salt
¼ teaspoon black pepper
Lettuce leaves

1. Cook corn and cut from cob (or cook according to package directions).

2. Combine corn, cabbage, red pepper, celery, and onion in a large bowl.

3. Whisk together olive oil, lemon juice, honey, mustard, salt, and pepper. Pour over salad and toss to coat. Cover and refrigerate at least 2 and up to 24 hours. To serve, spoon salad onto a lettuce leaf. Makes 6 servings.

❖ JOAN KEEFFE | Methow Valley United Methodist Church, Twisp, Washington

Green Bean-Zucchini Salad

½ lb. fresh green beans,
    trimmed and snapped
2½ teaspoons olive oil
1 garlic clove, minced
½ teaspoon dried tarragon, crumbled
⅛ teaspoon pepper

1 small zucchini (4 oz.), cut into
    matchstick strips
1 small red onion, sliced thin and
    punched into rings
1½ teaspoons tarragon vinegar

1. Place green beans in a saucepan, add boiling salted water to cover, and cook over medium heat until tender but still crisp, 3 to 5 minutes.

2. Drain in a colander, rinse under cold running water to stop the cooking, and drain again.

3. Combine olive oil, garlic, tarragon, and pepper in a large bowl. Add green beans, zucchini, and onion and toss well. Cover and chill, tossing occasionally, 2 to 3 hours. Sprinkle with vinegar and toss again just before serving. Makes 2 servings.

❖ BECKY ROWELL | Christ Church, Frederica, St. Simons Island, Georgia

Fruit and Nut Tropical Slaw

1 can (8.25 oz.) pineapple chunks
1 tablespoon lemon juice
1 medium banana, sliced
3 cups finely shredded cabbage
1 can (11 oz.) mandarin oranges, drained

½ cup chopped walnuts
¼ cup raisins
1 container (8 oz.) orange- or
    lemon-flavored yogurt
½ teaspoon salt

1. Drain pineapple, reserving 2 tablespoons juice. Combine reserved pineapple juice and lemon juice.

2. Place banana slices in bowl and toss with 1 tablespoon of the juice mixture.

3. Combine pineapple, bananas, cabbage, mandarin oranges, walnuts, and raisins in a large bowl.

4. Combine yogurt, salt, and reserved juice mixture. Add to cabbage mixture and toss lightly to coat. Cover and chill. Makes 8 servings.

❖ JUNE FOREMAN | Vincent Memorial United Methodist Church, Nutter Fort, West Virginia

Gazpacho

1 can (46 oz.) tomato juice
1 tablespoon minced parsley
¾ cup chopped cucumber
2 tomatoes, coarsely chopped
¾ cup chopped green onion
½ cup chopped Vidalia onion
1 garlic clove, crushed

2 tablespoons white wine vinegar
1 tablespoon olive oil
½ teaspoon Worcestershire sauce
3 drops Tabasco sauce
½ teaspoon salt
¼ teaspoon freshly ground pepper
Finely chopped cucumber, pepper, and onion

1. Pour tomato juice into a large stainless steel bowl.

2. Add parsley, cucumber, tomatoes, green onion, Vidalia onion, garlic, vinegar, olive oil, Worcestershire sauce, Tabasco sauce, salt, and pepper. Stir to combine. Cover and chill. To serve, ladle into bowls and garnish with finely chopped cucumber, pepper, and onion. Makes 8 to 10 servings.

❖ ANN CARMICHAEL | Christ Episcopal Church, Charlotte, North Carolina

Cucumber and Onion Salad

3 cucumbers, each 6 inches long
1 bunch green onions
½ cup white wine vinegar
½ cup sugar
1 tablespoon dill weed

1 tablespoon salt
½ teaspoon white pepper
Butter or leaf lettuce
Tomato wedges

1. Slice cucumbers and green onions very thin in a food processor. Place in a large bowl.

2. Whisk together vinegar, sugar, dill weed, salt, and white pepper. Pour over cucumbers and toss until evenly coated. Marinate in refrigerator 1 hour or more. To serve, drain off some of the marinade and set on lettuce leaves, garnished with tomato wedges. Makes 4 servings.

❖ TONYA MINOR | Christ Church, Frederica, St. Simons Island, Georgia

Easy Pasta Salad

½ lb. macaroni or small shells
1 broccoli, cut into florets
1 red onion, coarsely chopped
1 jar (2 oz.) pimientos or
    roasted red sweet peppers
½ cup slivered almonds

½ to ¾ cup light mayonnaise or
    yogurt dressing
½ cup grated Parmesan or mozzarella
Celery salt
Pepper
1 tomato, quartered

1. Cook macaroni in boiling water for 5 minutes. Add broccoli florets and cook 5 minutes more, or until pasta is al dente. Drain well. Transfer to a large bowl.

2. Add red onion, pimientos, almonds, light mayonnaise, and Parmesan or mozzarella. Toss gently to combine. Season with celery salt and pepper. Spoon onto a serving platter and garnish with tomato wedges. Makes 8 to 10 servings.

✧ **MARY E. KENNEY** | Methow Valley United Methodist Church, Twisp, Washington

Potato Salad for Fifty

20 lbs. potatoes, peeled
4 medium onions, grated
4 green peppers, cut fine
2 jars (2 oz. each) chopped pimiento
2 celery ribs, finely chopped
2 cups chopped parsley
2 large dill pickles, chopped
Salt and pepper
2 quarts mayonnaise

Here are some potato salad seasonings ideas:
• mustard
• pickle juice
• salt and pepper
• capers
• pimientos
• olives
• green peppers
• green onions

1. Fit a large stockpot with a steamer basket, add water, and bring to a boil over high heat. Add potatoes, cover, and steam until tender, 8 to 10 minutes. Cook in batches if necessary.

2. When potatoes are cool enough to handle, cut them into small pieces.

3. Combine potatoes, onions, green peppers, pimiento, celery, parsley, and pickles in a large bowl or clean plastic basin. Sprinkle with salt and pepper. Add mayonnaise and stir to combine. Makes 50 servings.

✧ **PRESBYTERIAN CHURCH OF GONZALES** | Gonzales, Illinois

Seashell Pasta Salad

1 package (12 oz.) large shell pasta, cooked, rinsed in cold water, and drained
1 can (28 oz.) cut tomatoes, drained
2 carrots, sliced
½ red pepper, cubed
½ green pepper, cubed

⅓ cup sliced green onion
1 can (2.25 oz.) sliced black olives, drained
¼ cup grated Parmesan
1 package (10 oz.) sliced pepperoni
Salt and pepper
1 cup Italian salad dressing

1. Combine pasta, tomatoes, carrots, red and green peppers, green onion, black olives, Parmesan, and pepperoni in a large bowl. Sprinkle with salt and pepper.

2. Pour dressing over salad and toss gently to combine. Cover and chill 1 hour. Makes 8 to 10 servings.

✧ **BONNIE SELLERS** | Trinity Presbyterian Church, Little Rock, Arkansas

Melon Salad

½ cup oil

¼ cup lemon juice

1 teaspoon sugar or sugar substitute

½ teaspoon salt

Pinch of pepper

4 cups cantaloupe balls

2 cups honeydew balls

2 cups watermelon balls

1 cup coarsely chopped mango

1½ cups diced cucumber

Romaine lettuce leaves

1. Combine oil, lemon juice, sugar, salt, and pepper in a jar with a tight lid. Cover and shake until sugar is dissolved.

2. Combine cantaloupe, honeydew, watermelon, mango, and cucumber in a large bowl. Drizzle with dressing. Cover and refrigerate 1 to 1½ hours before serving. Serve over lettuce leaves. Makes 14 servings.

❖ DANI FLEMING | Christ Church, Frederica, St. Simons Island, Georgia

Pennsylvania Dutch Potato Salad

¼ cup vinegar

Salt and pepper

1 teaspoon sugar

1 egg, beaten

4 cups hot cubed cooked potatoes

½ cup chopped onion

4 slices of bacon, diced and fried

2 hard-boiled eggs, sliced

1. Combine vinegar, salt and pepper, sugar, and beaten egg in a small saucepan over low heat. Cook just until egg begins to solidify, about 1 minute. Pour mixture over hot potatoes.

2. Add onion, bacon, and egg slices. Toss gently. Serve hot. Makes 4 to 6 servings.

❖ JEAN MURPHY | Vincent Memorial United Methodist Church, Nutter Fort, West Virginia

Summer Spiral Salad

4 cups cooked spiral pasta

1 can (15 oz.) garbanzo beans

1 cup diced tomatoes

4 oz. shredded mozzarella

2 oz. salami or ham, thinly sliced
    and cut into strips

½ cup ripe olives

3 tablespoons olive oil

⅓ cup cider vinegar

1½ teaspoons salt

1½ teaspoons oregano

1½ teaspoons basil

⅛ teaspoon pepper

1. Combine spiral pasta, garbanzo beans, tomatoes, mozzarella, salami or ham, and olives in a large bowl.
2. Combine olive oil, vinegar, salt, oregano, basil, and pepper in a jar with a tight lid. Cover and shake until well mixed. Pour over pasta salad and toss to coat. Cover and chill 1 hour. Makes 8 servings.

❖ **KARI RICHARDSON** | Unity Baptist Church, Morgantown, Indiana

Fresh Fruit Salad

1 cup cored and cubed apple

1 cup seedless red grapes

1 cup canned pineapple chunks, drained, with juice reserved

½ cantaloupe, cubed

½ honeydew melon, cubed

1 cup sliced strawberries

½ cup water

½ cup sugar

¼ cup lemon juice

1½ teaspoons grated lemon zest

3 tablespoons lime juice

1½ teaspoons grated lime zest

1. Combine apple, grapes, pineapple, cantaloupe, honeydew, and strawberries in a large bowl.
2. Heat water in a saucepan over medium heat until boiling. Add sugar, lemon juice, lemon zest, lime juice, and lime zest. Cook until sugar is dissolved. Cool to room temperature.
3. Pour sugar syrup over fruit and toss to combine. Chill at least 2 hours or overnight. Makes 8 to 10 servings.

❖ **LINDA S. THOMPSON** | Christ Church, Frederica, St. Simons Island, Georgia

Picnic Potato Salad

¼ cup mayonnaise or salad dressing

¼ cup French dressing

1 teaspoon mustard

½ teaspoon salt

¼ teaspoon pepper

6 cups cubed cooked potatoes

1 lb. cooked green beans, cut in short lengths

4 hard-boiled eggs, sliced, with a few slices reserved for garnish

1 cup sliced radishes

1 cup diced celery

¼ cup chopped sweet pickle

¼ cup minced onion

1. Combine mayonnaise, French dressing, mustard, salt, and pepper in a large bowl.
2. Add potatoes, green beans, eggs, radishes, celery, pickle, and onion. Toss lightly to combine. Chill. Makes 3 quarts.

❖ **MARY EVELYN HILL** | First Baptist Church, Russell, Kentucky

Baked German Potato Salad

2 quarts red potatoes, boiled, peeled,
    and sliced ⅛-inch thick
8 strips of bacon, cut into dice
1 cup chopped celery
1 cup chopped onion
3 tablespoons flour
1 teaspoon salt

½ teaspoon pepper
⅔ cup sugar
⅔ cup cider vinegar
1½ cups water
⅓ cup chopped parsley or
    1 tablespoon dried parsley
2 teaspoons celery seed

1. Preheat oven to 375°F. Grease an 11 x 7 x 2-inch baking dish. Layer potatoes in dish.
2. Fry bacon in a skillet over high heat until crisp. Drain on paper towels. Pour off all but ¼ cup of fat from skillet.
3. Reduce heat to medium. Add celery and onion to hot fat and cook just until softened, 3 minutes. Stir in flour, salt, and pepper and cook 2 minutes more.
4. Combine sugar, vinegar, and water. Pour over onions and celery all at once and whisk to combine. Bring to a boil and cook for 1 minute. Stir in parsley, celery seed, and bacon. Pour dressing over potatoes and mix gently, so potatoes are not broken. Bake uncovered until the middle of the casserole bubbles, 45 minutes. Serve warm. Makes 10 to 12 servings.

❖ **FAY S. MILLER** | Trinity Evangelical Lutheran Church, Lansdale, Pennsylvania

Garlicky Roasted Potato Salad

3 lbs. medium red potatoes, quartered
1 tablespoon vegetable oil
1 tablespoon stone-ground mustard
2 teaspoons coriander seeds, crushed
6 garlic cloves, halved
½ cup chopped fresh parsley

½ cup plain low-fat yogurt
⅓ cup thinly sliced green onions
    plus more for garnish
¾ teaspoon salt
¼ teaspoon black pepper

1. Preheat oven to 400°F.
2. Gently toss potatoes, oil, mustard, coriander seeds, and garlic in a shallow roasting pan. Bake, stirring occasionally, until tender, 30 minutes. Cool to room temperature.
3. Combine parsley, yogurt, green onions, salt, and pepper in a large bowl. Add cooled potato mixture and toss gently. Serve at room temperature or chilled, garnished with green onions. Makes 8 servings

❖ **ROSE REED** | Christ Church, Frederica, St. Simons Island, Georgia

Spinach Salad

1 lb. fresh baby spinach
¼ lb. fresh mushrooms, sliced
3 or 4 slices of bacon, cooked until
   crisp and crumbled
2 hard-boiled eggs, chopped
½ cup crumbled Feta
¼ cup sunflower seeds

1 cup water chestnuts, sliced
1 tablespoon wine vinegar or juice of 1 lemon
½ to 1 tablespoon Dijon mustard
¼ to ½ cup mayonnaise
1 teaspoon sugar
1 tablespoon grated Parmesan

1. Tear spinach into bite-size pieces into a large bowl.

2. Add mushrooms, bacon, eggs, Feta, sunflower seeds, and water chestnuts.

3. Combine vinegar, mustard, mayonnaise, and sugar in a small jar with a tight-fitting lid. Cover and shake well.

4. Pour dressing over salad and toss to combine. Sprinkle Parmesan on top. Makes 4 servings.

FAE NOVOTNY | Methow Valley United Methodist Church, Twisp, Washington

Zucchini-Potato Salad

6 medium red or white potatoes, skins on
2 tablespoons olive oil
2 medium zucchini, cut into chunks
½ teaspoon salt
1 large red pepper, cut into 1½-inch pieces
¼ cup fresh basil leaves, cut into 1-inch strips
Basil sprig

DRESSING:
½ cup regular or light mayonnaise
2 tablespoons cider vinegar
2 tablespoons milk
½ teaspoon cracked black pepper
¼ teaspoon salt

1. Place potatoes in a large stockpot, add 4 quarts of water, and bring to boiling over high heat. Reduce heat to low, cover, and simmer until tender, 25 to 30 minutes. Drain and cool. Cut into bite-size chunks.

2. Heat oil in skillet over medium heat, add zucchini and salt, and cook, stirring occasionally, until lightly browned and tender but still crisp, 4 to 6 minutes. Remove with a slotted spoon. Cook red peppers in same way and add to zucchini.

3. To make dressing: Combine mayonnaise, vinegar, milk, pepper, and salt in a large bowl. Add potatoes, zucchini, red pepper, and basil. Toss gently to coat. Cover and refrigerate. Garnish with basil sprig. Makes 6 to 8 servings.

LORI O. MORRISSEY | Trinity Evangelical Lutheran Church, Lansdale, Pennsylvania

Tomato Salad from Great-Grammy Beatty

4 large ripe tomatoes, peeled
   and quartered
1 Vidalia onion, chopped
½ cup sugar
½ cup apple cider vinegar
Dash of cinnamon

The tomatoes in this recipe are peeled so that they can soak up the dressing. Make this chilled salad late in the summer, when the tomato harvest is at its peak. Serve with grilled steak or chicken and corn on the cob.

1. Combine tomatoes and onion in a bowl.
2. Whisk together sugar, vinegar, and cinnamon. Pour over tomatoes and onions and toss gently to combine. Chill for 1 hour. Serve in small bowls. Makes 4 to 6 servings.

BETH CRIMMINS | Trinity Evangelical Lutheran Church, Lansdale, Pennsylvania

Wonderful Fresh Tomato Pie

3 or 4 medium ripe tomatoes, sliced
1 sweet onion, thinly sliced
¾ cup grated cheddar cheese
1 unbaked 9-inch pie shell

3 eggs, lightly beaten
Dash of salt
Dash of pepper
4 strips of bacon, cut in half

1. Preheat oven to 350°F.
2. Layer tomatoes, onion, and cheese alternately in pie shell until filled.
3. Whisk together eggs, salt, and pepper. Pour over tomatoes. Top with bacon. Bake until eggs are set and bacon is crisp, 35 to 40 minutes. Makes 6 to 8 servings.

PAT POLLARD | Christ Episcopal Church, Charlotte, North Carolina

Peaches and Cream Cheese Pie

¾ cup flour
1 teaspoon baking powder
½ teaspoon salt
1 package (3 oz.) cook-and-serve
   vanilla pudding mix
3 tablespoons butter

1 egg
½ cup milk
1 can (16 oz.) sliced peaches, drained, juice reserved
1 package (8 oz.) cream cheese
½ cup plus 2 tablespoons sugar, divided
1 teaspoon cinnamon

1. Preheat oven to 350°F. Grease a 9- or 10-inch glass pie plate.

2. Combine flour, baking powder, salt, vanilla pudding mix, butter, egg, and milk in a mixer bowl. Beat for 2 minutes. Pour filling into pie plate. Layer peaches on top of filling.

3. Combine cream cheese, ½ cup of the sugar, and 3 tablespoons of the reserved peach juice. Spoon over top of peaches to within 1 inch of the sides of the pie plate. Stir remaining 2 tablespoons sugar with cinnamon and sprinkle over the top. Bake for 30 to 35 minutes. Cool and chill before serving. Makes 6 to 8 servings.

EILEEN K. PETERS and **PAT CONNOLLY** | Trinity Evangelical Lutheran Church, Lansdale, Pennsylvania

Lemon Pecan Pie

3 eggs

1½ cups sugar

⅓ cup butter, melted

1 tablespoon lemon juice

1 teaspoon lemon extract

Pinch of salt

¾ cup pecans, chopped

1 unbaked 9-inch pie shell

1. Preheat oven to 400°F.

2. Beat eggs well until frothy and lemon-colored. Add sugar, melted butter, lemon juice, lemon extract, salt, and pecans. Mix until well combined.

3. Pour filling into pie shell. Set in oven and immediately reduce temperature to 300°F. Bake for 45 minutes or until set. Cool and chill before serving. Makes 6 to 8 servings.

ELAINE HUTSLER | Trinity Presbyterian Church, Little Rock, Arkansas

Two-Minute Coconut Custard Pie

4 eggs

2 cups milk

1 cup sugar

½ teaspoon salt

¼ teaspoon nutmeg

½ cup flour

½ cup butter, room temperature

1 teaspoon vanilla

1 cup shredded coconut

 This amazing coconut custard pie makes its own crust as it bakes!

1. Preheat oven to 350°F. Grease a 10-inch pie plate.

2. Combine eggs, milk, sugar, salt, nutmeg, flour, butter, vanilla, and coconut in a blender. Blend for 10 seconds, to make a lumpy mixture.

3. Pour mixture into pie plate. Bake for 45 minutes to 1 hour. Cool and chill before serving. Makes 8 to 10 servings.

CRICKET SNEARING | Trinity Evangelical Lutheran Church, Lansdale, Pennsylvania

Luby's Chocolate Icebox Pie

2½ cups whole milk, divided
1½ cups sugar
1 tablespoon butter
1 square (1 oz.) unsweetened chocolate
3 tablespoons cornstarch

3 egg yolks
1 teaspoon vanilla
1 cup mini marshmallows
1 baked 9-inch pie shell
Whipped cream

1. Combine 2 cups of the milk, sugar, butter, and chocolate in a large heavy saucepan over medium heat. Bring to a boil and remove from heat.

2. Whisk together cornstarch, remaining ½ cup milk, egg yolks, and vanilla. Add to chocolate mixture, stirring constantly, until well blended.

3. Set saucepan over low heat. Continue cooking, stirring with a wire whisk until thick and smooth. Stir in marshmallows until melted.

4. Pour filling into pie shell and refrigerate. After filling begins to set, 1 to 2 hours, pat waxed paper over it to prevent cracking. Serve topped with whipped cream. Makes 6 to 8 servings.

JEAN BARNETT | Presbyterian Church of Gonzales, Gonzales, Texas

Chilled Strawberry Pie

3 egg whites
1 cup sugar
1 teaspoon vanilla
1 cup vanilla wafer crumbs
1 cup chopped pecans

FILLING:
1 cup whipping cream
2 tablespoons confectioners' sugar
2 cups sliced strawberries
Whole strawberries

VARIATION:
Instead of 1 cup of vanilla wafer crumbs, use 10 crushed saltines, ¼ teaspoon baking powder, ⅛ teaspoon salt, and ⅛ teaspoon baking soda.

1. Preheat oven to 350°F. Grease a 10-inch pie plate.

2. Beat egg whites until soft peaks form. Gradually add sugar and vanilla and beat until stiff peaks form. Fold in vanilla wafer crumbs and pecans.

3. Transfer meringue to pie plate, spreading slightly higher at sides. Bake for 30 minutes or until lightly browned. Cool.

4. To make filling: Beat whipping cream until foamy. Gradually add confectioners' sugar, beating until soft peaks form. Fold in sliced strawberries and spread evenly in pie shell. Garnish with whole strawberries. Chill at least 4 hours before serving. Makes 8 to 10 servings.

PATTY ADAMS | Christ Episcopal Church, Charlotte, North Carolina

Red, White & Blueberry Pie

1 package (15 oz.) refrigerated
    piecrust pastry
1 quart fresh strawberries
4 squares (1 oz. each) white
    baking chocolate
1 package (8 oz.) cream cheese,
    room temperature

¾ cup cold milk
1 package (3.4 oz.) white chocolate
    instant pudding mix
1½ cups fresh blueberries, rinsed and drained
1 cup frozen light whipped topping, thawed

1. Preheat oven to 425°F. Place piecrust pastry in a 10-inch deep dish pie plate, following package directions. Prick bottom. Bake for 10 to 12 minutes or until golden brown. Cool completely.

2. Rinse strawberries and pat dry. Select 8 uniformly sized strawberries. Slice each one in half so that some green stem remains on each half. Hull and slice remaining strawberries.

3. Heat white chocolate in microwave until melted and smooth. Dip strawberry halves in melted chocolate and place, cut side down, on parchment or waxed paper. Chill in refrigerator until set, 15 minutes.

4. Spread remaining melted chocolate on bottom and sides of piecrust. Layer sliced strawberries over bottom of crust.

5. Beat cream cheese in a mixer bowl until smooth. Gradually add milk, mixing until well blended. Add pudding mix. Beat until mixture begins to thicken.

6. Spread cream cheese filling over strawberries in pie plate. Arrange blueberries evenly over top of pie filling. Pipe whipped topping around edge of pie. Place white chocolate–covered strawberry halves in whipped topping border. Chill until ready to serve. Makes 8 to 10 servings.

MELANIE SQUIRES | Vincent Memorial United Methodist Church, Nutter Fort, West Virginia

Toll House Pie

2 eggs
½ cup flour
½ cup sugar
½ cup brown sugar
1 cup butter, melted and cooled to
    room temperature

1 package (6 oz.) semisweet chocolate chips
1 cup chopped walnuts
1 unbaked 9-inch pie shell
Whipped cream or vanilla ice cream

1. Preheat oven to 325°F.

2. Beat eggs in a large mixer bowl until foamy. With mixer running on low speed, add flour, sugar, and brown sugar. Increase speed to high and beat until well blended.

3. Stir in melted butter, chocolate chips, and walnuts. Pour into pie shell. Bake for 1 hour. Remove from oven and allow to cool for 15 minutes. Serve warm topped with whipped cream or vanilla ice cream. Makes 6 to 8 servings.

NANCY HARRIS | Messiah United Methodist Church, York, Pennsylvania

Preserved Fun

½ dozen children
2 or 3 small dogs
1 large grassy field
1 shallow brook

Assorted pebbles
Assorted flowers
A deep blue sky

1. Mix the children and dogs and add them, stirring occasionally, to a field that is well fenced.

2. Pour the brook over the pebbles. Add the flowers as garnish. Cover with a deep blue sky.

3. Bake in a hot sun. Do this every day in summertime, cooling the children in a bathtub once a day. Preserved in this way, the memory of a childhood on the farm lasts indefinitely.

RECIPE VARIATIONS: I prefer to use assorted farm animals along with the dogs. Occasionally, I substitute a spring-fed lake for the bathtub.

MARY ELLEN GAITHER | Unity Baptist Church, Morgantown, Indiana

Apricot Bars

⅔ cup dried apricots
½ cup butter, room temperature
¼ cup sugar
1⅓ cups flour, divided
½ teaspoon baking powder
¼ teaspoon salt

2 eggs, beaten
1 cup brown sugar
½ teaspoon vanilla
½ cup chopped walnuts or pecans
Confectioners' sugar

1. Rinse apricots, place in a small saucepan, and add water to cover. Bring to a boil over medium-high heat. Boil for 10 minutes. Drain, cool, and chop coarsely.

2. Preheat oven to 350°F. Grease an 8 x 8 x 2-inch baking pan.

3. Combine butter, sugar, and 1 cup of the flour until crumbly. Press mixture into bottom of pan. Bake for 25 minutes.

4. Sift together remaining ⅓ cup flour, baking powder, and salt into a mixer bowl. Add eggs and beat well. Stir in brown sugar, vanilla, chopped walnuts or pecans, and apricots. Spread mixture over baked layer in pan. Bake 30 minutes more. Cool in pan. Cut into bars and dip in confectioners' sugar. Makes 15 to 20 bars.

BETTY JOAN CRABTREE | Trinity Presbyterian Church, Little Rock, Arkansas

Almond Cookies

1½ cups butter, room temperature
2½ cups sugar
2½ cups brown sugar
4 or 5 eggs
3 tablespoons honey
1 teaspoon almond extract

6 cups flour
1 teaspoon baking powder
1 teaspoon baking soda
1 package (1 lb.) chopped almonds
1 package (14 oz.) shredded coconut

1. Cream butter, sugar, and brown sugar in a large mixer bowl. Beat in eggs, honey, and almond extract.
2. Whisk together flour, baking powder, and baking soda. Add to egg mixture, blending to combine. Stir in almonds and coconut.
3. Divide dough in half. Shape each half into a log, wrap in plastic wrap, and chill for 1 hour.
4. Preheat oven to 350°F. Lightly grease several baking sheets. Use a sharp knife dipped in flour to cut slices ¼ inch thick from log. Set slices on baking sheet 1 inch apart. Bake for 12 to 15 minutes or until golden brown. Makes 60 cookies.

BETTY FUNK | Vincent Memorial United Methodist Church, Nutter Fort, West Virginia

Chocolate Blueberry Dessert Squares

1 package (8.5 oz.) chocolate wafer
   cookies, crushed
½ cup butter, melted
2 egg whites, room temperature
2 cups confectioners' sugar
1 package (8 oz.) cream cheese,
   room temperature

1 can (21 oz.) blueberry pie filling
1 cup chopped pecans, divided
1½ cups whipping cream
3 tablespoons sugar
½ teaspoon vanilla
½ cup semisweet chocolate chips
2 tablespoons milk

1. Preheat oven to 350°F. Set aside a 9 x 9 x 2-inch baking pan. Do not grease.
2. Combine cookie crumbs and melted butter in a small bowl, stirring well. Press mixture into bottom of pan. Bake for 10 minutes. Allow to cool.
3. Beat egg whites until foamy. Gradually add confectioners' sugar, beating until well blended. Add cream cheese and beat until smooth. Spread mixture evenly over crust. Top with blueberry pie filling and ¾ cup of the pecans.
4. Whip the cream until foamy. Add sugar and vanilla and continue whipping until soft peaks form. Spread whipped cream evenly over pie filling.
5. Combine chocolate chips and milk in a small saucepan over low heat. Cook, stirring constantly, until chocolate is melted and sauce is smooth. Drizzle chocolate sauce over whipped cream. Sprinkle remaining ¼ cup pecans on top. Chill several hours before serving. Makes 8 to 10 servings.

SHARON FITTS | Trinity Presbyterian Church, Little Rock, Arkansas

Chocolate-Orange Muffins

3 oz. bittersweet chocolate bar (for eating)

2 oranges

1 cup sugar

½ cup butter, room temperature

2 large eggs

½ cup plain low-fat yogurt or buttermilk

½ cup freshly squeezed orange juice

1 teaspoon baking powder

½ teaspoon baking soda

2 cups flour

1. Preheat oven to 375°F. Grease a 12-cup muffin pan or insert paper liners.

2. Break chocolate into chunks. Chop coarsely in a food processor and tip out onto waxed paper.

3. Use a vegetable parer to remove orange part only from orange peels; do not include white pith. Put peels and sugar into food processor and chop fine, about 2 minutes. Blend in butter until creamy. Scrape down sides of processor.

4. Add eggs, one at a time, pulsing to blend after each addition. Add yogurt, orange juice, baking powder, and baking soda. Pulse until blended.

5. Scrape batter into a large bowl. Sift flour onto batter, add chopped chocolate, and fold gently by hand, just until flour is incorporated. Spoon batter into muffin cups. Bake for 20 to 25 minutes or until golden brown and springy to the touch. Turn out onto a wire rack. Serve hot or warm. Makes 12 muffins.

❖ CAROL NASE | Trinity Evangelical Lutheran Church, Lansdale, Pennsylvania

Chocolate-Orange Muffins are fabulous anytime, but they are especially delicious served with freshly brewed coffee or espresso. With the speedy food processor method, the muffin batter can be prepared in the time it takes the oven to preheat and the coffee to brew.

Individual Cheesecakes

12 vanilla wafers

2 packages (8 oz. each) cream cheese

¾ cup sugar

1 tablespoon lemon juice

1 teaspoon vanilla

2 eggs

1 can (21 oz.) cherry pie filling

1. Preheat oven to 325°F. Insert paper liners in a 12-cup muffin pan. Place a vanilla wafer in bottom of each liner.

2. Beat cream cheese, sugar, lemon juice, vanilla, and eggs until well blended. Fill cups half full. Bake for 15 minutes. Cool 15 minutes. Spoon cherry pie filling on top of each cake. Chill. Makes 12 servings.

❖ EDNA MOSCAR and JOLURAY SMITH | Vincent Memorial United Methodist Church, Nutter Fort, West Virginia

Brown Bottom Cupcakes

1 package (8 oz.) cream cheese
1 egg
⅓ cup sugar
⅛ teaspoon salt
1 package (6 oz.) chocolate chips

FILLING:
1½ cups flour
1 cup sugar
¼ cup cocoa
½ teaspoon salt
¼ teaspoon baking soda
1 cup water
1 teaspoon vanilla
⅓ cup oil
1 tablespoon vinegar

1. Preheat oven to 350°F. Coat a 12-cup muffin pan with cooking spray and insert paper liners.

2. Beat cream cheese, egg, sugar, and salt in a mixer bowl. Stir in chocolate chips. Spoon into paper liners until one-third full.

3. To make filling: Whisk together flour, sugar, cocoa, salt, and baking soda. Stir in water, vanilla, oil, and vinegar. Beat until well combined. Add a heaping teaspoon of filling to each cupcake liner. Bake for 30 to 35 minutes. Cool on a wire rack. Makes 12 cupcakes.

KRIS HACHAT | Vincent Memorial United Methodist Church, Nutter Fort, West Virginia

Peaches and Cream

1½ cups flour
1 teaspoon salt
6 tablespoons butter, room temperature
2 eggs
2 teaspoons baking powder
2 packages (3 oz. each) cook-and-serve vanilla pudding mix
1 cup milk

1 can (29 oz.) sliced peaches, drained with juice reserved
2 packages (8 oz. each) cream cheese, room temperature
8 tablespoons peach juice
1 cup plus 1 tablespoon sugar, divided
½ teaspoon cinnamon

1. Preheat oven to 350°F. Lightly grease a 13 x 9 x 2-inch baking pan.

2. Combine flour, salt, butter, eggs, baking powder, pudding mix, and milk in a mixer bowl. Beat until well blended. Pour into pan and top with peach slices.

3. Beat cream cheese, 1 cup of the sugar, and peach juice for 2 minutes. Mix remaining tablespoon sugar with cinnamon. Spread cheese mixture on peaches and sprinkle with cinnamon sugar. Bake for 35 to 40 minutes. Cool on a wire rack. Makes 8 to 10 servings.

ED and **BRENDA HASLEBACHER CHAPMAN** | Vincent Memorial United Methodist Church, Nutter Fort, West Virginia

Carrot Bars

2 cups sugar

4 eggs

1¼ cups oil

3 jars (4 oz. each) strained carrots for babies

2 cups flour

2 teaspoons baking soda

1 teaspoon salt

2 teaspoons cinnamon

ICING:

½ package (4 oz.) cream cheese,
    room temperature

¼ cup butter

1⅓ cups confectioners' sugar

1 teaspoon vanilla

Chopped walnuts or pecans

1. Preheat oven to 350°F. Grease a 15½ x 10½ x 1-inch sheet pan.

2. Beat sugar, eggs, oil, and strained carrots in a mixer bowl. With mixer running on low speed, add flour, baking soda, salt, and cinnamon. Mix until well blended. Spread batter in pan. Bake for 30 to 40 minutes. Cool in pan.

3. To make icing: Combine cream cheese, butter, confectioners' sugar, and vanilla. Beat until smooth.

4. Spread icing on cake and top with chopped walnuts or pecans. Cut into bars. Makes 20 bars.

❖ KAREN OLSON | Trinity Evangelical Lutheran Church, Lansdale, Pennsylvania

Strawberry Shortcake

1½ quarts fresh strawberries

½ cup sugar or ¾ cup brown sugar

2¼ cups flour

4 teaspoons baking powder

½ teaspoon salt

Dash of nutmeg

⅓ cup plus 3 tablespoons butter,
    room temperature, divided

1 egg, well beaten

⅓ cup milk

1½ pints whipping cream, stiffly beaten

1. Set aside 12 strawberries for garnish. Slice remaining strawberries, toss with sugar or brown sugar, and let stand in a warm place.

2. Preheat oven to 400°F. Grease a 9 x 2-inch round cake pan.

3. Sift together flour, baking powder, salt, and nutmeg. Work in ⅓ cup of the butter with your fingertips until crumbly. Stir in egg and then milk until moistened. Do not overmix. Turn dough into pan and pat into shape. Bake for 15 minutes or until lightly golden.

4. Split warm shortcake into two layers. Butter cut sides with remaining 3 tablespoons butter. Place one shortcake layer, buttered side up, on a plate and spread with half of sliced strawberries. Top with remaining layer, buttered side up, and spread with remaining strawberries. Cut assembled shortcake into wedges and set on individual serving plates. Top with whipped cream and 2 whole strawberries. Makes 4 to 6 servings.

❖ MICHAELLE MOON | Christ Episcopal Church, Charlotte, North Carolina

Pineapple Sheet Cake

2 cups flour
2 teaspoons baking soda
2 cups sugar
2 eggs
1 teaspoon vanilla
1 can (20 oz.) crushed pineapple
½ cup chopped nuts

ICING:

1 package (8 oz.) cream cheese,
   room temperature
½ cup butter, room temperature
1¾ cups confectioners' sugar
1 teaspoon vanilla
½ cup chopped nuts

1. Preheat oven to 350°F. Grease a 15½ x 10½ x 1-inch sheet pan.

2. Combine flour, baking soda, sugar, eggs, vanilla, pineapple, and nuts in a large mixer bowl. Mix until well combined. Spread batter in pan. Bake for 20 minutes or until a tester inserted in center comes out clean. Cool in pan on a wire rack.

3. To make icing: Blend cream cheese and butter. Gradually add confectioners' sugar and vanilla, beating until well combined. Spread icing over cake. Sprinkle nuts on top. Makes 12 to 15 servings.

❖ **MARY APPUHN** and **YVONNE DAVISON** | First Presbyterian Church, Du Quoin, Illinois

Red Satin Punch

1 quart cranberry juice

1 quart apple juice

1 large bottle (2 liters) 7-Up

2 ice cube trays of frozen 7-Up

1. Combine cranberry juice and apple juice in a large punch bowl.

2. Slowly pour in 7-up soft drink. Add frozen soft drink cubes. Serve in punch cups. Makes 35 servings.

MRS. WILLIAM GRIFFIN | Pittsboro Baptist Church, Pittsboro, North Carolina

Lemonade Ice Tea

4 quarts water, divided

¾ cup sugar

4 family size tea bags

4 or 5 mint leaves

1 can (12 oz.) frozen lemonade concentrate, thawed

 Make hot lemonade for a winter warm-me-up. Instead of mint leaves, add 8 cloves.

1. Heat 2½ quarts of the water in a large saucepan over high heat until boiling. Remove from heat. Add sugar, tea bags, and mint leaves. Steep 5 minutes.

2. Remove tea bags. Stir in lemonade concentrate. Pour mixture into a 1-gallon pitcher or beverage cooler. Add enough of the remaining water to fill container. Makes 1 gallon.

FRED REES and MARGARET WILLIAMS | Christ Episcopal Church, Charlotte, North Carolina

Sangria for a Crowd

5 liters red wine

4 or 5 oranges, seeds removed and juiced

1 large bottle (2 liters) Sprite

½ bottle (375 ml) vodka

2 to 4 cups sugar

Lemons, cut in half and sliced

Oranges, cut in half and sliced

Apples, cored and cubed

Peaches, peeled and sliced

Bananas, sliced

1. Combine red wine, oranges, Sprite, and vodka in a large stockpot. Stir in sugar small amounts at a time, to obtain desired sweetness. Refrigerate overnight.

2. Four hours before serving, add lemons, oranges, apples, peaches, and bananas. Chill. To serve, pour into glasses and set a half slice of orange on the rim. Makes 30 to 35 servings.

TERI BARAKAT | Trinity Presbyterian Church, Little Rock, Arkansas

Honey Raspberry Iced Tea

2 cups freshly brewed tea
2 cups cranberry-raspberry juice
¼ cup honey

1. Combine tea, cranberry-raspberry juice, and honey in a large glass pitcher. Whisk to dissolve honey.
2. Chill in refrigerator. Serve over ice. Makes 4 servings.

❖ **ROSE REED** | Oakwood Church of God in Christ, Godfrey, Illinois

Sweetly Mint Iced Tea

½ cup fresh mint leaves
2 tea bags
4 cups boiling water
¼ cup honey

1. Place mint leaves and tea bags in a large glass pitcher.
2. Pour boiling water into pitcher. Whisk in honey. Let steep 5 minutes.
3. Remove tea bags and cool to room temperature. Chill in refrigerator. Serve over ice. Makes 4 servings.

❖ **ROSE REED** | Oakwood Church of God in Christ, Godfrey, Illinois

Spiced Orange Tea

3 cups water
1 cup orange juice
2 tablespoons lemon juice
¼ cup sugar
1 cinnamon stick

½ teaspoon whole cloves
2 tea bags
Ice cubes
Mint sprigs

1. Combine water, orange juice, lemon juice, sugar, cinnamon stick, cloves, and tea bags in 2-quart saucepan over medium heat. Cook, stirring occasionally, until sugar is dissolved. As soon as liquid begins to steam, cover and remove from heat. Steep for 5 minutes.
2. Strain tea into a 1½-quart container with a tight-fitting lid. Cool to room temperature, cover, and refrigerate until very cold. Serve in ice-filled tumblers garnished with mint. Tea may also be served hot. Makes 4 servings.

❖ **LINDA S. THOMPSON** | Oakwood Church of God in Christ, Godfrey, Illinois

Springtime Punch

2½ cups water
2 cups sugar
Juice of 3 or 4 lemons (1 cup)

Juice of 2 or 3 oranges (1 cup)
1 can (6 oz.) frozen pineapple juice concentrate
2 bottles (1 liter each) ginger ale

1. Heat water and sugar in a large saucepan over high heat. Bring to a boil and cook for 10 minutes. Remove from heat. Cool to room temperature.
2. Stir in lemon juice, orange juice, and pineapple juice. Chill in refrigerator until ready to serve. Combine with ginger ale in a large punch bowl. Serve in punch cups. Makes 16 servings.

❖ **MARY RIFE** | Messiah United Methodist Church, York, Pennsylvania

Apricot Punch

2 cans (46 oz. each) apricot juice
1 can (6 oz.) frozen orange
    juice concentrate

1 can (46 oz.) pineapple juice
½ liter Sprite
½ gallon pineapple sherbet

1. Combine apricot juice, orange juice concentrate, and pineapple juice in a large punch bowl.
2. Just before serving, pour in Sprite. Scoop spoonfuls of sherbet and float them on top. Makes 50 servings.

❖ **SONDRA NASSERI** | Vincent Memorial United Methodist Church, Nutter Fort, West Virginia

Sparkling Citrus Punch

¾ cup apricot nectar, chilled
¾ cup pink grapefruit juice cocktail, chilled
1 can (12 oz.) orange-tangerine juice concentrate, thawed
3 cups sparkling water, chilled

1. Combine apricot nectar, pink grapefruit juice cocktail, and orange-tangerine juice concentrate in a pitcher. Chill.
2. To serve, add sparkling water and pour over ice. Makes 10 to 12 servings.

❖ **LINDA S. THOMPSON** | Oakwood Church of God in Christ, Godfrey, Illinois

Cranberry-Lime Margarita Punch

6 cups water

1 can (12 oz.) frozen cranberry juice cocktail

½ cup fresh lime juice

¼ cup sugar

2 cups ice cubes

1 cup ginger ale

1 lime, sliced

Fresh cranberries

1. Combine water, cranberry juice cocktail, lime juice, and sugar in a small punch bowl. Stir until sugar dissolves.

2. Stir in ice cubes, ginger ale, and lime. Garnish with fresh cranberries. Makes 10 servings.

❖ LINDA S. THOMPSON | Oakwood Church of God in Christ, Godfrey, Illinois

Pineapple-Lemon Cocktail

1 can (20 oz.) pineapple juice

⅔ cup lemon juice

⅓ cup sugar

½ cup water

2 egg whites

1 cup finely crushed ice

1. Combine pineapple juice, lemon juice, sugar, water, egg whites, and crushed ice in a cocktail shaker or a large jar with a lid.

2. Cover and shake until frothy. Pour into cocktail glasses. Makes 6 servings.

❖ JEAN THOMAS | Oakwood Church of God in Christ, Godfrey, Illinois

Double Lime Punch

1 cup lime sherbet, room temperature

1 can (6 oz.) frozen limeade concentrate, thawed

2 cups water

½ bottle (½ liter) ginger ale, chilled

1. Combine sherbet, limeade concentrate, and water in a punch bowl.

2. Add ginger ale just before serving. Serve in punch cups. Makes 10 servings.

❖ TIM TRAPP | Miracle Deliverance Holiness Church, Columbia, South Carolina

Karen's Lemonade

1½ cups sugar
4 cups milk

1 can (12 oz.) frozen lemonade concentrate
5⅓ cups ginger ale

Combine sugar, milk, lemonade concentrate, and ginger ale. Mix well and chill. Makes 3 quarts.

❖ GUYLIA BUNGE | Unity Baptist Church, Morgantown, Indiana

Cape Cod Cooler

1 cup white grapefruit juice
1 large scoop orange sherbet

Place white grapefruit juice and orange sherbet in a blender. Blend on high speed to combine, about 5 seconds. Makes 1 serving.

❖ YVONNE M. HAYWOOD | Oakwood Church of God in Christ, Godfrey, Illinois

Della Robbia Punch

2 cups sugar
3 cups water, divided
2 apples
3 bananas
1 can (24 oz.) unsweetened pineapple juice
2 cans (6 oz. each) frozen orange
    juice concentrate

1 can (6 oz.) frozen lemonade concentrate
3 bottles (1 liter) ginger ale
1 orange, thinly sliced
1 lemon, thinly sliced

1. Combine sugar and 1½ cups of the water in a large saucepan over high heat. Bring to a boil. Remove from heat, stir, and allow to cool. Chill.
2. Peel and core one apple and cut into quarters. Core and quarter the second apple, but leave the peel intact. Slice bananas. Combine apples, bananas, and remaining 1½ cups water in a blender to make a slushy punch mix. Fill one ice cube tray with punch mix and freeze. Chill the remainder in the refrigerator.
3. To serve, combine sugar syrup, fruit punch mix, and ginger ale in a punch bowl. Drop in frozen punch mix cubes. Float orange and lemon slices on the surface. Makes 30 servings.

❖ JANE BOLT | Christ Episcopal Church, Charlotte, North Carolina

Potluck Suppers

AMERICA'S POTLUCK CLASSIC

Garrison Keillor once observed that when Lutheran women reach heaven they think they are in church and immediately look for the basement stairs to find the kitchen.

Naturally. For they are carrying a casserole to a potluck dinner.

From the beginning, church cookbooks have included recipes for macaroni, meat, and tomatoes. In the late 1930s a new staple was added: condensed cream of mushroom soup. Other recipes served as main dishes, but the one that appears over and over is listed under various names, such as Favorite Hot Dish, EZ Casserole, Mom's Supper Dish, or—and usually—Hamburger Hot Dish.

Not so different is the 1990s recipe on page 142 called confidently "The" Casserole. In this chapter are newer variants on the classics, too, like Greek Moussaka (page 145) and Taco Bake (page 144) that busy women today are setting on their tables—when they're not carrying them to the church kitchen, or to heaven.

Adapted from *The Best of the Old Church Cookbooks*
by Florence Ekstrand

Garlic Parmesan Pita Crisps

4 pitas

½ cup butter, room temperature

2 teaspoons garlic salt

3 tablespoons grated Parmesan

2 teaspoons dried basil

1. Preheat oven to 325°F.

2. Use scissors or a sharp knife to cut along the outside edge of each pita. Split each pita into two rounds.

3. Mix butter and garlic salt until well blended. Spread butter over the coarse side of each pita. Sprinkle with Parmesan and basil. Cut each round into 6 wedges.

4. Set wedges on ungreased baking sheets in a single layer. Bake in batches until crisp, 8 to 10 minutes. Cool on wire racks. Store at room temperature in resealable food storage bags. Makes 4 dozen.

KATHY HOAGLAND | Terrace Acres Baptist Church, Fort Worth, Texas

Party Cheese Ball

2 packages (8 oz. each) cream cheese, room temperature

2 cups shredded cheddar cheese

1 tablespoon chopped pimiento

1 tablespoon chopped green pepper

1 tablespoon finely chopped onion

2 teaspoons Worcestershire sauce

1 teaspoon lemon juice

Dash of salt

½ cup finely ground pecans

1. Combine cream cheese and cheddar cheese until well blended.

2. Stir in pimiento, green pepper, onion, Worcestershire sauce, lemon juice, and salt. Mix until well blended. Cover and chill 2 hours.

3. Roll cheese mixture into a ball. Roll ball in pecans until evenly coated. Serve with assorted crackers. Makes 8 to 10 servings.

KRISTI BETLER MILES | Vincent Memorial United Methodist Church, Nutter Fort, West Virginia

Cucumber Dunk

1 package (8 oz.) cream cheese, room temperature

6 tablespoons grated cucumber

1 tablespoon grated onion

1 teaspoon mayonnaise

Paprika

Combine cream cheese, cucumber, onion, and mayonnaise to make a soft dip. Spoon into a small bowl and sprinkle with paprika. Serve with chips or raw vegetables. Makes 1¼ cups dip.

JANIS McCASKILL | Presbyterian Church of Gonzales, Gonzales, Texas

Tomato Casserole

3 or 4 large tomatoes

Bread crumbs or croutons

Grated cheddar cheese

4 slices bacon, cooked and crumbled

1. Preheat oven to 325°F. Grease an 8 x 8 x 2-inch baking dish.

2. Peel and slice tomatoes. Drain on paper towels.

3. Place a single layer of tomato slices in baking dish. Top with some bread crumbs or croutons and grated cheese. Repeat layers. Top with bacon. Bake until cheese is bubbly and melted, about 30 minutes. Makes 6 servings.

❖ **PATSY FEREBEE** | St. Andrew's Episcopal Church, Rocky Mount, North Carolina

Chinese Spring Rolls

1 lb. ground beef

1 garlic clove, minced

1 teaspoon ginger

1 large bag slaw mix

½ cup thinly sliced green onions

2 tablespoons soy sauce

1 teaspoon dry cooking sherry

1 teaspoon oil

24 egg roll wrappers

1. Preheat oven to 400°F.

2. Combine ground beef, garlic, and ginger in a skillet over medium-high heat. Cook, stirring occasionally, until beef is browned, 5 to 7 minutes. Drain off fat.

3. Combine ground beef mixture, slaw mix, onions, soy sauce, sherry, and oil in a large bowl. Toss to combine. Working on a clean, dry counter, assemble spring rolls following directions on package of egg roll wrappers package. Place completed rolls on a baking sheet. Bake until golden brown, 14 to 16 minutes. Makes 24 spring rolls.

❖ **MARY JACKSON** | Terrace Acres Baptist Church, Fort Worth, Texas

Cocktail Franks

2 tablespoons vegetable oil

1 medium onion, chopped

½ cup chopped celery

1 package hot dogs, cut in bite-size pieces

2 tablespoons brown sugar

2 tablespoons mustard

1 tablespoon Worcestershire sauce

½ cup water

½ cup ketchup

1 can (8 oz.) tomato sauce

1. Heat oil in a large skillet over medium-high heat. Add onion and celery and sauté until soft, 3 to 4 minutes.

2. Add hot dogs, brown sugar, mustard, Worcestershire sauce, water, ketchup, and tomato sauce to skillet. Mix well. Bring to a boil, reduce heat, and simmer, uncovered, for 45 minutes. Serve hot; can also be frozen and reheated in microwave. Makes 8 servings.

CATHERINE DAVIS | Presbyterian Church of Gonzales, Gonzales, Texas

Crusty Tomato Bites

4 Roma tomatoes, seeded and chopped
2 tablespoons finely chopped green
   or red pepper
1 tablespoon finely chopped red onion
2 garlic cloves, pressed

8 large basil leaves
2 tablespoons olive oil
Salt and pepper
1 baguette
½ cup Parmesan

1. Combine tomatoes, pepper, onion, and garlic in a bowl.

2. Stack basil leaves and cut into long thin strips. Add basil strips and olive oil to tomato mixture. Season with salt and pepper. Cover and marinate 1 to 2 hours.

3. Cut baguette diagonally into long thin slices. Set bread on a baking sheet and place under a broiler, turning once, until both sides are lightly browned, 1 to 2 minutes per side. Spoon tomato mixture onto bread. Sprinkle Parmesan and pepper on top. Makes 8 to 10 servings.

KATHY HOAGLAND | Terrace Acres Baptist Church, Fort Worth, Texas

Cranberry Mousse

1 can (20 oz.) crushed pineapple,
   drained with juice reserved
2 packages (3 oz. each) strawberry gelatin
1 cup water
1 can (16 oz.) whole berry cranberry sauce

3 tablespoons fresh lemon juice
1 teaspoon grated lemon zest
¼ teaspoon nutmeg
2 cups sour cream
½ cup chopped pecans

1. Combine pineapple juice and gelatin mix in a 2-quart saucepan over medium-high heat. Add water, bring to a boil, and stir until gelatin dissolves. Remove from heat.

2. Add cranberry sauce to gelatin and stir to combine. Stir in lemon juice, lemon zest, and nutmeg. Chill until mixture thickens slightly, 10 to 20 minutes.

3. Blend in sour cream. Fold in pineapple and pecans. Pour into a 2-quart mold. Chill until firm, at least 4 hours. Release from mold onto a serving plate. Makes 8 servings.

ALICE YODER | Trinity Evangelical Lutheran Church, Lansdale, Pennsylvania

Green Chili Pie

2 cans (4 oz. each) chopped green chilies
1 lb. Monterey Jack, grated
1 lb. longhorn, grated
6 eggs, slightly beaten
2 or more tablespoons hot sauce
1 can (12 oz.) evaporated milk

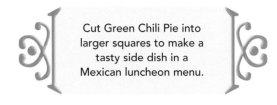

Cut Green Chili Pie into larger squares to make a tasty side dish in a Mexican luncheon menu.

1. Preheat oven to 350°F. Grease a 13 x 9 x 2-inch baking dish.

2. Layer chilis, Monterey Jack, and longhorn into bottom of baking dish.

3. Whisk together eggs, hot sauce, and evaporated milk. Pour over chilis and cheese. Bake for 40 minutes or until eggs are set. Cut into 1-inch squares. Serve warm with toothpicks. May be frozen, thawed, and reheated. Makes 96 appetizers.

BETTY DAVIS | Presbyterian Church of Gonzales, Gonzales, Texas

Brie with Chutney

1 round (13.2 oz.) Brie   Wheat crackers
1 jar (8 oz.) chutney with nuts

1. Preheat oven to 350°F.

2. Split Brie horizontally. Place bottom half in a baking dish, cut side up. Spread with chutney. Set top half in place, cut side down.

3. Bake until bubbly and brown on top, 10 to 12 minutes. Serve with wheat crackers. Makes 4 to 6 servings.

DOT OSHER | Christ Episcopal Church, Charlotte, North Carolina

Sour Cream Muffins

2 cups self-rising flour
¾ cup butter, melted
1 container (8 oz.) sour cream

VARIATION:
Add 1 to 2 cups grated cheddar cheese to the muffin batter.

1. Preheat oven to 350°F.

2. Combine self-rising flour, melted butter, and sour cream until well blended.

3. Spoon batter into a 24-cup mini muffin pan. Bake for 30 minutes. Serve hot or warm. May be frozen and reheated. Makes 24 mini muffins.

PATTY ADAMS | Christ Episcopal Church, Charlotte, North Carolina

South Texas Nachos

2 cups water
½ lb. unpeeled medium fresh shrimp
1 can (4 oz.) diced green chilies, drained
1 can (2.25 oz.) sliced black olives, drained

1½ cups (6 oz.) shredded cheddar cheese
½ cup sliced green onions
½ cup mayonnaise
8 dozen round tortilla chips

1. Preheat oven to 350°F.

2. Heat water in a large saucepan over high heat. Bring to a boil, add shrimp, and cook until shrimp turn pink, 3 to 5 minutes. Drain. Rinse with cold water. Peel and devein shrimp. Chop coarsely.

3. Combine shrimp, chilies, olives, cheese, and onions in a bowl. Toss with mayonnaise until combined.

4. Arrange tortilla chips on baking sheets in a single layer. Top each with 1½ teaspoons of shrimp mixture. Bake until cheese melts, 5 minutes. Makes 8 to 10 servings.

PRESBYTERIAN CHURCH OF GONZALES | Gonzales, Texas

Potluck Supper

SUGGESTED MENU

Cranberry Mousse
PAGE 117

Broccoli Salad
PAGE 170

Tossed Taco Salad
PAGE 172

Calico Bean Bake
PAGE 159

Baked Spaghetti
PAGE 129

Easy Lasagna
PAGE 128

Baked Chicken Parmesan
PAGE 137

Zucchini Bake
PAGE 169

Jewish Apple Cake
PAGE 176

Texas Sheet Cake
PAGE 186

TRINITY EVANGELICAL LUTHERAN CHURCH
Lansdale, Pennsylvania

Garden Pizza

2 tubes (8 oz. each) refrigerated
    crescent rolls
2 packages (8 oz. each) cream cheese,
    room temperature
¼ cup mayonnaise
1 envelope (4 oz.) ranch dressing mix
½ cup chopped green onions
½ cup chopped green pepper

½ cup chopped celery
½ cup chopped broccoli
½ cup chopped cauliflower
1 cup fresh chopped tomato
Sliced pitted olives
Shredded cheese
Pimientos

1. Preheat oven to 375°F.

2. Unroll and press dough flat to cover the bottom of a 12-inch round pizza pan. Turn up outer edges slightly. Bake for 9 minutes. Cool in pan.

3. Combine cream cheese, mayonnaise, and ranch dressing mix. Spread onto warm crust.

4. Combine green onions, green pepper, celery, broccoli, cauliflower, and tomato. Press into cream cheese mixture and allow to set. Strew olives, shredded cheese, and pimientos over the top. Chill 4 hours before serving. Makes 8 to 10 servings.

GINNY SAWYER | First Presbyterian Church, Du Quoin, Illinois

Spinach Cheese Squares

4 tablespoons butter
3 eggs
1 cup flour
1 cup milk
1 teaspoon salt
¼ teaspoon pepper
1 teaspoon baking powder
1 lb. grated Monterey Jack
2 packages (10 oz. each) frozen chopped spinach,
    thawed, drained, and pressed dry
1 tablespoon minced onion

Spinach Cheese Squares can be made ahead and frozen. To prevent sticking, place the squares on a baking sheet and set in the freezer for 30 minutes, just enough to become cold and stiff. Then drop the squares into a resealable freezer bag, seal, and return to the freezer. Reheat on a baking sheet in a 325°F oven for 12 minutes.

1. Preheat oven to 350°F. Place butter in a 13 x 9 x 2-inch baking dish and set in oven. Remove as soon as butter is melted.

2. Beat eggs in a large bowl. Whisk in flour, milk, salt, pepper, and baking powder. Stir in Monterey Jack, spinach, and onion.

3. Pour mixture into baking dish. Bake for 35 minutes. Cool in baking dish for 45 minutes or until set. Cut into squares. Makes 40 appetizers.

GINA RUDOLPH | Trinity Evangelical Lutheran Church, Lansdale, Pennsylvania

Olive Cheese Puffs

1 cup grated sharp cheddar cheese
3 tablespoons butter, softened
½ cup flour

¼ teaspoon salt
½ teaspoon paprika
24 stuffed olives, drained

1. Combine cheese, butter, flour, salt, and paprika with a fork or your fingers to make a soft dough.

2. Wrap 1 teaspoon cheese dough around each olive, covering it completely. Set puffs on a baking sheet, freeze for 30 minutes, and then transfer to a resealable food storage bag.

3. To serve puffs, place the desired quantity on an ungreased baking sheet. Bake in a preheated 400°F oven until golden brown and heated through, 10 to 15 minutes. Serve warm. Makes 24 appetizers.

❖ **INEZ HENNIGAN** | Trinity Presbyterian church, Little Rock, Arkansas

Mini Muffin–Puffs

4 oz. cooked ham, finely chopped
¼ onion, finely chopped
½ cup shredded cheddar cheese
1 egg

⅛ teaspoon pepper
1½ teaspoons Dijon mustard
1 tube (8 oz.) refrigerated crescent rolls

1. Preheat oven to 350°F. Coat two 12-cup mini muffin pans with nonstick cooking spray.

2. Combine ham, onion, cheddar cheese, egg, pepper, and mustard.

3. Unroll crescent roll dough. Press dough into one large rectangle. Cut into 24 pieces and place in muffin cups. Divide filling evenly among cups. Bake for 15 minutes or until lightly browned. Makes 24 puffs.

❖ **APRIL LEWIS** | Memorial Baptist Church, Tulsa, Oklahoma

Artichoke Dip

1 cup shredded Parmesan
¾ cup light mayonnaise
1 can (14 oz.) artichokes in water,
    chopped and drained
1 can (4 oz.) green chilies, drained

1 garlic clove, minced
2 tablespoons chopped green onions
1 tomato, coarsely chopped
Crackers

1. Preheat oven to 350°F.

2. Combine Parmesan, mayonnaise, artichokes, chilies, and garlic. Spread in a 9-inch glass pie plate. Top with green onions and tomato. Bake for 20 minutes. Serve hot with crackers. Makes 4 to 6 appetizer servings.

❖ **MARY CERNY** | Memorial Baptist Church, Tulsa, Oklahoma

Teriyaki Meatballs

1 cup soy sauce

½ cup water

2 tablespoons crushed or powdered ginger

2 garlic cloves, finely chopped

3 lbs. ground chuck

1. Preheat oven to 275°F.

2. Stir together soy sauce, water, ginger, and garlic.

3. Break up ground chuck in a large bowl. Pour soy sauce mixture on top and stir to combine. Form into 1-inch meatballs. Place meatballs in a 17 x 12 x 2-inch roasting pan. Bake uncovered for 1 hour. Transfer to a platter and spear with toothpicks for serving. Makes about 100 meatballs.

❖ **INEZ HENNIGAN** | Trinity Presbyterian Church, Little Rock, Arkansas

Guacamole

3 ripe avocados

1 medium tomato, seeded and chopped

½ cup mayonnaise

2 tablespoons finely chopped onion

2 tablespoons fresh lemon juice

2 tablespoons chili sauce

Dash of hot pepper sauce

Here's a trick for removing the pit from an avocado: Cut the avocado in half lengthwise and separate the halves. Stick the point of a sharp knife directly into the pit and twist gently to lift it out.

1. Cut avocados in half lengthwise and remove pits. Scoop out pulp into a bowl and mash with a fork.

2. Add tomato, mayonnaise, onion, lemon juice, chili sauce, and hot pepper sauce. Stir until well blended. Serve with tortilla chips. Makes about 2 cups.

❖ **VANESSA DRAPER** | Oakwood Church of God in Christ, Godfrey, Illinois

Pepper Poppers

1 package (8 oz.) cream cheese,
　room temperature

1 cup shredded sharp cheddar cheese

1 cup shredded Monterey Jack

⅛ teaspoon salt

¼ teaspoon chili powder

¼ teaspoon garlic powder

3 slices of bacon, fried crisp and finely crumbled

1 lb. fresh jalapeños

Dry bread crumbs

1. Preheat oven to 300°F. Grease a baking sheet.

2. Combine cream cheese, cheddar cheese, Monterey Jack, salt, chili powder, garlic powder, and bacon.

2. Wash jalapeños, cut in half lengthwise, and remove seeds. Fill each pepper with cheese mixture. Roll in dry bread crumbs to coat. Bake for 30 to 50 minutes; the shorter the baking time, the hotter and spicier the taste. Serve hot. Makes 24 to 30 appetizers.

✦ **ANNA BERRYHILL** | Memorial Baptist Church, Tulsa, Oklahoma

Vidalia Onion Dip

1 cup chopped Vidalia onion	**½ cup grated cheddar cheese**
1 cup mayonnaise	**½ cup grated Swiss cheese**

1. Preheat oven to 325°F. Grease a 9-inch pie plate.

2. Combine onion, mayonnaise, cheddar cheese, and Swiss cheese. Transfer to pie plate. Bake for 30 minutes or until heated through. Serve with crackers. Makes 4 to 6 appetizer servings.

✦ **HENRIETTA PALMER** | Christ Episcopal Church, Charlotte, North Carolina

Seven-Layer Taco Dip

1 can (8 oz.) jalapeño bean dip	**Pepper**
2 avocados, pits and skins removed	**Tabasco sauce**
1 tablespoon mayonnaise	**1 cup chopped onion**
1 package (1 oz.) taco seasoning mix	**Coarsely chopped black olives**
2 cups sour cream	**2 tomatoes, chopped**
Garlic salt	**Shredded cheese**
Chili powder	**Tortilla chips**

1. Spread bean dip over the bottom of a 13 x 9 x 2-inch baking dish.

2. Combine avocados and mayonnaise, mash with a fork, and spread in an even layer over the bean dip.

3. Stir taco seasoning into sour cream. Spread over avocado layer. Sprinkle with garlic salt, chili powder, and pepper. Add a few dashes of Tabasco sauce.

4. Layer onions, olives, and tomatoes over sour cream. Top with shredded cheese. Cover with plastic wrap and refrigerate overnight to meld the flavors. Serve with tortilla chips. Makes 6 to 8 appetizer servings.

✦ **L. WIEMAN** | Presbyterian Church of Gonzales, Gonzales, Texas

Cucumber Cream Cheese Spread

2 packages (8 oz. each) cream cheese,
  room temperature
2 teaspoons lemon juice
¼ teaspoon prepared horseradish

¼ teaspoon salt
⅛ teaspoon hot sauce
2 teaspoons minced onion
½ medium cucumber, peeled and finely chopped

1. Beat cream cheese until smooth. Add lemon juice, horseradish, salt, and hot sauce and mix well.
2. Stir in onion and cucumber. Cover and chill 1 hour before serving. Serve with crispbread or cocktail bread. Makes 2½ cups.

GRACE ON THE HILL UNITED METHODIST CHURCH | Corbin, Kentucky

Monica's Salsa

3 large tomatoes, finely chopped
1 small chipotle, minced
¼ cup lime juice
½ cup fresh cilantro, finely chopped
1 red onion, finely chopped
½ cup tomato juice

2 garlic cloves, minced
1 tablespoon sugar
Salt

 Adjust salsa ingredients and quantities to your individual taste. Experiment and have fun!

1. Combine tomatoes, chipotle, lime juice, cilantro, onion, tomato juice, garlic, and sugar in a bowl. Sprinkle with salt. Stir until well combined.
2. Cover salsa with plastic wrap and chill at least 1 hour before serving. Can be stored in refrigerator up to 5 days. Serve with tortilla chips. Makes 5 cups.

MONICA HESEMAN | Trinity Presbyterian Church, Little Rock, Arkansas

Party Meatballs

3 lbs. ground beef
1 onion, chopped
2 eggs
Garlic powder
Salt and pepper

SAUCE:
2 bottles (12 oz. each) chili sauce
1 jar (8 oz.) grape jelly
2 teaspoons chili powder

1. Combine ground beef, onion, eggs, and garlic powder in a large bowl. Sprinkle with salt and pepper. Toss to combine. Roll into tiny meatballs.

After the Service Soup

A church in California has a celebrative meal each Sunday without causing anyone to miss church school or worship service. One member comes early and puts a soup bone on to cook. As others come, they drop prepared vegetables brought from home into the soup pot. All during the service, the soup is cooking, and when the service ends, lunch is ready. Bread and fruit are set out and the congregation enjoys a family meal. Simple, but a celebration!

Adapted from *Simply Delicious* by Grace Winn,
©1983, Alternative, Inc.

2. To make sauce: Combine chili sauce, grape jelly, and chili powder in a large skillet over medium-low heat. Simmer for 20 minutes.

3. Add half of meatballs to sauce and cook for 15 minutes. Remove meatballs from sauce with a slotted spoon. Add remaining meatballs and cook for 15 minutes. Return all meatballs to sauce and continue simmering until done, 10 to 15 minutes more. Makes about 100 meatballs.

JILL RUZISKA | Vincent Memorial United Methodist Church, Nutter Fort, West Virginia

Three-Cheese Manicotti

2 cups grated mozzarella, divided

1 cup ricotta or creamed cottage cheese

½ cup Parmesan

2 eggs, beaten

¼ cup snipped parsley

½ teaspoon salt

⅛ teaspoon pepper

8 manicotti shells, cooked and drained

1 jar (14 oz.) spaghetti sauce with herbs

1. Preheat oven to 350°F. Grease a 2-quart casserole.

2. Combine 1 cup of the mozzarella, ricotta, and Parmesan. Stir in eggs, parsley, salt, and pepper.

3. Stuff manicotti shells with cheese mixture, using about ¼ cup each.

4. Pour ½ cup of the spaghetti sauce into casserole. Arrange stuffed manicotti in dish. Pour remaining sauce over top and sprinkle with remaining cup mozzarella. Bake uncovered 25 to 30 minutes or until bubbly. Makes 4 servings.

JANE BRUCE | Christ Episcopal Church, Charlotte, North Carolina

Veggie Spinach Lasagna

1 box (16 oz.) wide lasagna noodles
½ lb. fresh spinach
2 yellow squash, sliced
2 zucchini, sliced
1 eggplant, sliced

1 teaspoon oregano
1 teaspoon tarragon
Salt and pepper
¼ lb. Swiss cheese, provolone,
    or Feta, shredded

1. Preheat oven to 350°F. Lightly coat a 15 x 10½ x 2-inch baking dish with nonstick cooking spray.
2. Layer noodles alternately with spinach, yellow squash, zucchini, and eggplant in baking dish; sprinkle oregano, tarragon, and salt and pepper over vegetables as you go. End with a noodle layer. Top with shredded cheese.
3. Cover dish tightly with aluminum foil. Bake for 25 to 35 minutes or until hot and bubbling. Dish will be very juicy. Makes 6 to 8 servings.

KEVIN DOUGLASS | Oakwood Church of God in Christ, Godfrey, Illinois

Penne Caprese

6 cups hot cooked penne, rinsed and drained
4 cups chopped plum tomatoes
1½ cups fresh basil leaves, thinly sliced
1 cup diced fresh mozzarella
2 tablespoons extra virgin olive oil

1 tablespoon capers
1 teaspoon salt
½ teaspoon pepper
2 garlic cloves, crushed
⅓ cup grated Parmesan or Romano

1. Combine penne, plum tomatoes, basil, and mozzarella in a large bowl.
2. Whisk together olive oil, capers, salt, pepper, and garlic. Pour over penne and toss gently. Sprinkle with Parmesan or Romano cheese and toss again. Makes 5 servings.

JEFF and BARBIE JACKSON | Vincent Memorial United Methodist Church, Nutter Fort, West Virginia

Linguine with Broccoli and Roasted Garlic

1 garlic bulb
3 oz. whole wheat linguine
1 head of broccoli
1 tablespoon toasted sesame oil

2 tablespoons minced garlic
¼ cup sesame seeds
1 tablespoon lemon juice
½ teaspoon salt

1. Preheat oven or toaster oven to 375°F. Place whole unpeeled garlic bulb in a small ovenproof dish. Roast until soft when squeezed, 30 to 35 minutes. Cool to room temperature and squeeze out garlic cloves from their skins.

2. Cook linguine following package directions. Drain and rinse.

3. Cut or break off bite-size florets from broccoli. Place in a steamer basket over boiling water. Steam just until tender, 4 to 6 minutes.

4. Heat sesame oil in a large skillet, add minced garlic and sesame seeds, and sauté for 3 minutes. Add roasted garlic cloves, linguini, broccoli, lemon juice, and salt. Toss all ingredients and serve immediately. Makes 4 to 6 servings.

TOM TILTON | Unity Baptist Church, Morgantown, Indiana

Lasagna

3 quarts water
1 tablespoon salt
1 tablespoon oil
½ package (8 oz.) lasagna noodles

Tomato Sauce (recipe follows)
1 lb. ricotta
1 lb. mozzarella
1 jar (3 oz.) grated Parmesan

1. Preheat oven to 350°F. Grease a 13 x 9 x 2-inch baking dish.

2. Heat water in a large stockpot over high heat. Add salt and bring to a rolling boil. Add oil and lasagna noodles, two or three pieces at a time, returning water to a boil after each addition. Cook, uncovered, for 15 minutes. Drain and rinse under hot water.

3. Spoon one-third of tomato sauce over bottom of baking dish. Layer one-third each of noodles, ricotta, mozzarella, and Parmesan. Repeat the layering two more times until all the ingredients are used. Bake uncovered for 45 to 50 minutes. Let stand 10 to 15 minutes before cutting. Makes 9 servings.

TOMATO SAUCE

¼ cup olive oil
½ cup finely chopped onion
1 garlic clove, crushed
2 tablespoons finely chopped fresh parsley
1 lb. ground chuck
1 can (35 oz.) Italian tomatoes, undrained

2 cans (6 oz.) tomato paste
1 teaspoon dried basil leaves, crushed
2 teaspoons dried oregano leaves, crushed
1 tablespoon salt
¼ teaspoon pepper
2 tablespoons sugar

1. Heat oil in a large, deep skillet over medium heat. Add onion, garlic, and parsley and sauté until onion is tender, 5 minutes.

2. Add ground chuck and brown, stirring occasionally. Drain off fat.

3. Stir in tomatoes and their juice, tomato paste, basil, oregano, salt, pepper, and sugar. Bring to a boil, reduce heat, and simmer, covered, for 3 hours. Makes 6 cups.

JENNIFER SMITH LYLE | Vincent Memorial United Methodist Church, Nutter Fort, West Virginia

Easy Lasagna

½ package (8 oz.) lasagna noodles
2 tablespoons butter
1 lb. ground beef
½ cup chopped onion
2 cans (8 oz. each) pizza sauce, divided
1 can (6 oz.) tomato paste

1 teaspoon garlic salt
½ teaspoon oregano
1 cup cottage cheese
¾ cup grated Parmesan
2 cups shredded mozzarella, divided

1. Preheat oven to 350°F. Grease a 13 x 9 x 2-inch baking dish.

2. Cook and drain noodles according to package directions.

3. Melt butter in a large skillet over medium heat. Add ground beef and onion. Cook, stirring occasionally, until beef is evenly browned, 5 to 6 minutes. Stir in 1 can of the pizza sauce, tomato paste, garlic salt, and oregano. Reduce heat and simmer, uncovered, for 10 to 15 minutes.

4. Combine cottage cheese, Parmesan, and 1¾ cups of the mozzarella.

5. Layer one-third of the noodles, one-third of the beef mixture, and one-third of the cheese in baking dish. Repeat once. Layer remaining noodles and beef and remaining can of pizza sauce. Top with remaining cheese mixture. Bake uncovered for 30 minutes. Strew remaining mozzarella over the top. Bake until mozzarella melts, 5 minutes more. Remove from oven and allow to set 10 minutes before cutting into squares. Makes 8 servings.

❖ **MARILYN J. TAYLOR** | Trinity Evangelical Lutheran Church, Lansdale, Pennsylvania

Live Longer Casserole

2 tablespoons butter
3 small zucchini or yellow squash,
    coarsely chopped
1 cup sliced mushrooms
3 large tomatoes, coarsely chopped
¼ cup chopped parsley

3 cups torn spinach leaves
½ teaspoon salt
½ box (8 oz.) pasta, cooked and drained
6 oz. Swiss cheese
6 oz. cheddar cheese
Parmesan

1. Preheat oven to 350°F. Lightly grease a 13 x 9 x 2-inch baking dish.

2. Heat butter in a large skillet over medium heat until melted. Add zucchini or yellow squash and mushrooms. Sauté until softened, 4 to 6 minutes.

3. Stir in tomatoes, parsley, and spinach. Sprinkle with salt.
Lower to a simmer and cook for 10 to 15 minutes. Mix in cooked pasta.

4. Transfer mixture to baking dish. Top with Swiss cheese and cheddar cheese. Sprinkle with Parmesan. Bake until casserole is heated through and cheese melts, about 20 minutes. Serve hot. Makes 10 to 12 servings.

Instead of Swiss cheese, try Monterey Jack, provolone, or mozzarella.

❖ **SUSIE HUGHES** | Sorento Assembly of God Church, Sorento, Illinois

Fresh Vegetable Lasagna

2 tablespoons oil
3 small zucchini, sliced and quartered
3 carrots, sliced in rounds
2 sweet red peppers, chopped
4 green onions, sliced
Salt and pepper
15 uncooked lasagna noodles

1 container (16 oz.) skimmed milk ricotta
1 lb. shredded mozzarella
1 can (28 oz.) Italian-style tomatoes,
   quartered
1 can (28 oz.) tomato purée
1 cup grated Parmesan
2 cups water

1. Preheat oven to 350°F. Lightly coat a 15 x 10½ x 2-inch baking dish with nonstick cooking spray.
2. Heat oil in a skillet over high heat. Add zucchini, carrots, red peppers, and onions and stir-fry for 5 minutes. Remove from heat. Sprinkle with salt and pepper.
3. Place three or four uncooked lasagna noodles in bottom of baking dish. Layer vegetables over noodles. Place three or four more noodles and layer ricotta cheese over them. Continue layering noodles alternately with mozzarella, tomatoes, and tomato purée. Top with grated Parmesan.
4. Add water to baking dish. Lightly coat a piece of foil with nonstick cooking spray, place facedown on dish, and crimp to seal the edges. Bake for 1½ hours. Allow to set ½ hour before cutting into squares. Makes 6 to 8 servings.

✦ **JUNE FOREMAN** | Vincent Memorial United Methodist Church, Nutter Fort, West Virginia

Baked Spaghetti

1 tablespoon butter
1 cup chopped onion
1 cup chopped green pepper
1 can (28 oz.) tomatoes, cut up,
   liquid reserved
1 can (4 oz.) mushrooms, drained
1 can (2.25 oz.) sliced black olives
2 teaspoons oregano

1 lb. ground beef, browned and partially
   drained of fat
¾ box (12 oz.) spaghetti
2 cups shredded cheddar cheese
1 can (10.5 oz.) cream of mushroom
   condensed soup
¼ cup water
¼ cup grated Parmesan

1. Preheat oven to 350°F. Grease a 13 x 9 x 2-inch baking dish.
2. Melt butter in a large skillet over medium heat. Add onion and green pepper and sauté until tender, 4 to 6 minutes. Add tomatoes and their liquid, mushrooms, olives, oregano, and browned beef. Simmer uncovered for 10 minutes.
3. Cook and drain spaghetti according to package directions. Place half of spaghetti in baking dish. Top with half of beef mixture followed by half of cheddar cheese. Repeat layers.
4. Mix condensed soup and water until smooth. Pour over casserole. Sprinkle Parmesan on top. Bake uncovered for 30 to 35 minutes. Makes 10 servings.

✦ **BERNICE SENSENIG** and **CAROL NASE** | Trinity Evangelical Lutheran Church, Lansdale, Pennsylvania

Chicken Delicious

3 to 4 whole boneless, skinless
    chicken breasts
Salt
½ cup finely chopped celery
½ cup finely chopped carrot
½ cup finely chopped onion
3 teaspoons chopped parsley

3 to 4 cups boiling water
1 small can (8 oz.) sliced water chestnuts
½ lb. mushrooms, sliced and sautéed
1 can (10.75 oz.) cream of mushroom condensed soup
1 cup mayonnaise
2 cups corn bread stuffing (such as Pepperidge Farm)
½ cup butter, melted

1. Preheat oven to 350°F. Lightly grease a 13 x 9 x 2-inch baking dish.

2. Sprinkle chicken breasts with salt. Combine chicken breasts, celery, carrot, onion, and parsley in a large stockpot. Add boiling water, adjust to a simmer, and cook until meat is tender, 20 to 30 minutes. Remove chicken from pot and set in baking dish. Reserve cooking liquid.

Prepare Chicken Delicious up to 1 day ahead and keep refrigerated until baking time. Leftovers can be frozen and reheated in the microwave.

3. Combine water chestnuts, mushrooms, cream of mushroom condensed soup, mayonnaise, and ¼ to ½ cup of the reserved cooking liquid. Pour sauce over chicken. Toss stuffing with butter and sprinkle over top of casserole. Bake until top is golden brown, 45 to 50 minutes. Serve hot. Makes 8 to 10 servings.

DORIS ROULEAU | Memorial Baptist Church, Tulsa, Oklahoma

Sherried Chicken

¾ cup flour
2 teaspoons salt
Garlic powder
6 chicken breasts or thighs
10 tablespoons butter

SAUCE:
6 tablespoons butter
¾ cup sherry
3 tablespoons soy sauce
3 tablespoons lemon juice
½ teaspoon ginger

1. Preheat oven to 350°F.

2. Whisk together flour, salt, and garlic powder. Lightly dredge chicken pieces in flour mixture and shake off excess.

3. Melt butter in a heavy skillet over medium heat. Add chicken in batches and cook, turning once, until browned on all sides, 4 to 6 minutes per side. Place chicken in casserole dish.

4. To make sauce: Melt butter in a saucepan over medium heat. Stir in sherry, soy sauce, lemon juice, and ginger. Bring to a boil, stirring constantly. Pour over chicken. Bake uncovered, turning chicken once and basting occasionally, until tender, about 1 hour. Makes 4 to 6 servings.

MIMI ROGERS | Christ Church, Frederica, St. Simons Island, Georgia

Chicken with Artichoke Hearts

1 large onion, finely chopped
Salt
⅜ cup butter
4 boneless, skinless chicken breasts
2 teaspoons paprika
4 tablespoons flour

½ cup chicken stock
¾ cup sour cream
1 cup white wine
1 can (14 oz.) artichoke hearts, drained
5 slices bacon, cooked crisp and crumbled
Slivered almonds

1. Preheat oven to 350°F.

2. Place onion in a shallow bowl. Sprinkle with salt.

3. Heat butter in a large skillet over medium-high heat until melted. Add chicken breasts and cook, turning once, until browned on both sides, 4 to 6 minutes per side. Remove from pan.

4. Add onion to skillet, sprinkle with paprika, and sauté until golden and translucent. Remove pan from heat and stir in flour. Return pan to heat. Gradually add chicken stock, stirring to combine. Cook, stirring continuously, until mixture boils and thickens. Reduce heat, stir in sour cream and wine, and simmer 5 minutes.

5. Transfer chicken and artichoke hearts to an ovenproof dish. Top with sauce. Cover and bake for 1 hour. Serve topped with bacon and almonds. Makes 4 servings.

❖ ANN SHADE | Trinity Evangelical Lutheran Church, Lansdale, Pennsylvania

Deborah's Simple Chicken Curry

1 teaspoon butter
2 teaspoons peanut oil
4 boneless, skinless chicken breasts, split
1 onion, chopped
3 garlic cloves, minced
1 tablespoon curry powder

Salt and pepper
1 apple, cored and coarsely chopped
½ cup chopped dried apricots
½ cup golden raisins
1 can (14.5 oz.) chicken broth
Cooked rice

1. Melt butter with peanut oil in heavy skillet over medium-high heat. Add chicken breasts and cook, turning once, until browned on both sides, 5 to 6 minutes per side. Transfer to a plate.

2. Reduce heat to medium, add onion and garlic to skillet, and cook until onions are translucent, 6 minutes. Stir in curry powder. Sprinkle with salt and pepper.

3. Add apples, apricots, and raisins to skillet and stir to combine. Add broth just to cover mixture. Return chicken to skillet. Cover and simmer until chicken is tender, about 10 minutes. Transfer chicken to a platter and cover with foil to keep warm.

4. Continue cooking curry sauce until it thickens, 5 minutes more. To serve, place chicken on hot cooked rice and spoon curry sauce over the top. Pass chutney on the side. Makes 6 to 8 servings.

❖ GINNY SAWYER | First Presbyterian Church, Du Quoin, Illinois

Chicken Casserole for a Crowd

10 cups cooked chicken, diced

10 cups chopped celery

2 bunches green onions with tops, sliced

2 cans (4 oz. each) chopped green chilies

1 can (5.75 oz.) pitted ripe olives,
    drained and sliced

2 cups slivered almonds

5 cups (20 oz.) shredded cheddar cheese, divided

2 cups mayonnaise

2 cups (16 oz.) sour cream

5 cups crushed potato chips

1. Preheat oven to 350°F. Grease two 13 x 9 x 2-inch baking dishes.

2. Combine chicken, celery, green onions, chilies, olives, and almonds in a large bowl. Add 2 cups of the cheddar cheese.

3. Combine mayonnaise and sour cream in a separate bowl, add to chicken mixture, and toss until evenly coated. Spoon mixture into baking dishes. Top with crushed potato chips and remaining 3 cups cheddar cheese. Bake until hot, 20 to 25 minutes. Makes 24 servings.

 **CAROL NASE** | Trinity Evangelical Lutheran Church, Lansdale, Pennsylvania

Chicken Pot Pie

1 broiler-fryer chicken, 2½ lbs.

2 quarts water

2 teaspoons salt, divided

5⅓ tablespoons butter

1 cup chopped onion

1 cup chopped celery

1 cup chopped carrots

1 or 2 potatoes, peeled and chopped

½ cup frozen green peas, thawed

½ cup plus 1 teaspoon flour, divided

2 cups chicken broth

1 cup half-and-half

½ teaspoon pepper

1 package (15 oz.) refrigerated piecrust pastry

1. Place chicken, water, and 1 teaspoon of the salt in a Dutch oven. Bring to a boil. Cover, reduce heat, and simmer 1 hour.

2. Remove chicken from Dutch oven. Strain broth, reserving 2 cups. Skim off fat from broth. Skin and bone chicken. Shred or cut meat into bite-size pieces.

3. Preheat oven to 400°F. Lightly grease an 11 x 7 x 2-inch baking dish.

4. Melt butter in a skillet over medium heat. Add onion, celery, carrots, potatoes, and peas. Cook until carrots are tender, 8 to 10 minutes. Stir in ½ cup of the flour until smooth.

5. Gradually stir in reserved broth and half-and-half. Cook over medium heat, stirring continuously, until mixture is thickened and bubbly. Stir in chicken, remaining teaspoon salt, and pepper. Pour filling into baking dish.

6. Unfold piecrust pastry, press out fold lines, and dust with remaining teaspoon flour. Roll into a 12 x 8-inch rectangle. Place pastry over filling, fold edges under, and crimp. Cut slits in top. Bake for 30 minutes, covering edges with foil after 20 minutes to prevent excess browning. Makes 6 servings.

JEANNE KUTROW | Christ Episcopal Church, Charlotte, North Carolina

Chicken à la King

1 chicken, 3½ to 4 lbs.
1 celery rib, chopped
½ onion, chopped
2 teaspoons salt
8 whole allspice
6 tablespoons butter

8 tablespoons flour
1 cup chopped celery, cooked,
    cooking water reserved
1 can (8 oz.) mushrooms, drained,
    liquid reserved
1 small jar (2 oz.) pimiento

1. Place chicken in a large stockpot, add water to cover, and set over medium-high heat. Add celery, onion, salt, and allspice. Bring to a boil, reduce to a simmer, and cook until chicken is tender, 35 to 45 minutes.
2. Remove chicken from broth and set on a platter. When cool enough to handle, tear or cut up chicken into bite-size pieces, removing and discarding bones and skin.
3. Strain chicken broth and skim off fat. Measure and set aside 3 cups of broth.
4. Melt butter in top half of a large double boiler. Add flour and stir to make a roux. Gradually add chicken broth, celery cooking water (do not add the celery), and mushroom liquid. Cook until sauce thickens. Stir in mushrooms, pimiento, and chicken. Simmer, uncovered, in double boiler until ready to serve. Serve in patty shells or potato baskets. Makes 8 to 10 servings.

❖ **LEONA WILKENS** | St. John's Guild, St. John's Church, West Bend, Wisconsin

Quiche Lorraine

1½ cups (6 oz.) grated Swiss cheese
8 slices of bacon, cooked until crisp
    and crumbled
1 unbaked 9-inch pie shell
3 eggs
1 cup heavy cream

½ cup milk
¼ teaspoon salt
¼ teaspoon pepper
Dash of cayenne pepper
½ teaspoon dry mustard

1. Preheat oven to 375°F.

2. Layer Swiss cheese and bacon into bottom of pie shell.

3. Whisk together eggs, heavy cream, milk, salt, pepper, cayenne pepper, and mustard. Pour into pie shell. Bake for 45 minutes or until firm and browned. Cut into wedges and serve hot. Makes 6 servings.

❖ **GINI WAGNER** | Methow Valley United Methodist Church, Twisp, Washington

Yogurt Parmesan Chicken

5 boneless, skinless chicken breasts
2 cups crushed buttery crackers
3 tablespoons Parmesan
1 teaspoon garlic salt

1 teaspoon seasoned salt
1 cup plain low-fat yogurt or sour cream
4 tablespoons butter, melted

1. Preheat oven to 350°F.

2. Cut chicken breasts into strips.

3. Combine crushed crackers, Parmesan, garlic salt, and seasoned salt in a shallow dish.

4. Dip chicken strips in yogurt or sour cream to coat and then roll in crumb mixture. Lay strips side by side in a 13 x 9 x 2-inch baking dish. Drizzle with melted butter. Bake uncovered for 45 minutes. Makes 8 to 10 servings.

❖ **LORRAINE PRIESTMAN** | Trinity Evangelical Lutheran Church, Lansdale, Pennsylvania

Chicken Casserole

1 box (7 oz.) long grain brown and wild rice
2 large chicken breasts, cooked and cubed
2 cans (10.75 oz. each) cream of chicken
    condensed soup
1 cup chopped celery

1 medium onion, chopped
1 green pepper, chopped
2 cans (8 oz. each) sliced water chestnuts, drained
¾ cup mayonnaise
½ to 1 cup bread crumbs

1. Butter a 13 x 9 x 2-inch baking dish.

2. Cook rice following package directions, reserving seasoning packet.

3. Combine rice and chicken in a large bowl. Stir in condensed soup, celery, onion, green pepper, water chestnuts, mayonnaise, and seasoning packet from rice until well combined. Transfer to baking dish and sprinkle bread crumbs on top. Cover and refrigerate overnight or freeze up to 1 week.

4. Preheat oven to 325°F. Bake casserole uncovered until heated through, 60 minutes. Add 15 minutes to baking time if casserole is frozen. Makes 6 to 8 servings.

MARY L. ZELLER | Methow Valley United Methodist Church, Twisp, Washington

Chunky Chicken for a Crowd

2 cans (4 oz. each) water chestnuts

1 can (10.75 oz.) cream of mushroom
    condensed soup

1 can (10.5 oz.) chicken broth, divided

3 cups diced celery

3 cups mayonnaise

24 boneless chicken breast halves or thighs

Salt and pepper

1 package (16 oz.) corn bread stuffing mix
    (such as Pepperidge Farm)

½ cup butter, melted

1. Preheat oven to 350°F.

2. Combine water chestnuts, condensed soup, half of the chicken broth, celery, and mayonnaise. Divide mixture into two or three large baking dishes. Distribute chicken pieces among pans and press into mixture. Sprinkle with salt and pepper.

3. Combine corn bread stuffing, melted butter, and remaining chicken broth. Distribute evenly over chicken. Bake until tender, 35 to 40 minutes. Makes 25 servings.

LYDA LISTER and DELORES BUSS | Vincent Memorial United Methodist Church, Nutter Fort, West Virginia

Oven-Fried Parmesan Chicken

1 cup fine cracker crumbs

¼ cup grated Parmesan

1 tablespoon dried parsley flakes

1 teaspoon salt

⅛ teaspoon pepper

Dash of garlic powder

1 chicken fryer (2½ to 3 lbs.), cut up and skinned

½ cup butter, melted

1. Preheat oven to 350°F. Lightly grease a 13 x 9 x 2-inch baking dish.

2. Combine cracker crumbs, Parmesan, parsley flakes, salt, pepper, and garlic powder. Mix well.

3. Dip chicken pieces in melted butter and then in crumb mixture. Place in baking dish. Bake for 1 hour or until outside is crispy and meat is heated through. Makes 4 servings.

DOTTIE O'LOONEY | Christ Church, Frederica, St. Simons Island, Georgia

Chicken Enchiladas with Spicy Sauce

¼ cup butter

¼ cup flour

2 cups chicken broth

1 container (16 oz.) sour cream

2 jalapeños, seeded and chopped

2 tablespoons corn oil

12 corn tortillas

1 whole chicken, cooked and chopped

2 cups shredded Monterey Jack, divided

¾ cup chopped onion

1. Preheat oven to 425°F. Lightly grease a 13 x 9 x 2-inch baking dish.

2. Melt butter in a saucepan over low heat. Stir in flour. Cook, stirring continuously, 1 minute.

3. Gradually add chicken broth, stirring continuously, until mixture thickens and is bubbly. Stir in sour cream and jalapeños.

4. Pour half of the sour cream sauce into baking dish.

5. Heat corn oil in a skillet over medium heat until hot. Fry tortillas one at a time, turning once, until softened, about 5 seconds per side. On each tortilla, place 1 tablespoon of chicken, Monterey Jack, and onion. Roll up tortillas and place seam side down in baking dish. Pour remaining sour cream sauce over top. Bake for 20 minutes. Sprinkle remaining 1¼ cup Monterey Jack on top and bake 5 minutes more. Garnish with Spicy Sauce (recipe follows). Makes 12 tortillas.

SPICY SAUCE

1 large tomato, finely chopped

½ cup finely chopped onion

2 canned jalapeños, chopped

½ teaspoon salt

Combine tomatoes, onion, jalapeños, and salt. Stir well. Chill until ready to serve.

ROSIE JAHNSEN | Presbyterian Church of Gonzales, Gonzales, Texas

Stir-Fried Chicken and Vegetables

¾ cup chicken broth

4 teaspoons cornstarch

3 tablespoons soy sauce, divided

3 tablespoons peanut oil, divided

3 or 4 drops chili oil

1 teaspoon sesame oil

2 boneless chicken breasts, cut into
　1-inch cubes

½ teaspoon ground ginger

½ cup raw cashews

4 oz. fresh mushrooms, sliced

1 onion, sliced into rings

¼ lb. Chinese peapods

Florets from 1 bunch broccoli

1 large carrot, cut lengthwise, then
　diagonally into 1-inch strips

Hot cooked rice

1. Whisk together chicken broth, cornstarch, and 2 tablespoons of the soy sauce.

2. Heat 1 tablespoon of the peanut oil in a wok or large skillet over high heat. Add chili oil and sesame oil. Add chicken cubes and stir-fry 1 minute. Sprinkle remaining tablespoon soy sauce and ground ginger over chicken and stir-fry 2 to 3 minutes more. Remove chicken from wok.

3. Add cashews to hot oil and stir-fry until slightly browned, about 1 minute. Remove with a slotted utensil.

4. Add another tablespoon peanut oil to wok. Add mushrooms and onions, stir-fry 2 to 3 minutes, and remove.

5. Add remaining tablespoon peanut oil to wok. Add pea pods, broccoli, and carrots. Stir-fry until crispy, 2 to 3 minutes. Add chicken broth mixture to vegetables and toss. Return mushrooms, onions, chicken, and cashews to wok. Toss until entire mixture is warmed. Serve over hot rice. Makes 6 servings.

❖ **ELAINE ROBERTS** | First Moravian Church, Greensboro, North Carolina

Curried Orange Chicken

3 to 3½ lbs. chicken breasts, thighs,
  and drumsticks
1 cup English orange marmalade
1 tablespoon curry powder

1 teaspoon salt
½ cup water
Hot cooked noodles or rice

1. Preheat oven to 350°F. Butter a 4-quart casserole.

2. Place chicken pieces in casserole. Combine marmalade, curry powder, salt, and water and spoon over chicken. Bake uncovered, basting occasionally, until heated through, at least 45 minutes.

3. Remove chicken from casserole. Skim off fat from sauce. To serve, arrange chicken pieces on a bed of noodles or rice and spoon sauce on top. Makes 4 to 6 servings.

❖ **JUDY GAINES** | Christ Episcopal Church, Charlotte, North Carolina

Baked Chicken Parmesan

1½ cups dried plain bread crumbs
½ cup Parmesan
1 teaspoon salt
1 teaspoon dried parsley
⅓ garlic clove, crushed

½ cup butter, melted
1 teaspoon Worcestershire sauce
1 tablespoon Dijon mustard
2 to 3 lbs. chicken tenderloins

1. Preheat oven to 350°F.

2. Combine bread crumbs, Parmesan, salt, parsley, and garlic in a shallow bowl.

3. In a separate bowl, whisk together melted butter, Worcestershire sauce, and Dijon mustard.

4. Dip chicken into butter mixture, then into bread crumbs to coat. Place in shallow baking dish. Bake uncovered, basting occasionally, until golden brown, about 30 minutes. Makes 4 to 6 servings.

❖ **LISA NASE** | Trinity Evangelical Lutheran Church, Lansdale, Pennsylvania

Curry-Cajun Spiced Chicken

⅔ cup honey

6 tablespoons water

6 tablespoons mustard

4 tablespoons butter, melted

4 to 6 teaspoons Cajun seasoning

4 to 5 teaspoons curry powder

2 teaspoons lemon juice

2 garlic cloves, minced

6 boneless, skinless chicken breasts

Hot cooked rice

1. Preheat oven to 350°F. Lightly grease a 13 x 9 x 2-inch baking dish.

2. Combine honey, water, mustard, melted butter, Cajun seasoning, curry powder, lemon juice, and garlic in baking dish. Stir until well blended.

3. Add chicken breasts, turning to coat. Bake uncovered until chicken is tender and no longer pink, about 30 minutes. Serve chicken and pan drippings over hot cooked rice. Makes 6 servings.

LINDA LUALLEN | Church of the Canyons Women's Ministries, Canyon Country, California

A Meal for Those in Mourning

When preparing to visit someone who has recently lost a loved one, one of the first questions that comes to mind is, "What do I say?"

Just being there is often far more important than saying the "right" thing. Your ministry of presence can be far more meaningful than words.

If you feel the need to say something, simply saying "I'm sorry" may be enough. The fact that you took the time to prepare something for them to eat, and were with them in their grief, often says more than words could ever express.

THE REVEREND FRED W. PASCHALL, JR., Associate Rector
Christ Episcopal Church, Charlotte, North Carolina

SUGGESTED MENU

Beef Tenderloin, page 140

Zoe's Rice Casserole, page 162

Marinated Green Beans, page 167

Sour Cream Muffins, page 118

Irwin's Super Brownies, page 186

Chicken Paella

2 to 2½ lbs. skinless chicken parts
1 teaspoon salt
1 teaspoon pepper
1 tablespoon olive oil
1 cup rice
1 medium onion, chopped
2 garlic cloves, minced
2½ cups chicken broth

1 can (8 oz.) stewed tomatoes, chopped,
   juice reserved
½ teaspoon paprika
½ teaspoon oregano
⅛ teaspoon ground saffron or pinch of turmeric
1 red pepper, cut in strips
1 green pepper, cut in strips
½ cup frozen green peas

1. Season chicken with salt and pepper. Heat oil in a Dutch oven over medium heat. Add chicken and cook, turning once, until browned on both sides, 4 to 6 minutes per side. Transfer chicken pieces to a platter and cover with foil to keep warm.

2. Add rice, onion, and garlic to Dutch oven. Cook, stirring continuously, until rice is lightly browned and onion is transparent, 4 to 6 minutes. Add broth, tomatoes, paprika, oregano, and saffron. Return chicken pieces to Dutch oven and bring to a boil. Reduce heat, cover, and simmer 10 minutes.

3. Add red and green pepper strips and peas. Cover and simmer 15 minutes more or until rice is tender and liquid is absorbed. Makes 6 servings.

❖ **JOANNE LELAND** | Christ Episcopal Church, Charlotte, North Carolina

Southern Creamy Chicken Breasts

8 boneless, skinless chicken breast halves
8 slices Swiss cheese
1 can (10.75 oz.) cream of chicken
   condensed soup
¼ cup dry white wine
1 cup herb-seasoned stuffing mix, crushed
¼ cup butter, melted

VARIATION:
Omit the white wine and use cream of mushroom instead of cream of chicken soup.

1. Preheat oven to 350°F. Grease a 4-quart casserole.

2. Arrange chicken breasts in casserole. Top with cheese slices.

3. Combine soup and wine and pour over chicken. Top with stuffing mix and drizzle with melted butter. Bake until chicken is thoroughly cooked and stuffing is lightly browned, 45 to 55 minutes. Makes 6 to 8 servings.

❖ **JANE SHOWALTER** | Christ Episcopal Church, Charlotte, North Carolina

Beef Tenderloin

1 beef tenderloin, 4 to 6 lbs.
Vinegar
Salt and pepper

1. Preheat oven to 500°F.
2. Rub tenderloin with a small amount of vinegar to prevent splattering. Season with salt and pepper.
3. Place tenderloin in shallow roasting pan and cook 7 minutes.
4. Without opening oven door, reduce heat to 350°F and cook 25 minutes more for a rare roast. Let stand 15 minutes before carving and serving. Makes 6 to 8 servings.

❖ **ANNE TOMLINSON** | Christ Episcopal Church, Charlotte, North Carolina

Meat Pot Pie

1½ lbs. round steak, cut in 1-inch cubes
1 teaspoon salt
¼ teaspoon pepper
Flour
4 tablespoons butter or
    vegetable shortening
1 heart of celery, chopped
1 medium onion, chopped
2 cups water
½ can (2 oz.) sliced mushrooms
3 carrots, cooked and sliced into
    ½-inch rounds
½ cup cooked peas

1 cup diced, cooked potatoes browned
    in ¼ cup shortening
1 teaspoon chopped parsley
1 package (15 oz.) refrigerated piecrust pastry

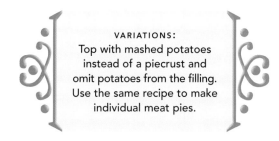

VARIATIONS:
Top with mashed potatoes
instead of a piecrust and
omit potatoes from the filling.
Use the same recipe to make
individual meat pies.

1. Sprinkle steak cubes with salt and pepper and dredge in flour.
2. Melt butter or shortening in a large skillet over medium heat. Add steak cubes and cook, turning occasionally, until browned on all sides. Add celery, onion, and water. Reduce heat and simmer until meat is tender, 1½ hours.
3. Preheat oven to 425°F. Stir mushrooms, carrots, peas, and potatoes into meat filling. Transfer filling to a 2-quart round casserole and sprinkle with chopped parsley. Layer pastry on top and crimp the edges. Slash crust with a knife to allow steam to escape. Bake for 20 minutes or until crust is golden brown. Makes 6 servings.

❖ **JUNE SPIELMAN** | St. John's Guild, St. John's Church, West Bend, Wisconsin

Mexican Import Casserole

1 lb. lean ground beef
1 tablespoon instant minced onion
½ teaspoon garlic salt
2 cans (8 oz. each) tomato sauce
1 cup chopped black olives

1 cup sour cream
1 cup small-curd cottage cheese
1 can (4 oz.) chopped chilies
1 bag (13 oz.) tortilla chips, crushed
2 cups grated Monterey Jack

1. Preheat oven to 350°F. Grease a 2½-quart casserole dish.

2. Brown beef in a large skillet over medium-high heat. Drain off excess fat. Add onion, garlic salt, tomato sauce, and olives.

3. Combine sour cream, cottage cheese, and chilies.

4. Line bottom of casserole with half of crushed tortilla chips. Add half of meat mixture, half of sour cream mixture, and half of grated Monterey Jack in layers. Repeat layers. Bake uncovered for 30 to 35 minutes or until bubbly. Makes 4 to 6 servings.

DARLA BROWN | Church of the Canyons Women's Ministries, Canyon Country, California

Shepherd's Pie

2 lbs. ground chuck
1 onion, chopped
½ cup finely chopped celery
Garlic powder
Salt and pepper
2 cans (10.75 oz. each) cream of
    mushroom condensed soup

8 to 10 Yukon gold potatoes,
    peeled and quartered
¼ cup butter
¼ cup milk, warmed in microwave

1. Preheat oven to 400°F. Lightly coat a casserole with nonstick cooking spray.

2. Combine ground chuck, onion, and celery in a large skillet over medium-high heat. Cook, stirring occasionally, until meat is evenly browned. Sprinkle with garlic powder, salt, and pepper. Remove from heat and stir in cream of mushroom soup.

3. Place potatoes in a large saucepan, add water to cover, and bring to a boil. Cook until tender when pierced with a fork, 20 to 25 minutes. Remove from heat and drain. Return potatoes to pan, add butter and warm milk, and mash with a potato masher. Potatoes should be thick.

4. Line bottom and sides of casserole with some of the mashed potatoes. Pour meat mixture into casserole. Top with remaining potatoes, spreading to seal all edges. Make a swirly design in potatoes, if desired. Bake for 20 to 30 minutes or until potatoes are golden brown. Cool 10 to 15 minutes before serving. Serve with a salad and vegetable. Makes 6 to 8 servings.

ROSE REED | Oakwood Church of God in Christ, Godfrey, Illinois

Beef Ragout

3 lbs. lean beef, cut in pieces
2 teaspoons salt
¼ teaspoon pepper
¼ cup butter
1 onion, chopped
1 carrot, chopped
2 celery ribs, chopped
2 garlic cloves, minced
¼ cup flour

2 cups water
¼ cup canned tomatoes
4 parsley sprigs
2 bay leaves
¼ teaspoon thyme
12 small onions
6 carrots, halved
12 small potatoes
1 tablespoon chopped parsley

1. Sprinkle beef with salt and pepper. Melt butter in a Dutch oven over high heat. Cook beef a few pieces at a time, turning occasionally, until well browned on all sides. Transfer browned pieces to a plate. Return meat to Dutch oven when all pieces have been browned. Reduce heat to medium.

2. Add onion, carrot, celery, and garlic. Cook until onion is lightly browned, 4 to 6 minutes. Stir in flour and cook until blended. Gradually add water, stirring to combine, and bring to a boil.

3. Add tomatoes, parsley, bay leaves, and thyme. Cover, reduce heat to low, and cook for 1½ hours. Add small onions, halved carrots, and potatoes. Cover and cook 1 hour more. Serve in bowls garnished with chopped parsley. Makes 8 to 10 servings.

❖ **LEOTA POWELL** | Memorial Baptist Church, Tulsa, Oklahoma

"The" Casserole

1½ lbs. ground chuck
1 onion, chopped
1 garlic clove, minced
1 can (2 lbs.) tomatoes
1 can (12 oz.) tomato paste

¼ teaspoon oregano
Salt and pepper
1 package (16 oz.) shell macaroni
1 package (16 oz.) sliced American cheese

1. Preheat oven to 325°F.

2. Combine ground chuck, onion, and garlic in a large skillet over medium-high heat. Cook, stirring occasionally, until chuck is evenly browned. Drain off fat.

3. Add tomatoes, tomato paste, oregano, and salt and pepper. Reduce heat and simmer 1 hour.

4. Cook shell macaroni following package directions. Drain well.

5. Layer half of macaroni, half of meat sauce, and half of cheese in a casserole. Repeat layering. Cover and bake 45 to 55 minutes. Makes 6 to 8 servings.

Most casseroles aren't fussy. If the serving time is delayed, they can sit in a warm oven (170°F) until everyone is ready to eat. That's one reason they are so popular for potluck suppers.

❖ **ELIZABETH WRIGHT** | Christ Church, Frederica, St. Simons Island, Georgia

Upside-Down Pizza Casserole

1 lb. ground beef
1 cup chopped onion
1 cup chopped green pepper
1 can (15 oz.) pizza sauce
¼ lb. pepperoni, chopped
½ teaspoon dried Italian seasoning
1 jar (2.5 oz.) sliced mushrooms, drained
6 oz. mozzarella, thinly sliced

TOPPING:
1 cup milk
1 tablespoon oil
2 eggs
1 cup flour
¼ teaspoon salt
¼ cup grated Parmesan

1. Preheat oven to 400°F. Lightly grease a 13 x 9 x 2-inch baking dish.

2. Combine ground beef, onion, and green pepper in a large skillet over medium-high heat. Cook until ground beef is lightly browned and onions are translucent. Drain off fat.

3. Stir in pizza sauce, pepperoni, Italian seasoning, and mushrooms.

4. To make topping: Beat milk, oil, and eggs in a mixer bowl for 1 minute. Add flour and salt and beat 2 minutes more. Pour mixture into a large saucepan and bring to a boil. Reduce to a simmer and cook uncovered, stirring occasionally, for 10 minutes.

5. Spoon meat mixture into baking dish. Layer mozzarella over meat mixture. Add topping, completely covering mozzarella. Sprinkle with Parmesan. Bake for 20 to 30 minutes. Makes 6 to 8 servings.

NORA KELLY | Grace on the Hill United Methodist Church, Corbin, Kentucky

Enchilada Casserole

2 lbs. ground chuck
1 onion, chopped
2 cans (8 oz. each) tomato sauce
1 can (11 oz.) Mexican-style corn, drained
1 can (10 oz.) enchilada sauce
1 teaspoon chili powder
½ teaspoon oregano

½ teaspoon pepper
¼ teaspoon salt
1 package (6½ oz.) corn tortillas, divided
2 cups shredded cheddar cheese, divided, plus more for topping
Chopped green chilies

1. Preheat oven to 375°F. Grease a 13 x 9 x 2-inch baking dish.

2. Cook ground chuck and onion in a large skillet over medium heat until lightly browned. Drain off fat.

3. Stir in tomato sauce, corn, enchilada sauce, chili powder, oregano, pepper, and salt. Bring to a boil, reduce heat to medium, and cook uncovered, stirring occasionally, 5 minutes.

4. Place half of tortillas in bottom of baking dish. Spoon half of beef mixture over tortillas. Top with 1 cup of the cheddar cheese. Repeat layers with remaining tortillas and beef mixture. Bake for 10 minutes, top with remaining cup cheese, and bake until cheese melts, 5 minutes more. Garnish with chopped green chilies. Makes 8 servings.

TANA BENTZEL | Messiah United Methodist Church, York, Pennsylvania

Noodle Strudel

½ package (8 oz.) fine noodles
1½ lbs. ground beef
1 onion, diced
1 teaspoon salt
½ teaspoon pepper

1 green pepper, chopped
1 can (15½ oz.) whole kernel corn
1 can (28 oz.) tomatoes
Bread crumbs

1. Preheat oven to 350°F. Lightly grease a 13 x 9 x 2-inch baking dish.

2. Cook noodles in salted water following package directions. Drain.

3. Brown ground beef and onion in a large skillet over medium-high heat. Drain off fat. Transfer beef and onions to a large bowl. Season with salt and pepper.

4. Add green pepper, corn, tomatoes, and noodles to ground beef. Mix gently. Spoon into baking dish. Top with bread crumbs. Bake for 45 minutes. Makes 4 to 6 servings.

❖ **MRS. ART ZIEGLER** and **MRS. FRED SAGER** | St. John's Guild, St. John's Church, West Bend, Wisconsin

Taco Bake

1 lb. ground beef
1 onion, chopped
1 package (1 oz.) taco seasoning mix
¾ cup water
1 can (15 oz.) tomato sauce

½ package (8 oz.) shell macaroni,
　cooked and drained
1 can (4 oz.) chopped green chilies
2 cups (8 oz.) shredded cheddar cheese, divided

1. Preheat oven to 350°F. Grease a 1½-quart baking dish.

2. Brown beef and onion in a large skillet over medium-high heat. Drain off fat.

3. Add taco seasoning, water, and tomato sauce. Bring to a boil, reduce heat, and simmer, stirring occasionally, 20 minutes. Stir in cooked macaroni, chilies, and 1½ cups of the cheddar cheese. Pour into baking dish. Top with remaining ½ cup cheese. Bake for 30 minutes. Makes 4 servings.

❖ **NORA KELLY** | Grace on the Hill United Methodist Church, Corbin, Kentucky

Zucchini Casserole

2 lbs. zucchini, sliced
1 lb. lean ground beef
1 cup chopped onion
1 teaspoon salt
¼ teaspoon pepper
¼ teaspoon garlic powder

3 cups cooked rice
2 eggs, beaten
1½ cups cottage cheese
2 tablespoons grated Parmesan
2 cups grated cheddar cheese

1. Preheat oven to 350°F. Lightly grease a 13 x 9 x 2-inch baking dish.

2. Bring a pot of salted water to a boil over high heat, add zucchini, and cook until soft, 5 minutes. Drain and set aside.

3. Brown ground beef and onion in a large skillet over medium-high heat. Drain off fat. Sprinkle with salt, pepper, and garlic powder. Stir in rice and zucchini.

4. Combine eggs, cottage cheese, and Parmesan. Stir into meat mixture. Transfer to a baking dish, top with cheddar cheese, and bake for 30 minutes. Makes 6 to 8 servings.

✦ EVELYN ASH | Vincent Memorial United Methodist Church, Nutter Fort, West Virginia

Greek Moussaka

16 tablespoons butter, divided	Salt and pepper
3 eggplants, peeled and sliced ½-inch thick	1 cup fine bread crumbs
3 large onions, chopped	6 tablespoons flour
2 lbs. ground lamb or beef	1 quart milk
3 tablespoons tomato paste	4 eggs, beaten until frothy
½ cup red wine	Dash of nutmeg
1 cup chopped parsley	2 cups ricotta or cottage cheese
¼ teaspoon cinnamon	1 cup freshly grated Parmesan

1. Melt 4 tablespoons of the butter in a large skillet over medium heat. Add eggplant in batches and cook, turning once, until lightly browned on both sides, 6 to 8 minutes per batch. Remove from pan and set aside.

2. Heat another 4 tablespoons of butter in same skillet, add onions, and cook, stirring occasionally, until browned, 8 to 10 minutes.

3. Add ground beef or lamb to skillet. Break up meat with a spoon as it cooks and browns, 10 minutes.

4. Combine tomato paste, wine, parsley, cinnamon, and salt and pepper. Stir into meat mixture. Reduce heat and simmer, stirring frequently, until all the liquid has been absorbed. Remove from heat.

> The flavor of moussaka improves after one day. Reheat in a 350°F oven for 20 minutes or warm individual servings in the microwave. Moussaka can also be prepared ahead and frozen before baking. There's no need to defrost but do allow an extra 20 minutes' baking time.

5. Preheat oven to 375°F. Grease a 15 x 10½ x 2-inch baking pan. Sprinkle bread crumbs on bottom of pan.

6. Melt remaining 8 tablespoons butter in a large saucepan. Blend in flour, stirring with a wire whisk, to make a roux. Bring milk to a boil in a separate saucepan. Gradually add milk to roux, stirring continuously, until thickened and smooth. Remove from heat. Cool slightly. Stir in eggs, nutmeg, and ricotta.

7. Layer eggplant and meat sauce alternately in pan, sprinkling each with a bit of Parmesan. Pour ricotta sauce over the top. Bake for 1 hour or until golden brown. Remove from oven, cool 20 minutes, and cut into squares. Makes 8 to 10 servings.

✦ JACQUELINE CURL | Christ Church, Frederica, St. Simons Island, Georgia

A Beehive of Activity

The kitchen at our church is a sunny place, with yellow countertops and two ovens. The major side entrance to the church takes you directly into the kitchen. If you stop by the church during the week, the kitchen is so very quiet, like a sleeping child.

But our kitchen quickly becomes a beehive of activity for our social gatherings. Often, the two ovens are filled to capacity with the settings on "warm" to keep casseroles hot during the service. The aroma of the kitchen wafts into church while the pastor is giving his message. It is hard to keep our minds off the things of the world (our tummies) when there is a potluck luncheon directly following the service.

I think about the occasions I have had to eat happily with the members of our church. We ladle goulash and strudels and salads and chocolate desserts onto our plates, reminding our offspring not to take too much, and trying to restrain ourselves as well.

Of course our church is more than a kitchen, a structure, and potluck luncheons. It is all about friendships, sharing in each other's lives, and God. Preparing food for each other is a visible act of kindness, a way to bring His love into reality.

LINDA HOLLINGSWORTH
Church of the Canyons Women's Ministries, Canyon Country, California

Layered Hamburger Pie

1 lb. lean ground beef
1 egg
¼ cup bread crumbs
1 teaspoon salt
1 teaspoon mixed Italian dried herbs
    (oregano, basil, marjoram)
1 teaspoon dry mustard
¼ teaspoon ground cumin

⅛ teaspoon garlic powder
3 or 4 potatoes, peeled and sliced thin
    (1½ cups)
1 onion, sliced and separated into rings
1¼ cups sliced fresh mushrooms, divided
1 cup shredded cheddar cheese
½ cup shredded Swiss cheese
2 tablespoons fresh minced parsley

1. Preheat oven to 350°F.

2. Toss ground beef, egg, bread crumbs, salt, Italian herbs, mustard, cumin, and garlic powder until well combined. Pat evenly into bottom and up sides of a 9-inch pie plate to make a "crust."

3. Layer potato slices, onions, and 1 cup of the mushrooms onto crust. Cover with foil. Bake for 1 hour or until potatoes are cooked through.

4. Remove pie plate from oven. Remove and discard foil. Add cheddar cheese and Swiss cheese to pie. Arrange remaining ¼ cup mushrooms in a ring around the rim. Return to oven just long enough to melt the cheese, 4 to 6 minutes. Garnish with parsley. Makes 4 to 6 servings.

✤ **MOTHER LILLIE DRAKEFORD** | Miracle Deliverance Holiness Church, Columbia, South Carolina

Favorite Veal Parmesan

3 tablespoons butter

¼ cup Parmesan

Dash of pepper

¼ cup herb-seasoned stuffing mix

1 lb. (about 5 pieces) veal for scaloppine

1 egg, beaten

1 teaspoon oregano

1 jar (14 oz.) basil-flavored tomato sauce

4 slices mozzarella

1 lb. angel hair pasta, cooked

1. Preheat oven to 400°F. Add butter to a 13 x 9 x 2-inch baking dish and set in oven. Remove when butter melts and begins to brown.

2. Combine Parmesan, pepper, and stuffing mix. Dip veal scaloppine in egg, then in cheese-stuffing mix to coat. Arrange veal in a single layer in baking dish. Bake for 15 minutes, turn veal over, and bake 10 minutes more or until browned.

3. Combine oregano and tomato sauce and pour over veal. Top with mozzarella. Return baking dish to oven and bake until cheese begins to brown, 5 to 10 minutes. Serve over angel hair pasta. Makes 4 to 5 servings.

✤ **MARY ANNE THOMAS** | Christ Episcopal Church, Charlotte, North Carolina

Veal Vermouth

2 lbs. veal cutlets

1 cup Parmesan

Salt and pepper

2 tablespoons butter

2 small or 1 medium onion, sliced

1 cup sliced mushrooms

4 carrots, thinly sliced

3 chicken bouillon cubes

1½ cups boiling water

½ cup dry vermouth

1. Sprinkle veal cutlets with Parmesan, salt, and pepper.

2. Melt butter in a heavy skillet over medium heat. Cook veal in batches, turning once, until browned on both sides, 8 to 10 minutes. Layer veal in a 3-quart casserole.

3. Sauté onions, mushrooms, and carrots in same skillet.

4. Dissolve bouillon cubes in boiling water. Stir in vermouth. Pour over vegetables; then pour all over veal. Cover and refrigerate for 2 to 5 hours.

5. Preheat oven to 325°F. Bake casserole, covered, for 1 hour. Serve accompanied by noodles, rice, or mashed potatoes. Spoon cooking liqueur over all. Makes 5 servings.

✤ **BETH CRIMMINS** | Trinity Evangelical Lutheran Church, Lansdale, Pennsylvania

Ben's Beef Stew

5 tablespoons flour, divided
1 teaspoon minced garlic
1 tablespoon Worcestershire sauce
½ teaspoon pepper
6 to 10 drops hot pepper sauce
3 lbs. lean stew beef, cut into bite-size pieces
1 large baking potato
2 onions
1 lb. carrots
2 zucchini
Salt
½ lb. mushrooms, sliced
1 can (10½ oz.) beef broth

1 cup red wine
¼ cup cold water
8 to 10 cups hot cooked rice

VARIATIONS:
Substitute lamb for beef.
For curried stew, rub 1
tablespoon of curry powder
into meat before baking
and add another
tablespoon of curry powder
to flour and water before
last hour of cooking.

1. Preheat oven to 350°F.

2. Rub 3 tablespoons of the flour, garlic, Worcestershire sauce, pepper, and 6 to 10 drops of hot sauce into beef. Put beef in large roaster.

3. Cut potato, onions, carrots, and zucchini into bite-size chunks. Add to roaster. Sprinkle beef and vegetables with salt. Top with sliced mushrooms.

4. Pour broth and wine over meat and vegetables. Cover roaster and bake for 2 hours.

5. Mix remaining 2 tablespoons flour with cold water and add to roaster. Cover and cook 1 hour more. Serve over hot rice. Makes 8 to 10 servings.

 BEN HUTTO | Christ Episcopal Church, Charlotte, North Carolina

Lamb Casserole

1 lb. ground lamb
1½ cups uncooked rice
2 cups water
2 cans (10¾ oz. each) condensed
    tomato soup

½ onion, chopped
½ green pepper, chopped
1½ teaspoon salt
1 teaspoon oregano
½ teaspoon pepper

1. Preheat oven to 350°F.

2. Brown ground lamb in a large skillet over medium-high heat, 6 to 8 minutes. Drain on paper towels.

3. Combine lamb, rice, water, tomato soup, onion, green pepper, salt, oregano, and pepper in a casserole. Stir well. Cover and bake for 1 hour or until all liquid is absorbed and rice and vegetables are cooked. Makes 4 servings.

BERT ROME | St. Mark's Lutheran Church, Conshohocken, Pennsylvania

Lamb Stew

3 tablespoons oil
2 onions, coarsely chopped
2½ to 3 lbs. boneless lamb shoulder,
    cut in 2-inch pieces
½ cup red wine, divided
4 large tomatoes, peeled, seeded,
    and chopped
2 garlic cloves

1 bay leaf
1½ tablespoons fresh rosemary
Grated zest and juice of 1 orange, divided
½ cup water
6 new potatoes, parboiled and halved
2 cups pearl onions, parboiled and skinned
½ cup orange liqueur
1 orange, cut into slices

1. Preheat oven to 350°F.

2. Heat oil in a large skillet over medium heat. Add onions and sauté until translucent, 3 to 4 minutes. Use a slotted spoon to transfer onions to a 3-quart casserole.

3. Add lamb to skillet in batches and cook, turning occasionally, until browned on all sides. Transfer lamb to casserole. Pour ¼ cup of the red wine into skillet and cook, stirring, to deglaze the browned bits. Pour deglazing liquid over lamb.

4. Add tomatoes, garlic, bay leaf, rosemary, orange zest, remaining ¼ cup wine, and water to casserole. Cover and bake until lamb is tender, 1 to 1½ hours.

5. Add potatoes, pearl onions, orange liqueur, and orange juice. Bake until potatoes and onions are heated through, 15 to 20 minutes more. Serve garnished with orange slices. Makes 6 to 8 servings.

JEANNE WADE | Christ Church, Frederica, St. Simons Island, Georgia

Lamb with Garlic and Olives

3½ lbs. lamb, cut into 1-inch cubes
1 cup pitted black olives, halved
2 garlic cloves, coarsely chopped
⅔ cup tomato purée
1 large onion, chopped
1 teaspoon basil

½ cup chopped celery
½ teaspoon oregano
½ cup fresh chopped dill
1 teaspoon salt
½ teaspoon sugar
1 cup chopped parsley, divided

1. Preheat oven to 350°F.

2. Combine lamb, olives, garlic, tomato purée, onion, basil, celery, oregano, dill, salt, sugar, and ½ cup of the parsley in a large casserole. Cover and bake for 1 hour.

3. Reduce heat to 300°F. Continue baking until meat is tender, 30 to 45 minutes more. Skim off fat. Garnish with remaining parsley and serve with rice. Makes 6 servings.

Buy a leg of lamb and ask the butcher to remove the bone. Use 3½ lbs. for this recipe and freeze the remainder for a later dish.

LOTTA M. HUNT | Christ Church, Frederica, St. Simons Island, Georgia

Pork Chop Casserole

¾ cup rice

4 lean center-cut pork chops

1 onion, sliced into rings

1 tomato, sliced into rounds

1 green pepper, sliced into rings

1 can (10.5 oz.) beef bouillon

1. Preheat oven to 375°F. Lightly grease a 2-quart casserole. Place rice in bottom of casserole.

2. Trim fat from pork chops. Heat a skillet over medium heat, add pork chops, and cook, turning once, until browned on both sides, 8 to 10 minutes.

3. Use tongs to arrange pork chops on top of rice. Place a few onion rings, a tomato slice, and a pepper ring on top of each chop. Pour beef bouillon over chops. Cover and bake 1 hour or until rice is fully cooked. Add water during baking if all liquid is absorbed. Makes 4 servings.

SUE HEAD | Christ Episcopal Church, Charlotte, North Carolina

Garden Supper Casserole

2 cups bread cubes

½ cup shredded cheddar cheese

2 tablespoons butter, melted

1 cup cooked peas

2 tablespoons chopped onion

3 tablespoons butter

3 tablespoons flour

1 teaspoon salt

⅛ teaspoon pepper

1½ cups milk

1 cup cooked cubed pork

1 large tomato, sliced

1. Preheat oven to 350°F. Grease a 1-quart casserole.

2. Combine bread cubes, cheddar cheese, and butter. Place half of mixture in casserole. Top with cooked peas.

3. Heat butter in a skillet over medium heat until melted. Add onion and sauté until tender, 4 to 6 minutes. Blend in flour, salt, and pepper. Reduce heat to low and cook until bubbly. Remove from heat and stir in milk.

4. Bring to a boil, stirring continuously, and cook for

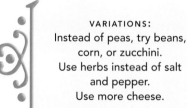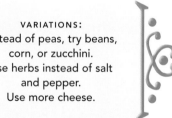

VARIATIONS:
Instead of peas, try beans, corn, or zucchini.
Use herbs instead of salt and pepper.
Use more cheese.

1 minute. Add cubed pork and stir to combine. Pour mixture over peas in casserole. Arrange tomato slices on top and sprinkle with remaining bread cube mixture. Bake uncovered for 25 to 35 minutes. Makes 4 servings.

EILEEN NOEGEL | St. John's Guild, St. John's Church, West Bend, Wisconsin

Ginger Pork Loin with Apple-Horseradish Sauce

1 teaspoon dry mustard

1 teaspoon thyme

5 lbs. boneless pork loin

2 large garlic cloves

1 piece ginger (¾ oz.), peeled and halved

½ cup dry sherry

½ cup soy sauce

Parsley

GLAZE:

½ cup red currant jelly

2 tablespoons dry sherry

Apple-Horseradish Sauce (recipe follows)

1. Combine mustard and thyme to make a dry rub. Massage dry rub all over pork loin with your fingers. Place pork loin in a resealable food storage bag. Set bag in a bowl.

2. Finely chop garlic and ginger in a food processor. Add sherry and soy sauce and pulse to combine. Pour the marinade over the pork, seal bag, and set bowl with bag in refrigerator. Marinate, turning bag occasionally, at least 2 hours or overnight.

3. Preheat oven to 325°F. Remove pork loin from marinade and set in a roasting pan with a rack. Discard marinade. Roast for 1 hour 40 minutes (20 minutes per lb.) or until a meat thermometer inserted in thickest part registers 155°F to 160°F. Remove from oven and transfer pork loin to a platter.

4. To make glaze: Heat red currant jelly in a 1-quart saucepan over medium heat until melted. Stir in sherry.

5. To serve, cut thin slices of pork, arrange on a platter, and spoon glaze over the top. Garnish with parsley. Serve apple-horseradish sauce on the side. Makes 10 to 12 servings.

APPLE-HORSERADISH SAUCE

1½ lbs. Granny Smith apples, peeled, cored, and sliced

¼ cup sugar

2 tablespoons horseradish

1. Combine apples and sugar in a large saucepan over medium-high heat. Cook, stirring occasionally, until very soft, 25 to 35 minutes.

2. Mash apples with a potato masher to a coarse consistency. Allow to cool.

3. Stir in horseradish until well blended. Makes about 2 cups.

MARIE E. STALTE | Trinity Evangelical Lutheran Church, Lansdale, Pennsylvania

Pork Stew

4 lbs. trimmed pork shoulder,
  cut into 1-inch cubes
2 tablespoons butter
2 tablespoons vegetable oil
2 large onions, sliced
4 garlic cloves, minced
¼ cup flour
1 can (14.5 oz.) chicken broth
1½ cups apple juice
1 cup dark beer
2 tablespoons Dijon mustard

½ teaspoon salt
1 teaspoon coriander
½ teaspoon cinnamon
1 cup chopped dried apricots
¾ cup chopped pitted prunes

 Allow ample time to cut the pork into cubes and chop the dried fruit. This delicious stew is worth the extra effort!

1. Preheat oven to 350°F.
2. Melt butter and oil in large skillet over medium-high heat. Add pork and cook, stirring occasionally, until evenly browned, 8 to 10 minutes. Transfer pork to a casserole.
3. Add onions and garlic to skillet and cook until tender, 10 minutes. Add flour and cook, stirring continuously, for 3 minutes. Stir in broth, apple juice, and beer. Add mustard, salt, coriander, and cinnamon, stirring to dissolve. Add apricots and prunes. Spoon mixture from skillet over pork in casserole. Cover and bake for 1 hour. Remove cover and bake 45 minutes more. Makes 6 to 8 servings.

❖ **JILL CUNNINGHAM** | Christ Church, Frederica, St. Simons Island, Georgia

Seafood Gumbo

½ cup flour
2 tablespoons vegetable oil
1½ cups chopped onion
½ cup chopped celery
4 cups frozen cut okra
1½ cups peeled, seeded, and chopped tomato
⅓ cup chopped smoked ham (about 2 oz.)

3 cans (16 oz. each) fat-free low-sodium
  chicken broth
2 garlic cloves, minced
1 lb. medium shrimp, peeled and deveined
8 oz. lump crabmeat, shell pieces removed
1 container (8 oz.) shucked oysters, drained
½ teaspoon hot sauce

1. Preheat oven to 350°F.
2. Add flour to a 9-inch pie plate. Set in oven for 45 minutes or until light brown. Cool on a wire rack.
3. Heat oil in a large Dutch oven over medium-high heat. Stir in 3 tablespoons of the toasted flour (reserve remaining flour for another use). Add onion and celery and sauté 2 minutes.
4. Add okra, tomatoes, ham, and broth. Bring to a boil, reduce heat, and simmer 45 minutes.
5. Stir in minced garlic. Return to a boil and add shrimp, crabmeat, and oysters. Boil until shrimp are pink and edges of oysters curl, about 2 minutes. Stir in the hot sauce. Ladle into deep soup bowls. Makes 6 servings.

❖ **LINDA S. THOMPSON** | Oakwood Church of God in Christ, Godfrey, Illinois

Jambalaya

2 tablespoons vegetable oil

¾ cup diced smoked ham

1 smoked sausage, sliced ½-inch thick

1 lb. boneless chicken, cubed

1½ cups chopped onion

1 cup chopped celery

1 green pepper, chopped

2 garlic cloves, minced

2 bay leaves

1½ teaspoons salt

1½ teaspoon oregano

1 teaspoon white pepper

½ teaspoon black pepper

1 teaspoon thyme

1 can (8 oz.) tomato sauce

1 can (14.5 oz.) chicken broth

2 cups rice

4 tomatoes, peeled and chopped

1. Preheat oven to 350°F.

2. Heat oil in a large Dutch oven over medium heat. Add ham, sausage, and chicken and sauté, stirring frequently, until lightly browned, 4 to 8 minutes.

3. Stir in onion, celery, and green pepper. Sauté until crisp-tender, about 5 minutes. Stir in garlic, bay leaves, salt, oregano, white pepper, black pepper, and thyme. Cook over medium heat, stirring continuously and scraping pan frequently, 5 minutes.

4. Add tomato sauce and chicken broth. Bring to a boil. Stir in rice and tomatoes. Remove from heat, cover, and set in oven until rice is tender, 20 to 25 minutes. Remove bay leaves before serving. Serve hot. Makes 10 servings.

❖ **DAWNA MASON JACOB** | Memorial Baptist Church, Tulsa, Oklahoma

Lizzy's Crab Casserole

2 green onions with tops, chopped

½ cup butter, divided

2 garlic cloves, pressed

35 to 40 saltines, crushed, divided

1 lb. fresh crabmeat

¼ teaspoon cayenne pepper

Salt and pepper

1 cup half-and-half

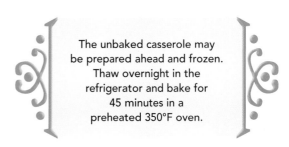

The unbaked casserole may be prepared ahead and frozen. Thaw overnight in the refrigerator and bake for 45 minutes in a preheated 350°F oven.

1. Preheat oven to 350°F. Grease a 2-quart casserole.

2. Melt 6 tablespoons of the butter in a large skillet over medium heat. Add onions and sauté until translucent, 4 to 6 minutes. Add garlic and sauté 1 minute; do not let garlic brown. Remove from heat.

3. Add three-fourths of the crushed saltines, crabmeat, and cayenne pepper. Sprinkle with salt and pepper. Stir to combine. Spoon into casserole and top with remaining crushed saltines. Pour half-and-half over casserole and dot with remaining 2 tablespoons butter. Bake for 30 minutes. Makes 4 servings.

❖ **CYNTHIA GASS** | Christ Episcopal Church, Charlotte, North Carolina

Crab Casserole

¼ cup butter

3 tablespoons flour

2 cups warm milk

2 tablespoons minced onion

¼ teaspoon celery salt

⅛ teaspoon grated orange zest

1 tablespoon minced parsley

1 tablespoon chopped green pepper

1 pimiento, minced

Dash of Tabasco sauce

2 tablespoons sherry

1 egg, beaten

1 teaspoon salt

Dash of pepper

4 cups deluxe lump crabmeat

1 cup buttery bread crumbs (see tip)

Paprika

1. Preheat oven to 350°F. Grease a 13 x 9 x 2-inch baking dish.

2. Melt butter in a saucepan over medium heat. Stir in flour until well combined. Cook, stirring continuously, until flour turns golden. Gradually add milk, stirring continuously, until sauce begins to thicken.

3. Stir in onion, celery salt, orange zest, parsley, green pepper, pimiento, and Tabasco sauce. Remove from heat and stir in sherry.

4. Ladle some of white sauce into beaten egg and whisk to combine. Return eggs to hot mixture. Add salt, pepper, and crabmeat. Ladle into casserole, top with bread crumbs, and dust with paprika. Bake until hot and bubbly, 12 to 20 minutes. Makes 6 servings.

❖ **MRS. WILLIAM J. HULL** | Christ Church, Frederica, St. Simons Island, Georgia

TO MAKE BUTTERY BREAD CRUMBS:
Combine 1 to 2 tablespoons melted butter with 1 cup of bread crumbs. Makes a crispy topping for casseroles that bake in the oven.

Light Tuna Noodle Casserole

3½ cups medium yolkless egg noodles

1 can (6.5 oz.) water-packed tuna, drained and flaked

¼ cup light mayonnaise

3 celery ribs, sliced crosswise at an angle

⅓ cup chopped onion

¼ cup chopped green pepper

1 package (10 oz.) frozen peas, cooked

1 tablespoon corn oil

3 tablespoons flour

¾ cup chicken stock, skimmed of fat

½ cup skim milk

½ teaspoon salt

⅛ teaspoon garlic powder

⅛ teaspoon pepper

½ cup grated reduced-fat cheddar cheese

¼ cup slivered blanched almonds, toasted

1. Preheat oven to 425°F. Lightly coat a 1½-quart casserole with nonstick cooking spray.

2. Cook noodles according to package directions, omitting salt and oil in the cooking water. Drain and rinse.

3. Combine noodles, tuna, mayonnaise, celery, onion, pepper, and peas in a large bowl. Set aside.

4. Heat oil in a large skillet over medium heat. Add flour and stir for 1 minute. Do not brown. Add chicken stock and milk and let come to a boil. Add salt, garlic powder, and pepper and cook 1 minute more. Stir in cheese until it melts. Pour sauce onto noodles and mix well. Turn into casserole and top with toasted almonds. Bake for 20 minutes or until bubbly. Makes 6 servings.

❖ JEANNE JONES | Presbyterian Church of Gonzales, Gonzales, Texas

Toasting brings out the flavor in nuts. Spread raw nuts on a rimmed baking sheet and toast in a 350°F oven for 8 to 10 minutes. To stop the toasting action and to capture just the right flavor, slide the nuts off the hot baking sheet and into a bowl as soon they come out of the oven. Nuts still warm from toasting are especially delicious in salads.

Seashell Tuna Casserole

1 tablespoon butter
¼ cup chopped green pepper
¼ cup chopped onion
1 can (10.75 oz.) cheddar cheese
    condensed soup

½ cup chopped canned tomatoes
1 can (7 oz.) tuna, drained and flaked
2 cups cooked shell macaroni
Dash of pepper

1. Preheat oven to 350°F.
2. Melt butter in a saucepan over medium heat. Add green pepper and onion and sauté until onion is translucent, 3 to 5 minutes.
3. Stir in cheese soup, tomatoes, tuna, macaroni, and pepper until well combined. Add a dash of pepper. Turn into a 1-quart casserole. Bake uncovered for 30 minutes. Makes 3 servings.

❖ MARIE HECKLER | Trinity Evangelical Lutheran Church, Lansdale, Pennsylvania

Garlic Shrimp

2 lbs. cooked shrimp, peeled and deveined
½ cup butter, room temperature
½ cup seasoned bread crumbs
2 tablespoons sour cream
2 tablespoons chopped parsley

1 garlic clove, chopped
1 teaspoon salt
½ teaspoon Worcestershire sauce
2 teaspoons lemon juice
Dash of pepper

1. Preheat oven to 450°F.
2. Layer shrimp in a 1-quart casserole.
3. Combine butter, bread crumbs, sour cream, parsley, garlic, salt, Worcestershire sauce, lemon juice, and pepper. Spread mixture over shrimp. Bake for 10 minutes or until bubbly and browned. Makes 4 servings.

❖ ANITA GRIFFIN | Christ Episcopal Church, Charlotte, North Carolina

Make-Ahead Buffet Shrimp Casserole

12 to 15 slices firm white bread, crusts removed, divided

3 lbs. cooked shrimp, peeled, divided

4 cups grated sharp cheddar cheese, divided

½ cup butter, melted

6 eggs, beaten

Salt and pepper

1 teaspoon dry mustard

1 quart milk

1. Break bread into small pieces. Line the bottom of a greased 13 x 9 x 2-inch baking dish with bread, using about half of it.

2. Layer half of the shrimp and half of the cheddar cheese in baking dish. Repeat the bread, shrimp, and cheese layers. Drizzle with melted butter.

3. Beat eggs. Sprinkle with salt and pepper. Whisk in mustard and milk. Pour over shrimp, cover with foil, and let stand in refrigerator at least 3 hours or overnight.

4. Preheat oven to 350°F. Bake casserole for 1 hour or until hot. Remove foil and continue baking until browned and bubbly, 10 to 15 minutes more. Makes 12 servings.

❖ **BETSY LOCKE, HOPE PARROTT,** and **JO GRIFFITH** | Christ Episcopal Church, Charlotte, North Carolina

Asparagus Onion Casserole

5 tablespoons butter, divided

1 lb. fresh asparagus, cut into 1-inch pieces

2 medium onions, sliced

2 tablespoons flour

1 cup warm milk

1 small package (3 oz.) cream cheese, cubed

1 teaspoon salt

⅛ teaspoon pepper

½ cup shredded cheddar cheese

1 cup soft bread crumbs

1. Preheat oven to 350°F. Set aside a 1½-quart baking dish; do not grease.

2. Melt 1 tablespoon of the butter in a skillet. Add asparagus and onions and sauté until asparagus is crisp-tender, about 8 minutes. Spoon into baking dish.

3. Melt another 2 tablespoons butter in a saucepan over medium heat. Stir in flour until smooth. Gradually add milk, stirring continuously. Bring to a boil and cook, stirring continuously, until thickened, 2 to 3 minutes.

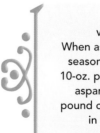

VARIATION:
When asparagus is not in season, substitute two 10-oz. packages of frozen asparagus for every pound of fresh asparagus in your recipe.

4. Reduce heat. Add cream cheese, salt, and pepper. Stir until cheese is melted. Pour sauce over asparagus. Top with cheddar cheese. Melt remaining 2 tablespoons butter, toss with bread crumbs, and sprinkle over top of casserole. Bake uncovered for 35 to 40 minutes or until heated through. Makes 4 to 6 servings.

❖ **MARGARET DEMEO** | Methow Valley United Methodist Church, Twisp, Washington

The Farmer's Love Letter

My sweet potato, do you carrot all for me?
You are the apple of my eye, with your radish hoar and turnip nose.
My heart beets for you. My love for you is as strong as onions.
If we cantaloupe, lettuce marry and we will be a happy pear.

FRED STAMPLEY
Christ Church, Frederica, St. Simons Island, Georgia

Garlicky Asparagus

1 lb. asparagus, trimmed and stalks,
  peeled if tough
1 tablespoon fresh lemon juice
½ teaspoon grated lemon zest

1 tablespoon olive oil
¼ teaspoon salt
⅛ teaspoon pepper
2 garlic cloves, crushed

1. Preheat oven to 350°F.
2. Place asparagus in a single layer in a 13 x 9 x 2-inch baking dish.
3. Whisk together lemon juice, lemon zest, olive oil, salt, and pepper. Drizzle over asparagus. Turn asparagus gently to coat. Place garlic on top. Bake for 25 minutes or until fork-tender. Remove and discard garlic. Makes 4 servings.

❖ **PEARL TALBERT** | Christ Church, Frederica, St. Simons Island, Georgia

Sautéed String Beans

1 lb. string beans, trimmed
2 tablespoons olive oil
3 garlic cloves, cut in half

¼ teaspoon salt
⅛ teaspoon pepper
1 tablespoon sliced almonds or chopped walnuts

1. Cook beans in lightly salted boiling water for 5 minutes. Drain in colander. Rinse under cold running water.
2. Heat oil in a large skillet over low heat. Add garlic and cook until fragrant, 5 minutes. Add beans, salt, pepper, and almonds or walnuts. Cook, stirring, until beans are heated through, 2 minutes. Remove garlic and discard. Makes 4 to 6 servings.

❖ **PEARL TALBERT** | Christ Church, Frederica, St. Simons Island, Georgia

Baked Beans

1 pint navy beans
¼ lb. salt pork or ¼ to ½ lb. pork
   shoulder cut in small pieces
1 onion, peeled
1 tablespoon molasses

3 tablespoons brown sugar
3 tablespoons corn syrup
1 tablespoon salt
½ teaspoon dry mustard
1 cup boiling water plus more for pot

1. Pick over and rinse beans. Place in a large stockpot, add cold water to cover, and let soak overnight.

2. In the morning, pour off water and add fresh water to cover. Set pot over medium-high heat and bring to a boil. Reduce heat to a simmer and cook, stirring occasionally, until skins break, 20 to 25 minutes.

3. Preheat oven to 350°F.

4. Scald the salt pork, scrape, and cut into 3 or 4 pieces. Put beans in bean pot or casserole, place onion in the center, and bury salt pork in beans, leaving zest exposed.

5. Dissolve molasses, brown sugar, corn syrup, salt, and mustard in boiling water. Pour over beans. Add more boiling water to cover beans. Bake for 5 to 6 hours. Makes 8 to 10 servings.

> Are your beans completely cooked? A good test is to take a few beans on a spoon and blow on them. The skins will break if they are cooked enough.

❖ **MRS. F. O. REINKE** | St. John's Guild, St. John's Church, West Bend, Wisconsin

Fiesta Stuffed Green Peppers

1 small onion, diced
1 teaspoon butter
½ lb. ground beef
1 can (11 oz.) Mexican-style corn, drained
1 cup celery, diced

½ cup finely crushed saltines
1 can (8 oz.) tomato sauce
Salt and pepper
4 large green peppers, cored, seeded,
   and pith removed

1. Preheat oven to 350°F. Set aside a 9 x 9 x 2-inch baking pan.

2. Combine onions and butter in a small skillet over medium heat. Cook for 10 minutes. Remove onions from skillet and drain.

3. Cook ground beef in same skillet, breaking up clumps with a spoon, until lightly browned, 5 to 6 minutes. Drain.

4. Combine ground beef, corn, celery, saltines, and tomato sauce in a medium-size bowl. Sprinkle with salt and pepper.

5. Stand green peppers upright in pan and slightly apart. Stuff peppers with meat mixture. Bake for 45 minutes to 1 hour or until peppers are tender. Makes 4 servings.

❖ **RUBY L. CARR** | Miracle Deliverance Holiness Church, Columbia, South Carolina

Scalloped Potatoes

8 to 10 medium potatoes, peeled
   and sliced thinly
1 medium onion, diced, divided
1 or 2 garlic cloves, minced, divided
¼ cup butter

⅓ cup flour
1½ to 2 cups milk
4 oz. shredded sharp cheddar cheese, divided
Bread crumbs

1. Preheat oven to 375°F. Grease a 13 x 9 x 2-inch baking dish.

2. Combine potatoes, half of the onion, and half of the garlic in a large bowl.

3. Heat butter in a saucepan over medium heat until melted. Add remaining onion and garlic and sauté 1 minute. Stir in flour and continue cooking, stirring continuously, to make a roux; do not let roux brown. Gradually add milk, stirring continuously, until mixture begins to thicken. Add one-third of the cheddar cheese and stir until melted.

4. Pour sauce over potatoes. Stir until evenly coated. Layer potatoes in pan with another third of the cheese. Combine remaining cheese with bread crumbs and sprinkle over the top. Add milk to baking dish if potatoes are not well coated. Cover and bake for 1 hour and 15 minutes. Remove cover and continue baking until top is browned and a fork pierces through potatoes with only slight resistance, 5 to 10 minutes more. Makes 4 to 6 servings.

❖ **HEATHER MCLEAN NICHOLS** | Methow Valley United Methodist Church, Twisp, Washington

Calico Bean Bake

½ lb. ground beef
1 onion, chopped
½ lb. bacon, cut into pieces, fried,
   and drained
½ cup ketchup
¾ cup brown sugar

1 teaspoon salt
1 teaspoon dry mustard
2 tablespoons vinegar
2 cans (16 oz. each) pork and beans
1 can (15 oz.) kidney beans
1 can (15 oz.) butter beans

1. Preheat oven to 300°F. Grease 13 x 9 x 2-inch baking dish.

2. Brown ground beef and onions in a large skillet over medium heat. Drain off fat.

3. Stir in bacon, ketchup, brown sugar, salt, mustard, and vinegar. Simmer until heated through, 8 to 10 minutes.

4. Add pork and beans, kidney beans, and butter beans. Mix well. Transfer mixture to a baking dish. Bake for 1½ hours or until bubbly. Makes 6 to 8 servings.

VARIATION:
Instead of baking beans in the oven, use a slow cooker set to low for the final stage of cooking.

❖ **NANCY J. CLARKE** | Trinity Evangelical Lutheran Church, Lansdale, Pennsylvania

Two-Corn Casserole

½ cup butter

¾ cup chopped green pepper

⅓ cup chopped onion

1 can (17 oz.) cream-style corn

1 can (15.5 oz.) whole kernel corn, liquid reserved

3 eggs, well beaten

1 package (8.5 oz.) corn muffin mix

4 oz. shredded cheddar cheese

1. Preheat oven to 350°F. Grease a 2-quart casserole.

2. Heat butter in a small skillet until melted. Add green pepper and onion and sauté until crisp-tender. Remove from heat.

3. Combine cream-style corn, whole kernel corn, eggs, and muffin mix in a large bowl. Add peppers and onions and mix well. Pour into casserole and top with cheddar cheese. Bake for 55 to 60 minutes or until eggs are firm. Let stand 5 minutes before serving. Makes 12 servings.

SUSI DAVISON-WEBER | First Presbyterian Church, Du Quoin, Illinois

Cauliflower Parmesan

1 medium head cauliflower,
   broken into bite-size florets

½ teaspoon salt

¼ cup butter, melted

Grated Parmesan

Salt and pepper

1. Pour water into a saucepan to a level of 1 inch. Set saucepan over high heat, add a dash of salt, and bring to a boil. Add cauliflower florets and return to a boil. Cover and cook until fork-tender, 10 to 15 minutes. Drain well.

2. Place cauliflower in a serving dish. Drizzle with melted butter. Sprinkle with Parmesan, salt, and pepper. Makes 4 to 6 servings.

PEARL TALBERT | Christ Church, Frederica, St. Simons Island, Georgia

Escalloped Corn

3 tablespoons butter, divided

1½ tablespoons flour

½ teaspoon salt

¼ cup cream

1 can (15.5 oz.) whole kernel corn

1 can (4 oz.) mushrooms

2 egg yolks, beaten

½ cup bread crumbs or crushed cornflakes

1. Preheat oven to 300°F. Grease a 1-quart casserole.

2. Melt 2 tablespoons of the butter in a saucepan over medium heat. Stir in flour and salt until combined. Gradually add cream and cook until thick. Remove from heat.

3. Stir in corn, mushrooms, and egg yolks. Pour into casserole. Melt remaining tablespoon butter, mix with bread crumbs or crushed cornflakes, and sprinkle on top of casserole. Bake until heated through, 15 minutes. Makes 4 servings.

❖ ESTHER KLEIN | St. John's Guild, St. John's Church, West Bend, Wisconsin

Gratin of Yukon Gold Potatoes

½ tablespoon butter

6 Yukon gold potatoes, peeled and
    sliced ⅛-inch thick

⅔ cup grated Gruyère, divided

1 teaspoon olive oil

1 tablespoon fresh thyme leaves

½ teaspoon salt

⅛ teaspoon pepper

⅓ cup low-salt chicken stock,
    canned or homemade

1. Preheat oven to 400°F. Grease a 9-inch round or oval baking dish.

2. Combine potatoes, ⅓ cup of the Gruyère, olive oil, thyme leaves, salt, and pepper in a large bowl. Toss gently to mix.

3. Arrange potatoes in a neat overlapping pattern in baking dish. Pour chicken stock over potatoes and sprinkle remaining ⅓ cup Gruyère over top. Bake uncovered until potatoes are tender and cheese and potatoes start to brown, about 45 minutes. Makes 4 servings.

❖ NANCY SCHARFF | Trinity Evangelical Lutheran Church, Lansdale, Pennsylvania

Hot German Potato Salad

4 medium potatoes

8 slices of bacon

¼ cup sugar

2 tablespoons flour

⅓ cup water

⅓ cup vinegar

1 small onion, chopped

1 small green pepper, chopped

¼ cup chopped celery

2 tablespoons chopped pimiento

1. Cook potatoes in boiling salted water until tender, 20 to 25 minutes. Drain well. When cool enough to handle, peel and cut into ½-inch cubes.

2. Heat a heavy skillet over medium heat, add bacon, and cook until crisp. Drain on paper towels, reserving ¼ cup drippings in skillet. Crumble bacon.

3. Add sugar, flour, water, and vinegar to pan drippings, stirring well. Cook over medium heat until slightly thickened.

4. Combine potatoes, bacon, onion, green pepper, celery, and pimiento in a large bowl. Top with warm vinegar mixture and toss gently. Serve warm. Makes 6 servings.

❖ LORRAINE SIENER | First Presbyterian Church, Du Quoin, Illinois

New Potatoes Gratinée

6 tablespoons butter, divided

12 medium red potatoes, thinly sliced

1 lb. mushrooms, trimmed and sliced

1 medium onion, finely chopped

½ cup finely chopped parsley

1¼ cups shredded Gruyère or
   Swiss cheese, divided

2 garlic cloves, finely chopped

1 teaspoon salt

½ teaspoon pepper

2 cups heavy cream

½ cup water

1. Preheat oven to 325°F. Generously grease a 13 x 9 x 2-inch baking dish, using 1 tablespoon of the butter.

2. Combine potatoes, mushrooms, onion, parsley, 1 cup of the Gruyère or Swiss cheese, garlic, salt, and pepper in a large bowl. Melt 2 tablespoons of the butter and drizzle over the top. Toss gently to combine. Transfer to baking dish.

3. Whisk together heavy cream and water. Pour over potato mixture. Sprinkle with remaining ¼ cup Gruyère or Swiss cheese. Dot with remaining 3 tablespoons butter. Bake for 1½ hours, covering with a loose tent of foil after the cheese has browned. Remove from oven and cover tightly with foil to keep potatoes hot until serving. Makes 8 to 10 servings.

CAM CALDWELL | Christ Church, Frederica, St. Simons Island, Georgia

Zoe's Rice Casserole

⅜ cup butter

1 cup long grain rice

1 can (10.75 oz.) onion soup

1⅓ cups water

1 can (8 oz.) water chestnuts,
   drained and thinly sliced

1 jar (4.5 oz.) button mushrooms, drained

1 cup pecan halves

1. Preheat oven to 350°F. Grease a 2-quart casserole.

2. Heat butter in a large saucepan over medium-high heat until melted. Add rice and stir to coat grains. Add soup and water. Bring to a boil, reduce heat, and simmer 2 minutes.

3. Pour rice mixture into casserole. Stir in water chestnuts and mushrooms. Bake until heated through and bubbly, 45 to 60 minutes. Top with pecans during last 15 minutes of baking. Makes 6 to 8 servings.

LIBBA ELEAZER | Christ Episcopal Church, Charlotte, North Carolina

Rosemary Roasted Potatoes

2 lbs. medium red potatoes (about 12), scrubbed and cut into quarters

2 tablespoons olive oil

1 teaspoon chopped fresh rosemary

½ teaspoon salt

⅛ teaspoon pepper

1. Preheat oven to 350°F.

2. Toss together potato quarters, olive oil, and rosemary in a large roasting pan until oil is evenly distributed. Sprinkle with salt and pepper and toss again.

3. Roast potatoes, turning once halfway through cooking, until jackets are tight and crisp and flesh is tender when pierced with a fork, 45 to 50 minutes. Makes 4 servings.

PEARL TALBERT | Christ Church, Frederica, St. Simons Island, Georgia

Spanish Tomato Rice

8 slices of bacon

1 cup chopped onion

¼ cup chopped green pepper

1 can (16 oz.) whole tomatoes

1½ cups water

½ cup chili sauce

1 teaspoon salt

Dash of pepper

1 teaspoon brown sugar or maple syrup

½ teaspoon Worcestershire sauce

¾ cup long grain rice

Parsley sprigs

1. Heat a large skillet over medium heat, add bacon, and cook until browned and crisp. Drain on paper towels. Drain off all but ¼ cup of the bacon drippings.

2. Add onion and green pepper to reserved drippings and sauté just until tender, 4 to 6 minutes. Do not brown.

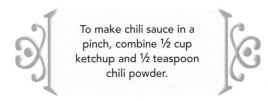

To make chili sauce in a pinch, combine ½ cup ketchup and ½ teaspoon chili powder.

3. Add tomatoes, water, chili sauce, salt, pepper, brown sugar, and Worcestershire sauce. Cook for 3 to 5 minutes. Add rice, cover, and simmer 35 to 40 minutes. Spoon into a serving dish, crumble bacon on top, and garnish with parsley. Makes 4 servings.

MICHELE WHITE | First Moravian Church, Greensboro, North Carolina

Squash Casserole

1 package (16 oz.) seasoned stuffing
   (such as Pepperidge Farm)
½ cup butter, melted
1½ lbs. yellow squash
1 small jar (2 oz.) pimiento, chopped
2 small onions, grated
1 cup sour cream
2 medium carrots, grated
1 can (10.75 oz.) cream of chicken condensed soup

For a more intense squash flavor, prepare the casserole one day ahead and refrigerate overnight before baking.

1. Preheat oven to 350°F. Lightly grease a 2-quart casserole.

2. Toss stuffing with melted butter until well combined. Press half of mixture into bottom and up sides of casserole.

3. Cook squash in boiling salted water until soft. Drain well.

4. Press squash through a sieve, pouring off and discarding excess liquid. Combine squash, pimiento, onions, sour cream, carrots, and all but 1 cup of the stuffing. Spoon squash mixture into casserole. Top with reserved stuffing. Bake for 30 minutes. Makes 8 to 10 servings.

VIRGINIA LEVEAU | Christ Church, Frederica, St. Simons Island, Georgia

Risotto

2 tablespoons butter
2 tablespoons olive oil
¼ cup sliced garlic
½ cup sliced green onion
2 large carrots, thinly sliced
1 cup long grain white rice
2 cups water
½ cup dry white wine

¾ teaspoon salt
½ teaspoon basil
¼ teaspoon thyme
¼ teaspoon pepper
1 small sweet red pepper, thinly sliced
1 small green pepper, thinly sliced
¼ cup fresh chopped parsley
¼ cup grated Parmesan

1. Heat butter and oil in a large skillet over medium heat until butter is melted. Add garlic, green onions, carrots, and rice. Sauté, stirring continuously, until rice is golden, about 3 minutes.

2. Add water, wine, salt, basil, thyme, and pepper. Reduce heat to low, cover, and cook until rice is almost tender, about 15 minutes.

3. Fold in red and green peppers, parsley, and Parmesan. Cook 5 minutes more. Serve hot. Makes 5 servings.

KATHERINE SCHWERINER | Trinity Evangelical Lutheran Church, Lansdale, Pennsylvania

Herbed Rice Pilaf

¼ cup butter

1 cup long grain rice

1 cup chopped celery

1 cup shredded carrots

¾ cup chopped onion

2½ cups chicken broth

1 package (2 to 2.5 oz.) dry chicken noodle soup mix

2 tablespoons minced parsley

½ teaspoon thyme

¼ teaspoon rubbed sage

¼ teaspoon pepper

1 tablespoon chopped pimientos

1. Heat butter in a large skillet over medium heat until melted. Add rice, celery, carrots, and onion and cook, stirring continuously, until rice is browned, about 4 minutes.

2. Stir in chicken broth, soup mix, parsley, thyme, sage, and pepper and bring to a boil. Reduce heat, cover, and simmer for 15 minutes.

3. Stir in the pimientos. Remove from heat and let stand, covered, for 10 minutes before serving. Makes 4 to 6 servings.

BETTY JOAN CRABTREE | Trinity Presbyterian Church, Little Rock, Arkansas

Bacon-Stuffed Yellow Squash

12 well-shaped small yellow squash

6 slices of bacon, fried and crumbled, drippings reserved

1 cup chopped onion

Salt and pepper

Dash of Worcestershire sauce

½ cup bread crumbs

Dash of cayenne

Paprika

Butter

1. Preheat oven to 325°F. Lightly grease a 13 x 9 x 2-inch baking dish.

2. Remove stems from squash. Cook whole squash in boiling salted water until tender but still firm, 8 to 10 minutes. Cool slightly.

3. Cut each squash in half lengthwise. Scoop out seeds and discard. Scoop out flesh from large end with a spoon or melon baller, leaving about ¼ inch of flesh on outside skin. Place squash flesh in a bowl and mash with a potato masher. Arrange squash shells cavity side up in baking dish.

4. Heat bacon drippings in a large skillet until hot. Add onion and sauté until tender, 3 to 4 minutes. Add mashed squash, salt, pepper, and Worcestershire sauce. Stir over medium heat for several minutes. Add bread crumbs, bacon, and cayenne. Stir to combine.

5. Spoon mixture into squash shells. Sprinkle with paprika. Dot with butter. Bake for 30 minutes or until heated through and lightly browned. Makes 6 to 8 servings.

KATHY HOAGLAND | Terrace Acres Baptist Church, Fort Worth, Texas

Vegetable Curry

2 teaspoons butter, divided

2 cups chopped red onion

1 cup sliced red pepper

2 cups diced eggplant

2 cups sliced zucchini

2 garlic cloves, crushed

1-inch piece fresh ginger, peeled and chopped

2 tablespoons flour

2 teaspoons ground cumin

1½ tablespoons curry powder

1 cup apple juice

¼ cup raisins

Salt and pepper

1. Melt 1 teaspoon of the butter in a large skillet over medium heat. Add onion, red pepper, and eggplant and sauté for 5 minutes. Add zucchini and garlic and sauté 5 minutes more.

2. Mix remaining teaspoon butter with ginger, flour, cumin, and curry. Add to skillet, stirring to blend. Add apple juice and cook until thick, about 1 minute. Stir in raisins. Sprinkle with salt and pepper. Serve with rice or potatoes. Makes 4 to 6 servings.

RUTH DABRITZ | Methow Valley United Methodist Church, Twisp, Washington

Marinated Green Beans

1½ lbs. green beans, steamed
    until tender but still crisp
1 lb. mushrooms, sliced
1 medium red onion,
    thinly sliced into rings
½ cup finely chopped celery

MARINADE:
1 cup tarragon wine vinegar
½ cup olive oil
½ cup vegetable oil
1 teaspoon oregano
1 teaspoon dry mustard
1 teaspoon basil
⅛ teaspoon salt
⅛ teaspoon pepper

1. Combine green beans, mushrooms, red onion, and celery in a bowl.

2. To make marinade: Combine vinegar, olive oil, vegetable oil, oregano, mustard, basil, salt, and pepper in a jar with a tight-fitting lid. Shake until well blended. Pour over green beans and toss gently to combine. Cover and refrigerate. Toss again just before serving. Makes 8 servings.

❖ **NIKKI MORRIS** | Christ Episcopal Church, Charlotte, North Carolina

Vegetables with Broccoli-Lemon Sauce

3 lbs. small red potatoes, quartered
2 carrots, sliced
2 cups fresh broccoli florets
1 large red pepper, cut into
    ½-inch thick strips
1 can (10.75 oz.) cream of broccoli
    condensed soup

½ cup mayonnaise
4 scallions, finely chopped (¼ cup)
1 tablespoon lemon juice
¼ teaspoon thyme

1. Set a steamer basket in a large saucepan over 1 inch of water. Bring to a boil, add potatoes and carrots, and steam for 6 minutes. Add broccoli and red pepper and steam until tender, 6 minutes more.

2. Combine soup, mayonnaise, scallions, lemon juice, and thyme in a small saucepan over medium heat. Cook, stirring occasionally, until heated through. To serve, arrange vegetables on platter and pour sauce over the top. Makes 8 servings.

❖ **DEBRA O'STEEN** | Christ Church, Frederica, St. Simons Island, Georgia

Nut-Glazed Acorn Squash

2 acorn squash, cut lengthwise
   with seeds removed
Salt
4 tablespoons butter
2 tablespoons brown sugar
½ cup chopped pecans or walnuts

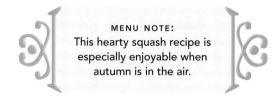

MENU NOTE:
This hearty squash recipe is
especially enjoyable when
autumn is in the air.

1. Preheat oven to 325°F.

2. Set squash halves cut side up in a baking dish. Add water to baking dish to the ½-inch level.

3. Sprinkle each half lightly with salt. Fill each cavity with 1 tablespoon butter, 1½ teaspoons brown sugar, and 2 tablespoons pecans or walnuts. Cover and bake for 1 hour 15 minutes or until squash is tender. Makes 4 servings.

❖ **JANE LEDBETTER** | Christ Church, Frederica, St. Simons Island, Georgia

Baked Turnips

4 medium turnips, peeled and cubed
1 tablespoon flour
1 tablespoon butter
2 tablespoons brown sugar

1 cup milk
1 egg, beaten
Salt and pepper

1. Preheat oven to 350°F. Lightly butter a 1-quart baking dish.

2. Cook turnips in boiling salted water until tender, 15 to 20 minutes. Drain well.

3. Mash turnips until smooth. Stir in flour. Add butter, brown sugar, milk, and egg and beat to combine. Season with salt and pepper. Spoon turnips into baking dish. Bake uncovered until puffed and browned, 45 to 50 minutes. Makes 4 to 6 servings.

❖ **GRACE KILLMER** | St. Mark's Lutheran Church, Conshohocken, Pennsylvania

Zucchini and Tomato

2 tablespoons butter
½ cup chopped green pepper
¼ cup chopped onion
2 cups sliced zucchini
½ cup soft bread crumbs

¼ cup grated Parmesan
1 teaspoon salt
Dash of pepper
2 cups tomato wedges
½ cup shredded cheddar cheese

1. Preheat oven to 375°F. Lightly grease a 1½-quart casserole.

2. Melt butter in a large skillet over medium heat. Add green pepper and onion and sauté, stirring occasionally, until tender, 6 to 8 minutes.

3. Stir in zucchini, bread crumbs, Parmesan, salt, and pepper. Spoon mixture into casserole. Cover and bake for 20 minutes. Add tomato wedges, cover, and bake 10 minutes more. Top with cheddar cheese, leave cover off, and bake just until cheese is melted, 2 to 3 minutes. Makes 6 to 8 servings.

⬥ **TERRACE ACRES BAPTIST CHURCH** | Fort Worth, Texas

Zucchini Bake

1 can (10.75 oz.) cream of mushroom
    condensed soup
½ cup sour cream
4 cups sliced zucchini, cooked

1 cup shredded carrots
¼ cup finely chopped onion
2 cups herbed stuffing mix
¼ cup butter, melted

1. Preheat oven to 350°F. Lightly grease a shallow 2-quart baking dish.

2. Combine mushroom soup, sour cream, zucchini, carrot, and onion. Spoon into baking dish.

3. Toss stuffing mix with melted butter. Spoon stuffing mix over vegetables. Bake for 30 minutes. Makes 4 to 6 servings.

⬥ **GLADYS REED** and **ARLENE M. LUTZ** | Trinity Evangelical Lutheran Church, Lansdale, Pennsylvania

Mixed Greens with Blue Cheese and Walnuts

¾ cup walnuts
12 cups torn mixed greens
4 oz. blue cheese, crumbled

DRESSING:
6 tablespoons extra virgin olive oil
¼ cup red wine vinegar
½ teaspoon salt
¼ teaspoon pepper

Here is an easy
mixed greens sampler:
Romaine lettuce
Bibb lettuce
Belgian endive
Radicchio
Red leaf lettuce

1. Spread walnuts on a baking sheet and toast in a preheated 350°F oven for 12 to 15 minutes.

2. To make dressing: Whisk together olive oil, vinegar, salt, and pepper.

3. Combine mixed greens, warm walnuts, and blue cheese in a large bowl. Pour dressing over salad and toss to combine. Makes 6 to 8 servings.

⬥ **JANICE MILLER** | Trinity Evangelical Lutheran Church, Lansdale, Pennsylvania

Broccoli Salad

2 heads of broccoli, rinsed and drained

10 slices of bacon, fried and crumbled

½ red onion, sliced or finely chopped

⅔ cup seedless raisins

3 tablespoons salted peanuts

1 cup mayonnaise

⅓ cup sugar

2 tablespoons vinegar

VARIATIONS:

Substitute ¼ cup walnuts for 3 tablespoons peanuts.

Substitute cider vinegar for wine vinegar.

Add 1 cup grated sharp cheddar cheese for color and flavor.

1. Break off bite-size florets from broccoli and place in a large bowl. Add bacon, onion, raisins, and peanuts.

2. In a separate bowl, whisk together mayonnaise, sugar, and vinegar. Pour over broccoli and toss to combine. Cover and marinate in refrigerator at least 2 hours or overnight. Make 8 servings.

✤ JERILYNN MILLER | Trinity Evangelical Lutheran Church, Lansdale, Pennsylvania

Creamy Curried Chicken Salad with Apple and Fusille

2 cups fusille pasta

2½ to 3 cups cooked chicken, cut into pieces

1 cup chopped celery

2 red apples, cored and chopped

½ cup raisins

½ cup green onion tops, cut in 1-inch pieces

⅓ cup slivered almonds, toasted

DRESSING:

1 cup mayonnaise

¼ cup light cream

2 teaspoons curry powder

1½ teaspoons salt

⅛ teaspoon cayenne

1 tablespoon lemon juice

1. Cook fusille in boiling salted water until al dente, following package directions. Drain and rinse in cold water. Drain again.

2. Combine fusille, chicken, celery, apples, raisins, green onions, and almonds in a large bowl. Chill.

3. To make dressing: Whisk together mayonnaise, light cream, curry powder, salt, cayenne, and lemon juice. Pour over salad and toss to combine. Makes 6 to 8 servings.

✤ CIVIL McGOWAN | Christ Episcopal Church, Charlotte, North Carolina

Fruit and Spinach Salad

1 lb. spinach, washed and drained

4 small heads Belgian endive,
    cut lengthwise into quarters

4 kiwifruit, peeled and sliced

1 small cantaloupe, cut into chunks

¼ lb. Feta, crumbled

2 oz. Jarlsberg or Swiss cheese,
    cut into ½-inch cubes

DRESSING:

1 tablespoon olive oil or vegetable oil

1 large red onion, thinly sliced

¾ teaspoon salt

⅛ teaspoon pepper

½ cup orange juice

2 tablespoons white wine vinegar

1. Arrange spinach and endive on individual serving plates. Add kiwifruit and cantaloupe.

2. To make dressing: Heat oil in a saucepan over medium heat. Add onion, salt, and pepper. Sauté, stirring frequently, until onion is golden and translucent, 4 to 6 minutes. Remove from heat. Stir in orange juice and vinegar.

3. Spoon warm dressing over salad. Top with crumbled Feta and cubed Jarlsberg or Swiss cheese. Makes 4 to 6 servings.

❖ **MEREDITH FORSHAW** | Christ Episcopal Church, Charlotte, North Carolina

Potluck Pasta Salad

¼ box (4 oz.) wagon wheel pasta

¼ box (4 oz.) tri-colored corkscrew macaroni

1 teaspoon red pepper flakes

1 medium red sweet pepper, thinly sliced

1 medium yellow squash, halved
    lengthwise and sliced

1 package (10 oz.) frozen peas, thawed

1 can (6 oz.) pitted olives, drained

4 oz. smoked cheddar cheese, cubed

1 cup unbleached whole almonds, toasted

½ cup sliced green onions

2 tablespoons snipped fresh oregano

2 tablespoons snipped fresh basil

2 tablespoons snipped fresh dill

1 bottle (8 oz.) Italian dressing

1. Combine wagon wheel pasta and corkscrew macaroni. Cook according to package directions, adding red pepper flakes to the cooking water. Rinse in cool water and drain. Cool to room temperature.

2. Combine pasta, red pepper, squash, peas, olives, cheddar cheese, almonds, green onions, oregano, basil, and dill. Shake salad dressing, pour over the salad, and toss lightly to combine. Cover and chill 2 hours or up to 24 hours. Toss again just before serving. Makes 12 servings.

❖ **JAN RAKESTRAW CLARK** | Methow Valley United Methodist Church, Twisp, Washington

Orzo Salad

1 cup orzo
½ oz. sun-dried tomatoes
1 cup water
1 cup crumbled Feta
¼ cup chopped red onion
¼ cup chopped green pepper
¼ cup chopped red pepper
¼ cup chopped yellow pepper

2 tablespoons chopped fresh parsley
2 tablespoons chopped green olives
2 tablespoons chopped black olives
¼ teaspoon pepper
2 tablespoons red wine vinegar
1 tablespoon balsamic vinegar
1½ tablespoons olive oil

1. Cook orzo in boiling salted water following package directions. Drain and rinse.

2. Combine sun-dried tomatoes and water in a small saucepan, bring to a boil, and cook 2 minutes. Cover and remove from heat. Let stand 5 minutes or until reconstituted. Drain and coarsely chop.

3. Combine orzo, tomatoes, Feta, red onion, green pepper, red pepper, yellow pepper, parsley, green olives, and black olives. Sprinkle with pepper.

4. Whisk together red wine vinegar, balsamic vinegar, and olive oil. Pour over salad and toss to combine. Makes 4 servings.

✦ **SUSAN DAISLEY** | Christ Episcopal Church, Charlotte, North Carolina

Tossed Taco Salad

1 tablespoon oil
1 large onion, chopped
2½ lbs. ground turkey
¼ cup chili powder
1 teaspoon oregano
1 teaspoon ground cumin
1 can (15 oz.) pitted olives, drained,
    rinsed, and cut in slivers
1 can (19 oz.) red kidney beans,
    drained and rinsed
1 can (16 oz.) chickpeas, drained and rinsed

2 cans (15 oz. each) pinto beans
2 medium tomatoes, diced
2 jalapeños, seeded and minced
2 heads iceberg lettuce, washed and
    torn in bite-size pieces
2 cups shredded low-sodium cheddar cheese
2 cups coarsely crushed tortilla chips
2 cups nonfat mayonnaise
½ cup taco sauce
1 teaspoon hot pepper sauce

1. Heat oil in a large nonstick skillet over medium heat, add onion, and cook until soft and translucent, 4 to 6 minutes.

2. Add ground turkey to onions and cook, breaking up chunks with a wooden spoon, until no longer pink, 8 minutes. Drain off cooking liquid.

3. Stir in chili powder, oregano, and cumin, cook 1 minute, and remove from heat. Stir in olives, kidney beans, chickpeas, pinto beans, tomatoes, and jalapeños.

4. Toss lettuce, cheddar cheese, and crushed tortilla chips in a large serving bowl. Add turkey mixture and toss to combine. Whisk together mayonnaise, taco sauce, and hot pepper sauce, pour into a decorative decanter, and serve on the side. Makes 10 servings.

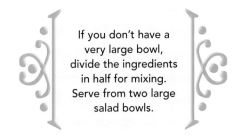
If you don't have a very large bowl, divide the ingredients in half for mixing. Serve from two large salad bowls.

CAROL NASE | Trinity Evangelical Lutheran Church, Lansdale, Pennsylvania

Thai Chicken Salad with Peanut Ginger Dressing

4 boneless, skinless chicken breast halves
Peanut Ginger Dressing (recipe follows)
3 oz. vermicelli, cooked and drained
4 cups torn romaine lettuce leaves
2 cups thinly sliced Chinese cabbage

2 medium carrots, grated
1 medium cucumber, julienned
1 large red pepper, julienned
½ cup chopped peanuts

1. Grill chicken, turning once, until heated through, 15 to 20 minutes. Cut into strips and combine with 3 tablespoons peanut ginger dressing. Cover and refrigerate 8 hours.

2. Toss vermicelli with 3 tablespoons peanut ginger dressing. Cover and refrigerate 8 hours.

3. To serve, toss lettuce, cabbage, carrots, cucumber, and red pepper in a bowl. Arrange on platter. Spoon vermicelli and chicken strips on top. Sprinkle with peanuts. Pass remaining dressing on the side. Makes 8 to 10 servings.

PEANUT GINGER DRESSING

½ cup rice vinegar
2 garlic cloves, minced
⅓ cup creamy peanut butter
¼ cup lime juice
2 tablespoons cider vinegar

1 tablespoon molasses
1 tablespoon hot sauce
2 teaspoons grated ginger
2 teaspoons soy sauce

Combine rice vinegar, cloves, peanut butter, lime juice, cider vinegar, molasses, hot sauce, ginger, and soy sauce in a bowl. Stir with a wire whisk until peanut butter is dissolved. Makes 1¼ cups.

ANN LINDE | Christ Episcopal Church, Charlotte, North Carolina

A Kitchen Prayer

Lord of all pots and pans and things,
Since I've not time to be a saint by doing things
Or watching late with Thee or dreaming in the dawn light,
Or storming heaven's gates,
Make me a saint by getting meals and
Washing up the plates.
Warm all the kitchen with Thy love,
And light it with Thy peace.
Forgive me all my worrying and make my grumbling cease.
Thou who didst love to give men food,
In room or by the sea, accept this service that I do,
I do it unto Thee.

CHRIST CHURCH
Frederica, St. Simons Island, Georgia

Chunk Apple Cake with Cream Cheese Frosting

½ cup butter, melted
2 cups sugar
2 large eggs
1 teaspoon vanilla
2 cups flour
1 teaspoon baking soda
1 teaspoon salt
2 teaspoons cinnamon
4 Granny Smith apples, peeled, cored, and cut into chunks
1½ cup walnuts, toasted and chopped, divided
Cream Cheese Frosting (recipe follows)

VARIATION:
Instead of Granny Smith apples, use Jonathan apples. Leave the skins on and reduce the sugar in step 2 to 1 cup.

1. Preheat oven to 350°F. Lightly grease a 13 x 9 x 2-inch baking pan.
2. Combine melted butter, sugar, eggs, and vanilla in a large bowl.
3. Whisk together flour, baking soda, salt, and cinnamon. Add to butter mixture, stirring until blended. Stir in apple chunks and 1 cup of the walnuts.

4. Transfer batter to pan. Bake for 45 minutes or until a tester inserted in center comes out clean. Cool in pan on a wire rack. Spread frosting on top of cake. Sprinkle with remaining ½ chopped nuts. Cut into squares. Makes 12 servings.

CREAM CHEESE FROSTING

1 package (8 oz.) cream cheese,
   room temperature
3 tablespoons butter, room temperature

1½ cups confectioners' sugar
⅛ teaspoon salt
1 teaspoon vanilla

1. Beat cream cheese and butter in a mixer bowl until smooth and creamy.
2. Beat in sugar and salt. Add vanilla and blend well. Makes 1½ cups.

EARLDEAN MCKENZIE | Trinity Presbyterian Church, Little Rock, Arkansas

Poppy Seed Torte

CRUST:
1 cup graham cracker crumbs
½ cup butter, melted
1 cup flour
½ cup chopped nuts

FILLING:
1½ tablespoons gelatin
¼ cup water
1½ cups milk
1½ cups sugar, divided
5 eggs, separated
¼ cup poppy seeds
2 tablespoons cornstarch
¼ teaspoon salt
½ teaspoon vanilla
½ teaspoon cream of tartar

Whipped cream

1. To make crust: Preheat oven to 325°F. Combine graham cracker crumbs, melted butter, flour, and nuts. Press mixture into bottom of a 13 x 9 x 2-inch baking pan. Bake for 10 to 15 minutes or until lightly browned.
2. To make filling: Dissolve gelatin in water. Combine milk, 1 cup of the sugar, and egg yolks in the top half of a double boiler over simmering water. Beat until sugar is dissolved. Add poppy seeds, cornstarch, and salt. Cook, stirring continuously, until thick. Stir in gelatin and allow to cool.
3. Beat egg whites until frothy. Add vanilla, cream of tartar, and remaining ½ cup sugar. Continue beating until stiff. Fold egg whites into cooled filling. Pour filling into crust and refrigerate for 4 hours. Cut into squares and top with whipped cream. Makes 10 to 12 servings.

MRS. WILLIAM WEILAND | St. John's Guild, St. John's Church, West Bend, Wisconsin

Chocolate Mint Torte

CRUST:

1 cup chocolate wafer crumbs

¼ cup finely chopped pecans

3 tablespoons butter, melted

FILLING:

1 envelope (.25 oz.) unflavored gelatin

½ cup cold water

½ cup boiling water

1 package (8 oz.) cream cheese,
    room temperature

1 cup sugar

1½ teaspoons vanilla

½ teaspoon peppermint extract

3 squares (1 oz. each) semisweet chocolate, melted

1 cup heavy cream, whipped, plus more for topping

Pecan halves

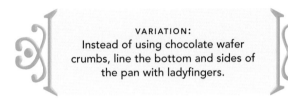

VARIATION:
Instead of using chocolate wafer crumbs, line the bottom and sides of the pan with ladyfingers.

1. Preheat oven to 325°F. Butter a 9 x 3-inch springform pan.

2. To make crust: Combine chocolate wafer crumbs, pecans, and melted butter. Press mixture into bottom and up sides of pan. Bake for 10 minutes.

3. To make filling: Soften gelatin in cold water. Add boiling water and stir until gelatin dissolves.

4. Beat cream cheese, sugar, vanilla, and peppermint extract in a mixer bowl. Stir in chocolate. Gradually add gelatin until well blended. Chill until slightly thickened, 10 minutes. Fold in whipped cream. Pour filling into crust. Chill until firm, 2 to 4 hours. Garnish with whipped cream and pecan halves. Makes 6 to 8 servings.

❖ **MRS. RAY HRON** | St. John's Guild, St. John's Church, West Bend, Wisconsin

Jewish Apple Cake

5 or 6 apples, peeled and cut into
    small chunks

2 teaspoons cinnamon

5 tablespoons sugar

3 cups flour

2 cups sugar

1 cup vegetable oil

4 eggs

¼ cup orange juice

1 teaspoon salt

3 teaspoons baking powder

1 teaspoon vanilla

1½ teaspoons almond extract

1. Preheat oven to 350°F. Grease a 10 x 4-inch tube pan.

2. Toss apple chunks with cinnamon and sugar.

3. Combine flour, sugar, vegetable oil, eggs, orange juice, salt, baking powder, vanilla, and almond extract in a large mixer bowl. Beat until smooth, 2 minutes. Batter will be very thick.

3. Pour half of batter into tube pan. Arrange half of the apple chunks on top of the batter. Add remaining batter and top with remaining apples. Bake for 1½ hours. Cool in pan for 20 minutes before turning out onto a wire rack. Makes 16 servings.

BETTY C. CLEMMER | Trinity Evangelical Lutheran Church, Lansdale, Pennsylvania

Fourteen-Karat Cake with Cream Cheese Frosting

2 cups flour
2 teaspoons baking powder
1½ teaspoons baking soda
1½ teaspoons salt
2 teaspoons cinnamon
2 cups sugar
1½ cups salad oil
4 eggs
2 cups shredded carrots
1 can (8 oz.) crushed pineapple, drained
½ cup walnuts, chopped
1 can (3.5 oz.) flaked coconut
Cream Cheese Frosting (recipe follows)

VARIATION:
Instead of a three-layer cake, make one large sheet cake. Use a 13 x 9 x 2-inch baking pan and increase the baking time to 60 minutes. Frost the cake right in the pan.

1. Preheat oven to 350°F. Grease and flour three 9 x 2-inch round cake pans.
2. Sift together flour, baking powder, baking soda, salt, and cinnamon into a mixer bowl. Add sugar, oil, and eggs. Beat at medium speed for 1 minute.
3. Stir in carrots, pineapple, walnuts, and coconut. Pour batter into cake pans. Bake for 40 minutes or until a tester inserted in center comes out clean. Cool in pan for 10 minutes before turning out onto a wire rack. Cool completely and assemble layers with cream cheese frosting. Makes 8 to 10 servings.

CREAM CHEESE FROSTING

½ cup butter, room temperature
1 package (8 oz.) cream cheese, room temperature

1 teaspoon vanilla
1 box (1 lb.) confectioners' sugar
Milk

1. Cream butter and cream cheese in a mixer bowl. Stir in vanilla.
2. With mixer running, gradually add confectioners' sugar, beating until smooth and creamy. Thin with a little milk if necessary. Makes 2 cups.

ARVA FINNEGAN | Trinity Presbyterian Church, Little Rock, Arkansas

Danish Cheesecake

CRUST:

½ cup butter, room temperature

6 tablespoons sugar

2 eggs

2 cups flour

1 teaspoon baking powder

FILLING:

2 packages (8 oz. each) cream cheese,
    room temperature

1¼ cups sugar

¼ cup flour

4 eggs

Juice of 1 lemon

3 cups milk

Cinnamon

1. Preheat oven to 300°F.

2. To make crust: Cream butter and sugar. Beat in eggs. Add flour and baking powder and mix well. Pat dough into bottom of a 13 x 9 x 2-inch baking pan.

3. To make filling: Combine cream cheese, sugar, flour, eggs, lemon juice, and milk in a mixer bowl. Beat until smooth. Pour over crust and sprinkle with cinnamon. Bake for 1½ hours. Cool to room temperature and refrigerate for 4 hours. Serve chilled, cut into squares. Makes 12 servings.

❖ **GRACE ON THE HILL UNITED METHODIST CHURCH** | Corbin, Kentucky

Luscious Lemon Layer Cake

½ cup vegetable shortening

1 cup sugar

1 teaspoon vanilla

1 teaspoon lemon extract

2 eggs

2 cups cake flour

1 teaspoon baking powder

¾ teaspoon baking soda

¼ teaspoon salt

1 cup sour milk

LEMON FILLING:

½ cup sugar

2 tablespoons flour

⅔ cup cold water

Juice and grated zest of 1 lemon

1 egg yolk, beaten

2 teaspoons butter

SEVEN-MINUTE ICING:

2 egg whites

1½ cups sugar

¼ teaspoon cream of tartar

⅓ cup water

1 teaspoon vanilla

Coconut

1. Preheat oven to 350°F. Grease two 9 x 2-inch round cake pans and line with parchment or waxed paper.

2. Cream shortening and sugar in a mixer bowl. Stir in vanilla and lemon extract. Add eggs one at a time, beating until fluffy after each addition.

3. Sift together flour, baking powder, baking soda, and salt. Add flour mixture and milk alternately to batter, beating until well blended. Pour batter into cake pans. Bake for 25 minutes or until a tester inserted in center comes out clean. Cool in pans 5 minutes before turning out onto wire racks. Cool completely.

4. To make lemon filling: Combine sugar and flour in a small saucepan, add cold water, and stir until blended. Stir in zest. Cook over low heat until thick. Stir in egg yolk, lemon juice, and butter. Continue cooking 2 minutes more. Remove from heat and cool.

5. To make seven-minute icing: Combine egg whites, sugar, cream of tartar, and water in the top of a double boiler. Cook over rapidly boiling water, beating continuously with a handheld electric mixer until stiff peaks form, 7 minutes. Remove from heat, add vanilla, and continue beating until icing is of spreading consistency, 2 minutes more.

6. Assemble cake layers with lemon filling. Ice sides and top with seven-minute frosting. Sprinkle coconut on top. Makes 8 to 10 servings.

❖ **MRS. FRED C. LANGE** | St. John's Guild, St. John's Church, West Bend, Wisconsin

Butter-Pecan Cheesecake

CRUST:

⅓ cup butter, melted

1½ cups graham cracker crumbs

⅓ cup sugar

½ cup chopped pecans

FILLING:

3 packages (8 oz. each) cream cheese

1½ cups sugar

3 eggs

2 cups sour cream

1 teaspoon vanilla

1 cup chopped pecans

Pecan halves

1. Preheat oven to 475°F.

2. To make crust: Combine melted butter, graham cracker crumbs, sugar, and pecans. Press mixture into bottom and partway up sides of a 9 x 3-inch springform pan.

3. To make filling: Combine cream cheese and sugar in a mixer bowl. Beat until well blended. Add eggs one at a time, beating well after each addition. Fold in sour cream. Stir in vanilla and pecans.

4. Pour filling into pan. Bake for 10 minutes. Reduce oven temperature to 300°F and bake 50 minutes more. Turn off oven, open oven door partway, and cool in oven 1 hour. Remove from oven and cool to room temperature. Arrange pecan halves around edge. Chill in refrigerator 2 to 4 hours, until cold. Cracking on top of cake is normal. Makes 10 to 12 servings.

❖ LINDA ALLEN | Christ Church, Frederica, St. Simons Island, Georgia

New York Cheesecake

1 cup graham cracker crumbs

¾ cup sugar, divided

6 tablespoons butter, melted

1½ cups sour cream

2 eggs

2 teaspoons vanilla

2 packages (8 oz. each) cream cheese, broken into small pieces

Puréed strawberries with lemon juice

1. Preheat oven to 325°F. Set aside an 8- or 9-inch springform pan. Do not grease.

2. Mix graham cracker crumbs with ¼ cup of the sugar and 4 tablespoons of the melted butter. Press mixture into bottom of pan.

3. Combine sour cream, remaining ½ cup sugar, eggs, and vanilla in a blender. Mix for 1 minute. Add cream cheese and blend until smooth. Blend in remaining 2 tablespoons melted butter.

4. Pour mixture into pan. Bake in lower third of oven for 45 minutes or until set. Place under broiler until top begins to bubble and turn brown, 2 to 3 minutes. Cool in pan. Refrigerate overnight. Slice and serve with a tart sauce of puréed strawberries mixed with lemon juice. Makes 12 servings.

❖ PEG MORRISSEY and BETSY ENNEY | Coastal Georgia Chapter of the Episcopal Synod of America and Prayer Book Society

Bing Cherry Cheesecake

CRUST:

16 graham crackers, crushed

3 tablespoons sugar

¼ cup butter

FILLING 1:

2 packages (8 oz. each) cream cheese,
   room temperature

½ cup sugar

2 eggs

1 teaspoon vanilla

1 teaspoon almond extract

FILLING 2:

1 cup sour cream

3 tablespoons sugar

TOPPING:

1 can (15 oz.) pitted Bing cherries,
   drained, juice reserved

1 cup juice

2 tablespoons cornstarch

2 tablespoons sugar

½ teaspoon almond extract

½ teaspoon vanilla

1. Preheat oven to 375°F.

2. To make crust: Combine graham cracker crumbs, sugar, and butter. Press mixture on the bottom and up sides of a 10 x 4-inch springform pan. Bake for 8 minutes. Cool.

3. To make filling 1: Reduce oven temperature to 350°F. Combine cream cheese, sugar, eggs, vanilla, and almond extract until well blended. Spoon mixture over crust. Bake for 20 minutes. Cool.

4. To make filling 2: Increase oven temperature to 400°F. Combine sour cream and sugar. Spread over filling 1. Bake for 10 minutes. Cool.

5. To make topping: Combine cherries, 1 cup reserved cherry juice, cornstarch, sugar, almond extract, and vanilla in a large saucepan over medium heat. Cook until juice turns thick and syrupy. Cool. Spread cherry topping over filling 2. Refrigerate until firm. Release and remove rim of pan. Makes 8 to 10 servings.

❖ SALLY McCAULEY | Christ Church, Frederica, St. Simons Island, Georgia

Lemon Chiffon Torte

1 can (14 oz.) sweetened condensed milk

Juice of 2 lemons

Grated zest of 1 lemon

1 cup heavy cream

3 teaspoons sugar

1 graham cracker piecrust

1. Combine condensed milk, lemon juice, and zest. Whip with a rotary beater.

2. In a separate bowl, whip the cream until soft peaks form. Add sugar and continue whipping until stiff. Fold into condensed milk mixture. Pour into piecrust. Chill 4 hours. Makes 6 to 8 servings.

❖ MRS. WILLARD WEGNER | St. John's Guild, St. John's Church, West Bend, Wisconsin

Pineapple Cheesecake

CRUST:

4 tablespoons butter

4 tablespoons sugar

1 egg, beaten

1 cup flour

½ teaspoon baking powder

1 can (15 oz.) crushed pineapple, drained

CHEESE FILLING:

2 packages (8 oz. each) cream cheese

¾ cup sugar

3 eggs

1 tablespoon vanilla

2 tablespoons flour

3 cups milk

Cinnamon

1. Preheat oven to 350°F. Set aside a 10 x 4-inch springform pan.

2. To make crust: Cream butter and sugar. Add egg, beating until well combined. Mix in flour and baking powder. Press mixture into bottom of pan. Spread pineapple over mixture in an even layer.

3. To make cheese filling: Combine cream cheese, sugar, eggs, vanilla, flour, and milk in a large mixer bowl. Mix on low speed until well blended. Pour over pineapples. Bake for 1 hour. Turn off oven, prop open door, and let stand in oven 15 minutes. Sprinkle cinnamon on top. Refrigerate overnight. Makes 10 to 12 servings.

❖ **FLORENCE BARCLAY** | Trinity Evangelical Lutheran Church, Lansdale, Pennsylvania

Black Bottom Cheesecake

1⅓ cups fine graham cracker, vanilla wafer, or zwieback crumbs

⅓ cup butter, melted

⅔ cup sugar, divided

1 box (3.5 oz.) vanilla pudding and pie filling mix

1 envelope (.25 oz.) unflavored gelatin

⅛ teaspoon salt

2 eggs, separated

1 cup milk

1 cup light cream

1 teaspoon vanilla

1½ squares (1.5 oz.) semisweet chocolate

1½ cups creamed cottage cheese

Whipped cream

Chocolate curls

 To make chocolate curls, scrape a vegetable peeler along the edge of a square of semisweet chocolate.

1. Combine crumbs, melted butter, and ⅓ cup of the sugar. Press mixture into bottom of a 10-inch pie plate or a 9 x 9 x 2-inch baking pan. Chill.

2. Whisk together vanilla pie filling mix, gelatin, and salt in a heavy saucepan. Beat in egg yolks, milk, and light cream. Cook over medium-high heat, stirring continuously, until mixture thickens and comes to a boil. Remove from heat. Stir in vanilla.

3. Place chocolate in a small bowl. Pour in ¾ cup of the hot vanilla mixture. Stir until melted and well blended. Pour chocolate mixture over crust. Chill.

4. Place cottage cheese in a blender. Blend until smooth. Gradually blend in remaining vanilla mixture. Pour into a bowl.

5. Beat egg whites until frothy. Gradually add remaining ⅓ cup of the sugar, beating until stiff. Fold egg whites into vanilla mixture. Pour over chocolate layer. Chill 4 hours or until firm. Decorate with whipped cream and chocolate curls. Makes 10 to 12 servings.

⬧ Adapted from *The Best of the Old Church Cookbooks* by Florence Ekstrand, courtesy of Welcome Press

Jelly Roll

4 eggs, beaten

1 cup sugar

1 cup sifted flour

½ teaspoon baking soda

1 teaspoon cream of tartar

4 tablespoons cream

¼ teaspoon salt

Confectioners' sugar

Jelly or jam

1. Preheat oven to 350°F. Line a 12 x 9 x 1-inch jelly roll pan with baking parchment.

2. Combine eggs and sugar in a mixer bowl and beat until frothy. Sift together flour, baking soda, and cream of tartar. Gradually blend into egg mixture. Stir in cream and salt. Pour batter into pan. Bake for 15 minutes. Cool in pan 5 minutes.

3. Lay out a clean dish towel and sprinkle with confectioners' sugar. Turn out warm cake onto towel. Spread jelly or jam evenly over entire surface. Roll up, wrap in towel, and cool completely. Cut into slices and serve. Makes 8 to 10 servings.

⬧ **MRS. R. SPIELMAN** | St. John's Guild, St. John's Church, West Bend, Wisconsin

Pears Baked in Cream

2 tablespoons butter, divided

2 tablespoons sugar, divided

2 pears, unpeeled, halved, and cored

½ cup heavy cream

1. Preheat oven to 400°F. Grease an 11 x 7 x 2-inch baking dish with 1 tablespoon of the butter. Sprinkle with 1 tablespoon of the sugar.

2. Arrange pears cut side down in baking dish. Dot with remaining tablespoon butter. Sprinkle remaining tablespoon sugar over top. Bake for 10 minutes.

3. Pour heavy cream over pears. Bake 20 minutes more. Serve warm. Makes 4 servings.

⬧ **NANCY EHRINGHAUS** | Christ Episcopal Church, Charlotte, North Carolina

Praline Cheesecake

¾ cup graham cracker crumbs

½ cup chopped pecans, toasted

¼ cup brown sugar

¼ cup butter, melted

4½ packages (36 oz.) cream cheese,
   room temperature

1½ cans (21 oz.) sweetened condensed milk

4 eggs

2 teaspoons vanilla

TOPPING:

⅔ cup brown sugar

⅔ cup heavy cream

⅔ cup chopped pecans, toasted

1. Preheat oven to 300°F. Set aside a 10- x 4-inch springform pan.

2. Combine graham cracker crumbs, pecans, brown sugar, and melted butter. Press mixture into bottom of pan.

3. Beat cream cheese in a mixer bowl until fluffy. Gradually add milk, beating until smooth. Beat in eggs and vanilla. Pour into pan. Bake for 55 to 60 minutes or until center is set. Cool in pan for 10 minutes. Run a knife along rim to loosen cheesecake from side of pan. Cool completely.

4. To make topping: Combine brown sugar and cream in a heavy saucepan over medium heat. Cook, stirring continuously, until mixture thickens slightly, 5 to 10 minutes. Cool to room temperature. Stir in pecans. Add topping to cheesecake. Refrigerate until ready to serve. Makes 12 servings.

❖ **GINNY HENDERSON** | Trinity Evangelical Lutheran Church, Lansdale, Pennsylvania

Cheese Torte

CRUST:

2 cups bread flour

¼ teaspoon salt

3 tablespoons sugar

1 cup butter

FILLING:

2 packages (8 oz. each) cream cheese

2 cups confectioners' sugar

2 cups heavy cream, whipped

BLUEBERRY TOPPING:

2 cans (15 oz. each) blueberries, drained,
   juice reserved

½ cup sugar

4 tablespoons cornstarch

2 tablespoons lemon juice

Whipped cream

1. Preheat oven to 375°F. Lightly grease a 13 x 9 x 2-inch baking dish.

2. To make crust: Whisk together flour, salt, and sugar. Cut in butter with a pastry blender or your fingers until crumbly. Press mixture into bottom of pan. Bake for 10 to 12 minutes or until lightly browned. Cool.

3. To make filling: Combine cream cheese and sugar in a mixer bowl. Beat until smooth. Fold in whipped cream. Spread filling over crust.

4. To make blueberry topping: Combine reserved blueberry juice, sugar, and cornstarch in a large saucepan over medium-low heat. Cook, stirring occasionally, until thick. Stir in lemon juice. Gently fold in blueberries. Cool to room temperature.

5. Spoon topping over filling. Chill for 4 hours. To serve, cut into slices and top with a dollop of whipped cream. Makes 16 servings.

❖ **VERA MARKS** | St. John's Guild, St. John's Church, West Bend, Wisconsin

VARIATION:
For a cherry topping, use 2 cans (15 oz. each) of sweetened cherries. Omit the lemon juice and add 3 or 4 drops of red food coloring.

Butter-Frosted Sponge Cake

5 eggs, separated
Pinch of salt
1½ cups sugar, divided
½ cup water
1 teaspoon vanilla
1½ cups sifted cake flour

FILLING/FROSTING:
4 egg yolks
¾ cup sugar
¾ cup milk
1 cup butter, room temperature
1 teaspoon vanilla
Toasted coconut or chopped nuts

1. Preheat oven to 350°F. Lightly grease and set aside a 10 x 4-inch tube pan.

2. Combine egg whites and salt in a mixer bowl. Beat until stiff. Beat in ½ cup of the sugar.

3. In a separate mixer bowl, beat egg yolks until light and frothy. Gradually beat in remaining cup of sugar. Mix in water, vanilla, and cake flour until well blended. Fold in egg whites.

4. Turn batter into pan. Bake for 45 minutes or until a tester inserted near center comes out clean. Cool in pan 20 minutes before turning out onto a wire rack. Cool completely.

5. To make filling/frosting: Whisk together egg yolks, sugar, and milk in a saucepan over medium-high heat. Gradually bring to a boil, stirring continuously, until mixture thickens and coats a spoon. Cool to room temperature. Cream butter in a mixer bowl. Gradually add cooled custard, mixing until well blended. Stir in vanilla.

6. Cut cake into three layers. Spread filling/frosting between layers. Frost sides and top of cake. Top with toasted coconut or chopped nuts. Makes 16 servings.

❖ **MRS. ROY BURGEMEISTER** | St. John's Guild, St. John's Church, West Bend, Wisconsin

Texas Sheet Cake

1 cup butter
1 cup water
4 tablespoons cocoa
2 cups flour
2 cups sugar
2 eggs, beaten
½ cup sour cream
1 teaspoon baking soda
1 teaspoon vanilla

FROSTING:

½ cup butter
¼ cup cocoa
6 tablespoons milk
1 box (1 lb.) confectioners' sugar, sifted

1. Preheat oven to 350°F. Grease a 15½ x 10½ x 1-inch sheet pan.

2. Combine butter, water, and cocoa in a large saucepan over medium-high heat. Bring to a boil. Remove from heat.

3. Add flour and sugar to cocoa mixture and mix well. Blend in eggs, sour cream, baking soda, and vanilla. Pour batter into pan. Bake for 25 minutes. Leave cake in pan.

4. To make frosting: Combine butter and cocoa in a saucepan over medium-high heat. Bring to a boil. Stir in milk and remove from heat. Gradually add confectioners' sugar, stirring continuously, until smooth.

5. Pour frosting over hot cake and spread quickly. Cool cake and frosting to room temperature. Makes 14 to 16 servings.

PEGGY HARTMAN | Trinity Evangelical Lutheran Church, Lansdale, Pennsylvania

Irwin's Super Brownies

1 package (14 oz.) caramels
⅔ cup evaporated milk, divided
1½ cups butter, room temperature

1 box (18.25 oz.) German chocolate cake mix
1 package (6 oz.) chocolate chips
1 cup chopped pecans

1. Preheat oven to 350°F. Grease a 13 x 9 x 2-inch baking pan.

2. Combine caramels and ⅓ cup of the milk in the top of a double boiler. Cook, stirring occasionally, until caramels are melted.

3. Cream butter in a mixer bowl. Alternately add cake mix and remaining ⅓ cup milk until well blended.

4. Pour half of batter into pan. Bake for 6 minutes. Layer chocolate chips in pan. Top with pecans and drizzle with caramel sauce. Dot with remaining batter, so chocolate chips, pecans, and caramel sauce peek through. Bake 15 to 18 minutes more. Cool in pan for 15 minutes, freeze for 30 minutes, and cut into bars. Makes 48 bars.

BETSY LOCKE | Christ Episcopal Church, Charlotte, North Carolina

Holidays
& Special
Occasions

ANNUAL MARINERS' CHRISTMAS PARTY

The lively Mariner Fellowship group (adult Sunday school class) at First Presbyterian Church in Berkeley, California, has a legacy of spirited Bible study and exciting entertainment. For more than 40 years, the Mariners' Christmas Party has been the social event of the year. In the past, it brought out the formal evening dresses, sequins, even feather boas; recently, the fashion statements have toned down—but only a bit. After-dinner programs usually involve a variety of entertainment—from choral groups from the neighboring University of California to pastors and their famous monologues to hilarious and irreverent skits. The evening always ends with a hearty, full-voiced round of favorite Christmas carols.

Food, of course, receives top billing at all the Mariners' gatherings, especially the Christmas Party, which often feature special ethnic menus. For many years, members of Mariners have prepared the food, beginning with a reception hour with an array of tasty homemade appetizers, dips, and punch. For the last few years, Patty Uhland and her Mariner team have created spectacular dinners that rival any 5-star restaurant. Last year's menu—featuring grilled tenderloin of pork over bread stuffing with chutney cream sauce and a fabulous dessert of lemon crunch sherbet dripping with fresh raspberry and strawberry purée—was unforgettable. Savoring moans could be heard even from the vegetarians! This year the Mariners are looking forward to another scrumptious feast, but mostly they look forward to another terrific evening of fun, friends, and fellowship.

FIRST PRESBYTERIAN CHURCH
Berkeley, California

BLT Valentine Bites

20 cherry tomatoes
1 lb. bacon, cooked and crumbled
½ cup mayonnaise

⅓ cup chopped green onions
3 tablespoons grated Parmesan
2 tablespoons fresh snipped parsley

1. Slice off and discard the top of each cherry tomato. Scoop out and discard the pulp. Invert tomatoes onto a paper towel to drain.
2. Combine bacon, mayonnaise, onions, Parmesan, and parsley in a small bowl. Mix well. Spoon into tomato cups. Refrigerate for 2 hours before serving. Makes 20 servings.

AMANDA LUCAS BETLER | Vincent Memorial United Methodist Church, Nutter Fort, West Virginia

Dianne's Deviled Easter Eggs

12 hard-boiled eggs
Assorted food colors
3 tablespoons mayonnaise
1 tablespoon sweet pickle relish

½ teaspoon salt
1 teaspoon sugar
½ teaspoon black pepper

1. Peel eggs and slice in half. Remove yolks and place in a broad, shallow soup bowl.
2. Prepare assorted food color baths following directions on package for coloring Easter eggs. Place egg whites in colored baths until desired tint is achieved. Remove and drain on paper towels.
3. Mash egg yolks until fine. Add mayonnaise, relish, salt, sugar, and pepper. Stir until well mixed. Place a teaspoonful of yolk mixture into each colored egg white. Sure to be a hit with children of all ages. Makes 24 servings.

PINEMOUNT BAPTIST CHURCH | McAlpin, Florida

Christmas Party Pinwheels

2 packages (8 oz. each) cream cheese,
    room temperature
1 envelope (4 oz.) ranch dressing mix
½ cup minced sweet pimiento

½ cup minced celery
¼ cup sliced green onions
¼ cup sliced stuffed olives
3 or 4 large flour tortillas

1. Beat cream cheese and salad dressing mix until smooth. Mix in pimiento, celery, onions, and olives until well combined.
2. Spread about ¾ cup of cheese mixture on each tortilla. Roll up tightly and wrap in plastic wrap. Refrigerate at least 2 hours. Slice into ½-inch pieces. Makes 15 to 20 servings.

MARTHA FREEMAN | First Presbyterian Church, Du Quoin, Illinois

Spicy Shrimp Spread

1 package (8 oz.) cream cheese,
    room temperature
¼ cup mayonnaise
5 green onions, finely chopped
½ teaspoon horseradish

½ tablespoon dry mustard
Garlic salt or garlic powder
½ lb. cooked shrimp, ground in blender
    or food processor

1. Combine cream cheese, mayonnaise, green onions, horseradish, mustard, and garlic salt or garlic powder until well blended. Stir in shrimp.

2. Chill for at least 6 hours or overnight. Serve with crackers. Makes 12 servings.

BECKY ROWELL | Christ Church, Frederica, St. Simons Island, Georgia

Hummus

1 can (12 oz.) chickpeas
2 tablespoons sesame oil
¼ to ½ cup lemon juice

1 garlic clove
3 tablespoons water
Olive oil

1. Purée chickpeas in food processor. Add sesame oil, lemon juice, garlic, and water. Pulse once or twice to combine.

2. Transfer hummus to a small serving bowl and smooth the top with a knife. Add just enough olive oil to cover the surface. Store at room temperature (up to 2 hours) or in refrigerator. Stir in olive oil just before serving. Serve with pita bread cut into triangles. Makes 4 servings.

DEEDEE DALRYMPLE | Christ Episcopal Church, Charlotte, North Carolina

Carolina Caviar

1 package (16 oz.) frozen black-eyed peas
2 cups zesty Italian dressing
1½ cups finely chopped onion

½ cup diced jalapeño
2 cups diced red pepper
1 tablespoon minced garlic

1. Cook peas following package directions. Drain well. Place peas in a large bowl. Pour Italian dressing over peas. Allow to cool.

2. Add onion, jalapeño, red pepper, and garlic. Toss to combine. Cover and refrigerate for 24 hours. Serve at room temperature with tortilla chips. Makes 12 servings.

SUSAN SMART | Christ Episcopal Church, Charlotte, North Carolina

Mother's Charleston Crab Dip

¼ to ½ cup mayonnaise

1 small package (3 oz.) cream cheese

1 to 3 teaspoons horseradish

1 cup freshly picked crabmeat

4 tablespoons French dressing

1 or 2 small onions, minced

Combine mayonnaise, cream cheese, horseradish, crabmeat, French dressing, and onions in a small bowl. Stir until well blended. Chill 2 hours. Serve with saltines. Makes 2 to 2¼ cups.

✦ SUSAN FITCH | Christ Episcopal Church, Charlotte, North Carolina

Mariners' Christmas Party

SUGGESTED MENU

Blue Cheese Cheeseball
PAGE 192

Artichoke Crab Dip
PAGE 196

Mexican Dip
PAGE 373

(above served with chips, breads, and crackers)

Mixed nuts

Fruit punch and hot mulled cider

✦ ✦ ✦

Butter lettuce, goat cheese, spicy pecans, and
craisins with vinaigrette dressing

Grilled Pork Tenderloin with Chutney Cream Sauce
PAGE 205

Baked butternut squash with apples

Roasted asparagus

Hard French rolls and butter

✦ ✦ ✦

Lemon crunch sherbet topped with
fresh raspberry and strawberry purée

FIRST PRESBYTERIAN CHURCH
Berkeley, California

Roasted Red Pepper and Garlic Dip

2 red peppers
2 garlic cloves, minced
1 package (8 oz.) cream cheese,
    room temperature
2 tablespoons fresh lime juice

3 tablespoons finely chopped basil
1 tablespoon parsley
½ teaspoon salt
¼ teaspoon white pepper

1. Set red peppers in a roasting pan. Place 6 inches under broiler and roast, turning frequently, until blackened on all sides. Remove from oven and let sit 10 minutes. Pull off and discard skins. Cut peppers in half and remove stem, seeds, and ribs.

2. Place peppers, garlic, cream cheese, lime juice, basil, parsley, salt, and white pepper in a food processor. Combine until creamy. Spoon dip into a bowl and serve with bread sticks or fresh raw vegetables. Makes 8 to 10 servings.

JANIE SELLERS | Christ Episcopal Church, Charlotte, North Carolina

Blue Cheese Cheeseball

1 package (8 oz.) cream cheese,
    room temperature
1 package (3 oz.) blue cheese,
    room temperature

1 can (8 oz.) crushed pineapple, well drained
½ teaspoon Worcestershire sauce
½ cup finely chopped pecans
Crackers

Combine cream cheese, blue cheese, pineapple, Worcestershire sauce, and pecans. Roll into a ball. Serve with crackers. Makes 6 servings.

FIRST PRESBYTERIAN CHURCH | Berkeley, California

Oriental Chicken Wontons

½ lb. ground chicken or pork
½ cup grated carrot
¼ cup finely chopped celery or
    water chestnuts
1 tablespoon soy sauce
1 tablespoon dry sherry

2 teaspoons cornstarch
2 teaspoons grated ginger
½ package (8 oz.) wonton wrappers
2 tablespoons butter, melted
Plum sauce or sweet-and-sour sauce

1. Cook chicken or pork in a large skillet, crumbling with a utensil, until no pink remains. Remove from heat and drain off fat.

2. Stir in carrot, celery or water chestnuts, soy sauce, sherry, cornstarch, and ginger until well combined.

3. Preheat oven to 375°F. Grease two baking sheets.

4. Spoon 1 tablespoon of filling onto a wonton wrapper. Dip your fingertip in a bowl of water and wet the edges of the wrapper. Bring two opposite points of the wrapper together above the filling and pinch to seal. Bring remaining two points together in same location, so edges flare out, and pinch to seal.

5. Repeat to fill and shape all wontons. Place wontons on baking sheets, brush with melted butter, and bake until lightly browned and crisp, 8 to 10 minutes. Serve with plum sauce or sweet-and-sour sauce. Makes 24 wontons.

JAN RICHARDS | Christ Episcopal Church, Charlotte, North Carolina

Mistletoe Cheeseball

2 packages (8 oz. each) cream cheese,
    room temperature

5 tablespoons mayonnaise

1 teaspoon mustard

¼ cup onions

¼ tablespoon sour pickles

5 tablespoons sweet pickles

15 saltines, crushed

4 pimiento-stuffed olives

1 tablespoon parsley

½ green pepper

½ cup coarsely chopped pecans

1. Beat cream cheese, mayonnaise, and mustard in a mixer bowl until creamy.

2. Combine onions, sour pickles, sweet pickles, crushed saltines, olives, parsley, and green pepper in a food processor. Pulse several times to finely chop. Add to cream cheese mixture and stir to combine.

3. Shape mixture into a ball. Roll in chopped pecans to coat. Refrigerate several hours or overnight. Serve with snack crackers. Makes 8 to 10 servings.

LINDA ADAMS | Trinity Presbyterian Church, Little Rock, Arkansas

Black-Eyed Pea Dip

4 cups black-eyed peas

1 or 2 canned jalapeños,
    drained and chopped

1 medium onion, chopped

1 or 2 garlic cloves, minced

1 can (4 oz.) chopped green chilies,
    liquid reserved

½ lb. shredded sharp cheddar cheese or
    sharp processed cheese spread

8 to 10 tablespoons butter

1. Combine black-eyed peas, jalapeños, onion, garlic, and chilies with liquid in a blender. Mix until smooth.

2. Heat cheese and butter in a double boiler until cheese melts. Stir in black-eyed peas mixture. Cook, stirring occasionally, until heated through. Transfer to a bowl and serve with tortilla chips. Makes 10 to 12 servings.

MARCIA GILBERT | Christ Episcopal Church, Charlotte, North Carolina

Caponata

½ cup olive oil

2 large eggplants, diced

2 large onions, chopped

2 green or red peppers, chopped

3 stalks celery, chopped

1 can (6 oz.) tomato paste

1 can (8 oz.) tomato sauce

5 garlic cloves, chopped

1 jar (10 oz.) black olives, drained

¼ cup sugar

⅓ cup vinegar

Dash of Tabasco sauce

¼ to ½ teaspoon oregano

Salt and pepper

1. Heat olive oil in a large skillet over medium-high heat. Add eggplant, onions, peppers, and celery. Sauté, stirring constantly, until soft, 4 to 6 minutes.

2. Add tomato paste, tomato sauce, garlic, black olives, sugar, vinegar, Tabasco sauce, oregano, and salt and pepper. Stir until well combined. Cook, stirring occasionally, 35 to 40 minutes. Cool to room temperature. Transfer to food storage containers and refrigerate at least 24 hours before serving, to allow flavors to blend. Can also be frozen or sealed in canning jars. Serve at room temperature with crackers. Makes 6 to 7 cups.

❧ **NANCY HEMMIG** | Christ Episcopal Church, Charlotte, North Carolina

Pâté

1 lb. chicken livers, fat removed

1¼ cups butter, room temperature, divided

3 tablespoons chopped onion

1 Granny Smith apple, peeled and chopped

1 teaspoon dry mustard

¼ teaspoon salt

¼ teaspoon nutmeg

Dash of cayenne pepper

Dash of ground cloves

1. Place chicken livers in a saucepan, add water to cover, and set over medium-high heat. Bring to a boil. Reduce heat and simmer until cooked through, 30 minutes. Cool in cooking liquid. Drain.

2. Melt 1 tablespoon of the butter in a large skillet over medium heat. Add onion and apple and sauté until softened, 5 minutes.

3. Combine chicken livers, onion and apple mixture, 1 cup of the butter, mustard, salt, nutmeg, cayenne pepper, and ground cloves in a food processor. Blend until smooth. Pack into a container that will tightly hold the pâté.

4. Melt remaining 3 tablespoons butter in a small saucepan over low heat. Remove from heat and let stand 5 minutes. Use a spoon to carefully remove and discard the foamy butterfat on top. Drain off the clarified butter (the clear liquid) and pour it over the pâté to form a seal. Refrigerate 24 hours.

5. To serve pâté, scrape clarified butter off top, invert onto a large plate, and surround with crackers or thin slices of French bread. Makes 6 to 8 servings.

❧ **JANIE SELLERS** | Christ Episcopal Church, Charlotte, North Carolina

Stuffed Mushrooms

2 tablespoons butter

1 package (8 oz.) cream cheese,
    room temperature

1 package (10.5 oz.) frozen chopped spinach,
    thawed and squeezed dry

Salt and pepper

15 large mushrooms or 4 portobello
    mushrooms, stems removed

1. Preheat oven to 350°F. Melt butter in a 11 x 7 x 2-inch baking dish set to warm in oven.

2. Combine cream cheese, spinach, and salt and pepper until well blended. Spoon mixture into mushroom caps. Set caps in baking dish. Bake for 15 minutes or until mushrooms are cooked through and filling is bubbly. Makes 15 appetizer servings or 4 main course servings.

MADIE TORLUEMKE | Trinity Evangelical Lutheran Church, Lansdale, Pennsylvania

Smoked Salmon Cheeseball

1 package (8 oz.) cream cheese, room temperature

1 can (7.5 oz.) smoked salmon, flaked

Pecan meal or parsley flakes

Combine cream cheese and smoked salmon with fork. Form into a ball and roll in pecan meal or parsley flakes to coat. Serve with crackers. Makes 6 servings.

GUYLIA BUNGE | Unity Baptist Church, Morgantown, Indiana

Curried Shrimp Appetizer

¼ cup butter

1 garlic clove, minced

1½ teaspoons curry powder

1 teaspoon mustard seeds, crushed

½ teaspoon red pepper flakes

1 lb. (about 36) medium raw shrimp,
    shelled and deveined

2 teaspoons lemon juice

½ cup chopped cilantro

1. Melt butter in a large skillet over medium heat. Add garlic, curry powder, mustard seeds, and red pepper flakes and stir.

2. Add shrimp and cook, stirring, just until shrimp turn pink; do not overcook. Remove from heat and stir in lemon juice and cilantro. Serve warm or chilled with toothpicks. Makes 8 to 10 servings.

LINDA DU LAC | Methow Valley United Methodist Church, Twisp, Washington

Annual Community Thanksgiving Dinner

I was hungry and you gave me food,
I was thirsty and you gave me drink,
I was a stranger and you welcomed me.

John 25:35

The sacrament of hospitality, giving thanks and help to the whole community—what better way to celebrate Thanksgiving? In November, the Cumming First United Methodist Church in Cumming, Georgia, welcomes parishioners, family, and friends to its annual Thanksgiving Dinner.

Each year the call goes out to more than 200 volunteers who bring 33 turkeys, 27 pans of homemade dressing, 200 lbs. of potatoes, 18 pans of sweet potatoes, corn, green beans, and cranberry sauce, 8 gallons of milk, 9 dozen eggs, and enough pies, cakes, and cookies to serve a crowd. The volunteers cook, set up and decorate the hall, greet guests, clean up, and deliver more than 170 meals to those who cannot attend in person.

Our Sweet Potato Casserole recipe (see page 197) has been a winner every year. We can even make it for as many as 240 people at one time!

CUMMING FIRST UNITED METHODIST CHURCH
Cumming, Georgia

Artichoke Crab Dip

2 cups Parmesan, grated
1 cup mayonnaise
1 can (6.5 oz.) crabmeat, drained,
    or 8 oz. surimi, chopped
1 can (14 oz.) artichoke hearts,
    drained and chopped

1 tablespoon horseradish mustard
2 tablespoons chopped parsley
    plus more for garnish
¼ teaspoon hot pepper sauce
Crackers

1. Preheat oven to 350°F.
2. Combine Parmesan, mayonnaise, crabmeat, artichoke hearts, horseradish mustard, parsley, and hot pepper sauce until well blended.
3. Spoon mixture into a shallow 1-quart baking dish. Bake for 25 minutes or until bubbly. Cool 5 minutes. Garnish with parsley and serve warm with crackers. Makes 16 servings.

FIRST PRESBYTERIAN CHURCH | Berkeley, California

Gravlax

2 lbs. fresh salmon (cross section from
    middle part of fish)

2 tablespoons coarse kosher salt

1 tablespoon sugar

1 teaspoon white pepper

1 large bunch fresh dill

MUSTARD SAUCE:

1 tablespoon tarragon vinegar

3 tablespoons oil

½ teaspoon salt

¼ to ½ cup minced dill

Dash of pepper

Dash of paprika

1 to 3 tablespoons Dijon mustard

1. Cut salmon in half lengthwise and remove all bones.

2. Combine kosher salt, sugar, and white pepper to make a dry rub. Rub into salmon flesh.

3. Place one piece of salmon skin-side down in a shallow glass dish. Pile dill on top. Layer second piece of salmon skin-side up, sandwiching dill in between. Cover with foil and add weights (cans of soup or soda). Marinate in refrigerator for 48 hours.

4. To make mustard sauce: Stir vinegar, oil, salt, dill, pepper, paprika, and mustard until well combined.

5. Lift off top layer of salmon and remove and discard dill. Cut very thin slices on the diagonal. Serve on dark bread with mustard sauce. Store in refrigerator 1 week or longer. Makes 10 to 15 servings.

FAY S. MILLER | Trinity Evangelical Lutheran Church, Lansdale, Pennsylvania

Sweet Potato Casserole

3 cups sweet potatoes, cooked

½ cup sugar

2 eggs

1 teaspoon vanilla

½ cup milk

½ cup butter, melted

TOPPING:

1 cup brown sugar

⅓ cup flour

1 cup chopped pecans

⅓ cup butter, room temperature

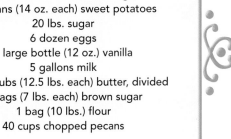

Here's the ingredient list to make the same
dish for a crowd (240 servings):
230 cans (14 oz. each) sweet potatoes
20 lbs. sugar
6 dozen eggs
1 large bottle (12 oz.) vanilla
5 gallons milk
4 large tubs (12.5 lbs. each) butter, divided
2 bags (7 lbs. each) brown sugar
1 bag (10 lbs.) flour
40 cups chopped pecans

1. Preheat oven to 350°F. Lightly grease a 1½-quart casserole.

2. Combine sweet potatoes, sugar, eggs, vanilla, milk, and melted butter in bowl. Mix until majority of lumps are gone. Pour into casserole.

3. To make topping: Combine brown sugar, flour, pecans, and butter with your fingers. Spoon over sweet potatoes. Bake uncovered for 30 minutes. Makes 4 to 6 servings.

LISA BURKE | Cumming First United Methodist Church, Cumming, Georgia

Curried Crab in Endive Spears

¼ cup mayonnaise

2 tablespoons minced celery

2 tablespoons minced onion

1 teaspoon curry powder

1 can (7 oz.) crabmeat

Pepper

4 heads Belgian endive, broken into spears

2 tablespoons minced fresh cilantro

1. Combine mayonnaise, celery, onion, and curry powder in a small bowl. Add crabmeat, sprinkle with pepper, and toss to combine.

2. Place a heaping tablespoon of crab mixture on base of each endive spear. Arrange leaves on a platter in spoke fashion. Sprinkle with cilantro. Can be prepared up to 8 hours ahead and refrigerated. Makes 6 to 8 servings.

❖ **MARIE E. STALTE** | Trinity Evangelical Lutheran Church, Lansdale, Pennsylvania

Cocktail Meatballs

3 lbs. ground beef

½ cup Italian-style bread crumbs

2 onions, minced

4 teaspoons horseradish

4 garlic cloves, crushed

1½ cups tomato juice

Salt and pepper

GRAVY:

¼ cup butter

2 onions, chopped

¼ cup flour

2 cans (13¾ oz. each) beef broth

½ cup red cooking wine

¼ cup brown sugar

¼ cup ketchup

2 teaspoons lemon juice

Salt and pepper

1. Preheat oven to 450°F. Lightly grease a large rimmed baking sheet.

2. Combine ground beef, bread crumbs, onion, horseradish, garlic, and tomato juice in a large bowl. Sprinkle with salt and pepper. Mix well. Form into 1-inch meatballs and place on baking sheet. Bake for 10 minutes or until browned. Drain on paper towels.

3. To make gravy: Melt butter in a large saucepan or skillet over medium heat. Add onion and cook until soft, 4 to 6 minutes. Stir in flour. Gradually add beef broth and wine, stirring continuously until gravy begins to thicken. Add brown sugar, ketchup, lemon juice, and salt and pepper. Reduce heat and simmer for 5 minutes.

4. Add meatballs to gravy, tossing gently to coat. Simmer 15 minutes more. Serve hot in a chafing dish with toothpicks. Makes 16 to 20 servings.

❖ **KAREN BROWN** | Trinity Evangelical Lutheran Church, Lansdale, Pennsylvania

Sugared Pecans

1 egg white
¼ teaspoon cinnamon
¼ teaspoon cloves
¼ teaspoon allspice

½ cup sugar
½ teaspoon salt
3 cups pecans

1. Preheat oven to 325°F.

2. Beat egg white until frothy. Stir cinnamon, cloves, allspice, sugar, and salt in a small bowl. Blend into egg white.

3. Toss pecans with the egg white mixture to coat. Place in a single layer on a rimmed baking sheet. Bake, stirring every 10 minutes, until lightly browned, 30 to 35 minutes. Turn out onto waxed paper to cool. Makes 3 cups.

❖ EVA K. JACKSON | Presbyterian Church of Gonzales, Gonzales, Texas

Winter Vegetable Soup

4 tablespoons butter
2 cups chopped onion
2 tablespoons flour
6 cups rich chicken broth
2 cups diced potatoes
1 small bunch parsley, tied with string
2 bay leaves
Salt and pepper
1 cup diced white turnip

1 or 2 stalks celery, chopped
½ to 1 cup heavy cream

GARNISH:
1 tablespoon butter
3 or 4 carrots, cut in julienne
6 large mushrooms, thinly sliced
    or cut into strips
2 large leeks, cut in julienne

1. Melt butter in a stockpot over medium heat. Add onion and sauté until soft but not browned, 3 to 4 minutes. Add flour and continue cooking, stirring continuously, for 2 minutes. Gradually add chicken broth, whisking until smooth.

2. Add potatoes, parsley, bay leaves, and salt and pepper. Simmer uncovered until potatoes are almost tender, 20 to 25 minutes.

3. Cook turnip in boiling salted water until tender, 20 to 25 minutes. Drain.

4. To make garnish: Melt butter in a large skillet over medium heat. Add carrots, mushrooms, and leeks. Sauté until soft but not browned, 4 to 6 minutes.

5. Stir celery and turnips into broth. Stir in heavy cream until smooth. Taste soup and adjust seasonings. Remove parsley bouquet and bay leaves. Serve very hot in soup bowls. Top with garnish. Makes 6 servings.

❖ ADELE AHLUM | Trinity Evangelical Lutheran Church, Lansdale, Pennsylvania

Holiday Brunch Casserole

4 cups cubed day-old bread

2 cups shredded sharp cheddar cheese

10 eggs

4 cups milk

1 teaspoon dry mustard

1 teaspoon salt

¼ teaspoon onion powder

Pepper

1 package (16 oz.) sausage, cooked, drained, and crumbled

½ cup chopped peeled tomatoes

½ cup chopped mushrooms

1. Butter a 13 x 9 x 2-inch baking dish. Layer bread cubes in bottom. Sprinkle with cheddar cheese.

2. Whisk together eggs, milk, mustard, salt, onion powder, and pepper. Pour evenly over cheese and bread layers. Top with sausage, tomatoes, and mushrooms. Cover and chill overnight.

3. Preheat oven to 325°F. Bake casserole uncovered for 1 hour, tenting with foil if top begins to brown too quickly. Makes 6 servings.

REBECCA JEHS | Memorial Baptist Church, Tulsa, Oklahoma

Split Pea Soup

1 package (16 oz.) dried green split peas

4 quarts water, divided

1 large yellow onion

2 whole cloves

1 ham hock

1 or 2 carrots, chopped

Salt and pepper

Liquid smoke

Freeze this thick, meaty split pea soup to enjoy on a busy day when you don't have time to cook. Just reheat and serve.

1. Pick over and rinse peas. Put peas and 2 quarts water in a large stockpot over medium-high heat. Bring to a boil. Reduce heat and simmer 2 minutes. Remove from heat and let sit 1 hour.

2. Pour off water and rinse and drain peas. Return peas to pot, add 2 quarts of fresh water, and set over medium-low heat. Press cloves into onion and add to pot. Add ham hock, carrots, and salt and pepper. Simmer until peas are very soft, 30 to 40 minutes.

3. Remove ham hock from soup and pull off meat. Remove cloves from onion. Put peas, carrots, and onion through a food mill or chop in small batches in a food processor. Return vegetables to pot. Stir in shredded ham and liquid smoke. Makes 2½ to 3 quarts.

KASSIE MINOR | Christ Episcopal Church, Charlotte, North Carolina

Crustless Springtime Quiche

2 tablespoons butter

½ cup shallots, chopped

5 plum tomatoes

1¾ cups milk (can use skim)

4 eggs

1½ cups shredded Monterey Jack

¼ cup chopped fresh dill

2 teaspoons grated lemon zest, grated

½ teaspoon salt

½ teaspoon pepper

2 packages (10 oz. each) frozen
chopped spinach, thawed, drained,
and squeezed dry

1 tablespoon dried bread crumbs

1 tablespoon grated Parmesan

1. Preheat oven to 350°F. Grease an 8 x 8 x 2-inch baking dish.

2. Melt butter in a small skillet over medium heat. Add shallots and sauté until translucent, 4 to 6 minutes.

3. Cut tomatoes in half. Squeeze out juice and seeds and discard. Coarsely chop flesh.

4. Whisk together milk and eggs. Stir in Monterey Jack, dill, lemon zest, salt, and pepper. Stir in spinach, tomatoes, and shallots. Pour mixture into pan. Sprinkle bread crumbs and Parmesan over the top. Bake 50 to 60 minutes or until topping is golden and a knife inserted in the center comes out clean. Makes 6 to 8 servings.

✦ **ANNE RITTER** | Trinity Evangelical Lutheran Church, Lansdale, Pennsylvania

French Onion Soup

¼ cup olive oil

5 cups yellow onion, thinly sliced and
separated into rings

2 tablespoons flour

3 cans (10.5 oz. each) beef broth plus
2 cans of water

½ teaspoon salt

¼ teaspoon pepper

¼ cup sherry

6 slices French bread, toasted

6 slices Swiss cheese or Gruyère

¼ cup Parmesan

1. Heat oil in a large saucepan or skillet over low heat. Add onion and sauté until golden, 6 to 8 minutes.

2. Add flour and stir continuously until browned, 4 to 6 minutes. Add broth and water. Stir in salt and pepper. Cover and simmer for 30 minutes.

3. Pour in sherry and simmer 2 minutes more. Ladle soup into ovenproof bowls set on a rimmed baking sheet. Set a slice of toasted French bread in each bowl and top with a slice of Swiss cheese or Gruyère. Set 4 inches under broiler until cheese is melted and golden, 2 to 3 minutes. Makes 6 servings.

✦ **BECKY ROWELL** | Christ Church, Frederica, St. Simons Island, Georgia

Winter Squash Soup

4 cups cubed butternut squash

⅛ teaspoon allspice

⅛ teaspoon cinnamon

4 to 5 cups chicken broth

2 tablespoons butter

2 onions, chopped

Chopped parsley

1. Combine squash, allspice, cinnamon, and 4 cups of the chicken broth in a large saucepan over medium-high heat. Bring to a boil. Reduce heat, cover, and simmer until squash is tender, 20 to 30 minutes.

2. Purée mixture in a food processor or blender, working in batches if necessary.

3. Melt butter in a clean saucepan over medium-high heat. Add onion and sauté until golden, 6 minutes. Stir in squash purée and cook until heated through, 3 to 4 minutes. Thin soup with additional broth or water if desired. Ladle into soup bowls and garnish with chopped parsley. Makes 6 servings.

❖ GINNY SHANK | Trinity Evangelical Lutheran Church, Lansdale, Pennsylvania

Cranberry Relish

1 cup sugar

1 small or medium onion, chopped

1 whole clove

1 teaspoon cinnamon

½ cup vinegar

1 teaspoon ginger

Pinch of red pepper flakes

½ teaspoon salt

½ cup water

⅓ cup brown sugar

1 cup seedless raisins

2 cups cranberries, washed and picked over

1. Combine sugar, onion, clove, cinnamon, vinegar, ginger, red pepper flakes, salt, and water in a large saucepan over medium-high heat. Bring to a boil and cook until sugar is dissolved, 4 to 5 minutes.

2. Add brown sugar, raisins, and cranberries. Continue boiling until cranberries burst.

3. Cool to room temperature, transfer to a covered container, and refrigerate for 2 to 3 hours before serving. Hot mixture can also be sealed in canning jars. Serve as relish or over cream cheese with crackers. Makes 2 pints.

JEAN SPRATT | Christ Episcopal Church, Charlotte, North Carolina

Orange-Roasted Turkey Breast

2 tablespoons frozen orange juice
concentrate, thawed

2 tablespoons honey

2 teaspoons snipped fresh thyme

4- to 5-lb. turkey breast

¼ teaspoon salt

¼ teaspoon pepper

GRAVY:

2 to 3 teaspoons cornstarch

2 teaspoons cold water

2 tablespoons frozen orange juice
concentrate, thawed

1 cup low-sodium chicken broth

Salt and pepper

1. Preheat oven to 325°F.

2. Stir orange juice concentrate, honey, and thyme in a small bowl.

3. Sprinkle turkey breast with salt and pepper. Place turkey, bone side down, on a rack in a shallow roasting pan. Roast uncovered for 1½ to 2¼ hours or until juices run clear and internal temperature reaches 170°F. Brush orange juice mixture on turkey during the last 15 minutes of cooking time.

4. Transfer turkey to a plate or cutting board. Cover with foil and let stand 15 minutes before carving.

5. To make gravy: Combine cornstarch and water in a small saucepan. Stir to make a smooth paste. Stir in broth and remaining 2 tablespoons orange juice. Cook over medium heat, stirring continuously, until slightly thickened and hot, 6 to 8 minutes. Season with salt and pepper.

6. To serve, arrange slices of turkey breast on a platter and pass gravy on the side. Makes 6 to 8 servings.

BRENDA MOYE | Grace on the Hill United Methodist Church, Corbin, Kentucky

Holiday Cranberry Sauce from Mom

1 package (16 oz.) whole cranberries, rinsed and chopped

2 medium apples, peeled, cored, and chopped

1 orange, peeled, seeded, and cut into bite-size pieces

¼ to ½ cup chopped pecans or English walnuts

1 to 1½ cups sugar

1. Combine cranberries, apples, oranges, and pecans or walnuts in a bowl.

2. Sprinkle with sugar and toss to combine. Store in a covered container in the refrigerator up to 2 weeks. Makes about 3 cups.

MARILYN J. TAYLOR | Trinity Evangelical Lutheran Church, Lansdale, Pennsylvania

Spicy Hopping John

2 cups dried black-eyed peas

8 cups water

8 oz. chopped ham

1 can (16 oz.) tomatoes, cut up

1 cup chopped onion

1 cup chopped celery

1 tablespoon salt

2 teaspoons chili powder

¼ teaspoon basil

1 bay leaf

1 cup long grain rice

1. Sort and rinse peas. Combine peas and water in a stockpot over medium-high heat. Bring to a boil. Reduce heat and simmer for 2 minutes. Remove from heat, cover, and let stand 1 hour. Do not drain.

2. Add ham, tomatoes, onion, celery, salt, chili powder, basil, and bay leaf to pot. Cover and simmer over medium-low heat until peas are tender, 50 to 60 minutes.

3. Add rice and simmer until rice is cooked through, 20 minutes more. Remove bay leaf. Makes 12 servings.

GENE PALMER | Christ Church, Frederica, St. Simons Island, Georgia

Linguine with Tomatoes and Basil

4 large ripe tomatoes, cut into ½-inch cubes

1 lb. Brie, rind removed, torn into pieces

1 cup fresh basil leaves, cut into strips

3 garlic cloves, finely minced

1 cup plus 1 tablespoon extra virgin olive oil, divided

2½ teaspoons salt, divided

¼ teaspoon pepper

6 quarts water

1½ lbs. linguine

1. Combine tomatoes, Brie, basil, garlic, 1 cup of the olive oil, ½ teaspoon of the salt, and pepper in large bowl. Cover and marinate at room temperature for at least 2 hours.

2. Heat water, remaining tablespoon oil, and remaining 2 teaspoons salt in a stockpot over medium-high heat. Bring to a boil. Add linguine and boil until tender but firm, 8 to 10 minutes. Drain well.

3. Toss hot pasta with tomato mixture. Serve in shallow bowls. Makes 4 to 6 servings.

JANE DOWD | Christ Episcopal Church, Charlotte, North Carolina

Grilled Pork Tenderloin with Chutney Cream Sauce

Grill or bake pork tenderloin (2 to 2½ lbs.) until internal temperature reaches 150°F. Remove from heat and cover loosely (do not seal) with foil until temperature reaches 155°F to 160°F.

CHUTNEY CREAM SAUCE

2 green onions, finely chopped
½ teaspoon minced fresh ginger
3 tablespoons Major Grey chutney
⅓ cup Madeira

¾ cup chicken broth
¾ cup whipping cream
2 tablespoons chopped crystallized ginger

1. Combine onions, ginger, chutney, Madeira, and broth in a saucepan over high heat. Bring to a boil and cook, stirring continuously, 5 minutes.

2. Add whipping cream and return to a boil. Continue cooking, stirring continuously, until sauce reduces to 1¼ cups. Pour over pork and sprinkle with crystallized ginger. Makes 4 to 6 servings.

FIRST PRESBYTERIAN CHURCH | Berkeley, California

Yorkshire Pudding

Roast beef drippings
2 cups flour
2 teaspoons baking powder

1 teaspoon salt
2 cups milk
4 eggs, separated

1. Preheat oven to 425°F. Spoon hot roast beef pan drippings into two shallow baking pans.

2. Sift together flour, baking powder, and salt.

3. Beat egg whites in a mixer bowl until foamy. Add milk and blend well. Gradually add flour mixture, mixing to form a very smooth batter. Add yolks last, beating well after each addition.

4. Pour batter into pans. Bake 20 to 25 minutes or until golden brown. Serve hot with roast beef. Makes 6 to 8 servings.

MRS. W. T. DAWE | *First Edition Presbyterian Cookbook* | Presbyterian Church of Gonzales, Gonzales, Texas

Good "Gracious" Friday

TRINITY EVANGELICAL LUTHERAN CHURCH
Lansdale, Pennsylvania

French Oven Beef Stew

2 tablespoons butter

6 tablespoons oil

6 lbs. beef chuck, cut into 1½-inch cubes

3 lbs. carrots, peeled and sliced

2 onions, sliced into rings

12 potatoes, peeled and sliced ¼-inch thick

1 cup white wine

1 can (10¾ oz.) beef broth

1 cup tomato purée

1 teaspoon salt

½ teaspoon pepper

1. Heat butter and oil in a Dutch oven over medium-high heat. Add beef chuck in batches and cook, turning occasionally, until browned on all sides, 6 to 8 minutes.

2. Transfer browned beef to a 13 x 9 x 2-inch baking dish. Arrange carrots, onions, and potatoes around beef.

3. Pour wine into Dutch oven and cook 3 minutes over high heat to deglaze. Stir in broth, tomato purée, salt, and pepper. Bring to a boil. Pour over beef and vegetables. Cover and refrigerate up to 24 hours.

4. Preheat oven to 325°F. Bake covered for 2 hours. Remove cover and bake 1 to 1½ hours more. Serve hot. Makes 6 to 8 servings.

⚜ **CAROLE KRIEBEL** | Trinity Evangelical Lutheran Church, Lansdale, Pennsylvania

Christmas Eve Chili

2 tablespoons butter
1 cup chopped green pepper
1 cup chopped onion
1 cup chopped celery
2 garlic cloves, minced
1 lb. ground beef
1 can (15 oz.) tomato paste

1 can (16 oz.) peeled tomatoes
1 can (15 oz.) kidney beans, drained
½ cup water
1 tablespoon chili powder
1½ teaspoons salt
½ teaspoon oregano
¼ teaspoon pepper

1. Melt butter in a large skillet or Dutch oven over medium heat. Add green pepper, onion, celery, and garlic. Cook until onion is soft and tender, 4 to 6 minutes.

2. Add ground beef and cook, stirring to break up clumps, until evenly browned.

3. Stir in tomato paste, peeled tomatoes, kidney beans, water, chili powder, salt, oregano, and pepper. Cover and simmer 3 or more hours or until flavors are blended. Makes 6 servings.

GAIL C. HAWORTH | First Moravian Church, Greensboro, North Carolina

Veal Scaloppine Marengo

12 veal scallops
½ cup flour
½ cup vegetable oil
8 tablespoons butter
½ teaspoon chopped garlic
1 tablespoon chopped parsley
Pinch each of thyme, oregano, and nutmeg

Salt and pepper
1 tablespoon tomato paste
1 cup chicken broth, divided
8 fresh mushrooms, sliced
¼ cup dry red wine
2 cups canned Italian tomatoes
2 leaves fresh chopped basil

1. Dust each veal scallops lightly with flour.

2. Heat oil in large skillet until very hot. Sauté scallops quickly on both sides in single layer. Transfer to a warm platter.

3. Melt butter in a saucepan over low heat. Add garlic and cook until soft, 3 minutes. Stir in parsley, thyme, oregano, nutmeg, salt and pepper, tomato paste, and one-third of the chicken broth. Mix until well blended. Cook for 5 minutes.

4. Add mushrooms and wine. Cook, stirring continuously, for 10 minutes. Add remaining broth as needed to thicken sauce to desired consistency. Add tomatoes and cook 25 minutes more. Cool slightly.

5. Pour sauce into a 15 x 10½ x 2-inch baking dish. Layer scaloppine in the sauce. Bake in a preheated 350°F oven for 6 minutes. To serve, arrange scaloppine on a platter, spoon sauce over them, and garnish with basil. Serve with a red wine, such as Barbaresco or Bardolino. Makes 8 servings.

JUDI E. MORGAN | Christ Church, Frederica, St. Simons Island, Georgia

Orange Ginger Catfish

1 lb. catfish fillets
¼ cup ginger teriyaki marinade (such as Golden Dip and Marinade for seafood and chicken)
1 orange, thinly sliced

1. Preheat oven to 350°F. Lightly coat a 13 x 9 x 2-inch baking dish with nonstick cooking spray.
2. Arrange catfish fillets in baking dish. Pour marinade evenly over fish. Top with orange slices. Bake for 25 minutes. Makes 2 to 3 servings.

JANET ROBERTS | Trinity Evangelical Lutheran Church, Lansdale, Pennsylvania

Lime Chicken

4 boneless, skinless chicken breasts
⅓ cup olive oil
Juice of 3 limes
4 garlic cloves, minced

1 teaspoon dried dill
½ teaspoon salt
½ teaspoon pepper
1½ tablespoons chopped parsley

1. Pound chicken between sheets of waxed paper to flatten. Place chicken breasts in a shallow bowl.
2. Combine olive oil, lime juice, garlic, dill, salt, and pepper. Pour over chicken breasts. Marinate for 1 hour at room temperature.
3. Grill or broil chicken to desired doneness. Serve garnished with chopped parsley. Makes 6 servings.

CELIA MARSHALL | Christ Episcopal Church, Charlotte, North Carolina

Lemon Honey Chicken

1 whole chicken (2½ to 3 lbs.),
    cut into 4 pieces
¼ cup oil
¼ cup honey

1 egg yolk, slightly beaten
2 tablespoons soy sauce
2 tablespoons lemon juice
1 teaspoon paprika
¼ teaspoon nutmeg

1. Preheat oven to 350°F.
2. Arrange chicken pieces in a single layer in a shallow baking dish.
3. Combine oil, honey, egg yolk, soy sauce, lemon juice, paprika, and nutmeg. Pour over chicken. Bake uncovered, turning once and occasionally basting with pan juices, for 1 hour. Makes 4 servings.

REBECCA FARNSWORTH | Christ Episcopal Church, Charlotte, North Carolina

Veal Picatta

1½ lbs. veal, cut into 2 oz. medallions
Flour
½ cup butter
1 cup dry white wine
Juice of 2 lemons

1½ cups chicken broth
Pinch of chicken base flour
White pepper
Salt

1. Pound veal into thin medallions with a meat mallet. Dredge with flour to lightly coat. Set aside 1 teaspoon of the dredging flour.

2. Melt butter in a large skillet over medium-high heat. Add veal in batches and sauté, turning once, until lightly browned on both sides, 6 to 8 minutes. Transfer browned medallions to a plate and cover to keep warm.

3. Add white wine and lemon juice to hot skillet. Stir to deglaze. Stir in chicken broth. Spoon a small amount of hot liquid into reserved flour, stir to combine, and then pour back into skillet. Simmer for 2 minutes. Raise heat and boil down to make a thin gravy.

4. Return medallions to skillet to warm through, 2 to 3 minutes. Serve medallions hot, smothered in gravy. Makes 4 servings.

✦ CAM CALDWELL | Christ Church, Frederica, St. Simons Island, Georgia

Roast Venison

1 venison roast, 3 to 4 lbs.
1 garlic clove, sliced
Salt and pepper
¼ cup water
1 large onion, sliced

1 can (10.75 oz.) cream of mushroom
   condensed soup
1 package (2 to 2.5 oz.) onion soup mix

1. Preheat oven to 350°F.

2. Make slits in top, bottom, and sides of roast and stuff with garlic slices. Sprinkle roast with salt and pepper.

3. Put water in roaster with a few slices of onion. Put roast on top of onions and cover with mushroom soup. Sprinkle onion soup mix over the top. Add remaining onion slices around roast. Cover tightly. Roast for 2 to 2½ hours or to desired doneness. If liquid boils, turn down oven to 300°F. This roast makes its own gravy. Makes 6 to 8 servings.

✦ M. MEHUS | Methow Valley United Methodist Church, Twisp, Washington

Eastern Shore Crab Cakes

1 lb. fresh backfin crabmeat
½ cup bread crumbs
1 egg, beaten
5 tablespoons plain or low-fat mayonnaise
1 tablespoon minced parsley

2 teaspoons prepared mustard
1 teaspoon Old Bay Seasoning
¼ teaspoon pepper
2 tablespoons butter

1. Remove cartilage from crabmeat. Shred crabmeat into a bowl.
2. Combine bread crumbs, egg, mayonnaise, parsley, mustard, Old Bay Seasoning, and pepper. Pour breading over crabmeat and fold in with a fork. Form mixture into six patties.
3. Melt butter in a skillet over medium-high heat. Add crab cakes and sauté, turning once, until golden brown on both sides, 3 to 5 minutes. Makes 6 servings.

BETH CRIMMINS | Trinity Evangelical Lutheran Church, Lansdale, Pennsylvania

Crown Pork Roast

4- to 5-lb. pork loin roast,
    arranged into a crown

STUFFING:
6 cups soft bread crumbs
½ cup butter, melted
1 teaspoon salt
¼ teaspoon pepper
½ teaspoon celery salt
4 tablespoons chopped onion
Sage or thyme

1. Preheat oven to 325°F.
2. Stand roast upright in a roasting pan.
3. To make stuffing: Combine bread crumbs, melted butter, salt, pepper, celery salt, onion, and sage or thyme. Spoon stuffing into center of crown.
4. Bake for 3½ hours. Cover roast with foil when meat is nicely browned. Makes 8 to 10 servings.

LUCILLE STENSCHKE | St. John's Guild, St. John's Church, West Bend, Wisconsin

Hobnob Scallops

¼ cup olive oil
¼ cup butter
2 lbs. sea scallops, washed, drained,
    and dredged in flour
½ cup chopped parsley
3 small shallots, diced

2 garlic cloves, minced
4 slices bacon, cooked and diced
1 cup dry white wine
Salt and pepper
Hot cooked rice

1. Heat olive oil and butter in large skillet over medium heat. Add scallops, parsley, shallots, and garlic. Cook just until scallops are heated through, about 8 minutes. Remove scallops to a heated dish. Cover to keep warm.

2. Add wine and bacon bits to skillet. Stir to deglaze. Increase heat and cook vigorously to reduce liquid by half. Remove from heat. Season with salt and pepper.

3. Place skillet on low heat. Return scallops to skillet just long enough to heat through. Serve over hot rice, spooning sauce over the top. Makes 4 servings.

✤ **ANNE RITTER** | Trinity Evangelical Lutheran Church, Lansdale, Pennsylvania

Broccoli, Cheese, and Rice

4 tablespoons butter	1 can (10.75 oz.) cream of chicken condensed soup
½ cup chopped celery	1 can (10.75 oz.) cream of celery condensed soup
½ cup chopped onion	1 jar (15 oz.) cheese sauce (such as Cheese Whiz)
2 packages (10 oz. each) frozen chopped broccoli, thawed and drained	¾ cup cooked rice
	Paprika

1. Preheat oven to 350°F. Lightly grease an 11 x 7 x 2-inch baking dish.

2. Melt butter in a large skillet over medium heat. Add celery and onions and sauté until onion is translucent and golden, 4 to 6 minutes.

3. Add broccoli, cream of chicken soup, cream of celery soup, and cheese sauce. Cook, stirring, until cheese is melted.

4. Layer rice in bottom of baking dish. Pour broccoli and cheese sauce over rice. Sprinkle with paprika. Bake uncovered for 30 minutes. Makes 4 to 6 servings.

✤ **MAXINE DETWEILER** | Trinity Evangelical Lutheran Church, Lansdale, Pennsylvania

Corn Pudding

2 eggs	2 cups corn, cut fresh from the cob
1 cup milk	1 small onion, chopped
1 tablespoon sugar	1 cup cracker crumbs
¼ teaspoon salt	3 tablespoons butter, melted
Dash of pepper	

1. Preheat oven to 350°F. Lightly grease a 1½-quart casserole.

2. Whisk together eggs, milk, sugar, salt, and pepper. Stir in corn and onion.

3. Stir cracker crumbs into melted butter and add to corn mixture. Spoon mixture into casserole and bake for 1¼ hours. Makes 4 to 6 servings.

✤ **MARY RENNINGER** | St. Mark's Lutheran Church, Conshohocken, Pennsylvania

Gingered Carrots and Apples

2 tablespoons butter
3 or 4 carrots, peeled and sliced
    crosswise on the diagonal
⅓ cup orange juice
2 to 3 teaspoons fresh ginger,
    slivered or grated

2 medium apples, cored and cut into ¼-inch slices
1 teaspoon brown sugar
1 teaspoon Grand Marnier liqueur
Snipped fresh chives

1. Melt butter in a large skillet over medium heat. Add carrots, orange juice, and ginger. Cook, stirring frequently, until carrots begin to soften, 5 to 6 minutes.
2. Add apples and simmer until crisp-tender, 2 to 4 minutes.
3. Stir in brown sugar and Grand Marnier liqueur. Cook until sugar melts, 1 minute more. Serve topped with chives. Makes 4 servings.

LINDA BRENNAN | Trinity Evangelical Lutheran Church, Lansdale, Pennsylvania

Brussels Sprouts in Orange Sauce

3 lbs. Brussels sprouts
⅓ cup butter
½ teaspoon grated orange zest

½ cup orange juice
Dash of nutmeg

1. Cook Brussels sprouts in rapidly boiling salted water until tender-crisp (bright green), 6 to 8 minutes. Drain.
2. Combine butter, orange zest, orange juice, and nutmeg in a small dish. Melt in microwave. Pour over sprouts. Serve immediately. Makes 8 servings.

LOUISE BEACH | Trinity Presbyterian Church, Little Rock, Arkansas

Ginger-Glazed Carrots

4 cups sliced carrots
¾ cup orange juice
2 teaspoons cornstarch

2 tablespoons brown sugar
3 tablespoons butter
½ teaspoon ginger

1. Cook carrots in boiling salted water until tender, 6 to 8 minutes. Keep warm in a covered serving dish.
2. Combine orange juice, cornstarch, brown sugar, butter, and ginger in a small saucepan over medium heat. Slowly bring to a boil and cook until thick, 8 to 10 minutes. Pour over carrots and serve. Makes 8 servings.

FRAN ZIMMERMAN | Trinity Evangelical Lutheran Church, Lansdale, Pennsylvania

Microwaved Asparagus

1 lb. asparagus, washed and trimmed
2 slices fresh ginger
¼ teaspoon lemon zest

Vinegar-based salad dressing of your choice
Freshly ground pepper
Garnish (optional)

1. Place asparagus, ginger, and lemon zest in resealable plastic bag. Close bag and microwave at medium (50%) power for 3 to 4 minutes.

2. Unseal bag and fill with cold water. Drain water, pour salad dressing in bag, and shake the bag to mix. Place asparagus on a serving platter. Makes 4 or 5 servings.

✦ **ROSEMARY VANDUYN** | Christ Episcopal Church, Charlotte, North Carolina

Corn Soufflé

5 slices of bacon
1 can (17 oz.) cream-style corn
1 can (15 oz.) whole kernel corn
1 cup sour cream

½ cup butter, melted
½ box (4.25 oz.) Jiffy corn bread
   or corn muffin mix
2 eggs, beaten

1. Preheat oven to 350°F.

2. Fry bacon in a skillet over high heat until crisp. Drain on paper towels. Crumble.

3. Combine cream-style corn and whole kernel corn in a large bowl. Stir in sour cream, melted butter, corn bread or corn muffin mix, and eggs. Pour mixture into a soufflé or casserole dish. Cover and bake for 1 hour. Uncover, sprinkle with bacon, and bake 15 minutes more. Makes 4 to 6 servings.

✦ **LEE MINOR** | Memorial Baptist Church, Tulsa, Oklahoma

Creamed Onions

2 lbs. small white onions, peeled
2 teaspoons salt
3 tablespoons butter
3 tablespoons flour

2 bouillon cubes
1½ cups milk
¼ cup chopped green pepper
2 tablespoons chopped pimiento

1. Fill a large saucepan halfway with water. Bring to a boil. Add onions and salt. Pour in more water, if needed, so onions are covered. Reduce to a simmer and cook, uncovered, until onions are tender, 20 minutes. Drain well.

2. Melt butter in a large skillet over medium heat. Add flour and bouillon cubes, stirring until cubes are dissolved. Add milk. Cook, stirring continuously, until mixture is smooth and thickened.

3. Spoon onions into sauce. Serve hot, garnished with chopped green pepper and pimiento. Makes 6 servings.

✦ **MARY EVELYN HILL** | First Baptist Church, Russell, Kentucky

Ratatouille

1 large or 2 small eggplants,
    cut in ½-inch slices
Salt
Olive oil
1 lb. courgettes (zucchini),
    cut into small chunks
1 lb. red and green peppers,
    cored and thinly sliced

8 oz. onions, peeled and chopped
1½ lbs. tomatoes, peeled,
    seeded, and chopped
3 garlic cloves, finely chopped
½ teaspoon sugar
Parsley sprigs
Chopped fresh thyme
9 to 10 basil leaves, cut into strips

1. Salt eggplant slices, layer in a colander, and drain for 30 minutes. Pat dry.
2. Heat 6 tablespoons olive oil in a large heavy skillet over medium heat. Add eggplant in batches and cook, turning once, until lightly browned on both sides, 6 to 8 minutes. Drain on paper towels.
3. Heat more oil in skillet. Add zucchini and cook just until moisture has evaporated; do not brown. Drain on paper towels. Cook peppers and onions in the same way. Leave onions in skillet.
4. Add tomatoes, garlic, sugar, parsley, and thyme to onions. Stir to combine. Simmer for 30 minutes. Return eggplant, zucchini, and peppers to skillet. Cook until heated through, 5 minutes. Stir in basil strips. Cover and refrigerate for 24 hours before serving. Serve warm or chilled. Makes 6 to 8 servings.

IDA H. McGARITY | Presbyterian Church of Gonzales, Gonzales, Texas

 This authentic recipe from the South of France may be served cold as an appetizer on French bread or warm as a vegetable dish or main course.

Vidalia Onions au Gratin

2 large Vidalia onions, sliced
1 beef bouillon cube
¾ cup boiling water
¼ teaspoon thyme
½ teaspoon salt

¼ teaspoon pepper
3 tablespoons butter, melted, divided
½ cup bread crumbs
¼ cup grated cheese

1. Preheat oven to 400°F.
2. Layer onion slices in a shallow baking dish.
3. Dissolve beef cube in boiling water. Add thyme. Pour mixture over onions. Sprinkle with salt and pepper. Drizzle with 1 tablespoon of the melted butter. Cover and bake for 20 minutes.
4. Toss bread crumbs with remaining 2 tablespoons melted butter and cheese. Sprinkle over onions. Bake uncovered 10 minutes more or until cheese is hot and bubbly. Makes 8 to 10 servings.

TOMELA KEENAN | Trinity Presbyterian Church, Little Rock, Arkansas

Harvest Home Sunday

SUGGESTED MENU

Stuffed Mushrooms
PAGE 195

Winter Squash Soup
PAGE 202

Irish Soda Bread
PAGE 215

French Oven Beef Stew
PAGE 206

Health Salad
PAGE 217

Corn Pudding
PAGE 211

Upside-Down Apple Pecan Pie
PAGE 245

Spiced Wassail
PAGE 262

TRINITY EVANGELICAL LUTHERAN CHURCH
Lansdale, Pennsylvania

Julia's Special Salad

½ package (5 oz.) fresh prewashed spinach
½ head romaine
½ head red-tipped lettuce
1 can (14 oz.) artichoke hearts
1 can (14 oz.) hearts of palm,
   cut into short pieces

DRESSING:

1 cup mayonnaise
2 tablespoons capers
2 garlic cloves, crushed
¼ cup beef bouillon
½ teaspoon curry powder
1 teaspoon Worcestershire sauce
Dash of Tabasco sauce
1 tablespoon dry mustard

1. Tear spinach, romaine, and red-tipped lettuce leaves into bite-size pieces. Combine with artichoke hearts and hearts of palm in a large salad bowl.
2. To make dressing: Whisk together mayonnaise, capers, garlic, bouillon, curry powder, Worcestershire sauce, Tabasco sauce, and mustard.
3. Pour dressing over salad greens. Toss to combine. Makes 6 to 8 servings.

 PERRI BELL | Presbyterian Church of Gonzales, Gonzales, Texas

Herbed Carrots

8 carrots, coarsely shredded
2 tablespoons horseradish
2 tablespoons grated onion
½ teaspoon salt
¼ teaspoon pepper

½ cup mayonnaise
¼ cup fine bread crumbs
1 tablespoon butter, melted
Dash of paprika

1. Preheat oven to 375°F. Lightly grease a shallow baking dish.

2. Pour ½ cup of water into a saucepan. Bring to a boil, add carrots, and cook for 2 minutes. Drain off cooking liquid, reserving ¼ cup. Arrange carrots in baking dish.

3. Combine horseradish, onion, reserved cooking liquid, salt, pepper, and mayonnaise. Pour over carrots.

4. Combine bread crumbs, butter, and paprika. Sprinkle over top of carrots. Bake for 15 to 20 minutes or until topping is lightly browned. Makes 4 to 6 servings.

✤ **OPAL WARD** | First Baptist Church, Russell, Kentucky

Potato Casserole

6 medium baking potatoes (about 2 lbs.),
    peeled and quartered
½ cup plain low-fat yogurt
2 tablespoons butter
¼ to ½ teaspoon salt

⅛ teaspoon red pepper
2 beaten eggs
¾ cup plain or herbed Feta, divided
1 package (10 oz.) prewashed fresh spinach
¼ teaspoon paprika

1. Preheat oven to 425°F. Lightly grease a shallow 2-quart baking dish.

2. Place potatoes in a large saucepan or stockpot, add boiling water to cover, and cook over high heat until tender, 20 to 25 minutes. Drain.

3. Mash potatoes with a potato masher. Transfer to a large mixer bowl. Stir in yogurt, butter, salt, and red pepper until combined. Add eggs and beat on low speed until fluffy. Fold in ½ cup of the Feta.

4. Heat ¼ cup of water in a 12-inch skillet over medium heat. Bring to a boil, toss in spinach, and cook until slightly wilted, 1 minute. Drain well and press out excess liquid. Chop coarsely.

5. Spread half of the potato mixture into baking dish. Layer spinach on top. Sprinkle with remaining ¼ cup Feta. Add remaining potato mixture and sprinkle with paprika. Bake uncovered for 15 minutes or until top is lightly browned. Makes 8 servings.

✤ **LINDA S. THOMPSON** | Christ Church, Frederica, St. Simons Island, Georgia

Health Salad

1 large cabbage, chopped
1 medium onion, chopped
1 green pepper, chopped
1 red pepper, chopped
1 medium carrot, grated
1 cup sugar

DRESSING:

2 tablespoons sugar
2 tablespoons salt
1 teaspoon celery salt
1 teaspoon dry mustard
½ cup cooking oil
1 cup white vinegar

1. Combine cabbage, onion, green and red peppers, and carrot in a large bowl. Sprinkle sugar over slaw but do not stir. Cover and refrigerate overnight.

2. To make dressing: The next day, combine sugar, salt, celery salt, mustard, oil, and vinegar in a saucepan over medium heat. Slowly heat to a boil.

3. Remove slaw from refrigerator. Pour boiling hot dressing over salad (do not stir). Cover immediately with foil to seal in steam. Cool to room temperature. Refrigerate overnight.

4. The next day, toss salad until well combined and transfer to a serving bowl. This salad will keep up to 3 weeks in the refrigerator. Makes 8 servings.

JOYCE W. LIGHTCAP | Trinity Evangelical Lutheran Church, Lansdale, Pennsylvania

Gourmet Baked Acorn Squash

3 acorn squash, halved and seeded
¼ cup butter
⅔ cup diced celery
1½ cups diced, unpeeled apples

1½ cups soft bread crumbs
1 cup grated cheese
½ teaspoon salt
⅛ teaspoon pepper

1. Preheat oven to 400°F.

2. Place squash halves cut side down in a baking pan. Add water to cover bottom of pan. Bake for 20 to 30 minutes or until almost tender.

3. Melt butter in a large skillet over medium heat. Add celery and apples. Sauté for 5 minutes. Stir in bread crumbs, grated cheese, salt, and pepper.

4. Turn squash halves right side up. Fill cavities with apple mixture. Return to oven and bake 10 to 15 minutes more or until squash is fork-tender. Makes 6 servings.

FREDA GANTT | Methow Valley United Methodist Church, Twisp, Washington

Christmas Cranberry Salad

2 packages (3 oz. each) raspberry gelatin
2 cups hot water
1 can (16 oz.) whole cranberry sauce
2 tablespoons lemon juice

1 package (8 oz.) cream cheese,
   room temperature
1 cup heavy cream, whipped
½ cup chopped pecans

1. Add gelatin to hot water and stir until dissolved, 2 minutes.

2. Add cranberry sauce and stir until dissolved. Stir in lemon juice. Pour mixture into a 13 x 9 x 2-inch baking dish. Refrigerate until firm, 2 to 4 hours.

3. Beat cream cheese in a mixer bowl until fluffy. Fold in whipped cream and pecans. Spread over top of gelatin.

4. Return salad to refrigerator and chill 2 hours more or until firm. To serve, cut into squares and place on a bed of lettuce leaves. Makes 12 servings.

ANGIE BURNS | Christ Church, Frederica, St. Simons Island, Georgia

Company Green Salad with Dijon Vinaigrette

2 medium heads romaine,
   torn into bite-size pieces
1 large red pepper, cored, seeded,
   and cut into strips
1 medium red onion, sliced into rings

1 can (11 oz.) mandarin oranges or
   grapefruit sections, halved and drained
4 oz. Feta or blue cheese, crumbled
Dijon Vinaigrette (recipe follows)

Combine romaine, red pepper, red onion, mandarin oranges or grapefruit sections, and Feta or blue cheese in a large salad bowl. Pour Dijon Vinaigrette over salad and toss until well combined. Makes 8 servings.

DIJON VINAIGRETTE

½ cup olive oil
¼ cup red or white vinegar
Pinch of salt
Pinch of sugar

1 teaspoon mixed Dijon mustard
1 tablespoon minced mixed fresh herbs
   (such as basil, oregano, and parsley)

Combine olive oil, vinegar, salt, sugar, mustard, and herbs in a glass jar with a tight-fitting lid. Cover and shake until well combined. Makes about ¾ cup.

BEN HUTTO | Christ Episcopal Church, Charlotte, North Carolina

Spinach Salad

1 package (10 oz.) prewashed fresh spinach
1 can (5 oz.) sliced water chestnuts
1 can (16 oz.) bean sprouts, drained
4 hard-boiled eggs, sliced
8 slices of bacon, crisply cooked
   and crumbled
Sliced mushrooms

DRESSING:

1 cup salad oil
⅓ cup ketchup
¾ teaspoon salt
¾ cup sugar
¼ cup vinegar
1 medium onion, finely chopped
1½ tablespoons Worcestershire sauce

1. Layer spinach, water chestnuts, bean sprouts, egg slices, bacon, and mushrooms in a large salad bowl. Do not toss. Cover and chill at least 4 hours or overnight.

2. To make dressing: Combine oil, ketchup, salt, sugar, vinegar, onion, and Worcestershire sauce in a jar with a tight-fitting lid. Cover and shake until well combined. Chill.

3. To serve, shake dressing, pour over salad, and toss until well combined. Makes 6 to 8 servings.

EVELYN K. BUCHER | Trinity Evangelical Lutheran Church, Lansdale, Pennsylvania

Greek-Style Salad

4 cups torn spinach or other mixed greens
½ medium cucumber, halved lengthwise and sliced
1 medium tomato, cut in thin wedges
1 medium onion, chopped
1 oz. Feta, crumbled
2 tablespoons sliced black olives
1 tablespoon snipped parsley

DRESSING:

2 tablespoons lemon juice
2 tablespoons olive oil
1 teaspoon honey
1 clove garlic, minced

VARIATION:
Add marinated artichoke hearts that have been drained of their liquid and chopped. Use one 16-oz. jar of artichoke hearts for every 4 cups of greens.

1. Combine spinach or mixed greens, cucumber, tomato, onion, Feta, black olives, and parsley in a large salad bowl.

2. To make dressing: Whisk together lemon juice, olive oil, honey, and garlic.

3. Pour dressing over salad and toss well to combine. Makes 4 servings.

GAIL CARR | Christ Episcopal Church, Charlotte, North Carolina

Shrimp Salad

1 lb. shrimp
1 large cucumber, sliced
2 medium tomatoes, cut into wedges
6 cups assorted lettuces, torn in
    bite-size pieces

DRESSING:
¼ cup olive oil
¼ cup sugar
2 tablespoons lime juice
2 tablespoons wine vinegar
1 garlic clove, minced
1 shallot, minced
1½ teaspoons chopped parsley

1. Grill and peel shrimp.

2. Combine cucumber, tomatoes, and lettuce in a large bowl.

3. To make dressing: Whisk together olive oil, sugar, lime juice, wine vinegar, garlic, shallot, and parsley. Pour over salad and toss to combine. To serve, place salad on individual plates and top with grilled shrimp. Makes 6 servings.

CLARA GODSHALL | Christ Episcopal Church, Charlotte, North Carolina

Marinated Asparagus and Hearts of Palm

1 lb. fresh asparagus, cooked
1 can (14 oz.) hearts of palm, drained,
    cut into bite-size pieces
¾ cup vegetable oil or olive oil

½ cup apple cider vinegar
1½ teaspoons salt
1 teaspoon pepper

1. Place asparagus and hearts of palm in a large resealable food storage bag.

2. Whisk together oil, vinegar, salt, and pepper. Pour over asparagus and seal bag. Marinate in refrigerator overnight. Serve at room temperature. Makes 6 servings.

ANN PERRY | Christ Episcopal Church, Charlotte, North Carolina

Layir's Tossed Salad for Thanksgiving

1 head romaine or iceberg lettuce,
    torn into bite-size pieces
1 green pepper
2 cucumbers, cut into thin slices
3 carrots, grated
1 cauliflower, broken into bite-size florets

½ to ¾ lb. assorted deli meats
    (smoked turkey, honey ham, chicken),
    cut into strips, divided
6 hard-boiled eggs, peeled and cut into wedges
1 cup shredded cheese
1 bottle (16 oz.) salad dressing

Babette's Feast

If you have seen the wonderful Danish film *Babette's Feast*, you will remember that it was Babette's gift and sacrifice of her talents as a chef that brought grace to a small community of people. At her feast, old wounds were healed, forgiveness discovered, and joy created. It is no accident that Jesus so often compared the Kingdom of God to a banquet. In the gift and sacrifice of the table, we might have life and have it abundantly.

THE REVEREND HENRY NUTT PARSLEY, JR.
Christ Episcopal Church, Charlotte, North Carolina

1. Layer lettuce, pepper, cucumbers, carrots, and cauliflower in a large salad bowl.
2. Layer half of the deli meats into the bowl. Layer in eggs, cheese, and remaining deli meats. Cover and chill overnight.
3. To serve, pour bottled dressing over the salad and toss until well combined. Makes 6 to 8 servings.

MINISTER LAYIR PEARCE ANTHONY | Miracle Deliverance Holiness Church, Columbia, South Carolina

Holiday Breakfast Bread

3 cups flour
2 cups sugar
1 teaspoon baking soda
1 teaspoon salt
1 teaspoon cinnamon
3 eggs

1½ cups oil
1 cup chopped pecans
1 cup coconut
2 cups dried bananas
1 can (20 oz.) crushed pineapple, drained
1½ teaspoons vanilla

1. Preheat oven to 350°F. Grease two 8½ x 4½ x 2½-inch loaf pans.
2. Whisk together flour, sugar, baking soda, salt, and cinnamon. Beat in eggs and oil until well blended. Stir in pecans, coconut, bananas, pineapple, and vanilla.
3. Pour batter into pans. Bake for 60 to 80 minutes or until lightly browned and fragrant. Cool in pans 5 to 10 minutes before turning out on a wire rack. Makes 2 loaves.

MARIAN COURT | Methow Valley United Methodist Church, Twisp, Washington

Christmas Stollen

2 cups milk

1 large cake (2 oz.) compressed
    wet yeast (such as Red Star)

8 cups sifted flour, divided,
    plus more for fruit

1 cup butter

1 cup sugar

4 eggs

Grated zest of 1 lemon

¾ cup golden raisins

¾ cup red glacéed pineapple

¾ cup green glacéed pineapple

¾ cup chopped glacéed cherries

1 cup chopped walnuts

1½ teaspoons salt

½ teaspoon nutmeg

1. Scald milk. Cool to lukewarm. Stir in yeast and 1 cup of the flour. Let rise ½ hour.

2. Cream butter and sugar in a mixer bowl. Beat in eggs one at a time. Stir in lemon zest.

3. Toss raisins, pineapple, cherries, and walnuts with a tablespoon of flour to coat.

4. Whisk together remaining 7 cups flour, salt, nutmeg, and fruits and walnuts. Fold sponge into egg mixture. Gradually add flour mixture to make a soft dough. Knead until smooth. Cover and let rise until doubled in bulk, 1½ to 2 hours.

5. Divide dough into three loaves. Place on greased baking sheets and set aside in a warm place to rise, 1 to 1½ hours.

5. Bake in a 350°F oven for 45 minutes or until lightly browned. Frost with confectioners' sugar glaze when still warm. Makes 3 stollen.

❖ **FRIEDA LANGE** | St. John's Guild, St. John's Church, West Bend, Wisconsin

Governor's Crème Brûlée

4¼ cups heavy cream

12 extra large egg yolks

1 cup sugar

2 teaspoons vanilla

1¼ cups light brown sugar

1. Heat heavy cream in a double boiler until hot.

2. Beat egg yolks and sugar until thick and light in color.

3. Slowly pour heated cream over the yolk mixture, beating continuously. Return mixture to double boiler and cook, stirring constantly, until custard coats a spoon heavily. Remove from heat and stir in vanilla.

4. Strain custard into individual 4-oz. ramekins or custard cups. Set cups on a tray and refrigerate at least 4 hours or overnight.

5. Before serving, sift 2 tablespoons light brown sugar in an even layer over each custard. Glaze sugar with a small propane torch on low flame or by placing custards, one or two at a time, under a preheated broiler for 1 to 2 minutes, just until sugar caramelizes but before it burns. Serve within 15 minutes of glazing. Makes 10 servings.

❖ **GOVERNOR ZELL MILLER** | Christ Church, Frederica, St. Simons Island, Georgia

Bubble Buns

24 frozen rolls

1 teaspoon cinnamon

½ cup sugar

1 cup brown sugar

1 package (3 oz.) cook-and-serve
    butterscotch pudding mix

½ to 1 cup chopped pecans or walnuts

½ cup butter, melted

1. Place rolls in a greased 10-cup Bundt pan or a 13 x 9 x 2-inch baking pan.

2. Toss together cinnamon, sugar, brown sugar, and pudding mix. Sprinkle over rolls. Top with pecans or walnuts. Drizzle with melted butter. Let stand uncovered at room temperature overnight.

3. Bake in a preheated 350°F oven for 30 minutes or until golden brown. Invert onto a serving plate. Makes 24 servings.

❖ **CAROL GASTON** | Methow Valley United Methodist Church, Twisp, Washington

Apple Dumplings

½ cup sugar

1 teaspoon cinnamon

2 refrigerated piecrust pastries

12 medium Granny Smith or
    Northern Spy apples, cored and peeled

Walnuts, coarsely chopped

Brown sugar

Butter

SAUCE:

2 cups water

¾ cup sugar

2 tablespoons butter

1 teaspoon vanilla

¼ teaspoon mace

¼ teaspoon nutmeg

1. Preheat oven to 375°F. Set aside two 11 x 7 x 2-inch baking dishes.

2. Mix sugar and cinnamon in a shallow bowl.

3. Roll out each piecrust pastry into an 18 x 12-inch rectangle. Cut each rectangle into six 6 x 6-inch squares, for 12 squares total.

4. Fill the hollow of each apple with walnuts, brown sugar, and butter. Roll each apple in cinnamon sugar.

5. Set an apple in the middle of a pastry square. Bring the four points of the pastry to the top. Moisten and press the points together, wrapping the pastry firmly around the apple. Place apple in baking dish. Repeat to wrap all apples with pastry. (Apples may be frozen at this stage. Thaw in refrigerator before baking.)

6. To make sauce: Heat water in a small saucepan over medium heat. Add sugar and bring to a boil. Cook, stirring continuously, until syrup is clear and begins to thicken. Remove from heat. Stir in butter, vanilla, mace, and nutmeg until fully blended and butter is melted. Pour sauce over dumplings. Bake uncovered, basting occasionally, for 1 hour or until apples are fork-tender. Cool 15 minutes before serving. Makes 12 servings.

❖ **LINDA BRENNAN** | Trinity Evangelical Lutheran Church, Lansdale, Pennsylvania

Éclairs or Cream Puffs

½ cup water
¼ cup butter
½ cup flour
¼ teaspoon salt
2 eggs
Confectioners' sugar or chocolate icing

CUSTARD:
⅓ cup plus 2 tablespoons sugar
⅛ teaspoon salt
2 tablespoons flour
2 egg yolks
1½ cups milk
2 teaspoons vanilla

1. Preheat oven to 450°F. Grease a baking sheet.

2. Heat water in a saucepan over medium-high heat. Bring to a boil, add butter, and stir until melted. Combine flour and salt and blend into water. Stir until dough no longer sticks to pan.

3. Remove from heat. Beat in eggs one at a time. Continue beating until stiff.

4. Form dough into oblong shapes or round mounds on baking sheet. Bake for 10 minutes. Reduce heat to 375°F and bake 25 minutes more or until lightly browned. Cool on wire racks.

5. To make custard: Whisk together sugar, salt, and flour in a saucepan. Stir egg yolks into milk and gradually whisk into sugar mixture over medium heat. Slowly bring to a boil, stirring continuously, until thick. Boil for 1 minute. Remove from heat and add vanilla. Cool completely.

6. Cut off tops and hollow out cavities of puffs. Spoon custard into cavities. Replace tops. Sprinkle with confectioners' sugar or drizzle with chocolate icing. Makes 6 éclairs or 12 to 18 cream puffs.

❖ ANNE TOMLINSON | Christ Episcopal Church, Charlotte, North Carolina

Misty Mountain Gingerbread with Lemon Sauce

1 cup molasses
1 cup butter
1 cup sugar
1 tablespoon cinnamon
1 tablespoon ginger
1 teaspoon allspice
1 teaspoon cloves

2½ cups flour
1 teaspoon salt
1 cup buttermilk
2 eggs, beaten
1 teaspoon baking soda
¼ cup hot water
Lemon Sauce (recipe follows)

1. Preheat oven to 350°F. Grease and flour an 11 x 7 x 2-inch baking pan.

2. Combine molasses, butter, sugar, cinnamon, ginger, allspice, and cloves in a large saucepan over medium-high heat. Bring to a boil, beating until butter melts. Remove from heat.

3. Combine flour and salt. Beat into boiled mixture. Beat in buttermilk and eggs.

4. Dissolve baking soda in hot water and stir into batter. Pour into pan and bake 50 to 60 minutes or until a tester inserted comes out clean. Turn out onto a wire rack and cool 10 to 15 minutes. Slice and serve warm with lemon sauce spooned over the top (recipe follows). Makes 12 servings.

LEMON SAUCE

½ cup sugar

2 tablespoons cornstarch

1 cup water

¼ cup butter

2 teaspoons grated lemon zest

¼ cup fresh lemon juice

Dash of salt

1. Combine sugar and cornstarch in a small saucepan over medium heat. Add water, stirring until smooth, and bring to a boil. Reduce heat and simmer, stirring continuously, until mixture thickens and turns translucent, 5 minutes.

2. Remove from heat. Stir in butter, lemon zest, lemon juice, and salt. Makes 1½ cups.

JANE BRUCE | Christ Episcopal Church, Charlotte, North Carolina

Boston Peach Layer Cake with Cream Filling

1 cup flour

1 teaspoon baking powder

½ teaspoon salt

3 eggs, separated

⅓ cup water

1 teaspoon grated lemon zest

½ teaspoon vanilla

1 cup sugar

2 tablespoons lemon juice

Whipped cream

CREAM FILLING:

1½ cups milk, divided

2 tablespoons butter

⅓ cup flour

¼ teaspoon salt

⅓ cup sugar

2 egg yolks, lightly beaten

1 teaspoon vanilla

1 can (29 oz.) sliced peaches,
   drained and patted dry

1. Preheat oven to 325°F. Grease two 8 x 1½-inch round cake pans. Line with waxed paper.

2. Sift together flour, baking powder, and salt.

3. Beat egg yolks, water, lemon zest, and vanilla in a mixer bowl until well blended. Add sugar gradually, beating until light and fluffy. Mix in lemon juice. Stir in flour mixture until well blended.

4. Beat egg whites until stiff but still foamy. Fold into batter. Pour batter into pans. Bake for 35 to 40 minutes. Turn out onto wire racks to cool.

5. To make cream filling: Heat 1 cup of the milk and butter in a large saucepan over medium-high heat. Whisk together flour, salt, and sugar, add remaining ½ cup milk, and stir until smooth. Pour into hot milk mixture and continue cooking, stirring continuously, until thick. Add some of the hot mixture to the egg yolks, stir to combine, and return yolks to saucepan, blending to combine. Cook about 2 minutes. Remove from heat, cool for 1 minute, and stir in vanilla.

6. Place one cake layer on a plate. Arrange peach slices on cake, reserving a few for top. Spread cream filling over peaches. Add second cake layer. Top with whipped cream and reserved peach slices. Makes 8 to 10 servings.

MRS. MAYNARD SCHOENBECK | St. John's Guild, St. John's Church, West Bend, Wisconsin

Hot Cross Buns

1 small cake (.6 oz.) compressed
    wet yeast (such as Red Star)
2 tablespoons sugar
2 cups lukewarm milk
6½ cups flour, divided
½ cup butter

⅔ cup sugar
2 eggs
½ teaspoon salt
2 teaspoons cinnamon
½ cup currants

1. Dissolve yeast and sugar in lukewarm milk. Add 3¼ cups of the flour to make a sponge. Beat until smooth. Let rise until light.

2. Cream butter and sugar in a large mixer bowl. Beat in eggs one at a time. Stir in salt, cinnamon, and currants. Fold in sponge. Add remaining 3¼ cups flour. Knead to make a soft dough. Cover and set in a warm place to rise, about 2 hours.

3. Lightly grease two or more baking sheets. Divide dough into three pieces. Roll out each piece into a log. Cut each log crosswise into 10 pieces. Shape each piece into a small, flat bun. Place buns 2 inches apart on baking sheets and grease tops. Let rise until very light, 1½ hours.

4. Preheat over to 375°F. Bake for 20 to 25 minutes or until golden brown. Cut a cross in the top and frost lightly with confectioners' sugar icing. Makes 30 hot cross buns.

Adapted from *The Best of the Old Church Cookbooks* by Florence Ekstrand, courtesy of Welcome Press

Cranberry Holiday Dessert

¾ cup butter
1 cup sugar
2 eggs, beaten
2¼ cups flour
1 teaspoon baking powder
1 teaspoon baking soda
¼ teaspoon salt
1 cup buttermilk

1 cup chopped walnuts
1 cup chopped dates
1 cup cranberries
Grated zest of 2 oranges

SAUCE:
1 cup sugar
1 cup orange juice

1. Preheat oven to 350°F. Grease a 10 x 4-inch tube pan.

2. Cream butter and sugar in a large mixer bowl. Blend in eggs.

3. Sift together flour, baking powder, baking soda, and salt. Add flour mixture and buttermilk alternately to batter, blending well after each addition. Stir in walnuts, dates, cranberries, and orange zest. Pour batter into pan. Bake for 1 hour. Cool in pan for 10 minutes before turning out onto a cake plate.

4. To make sauce: Combine sugar and orange juice. Stir until sugar is dissolved. Pour over warm cake and let stand 24 hours. Serve with whipped cream or hard sauce. Makes 16 servings.

Adapted from *The Best of the Old Church Cookbooks* by Florence Ekstrand, courtesy of Welcome Press

Red Velvet Cake

1 teaspoon vinegar
1 teaspoon baking soda
½ cup butter
½ cup oil
1½ cups sugar
2 eggs
2 bottles (1 oz. each) red food coloring
2 tablespoons cocoa
1 cup buttermilk

1 teaspoon salt
2¼ cups flour
1 teaspoon vanilla

ICING:

1 package (8 oz.) cream cheese, room temperature
½ cup butter
2 cups confectioners' sugar
1 teaspoon vanilla

1. Preheat oven to 350°F. Grease a 13 x 9 x 2-inch baking pan.

2. Mix vinegar and baking soda in a small cup. Let stand until baking soda is dissolved.

3. Cream butter, oil, sugar, and eggs in a mixer bowl until light. Stir food coloring into cocoa to make a paste. Blend paste into butter mixture.

4. With mixer running on medium speed, add buttermilk and salt alternately with flour. Stir in vanilla. Add soda and vinegar mixture and beat until well combined. Turn batter into pan. Bake for 35 minutes. Cool in pan on a wire rack.

5. To make icing: Beat cream cheese, butter, confectioners' sugar, and vanilla until smooth and creamy.

6. Set cake on a large platter. Spread frosting over top and sides. Makes 12 to 14 servings.

❖ LINDA S. THOMPSON | Oakwood Church of God in Christ, Godfrey, Illinois

Christmas Carol Cake

1 cup oil
2 cups white sugar
3 eggs
2 cups flour
2 teaspoons vanilla

1½ teaspoons cinnamon
1 teaspoon baking soda
3 Golden Delicious apples, diced
1 cup chopped nuts
¾ cup raisins

1. Preheat oven to 325°F. Grease and flour a 10 x 4-inch tube pan.

2. Combine oil and sugar in a mixer bowl. With mixer running on low speed, add eggs one at a time, flour, vanilla, cinnamon, and baking soda. Increase speed and beat until well blended. Stir in apples, nuts, and raisins.

3. Pour batter into pan. Bake for 1 hour and 10 minutes or until a tester inserted comes out clean. Cool in pan for 10 minutes before turning out onto a wire rack. Cake may be glazed and decorated if desired. Makes 16 servings.

❖ JOAN HOLOHAN | St. Mark's Lutheran Church, Conshohocken, Pennsylvania

Cinnamon Wreath

2 cups milk

2 packages (.25 oz. each) active dry yeast

¾ cup vegetable shortening

¼ cup butter

½ cup sugar

2 teaspoons salt

2 eggs

6 to 7 cups flour

COATING:

1 cup butter, melted

2 cups sugar

2 tablespoons cinnamon

1. Scald milk. Let cool. Sprinkle yeast on top.

2. Cream shortening, butter, sugar, and salt in a mixer until fluffy. Add eggs, milk with yeast, and 6 cups of the flour. Knead with a dough hook, adding more flour if needed, until dough is smooth and elastic.

3. Place dough in a greased bowl and turn once so greased side is on top. Cover and set in warm place to rise until doubled in bulk, 2 to 4 hours.

4. Punch down dough. Roll out to a ¼-inch thickness. Cut into rounds with a biscuit cutter.

5. To make coating: Grease two ring molds. Stir sugar and cinnamon in a shallow bowl. Dip cut dough rounds one at a time into melted butter and then into cinnamon sugar to coat both sides. Stand up side by side in ring molds. Set aside to rise, ½ hour.

6. Preheat oven to 350°F. Bake in molds for 30 to 40 minutes or until lightly browned. Cool 10 minutes in molds before turning out onto wire racks. Makes 16 to 20 servings.

❖ **JULIE GRIFFO** | United Methodist Church, Estancia, New Mexico

Philly Christmas Cake

1 package (8 oz.) cream cheese,
    room temperature

1 cup butter, room temperature

1½ cups sugar

1 teaspoon vanilla

4 eggs

2¼ cups flour, divided

1½ teaspoons baking powder

1 cup candied fruit

¾ cup chopped nuts, divided

1. Preheat oven to 350°F. Grease a 10 x 4-inch tube pan.

2. Blend cream cheese, butter, sugar, and vanilla in a mixer bowl. Beat in eggs one at a time. Gradually beat in 2 cups of the flour and baking powder.

3. Combine remaining ¼ cup flour with candied fruit and ½ cup of the nuts. Fold into batter. Pour batter into pan. Bake for 1 hour and 20 minutes or until a tester inserted comes out clean. Cool in pan 10 minutes before turning out onto a wire rack. Makes 16 servings.

❖ **BETTY ROTA** | Trinity Evangelical Lutheran Church, Lansdale, Pennsylvania

Love Cake for Mother

1 can obedience
1 pint neatness
1 can running errands
   (Willing Brand)
1 bottle Keep Sunny All Day
1 can pure thoughtfulness

Several lbs. affection
Some holiday, birthday, and
   everyday surprises
1 box powdered get-up-
   when-I-should

Mix well, bake in a warm heart, and serve to Mother every day in big slices.

LOIS M. MCLEAN | Methow Valley United Methodist Church, Twisp, Washington

Pumpkin Nut Cake

3 eggs
1 can (16 oz.) pumpkin
¾ cup vegetable oil
½ cup water
2½ cups flour
1½ teaspoons baking soda
¾ teaspoon nutmeg
2¼ cups sugar
1¼ teaspoons salt

¾ teaspoon cinnamon
1 cup golden raisins
½ cup chopped walnuts plus more for topping

ICING:

½ package (4 oz.) cream cheese, room temperature
½ box (8 oz.) confectioners' sugar
3 tablespoons butter
1 teaspoon vanilla or lemon juice

1. Preheat oven to 350°F. Grease two 9 x 2-inch round cake pans.
2. Combine eggs, pumpkin, oil, and water in a mixer bowl. Whisk together flour, baking soda, nutmeg, sugar, salt, and cinnamon. Add to pumpkin mixture and beat until well combined. Stir in raisins and walnuts. Pour batter into pans. Bake for 40 to 50 minutes or until a tester comes out clean. Cool on wire racks.
3. To make icing: Beat cream cheese, confectioners' sugar, butter, and vanilla or lemon juice in a mixer bowl until smooth.
4. Assemble cake layers, spreading icing as a filling and on top of cake; do not frost sides. Top with walnuts. Makes 8 to 10 servings.

Enjoy this rich, delicious cake in the fall.

DONNA LEIS | Unity Baptist Church, Morgantown, Indiana

Chocolate Trifle

1 package (19.8 oz.) brownie mix
1 package (5.9 oz.) chocolate fudge pudding
8 English toffee bars (4 oz. each),
    frozen and crushed, 1 heaping
    tablespoon reserved for topping

½ cup coffee-flavored liqueur,
    such as Kahlúa
12 oz. whipped cream, frozen
    whipped cream, or frozen
    whipped topping, thawed

1. Prepare brownies according to package directions. Cook, cool, and crumble.

2. Prepare pudding according to package directions. Chill.

3. Layer one-third of crumbled brownies in bottom of a glass trifle bowl. Add one-third of the pudding and one-third of the crushed toffees. Drizzle with one-third of the liqueur. Top with one-third of the whipped cream.

4. Repeat layers two more times until all ingredients are used. Sprinkle reserved crushed toffees on top. Chill until ready to serve. Makes 16 to 18 servings.

❖ **GENIE HUFHAM** | Christ Episcopal Church, Charlotte, North Carolina

Hot Cranberry Bake

4 cups cooking apples, peeled and chopped
2 cups fresh cranberries
1½ teaspoons lemon juice
1 cup sugar

1⅓ cups quick-cooking rolled oats
1 cup chopped walnuts
⅓ cup brown sugar
½ cup butter, melted

1. Preheat oven to 325°F. Lightly grease a 2-quart baking dish.

2. Layer apples and cranberries in baking dish. Sprinkle with lemon juice. Spoon sugar over fruit.

3. Combine oats, walnuts, brown sugar, and melted butter, stirring just until oats are moistened and mixture is crumbly. Sprinkle over fruit. Bake uncovered for 1 hour. Serve warm as a dessert or side dish. Makes 4 to 6 servings.

❖ **CAROL REEDER** and **CAROL NASE** | Trinity Evangelical Lutheran Church, Lansdale, Pennsylvania

Schnecken

1 cup butter, room temperature
2 cups flour
1 egg yolk
⅔ cup sour cream

FILLING:

1 cup sugar
2 teaspoons cinnamon
1 cup chopped walnuts
1 cup raisins

1. Cut butter into flour with a pastry blender until crumbly. Fold egg yolk into sour cream. Blend both mixtures together to make a dough.

2. Divide dough into five parts. Roll each piece into a ball, flatten slightly into a disk, dust with flour, and wrap in waxed paper. Refrigerate overnight or up to 1 week.

3. Preheat oven to 350°F. Grease baking sheets.

4. Combine sugar and cinnamon. Sprinkle work surface with cinnamon sugar. Roll out one dough disk to an 8-or 9-inch circle. Sprinkle cinnamon sugar, walnuts, and raisins on top. Cut like pizza into 12 slices. Roll up each slice, starting at wide end, and set on baking sheet. Repeat until all dough and filling ingredients are used. Bake for 20 minutes. Cool on wire racks. Makes 5 dozen.

MARGUERITE HANNA | Trinity Evangelical Lutheran Church, Lansdale, Pennsylvania

Cammie's Layer Cake with Caramel Frosting

1½ sticks butter, softened	½ teaspoon salt
1½ cups sugar	½ cup milk
4 extra large eggs, divided, room temperature	1 teaspoon vanilla
2 cups flour	¼ teaspoon almond flavoring
2 teaspoons baking powder	Caramel Frosting (recipe follows)

1. Preheat oven to 325°F. Grease and flour two 9 x 2-inch round cake pans.

2. Cream butter and sugar. Mix 3 eggs into the butter and sugar, adding one at a time.

3. Sift together flour, baking powder, and salt. Add to the creamed mixture, alternating with milk. Stir in vanilla and almond flavoring. Add remaining egg and mix well.

4. Pour batter into cake pans. Bake 25 minutes or until toothpick comes out clean. Cool cake thoroughly before frosting.

5. To frost, set cakes on a large platter. Spread frosting over top and sides of each and then stack. Makes 8 to 12 servings.

CARAMEL FROSTING

2 sticks butter	3½ to 4 cups powdered sugar
2 cups packed brown sugar	1 teaspoon vanilla
½ cup milk	

1. Slowly melt butter and then add brown sugar. Bring to a boil. Boil 2 minutes and add milk. Bring back to a boil and remove from heat.

2. Add powdered sugar, mix, and let sit until cool. Beat and add vanilla. Makes enough for 1 cake.

MARY ANNE THOMAS | Christ Episcopal Church, Charlotte, North Carolina

Resurrection Cookies

Make these cookies the night before Easter.

1 cup whole pecans, to be broken   Pinch of salt
1 teaspoon vinegar   1 cup sugar
3 egg whites

1. Preheat oven to 350°F. Grease a baking sheet.

2. Put pecans in a resealable bag. Let the children pound the pecans into pieces with a wooden spoon. Explain that Jesus was beaten and then nailed to a wooden cross. (Read John 19:1–3.)

3. Put vinegar in a mixer bowl. Let the children smell the vinegar. Explain that Jesus was thirsty while on the cross and was offered vinegar to drink. (Read John 19:28–30.)

4. Add egg whites to vinegar. Explain that eggs represent life. Jesus gave His life to give us eternal life. (Read John 10:10–11, 28.)

5. Sprinkle salt into each child's hand and then brush it into the mixture. Have children taste their salty hand. Explain that this reminds us of the tears of those saddened by Jesus' death. (Read Luke 23:27.)

6. Add sugar to mixture. Explain that the sweetest part of the story is that Jesus died because He loves us. His death makes it possible to know Him and believe in Him. (Read Psalm 34:8 and John 3:16.)

7. Beat mixture on high for 12 to 15 minutes or until stiff peaks form. Point out the pearly white color, which represents us being cleansed from sin because of Jesus' death. (Read Isaiah 1:18 and John 3:1–3.)

8. Fold in pecans. Drop by rounded teaspoonful onto baking sheet. Explain that each mound of dough resembles the rocky tomb in which Jesus was placed. (Read Matthew 27:57–60.)

9. Put cookies in oven, close the oven door, and turn oven off. Tape the door shut, allowing each child to help. Explain that Jesus' tomb was sealed. (Read Matthew 27:65–66.)

10. Tell your children it is time to go to bed, even though they may feel sad and disappointed to leave the cookies in the oven with the door taped shut. Explain that Jesus' death seemed final to His followers and they were in despair when His tomb was sealed. (Read John 16:20, 22.)

11. The first thing Easter morning, open the oven and give each child a cookie to eat. They will find each cookie hollow in the middle. Explain that on that first Easter morning, Jesus' followers were amazed to find His tomb open and empty. Jesus is alive! (Read Matthew 28:19.) Makes 2 dozen.

B. K. DREYER | Memorial Baptist Church, Tulsa, Oklahoma

Christmas Cookies

3 cups flour
2 teaspoons baking soda
1 teaspoon salt
2 teaspoons cinnamon
2 cups raisins
1 cup pecans
8 oz. candied mixed fruit

1 cup butter
2 cups sugar
4 eggs
½ cup milk
3 cups rolled oats
1 package (6 oz.) chocolate chips
1 package (14 oz.) shredded coconut

1. Sift together flour, baking soda, salt, and cinnamon.

2. Soak raisins in hot water until plump. Drain well. Pat dry with paper towels. Combine raisins, pecans, and candied mixed fruit. Add 1 tablespoon of the flour mixture and toss to lightly coat.

3. Cream butter and sugar in a mixer bowl. Beat in eggs one at a time. Add flour mixture and milk alternately, mixing well after each addition. Stir in rolled oats, chocolate chips, raisin-pecan-fruit mixture, and coconut. Cover and refrigerate until ready to bake.

4. Preheat oven to 350°F. Drop dough by teaspoonful onto greased baking sheets. Bake for 12 to 15 minutes or until lightly browned. Cool on wire racks. Makes 6 dozen.

VIRGINIA RATLIFF | Memorial Baptist Church, Tulsa, Oklahoma

Daisy Dearing's Christmas Lizzies

5½ cups flour
1 teaspoon baking soda
1 teaspoon cinnamon
1 teaspoon nutmeg
1 teaspoon cloves
1 teaspoon allspice
6 cups pecans
2 lbs. candied cherries

1 lb. white raisins
1 lb. dark raisins
2 lbs. candied pineapple
½ cup butter
1½ cups brown sugar
4 eggs
2 tablespoons milk
1 cup whiskey or lemon-lime soft drink (such as 7-Up)

1. Preheat oven to 325°F. Grease baking sheets.

2. Whisk together flour, baking soda, cinnamon, nutmeg, cloves, and allspice.

3. Combine pecans, cherries, white raisins, dark raisins, and pineapple in a large bowl. Add 1 cup of the flour mixture and toss to coat.

4. Cream butter in a mixer bowl. Gradually blend in brown sugar. Add eggs one at a time, beating well after each addition. Stir milk into whiskey or soft drink. Add flour mixture and milk mixture alternately, blending well after each addition.

5. Drop by teaspoonful onto baking sheets. Bake for 12 to 15 minutes or until lightly browned. Makes 6 dozen.

KATHY NICHOLS | Terrace Acres Baptist Church, Fort Worth, Texas

Sugar Cookies

½ cup butter, room temperature
1 cup sugar
1 teaspoon vanilla
2 medium eggs
2 to 2½ cups flour, divided

1 teaspoon baking powder
½ teaspoon salt
¼ teaspoon nutmeg
Colored sugar, silver balls, or citron

1. Cream butter in a mixer bowl. Cream in sugar and vanilla. Beat in eggs one at a time until light and fluffy.

2. Sift together 2 cups of the flour, baking powder, salt, and nutmeg. Add flour mixture and mix until blended. Add more flour, up to ½ cup, if dough is too moist or sticky for rolling. Cover and chill at least 2 hours or overnight.

3. Preheat oven to 375°F. Grease baking sheets.

4. Roll out dough on a floured board or waxed paper. Cut dough with cookie cutters and transfer to baking sheets with a wide, flat spatula. Decorate with colored sugar, silver balls, or citron. Bake for 10 minutes or until light golden. Cool on wire racks. Makes 3 dozen.

 **RUTH B. JOSEPH** | Trinity Evangelical Lutheran Church, Lansdale, Pennsylvania

California Christmas Fruitcake

1 cup pitted prunes, chopped
1 jar (4 oz.) candied mixed fruits
1 cup chopped walnuts
¼ cup flour
1 package (1 lb.) pound cake mix
1 tablespoon grated orange zest
½ teaspoon ground mace

½ cup milk
2 eggs
¼ cup brandy or fruit juice
¼ cup light corn syrup, warmed
   until bubbly
Confectioners' sugar icing

1. Preheat oven to 350°F. Grease a 9 x 5 x 3-inch loaf pan, dust lightly with flour, and tap out excess.

2. Combine prunes, mixed fruits, and walnuts in a large bowl. Sprinkle with flour and toss to coat.

3. Combine pound cake mix, orange zest, and mace in large mixer bowl. Add milk and beat at medium speed 2 minutes. Add eggs and brandy or fruit juice and beat 2 minutes more.

4. Pour batter over prunes, mixed fruit, and walnuts and fold gently until well blended. Spoon batter into pan. Bake for 1 hour and 15 minutes or until center springs back when lightly pressed with fingertip. Cool in pan on a wire rack for 30 minutes. Loosen edges with a knife, turn out onto rack, and cool completely.

5. Brush warm corn syrup over top of loaf. Drizzle with confectioners' sugar icing. Makes 8 to 10 servings.

NORMA WHITE | St. Mark's Lutheran Church, Conshohocken, Pennsylvania

Old Fashioned Fruitcake

2¼ cups flour
1½ teaspoons baking powder
½ teaspoon baking soda
½ teaspoon salt
1 jar (27 oz.) mincemeat
1 cup raisins

1 cup chopped nuts
1 cup sugar
1 cup butter, melted
1 teaspoon vanilla
2 eggs

1. Preheat oven to 325°F. Grease a 10 x 4-inch tube pan and line with waxed paper.
2. Sift together flour, baking powder, baking soda, and salt in a large bowl.
3. In a separate bowl, combine mincemeat, raisins, nuts, sugar, melted butter, and vanilla. Whisk in eggs. Fold egg mixture into flour mixture. Pour batter into pan. Bake for 1½ hours or until a toothpick inserted near center comes out clean. Cool in pan 10 minutes before turning out onto a wire rack. Makes 16 servings.

EVELYN ASH | Vincent Memorial United Methodist Church, Nutter Fort, West Virginia

Spiced Ornaments

⅓ cup applesauce
1 teaspoon allspice
1 teaspoon cinnamon
1 teaspoon cloves
1 teaspoon ginger

1 teaspoon mace
1 teaspoon nutmeg
2 teaspoons orrisroot powder
Ribbon or string

1. Stir applesauce, allspice, cinnamon, cloves, ginger, mace, nutmeg, and orrisroot powder in a small bowl until thoroughly combined.
2. Form mixture into small balls, bells, Christmas trees, and other holiday shapes, no larger than 1½ inches across; or roll out to a ¼-inch thickness and cut with tiny cookie cutters. Add a few drops of water if mixture dries.
3. Insert toothpicks in top of ornaments to make holes for ribbon or string hangers.
4. Preheat oven to 250°F. Place ornaments on a baking sheet. Bake, turning once, for 2 to 2½ hours or until dry. (Or heat in microwave on low, turning once, for 15 to 20 minutes. Ornaments may be slightly soft but will harden over time.)
5. Remove toothpicks, run ribbon or string through the holes, and tie the ends together. Use as tree ornaments or gift toppers. Store from year to year in resealable plastic bags to retain fragrance. Makes 12 to 16 ornaments

SUSAN BISHOP | Trinity Evangelical Lutheran Church, Lansdale, Pennsylvania

Our Favorite Christmas Cookies

1 cup vegetable shortening

1 cup sugar

1 cup brown sugar

2 eggs

1 teaspoon vanilla

1½ cups flour

1 teaspoon baking soda

1 teaspoon salt

3 cups quick-cooking rolled oats

½ cup chopped walnuts

1. Cream shortening, sugar, and brown sugar. Beat in eggs and vanilla.

2. Sift together flour, baking soda, and salt. Add to egg mixture and beat to combine. Stir in oats and walnuts.

3. Form dough into one or two rolls, 1 to 1½-inches in diameter. Wrap in waxed paper and chill in refrigerator for at least 30 minutes or overnight.

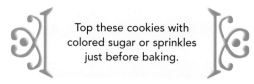

Top these cookies with colored sugar or sprinkles just before baking.

4. Preheat oven to 350°F. Slice dough into ¼-inch-thick rounds and place on ungreased baking sheets. Bake for 10 minutes or until lightly browned. Transfer to wire racks and allow to cool. Makes 5 dozen.

❖ **THE CRAIG DAVISON FAMILY** | First Presbyterian Church, Du Quoin, Illinois

Cranberry Christmas Cookies

⅔ cup butter

⅔ cup brown sugar

2 eggs

1½ cups rolled oats

1½ cups flour

1 teaspoon baking soda

½ teaspoon salt

1 package (6 oz.) dried cranberries

⅔ cup white or semisweet chocolate chips

⅓ cup coconut flakes

1. Preheat oven to 375°F.

2. Cream butter and brown sugar in a mixer bowl until fluffy. Add eggs and mix well.

3. Whisk together oats, flour, baking soda, and salt. Add to butter mixture in batches, mixing well after each addition. Stir in cranberries, chocolate chips, and coconut flakes.

4. Drop by rounded teaspoonfuls onto ungreased baking sheets. Bake for 10 to 12 minutes. Cool on wire racks. Makes 3½ dozen.

❖ **BARBARA LASLEY** | Memorial Baptist Church, Tulsa, Oklahoma

Coconut Cream Eggs

½ cup butter, room temperature
1 teaspoon vanilla
⅔ cup condensed milk
6 cups confectioners' sugar

Shredded coconut
8 squares (1 oz. each) unsweetened
   or semisweet chocolate

1. Cream butter in a large mixer bowl until light and fluffy. Add vanilla and condensed milk and beat until thoroughly blended. Add sugar 2 cups at a time, blending well after each addition. Stir in coconut.
2. Turn out mixture onto a counter and knead to a smooth fondant consistency.
3. Pinch off about 2 tablespoons of fondant and form into a small egg shape, no larger than 1 inch. Set on a tray or plate lined with waxed paper. Repeat until all fondant is used. Refrigerate eggs for 2 to 3 hours (chilling helps the chocolate adhere).
4. Melt chocolate in a microwave or the top of a double boiler. Transfer melted chocolate to a small round glass baking dish and cool slightly.
5. To coat eggs, tilt dish so chocolate pools and drop in one egg, rounded side down. Turn the egg to coat with a long-tined fork and lift it back onto the waxed paper to cool. Reheat the chocolate if it becomes too firm to handle. Makes 4 to 5 dozen candies.

DONNA LEIS | Unity Baptist Church, Morgantown, Indiana

Peanut Butter Eggs

¾ cup peanut butter
½ teaspoon salt
1 teaspoon vanilla
1 can (14 oz.) sweetened condensed milk
1 box (1 lb.) confectioners' sugar
8 squares (1 oz. each) unsweetened
   milk chocolate

Chocolate-covered fondant eggs do take time to make but everyone seems to love them. Semisweet and white chocolate are especially delicious on coconut cream eggs!

Cream peanut butter and salt in a large mixer bowl. Add vanilla and condensed milk and beat until thoroughly blended. Add sugar 2 cups at a time, blending well after each addition. Follow steps 2–5 in recipe above (Coconut Cream Eggs) to form eggs and coat with chocolate. Makes 5 dozen candies.

DONNA LEIS | Unity Baptist Church, Morgantown, Indiana

Pizelle

3 eggs
¾ cup sugar
¾ cup butter, melted
2 teaspoons vanilla
1 teaspoon anise extract
1½ cups flour

Shape warm pizelle into tubes by rolling around them around a narrow rolling pin or dowel. Let cool until crisp and use for Italian-style pastry desserts.

1. Heat electric pizelle maker following manufacturer's instructions.
2. Whisk together eggs, sugar, melted butter, vanilla, and anise extract.
3. Blend in flour to make a smooth batter.
4. Pour ¼ cup of mixture into hot pizelle maker. Cook until steam stops, typically 1 minute or less. Remove pizelle and set on a wire rack to cool. Repeat until all batter is used. Makes 5 dozen.

MARGUERITE HANNA | Trinity Evangelical Lutheran Church, Lansdale, Pennsylvania

Cindy's Swedish Kringle

½ cup softened butter
1 cup flour
1 tablespoon water

TOP LAYER:
1 cup water
½ cup butter
1 cup flour
3 eggs
½ teaspoon almond or lemon extract

FROSTING:
2 cups confectioners' sugar
2 tablespoons butter, room temperature
1 teaspoon almond or lemon extract
Enough cream or milk to spread

1. Preheat oven to 350°F. Lightly grease a baking sheet.
2. Cut butter into flour until crumbly. Add water and stir to make a dough. Form into a doughnut shape and place on baking sheet.
3. To make top layer: Combine water and butter in a large saucepan over medium-high heat. Bring to a boil. Remove from heat, add flour all at once, and mix well. Beat in eggs one at a time. Stir in almond or lemon extract. Spread mixture on top of the dough. Bake for 40 minutes. Cool on a wire rack.
4. To make frosting: Combine confectioners' sugar, butter, and almond or lemon extract in a bowl. Mix in cream or milk 1 tablespoon at a time until frosting is of spreading consistency but not too runny. Spread on top of kringle. Makes 12 to 14 servings.

STEPHANIE LAGERS | Memorial Baptist Church, Tulsa, Oklahoma

Double Chocolate Brownies

¾ cup flour

¼ teaspoon baking soda

¼ teaspoon salt

⅓ cup butter

¾ cup sugar

2 tablespoons water

1 package (12 oz.) semisweet chocolate chips, divided

2 eggs

1 teaspoon vanilla

½ cup chopped pecans

1. Preheat oven to 325°F. Grease and flour a 9 x 9 x 2-inch baking pan.

2. Sift together flour, baking soda, and salt.

3. Combine butter, sugar, and water in a small saucepan over medium heat. Bring to a boil, remove from heat, and add half of the chocolate chips. Stir until butter and chocolate are melted and sauce is smooth.

4. Transfer chocolate sauce to a large mixer bowl. Add eggs one at a time, beating well after each addition. Gradually blend in flour mixture. Stir in remaining chocolate chips, vanilla, and pecans. Pour batter into pan. Bake for 40 to 45 minutes. Cool in pan 30 minutes. Cut into squares. Makes 8 to 10 servings.

❖ **SENATOR SAM NUNN** | Christ Church, Frederica, St. Simons Island, Georgia

Christmas Snowball Cookies

1 cup butter

½ cup confectioners' sugar,
   plus more for coating

1 teaspoon vanilla

2¼ cups all-purpose flour

¼ teaspoon salt

¾ cup almonds, finely ground

For fresh almond flavor, grind whole almonds in a blender, food processor, or mini chopper. Allow 1¼ cups of whole almonds for every 1 cup of ground almonds.

1. Cream butter in the large bowl of an electric mixer. Add sugar and beat until light and fluffy. Stir in vanilla.

2. Sift together flour and salt. Add gradually to butter mixture, mixing until well combined. Stir in ground almonds. Wrap dough in plastic wrap and chill for 1 hour.

3. Preheat oven to 350°F. Shape dough into walnut-size balls and place on a baking sheet. Bake for 15 minutes. Roll cookies in confectioners' sugar while still warm. Store in a covered tin at room temperature. Makes 3 dozen.

❖ **ANNE RITTER** | Trinity Evangelical Lutheran Church, Lansdale, Pennsylvania

Jack-o'-Lantern Cookies

1½ packages (12 oz.) cream cheese,
    room temperature
1½ cups butter
1 cup sugar plus more for coating
1 teaspoon vanilla
3¼ cups flour

FROSTING:

½ package (4 oz.) cream cheese,
    room temperature
1 tablespoon milk
1 teaspoon grated orange zest
3 cups confectioners' sugar
Red and yellow food coloring
Raisins, licorice laces, and candy corn

1. Combine cream cheese, butter, sugar, and vanilla in a mixer bowl. Add flour and mix until well blended. Cover and chill several hours or overnight.

2. Preheat oven to 350°F. Lightly grease baking sheets.

3. Shape dough into 1½-inch balls. Set balls on baking sheet. Flatten with a drinking glass dipped in sugar to make 3-inch circles. Bake for 12 to 15 minutes or until edges are lightly browned. Cool on wire racks.

4. To make frosting: Combine cream cheese, milk, and orange zest until well blended. Gradually add confectioners' sugar, beating smooth after each addition. Add red and yellow food coloring to tint frosting orange.

A little food coloring goes a long way. Follow the package instructions to add just the amount you need and to mix colors. You can also use paste food colors, sold in the decorative baking aisle of craft stores.

5. Spread frosting on cookies. Decorate with raisins, licorice laces, and candy corn to resemble jack-o'-lanterns. Makes 3 dozen.

❖ LINDA SCHECKENBACH | Trinity Evangelical Lutheran Church, Lansdale, Pennsylvania

Bridegroom's Cake

2 cups sugar
4 eggs
1½ cups oil
¼ teaspoon vanilla
1 teaspoon cinnamon

2 cups flour
2 teaspoons baking soda
¼ teaspoon salt
3 cups grated carrots
½ cup chopped nuts

1. Preheat oven to 350°F. Grease a 13 x 9 x 2-inch baking pan. Line pan with waxed paper.

2. Combine sugar, eggs, oil, vanilla, and cinnamon in a mixer bowl. Add flour, baking soda, and salt until well blended. Stir in carrots and nuts. Pour batter into pan. Bake for 45 minutes. Cool in pan 5 minutes before turning out onto a wire rack. Makes 12 to 14 servings.

❖ MARY L. ZELLER | Methow Valley United Methodist Church, Twisp, Washington

A Dinner for a Couple to Be Married

O gracious God, you consecrate all that is lovely, good and true.
Bless thou who in your presence wait and every day their love renew.

—Russell Schulz-Widmar (b.1944) [Hymn 353, v. 2]

A dinner party celebrating the soon-to-be-wed couple is the perfect time to indulge in favorites and fantasies. When I am preparing a meal for such an occasion, I banish the idea of a heavy traditional meal and head in the direction of the light and unusual. In honoring this new bond and covenant of husband and wife, the food should be light and elegant with a contrast of color, shape, and texture. It is a time in life when thoughts are turned to romance and love.

Celebrations like these call for professions of love and passion. Invite other couples who will be willing to speak of their love, their faith together, their times of struggle and disappointment, their moments of joy and of mystical union. I once attended such a party where an older gentleman who had been married for many years stood up, wished the couple well, and quoted from an Elizabeth Barrett Browning sonnet to describe the love he and his wife still shared:

How do I love thee? Let me count the ways.
I love thee to the depth and breadth and height
My soul can reach, when feeling out of sight
. . . and, if God choose,
I shall but love thee better after death.

THE REVEREND BRIAN S. SUNTKEN
Christ Episcopal Church, Charlotte, North Carolina

SUGGESTED MENU

Oriental Chicken Wontons, page 192
Split Pea Soup, page 200
Make-Ahead Buffet Shrimp Casserole, page 156
Microwaved Asparagus, page 213
Poppy Seed Bread, page 278
Cammie's Layer Cake with Caramel Frosting, page 231

Mexican Wedding Cake

2 cups sugar
2 cups flour
2 teaspoons baking soda
1 can (20 oz.) crushed pineapple,
    juice reserved
2 eggs
1 cup chopped nuts

FROSTING:

1 small package (3 oz.) cream cheese,
    room temperature
¼ cup butter
1 teaspoon vanilla
1 to 2 cups confectioners' sugar

1. Preheat oven to 350°F. Grease and flour a 13 x 9 x 2-inch baking pan.

2. Combine sugar, flour, baking soda, pineapple and juice, eggs, and nuts in a mixer bowl. Beat until well blended. Pour batter into pan. Bake for 30 to 35 minutes. Cool in pan on a wire rack.

3. To make frosting: Beat cream cheese, butter, and vanilla in a mixer bowl until smooth. Beat in confectioners' sugar ¼ cup at a time until frosting reaches desired consistency. Spread frosting on cooled cake. Makes 12 to 14 servings.

WILMA BOWER | Memorial Baptist Church, Tulsa, Oklahoma

Southern Christening Cake

1½ cups butter
4 cups sugar
7 eggs, separated
4 cups flour
2 or 3 teaspoons baking powder

3 teaspoons nutmeg
1 cup sherry
1½ lbs. raisins or currants
1 cup chopped pecans
White icing

1. Preheat oven 300°F. Generously butter a 15½ x 10½ x 1-inch sheet pan.

2. Cream butter and sugar in the large bowl of an electric mixer. Whisk egg yolks until light and lemon colored, add to butter mixture, and beat until well blended.

3. Sift together flour, baking powder, and nutmeg. Add flour mixture and sherry alternately to batter, beating after each addition. Stir in raisins and pecans.

4. In a separate bowl, beat egg whites until stiff. Fold into batter. Gently transfer batter to pan. Bake for 4 hours. Cool in pan to room temperature. Frost with white icing. Makes 16 to 20 servings.

MARTHA RUSSELL | Christ Church, Frederica, St. Simons Island, Georgia

Our Family's Favorite Birthday Cake

1 cup butter

2 cups sugar

3 or 4 eggs

3 cups flour

3 teaspoons baking powder

¼ teaspoon salt

1 cup milk

1 teaspoon vanilla

ICING:

4½ teaspoons butter

3 cups sugar

1½ to 2 tablespoons orange juice

Grated zest and pulp of small orange

1 egg white, beaten until stiff

ORANGE FILLING:

¼ cup sugar

1½ teaspoons flour

¼ teaspoon salt

½ cup orange juice

2 teaspoons grated orange zest

1 egg yolk

2 teaspoons butter

1 teaspoon lemon juice

1. Preheat oven to 350°F. Grease and flour two 9 x 2-inch round cake pans.

2. Cream butter and sugar in a large mixer bowl. Add eggs one at a time, beating well after each addition.

3. Whisk together flour, baking powder, and salt. Add flour mixture and milk alternately to batter, mixing until well blended. Stir in vanilla. Pour batter into pans. Bake for 35 minutes or until a tester inserted in center comes out clean. Cool in pans 5 minutes before turning out onto wire racks.

4. To make orange filling: Combine sugar, flour, and salt in a medium saucepan. Stir in orange juice, orange zest, egg yolk, and butter. Cook on low heat until smooth and thickened. Remove from heat and blend in lemon juice.

5. To make orange icing: Cream butter and sugar until smooth. Beat in orange juice and orange zest and pulp. Mix well. Fold in egg white.

6. Layer cakes on a plate with orange filling in between. Spread orange icing over sides and top of the cake. Makes 8 servings.

❖ **JOYCE BITNER** | Trinity Evangelical Lutheran Church, Lansdale, Pennsylvania

Extra Elegant Apple Pie

2 tablespoons flour
½ teaspoon salt
¾ cup sugar
1 egg, beaten
1 cup sour cream
½ teaspoon vanilla
2 to 3 cups sliced apples
1 unbaked 9-inch pie shell

TOPPING:
⅓ cup sugar
⅓ cup flour
1 teaspoon cinnamon
¼ cup butter

1. Preheat oven to 425°F.
2. Sift together flour, salt, and sugar in a large bowl. Mix in egg, sour cream, and vanilla until well blended. Fold in apples. Spread mixture in pie shell. Bake for 15 minutes. Reduce heat to 350°F and bake 30 minutes more.
3. To make topping: Whisk together sugar, flour, and cinnamon. Cut in butter to resemble coarse crumbs.
4. Remove pie from oven. Increase oven temperature to 400°F. Sprinkle topping on pie, return to oven, and bake 10 minutes more. Cool at least 30 minutes before serving. Makes 6 to 8 servings.

SANDY BIXBY | Trinity Evangelical Lutheran Church, Lansdale, Pennsylvania

Banana Cream Pie

2 large bananas
1 baked 9-inch pie shell
¾ cup sugar
2 tablespoons flour
2 tablespoons butter
Pinch of salt
3 egg yolks
1 can (12 oz.) evaporated milk plus
　　whole milk to measure 2 cups
1 teaspoon vanilla

MERINGUE:
3 egg whites
6 tablespoons sugar
Pinch of salt
1 teaspoon vanilla

 The bananas and filling can also be served without the piecrust as a banana pudding. Evaporated milk makes this filling extra rich.

1. Preheat oven to 350°F.
2. Slice bananas and layer into pie shell.
3. Combine sugar and flour in the top of a double boiler. Add butter, salt, egg yolks, and milk. Cook over simmering water, stirring continuously, until thick, 10 to 12 minutes. Remove from heat and stir in vanilla. Pour filling into pie shell. Do not cool.
4. To make meringue: Beat egg whites until stiff. Gradually beat in sugar, salt, and vanilla. Spread meringue over hot pie filling. Bake until meringue is lightly browned, 12 to 15 minutes. Makes 8 servings.

JEANNE ALAIMO | Christ Church, Frederica, St. Simons Island, Georgia

Let the Women Lead the Way

Do you know what would have happened if it had been three wise women instead of three wise men? They would have asked for directions, arrived on time, helped deliver the baby, cleaned the stable, made a casserole, and brought practical gifts.

LORRAINE SIMPSON | Garden City, Georgia
from Dinner on the Grounds by Darrell Huckaby

Upside-Down Apple Pecan Pie

1 cup chopped pecans
½ cup brown sugar
⅓ cup butter, melted
1 package (15 oz.) refrigerated
    piecrust pastry

6 cups apples, peeled and sliced
¼ cup sugar
2 tablespoons flour
½ teaspoon cinnamon
⅛ teaspoon nutmeg

1. Preheat oven at 375°F. Lightly grease a 9-inch pie plate.

2. Combine pecans, brown sugar, and melted butter. Layer mixture in bottom of pie plate.

3. Prepare piecrust pastry following package directions. Layer pastry for bottom crust over pecan mixture in pie plate.

4. Combine apples, sugar, flour, cinnamon, and nutmeg in a large bowl. Spoon over pastry in pan. Top with remaining pastry. Flute the edges to seal in the apple filling. Cut slits in the top. Place on a baking sheet in oven. Bake for 40 to 50 minutes or until lightly browned. Cool in pie plate for 20 minutes.

5. Invert pie onto a serving plate. Use a knife to loosen pecans that remain stuck to the bottom of the pie plate. Layer them on top. Cool at least 1 hour before serving. Makes 6 to 8 servings.

JUDY LORENSON | Trinity Evangelical Lutheran Church, Lansdale, Pennsylvania

How to invert an upside-down pie: Turn a serving plate over and place it facedown on the pie plate. Grab both pieces with your hands, hold them together firmly, and flip them over in one smooth motion, so that the serving plate is on the bottom. Slowly and carefully lift off the pie plate, using a knife to loosen any parts that are sticking.

Brandy Alexander Pie

1 envelope (.25 oz.) unflavored gelatin
½ cup cold water
⅔ cup sugar, divided
⅛ teaspoon salt
3 eggs, separated

¼ cup brandy
¼ cup crème de cacao
2 cups heavy cream, whipped, divided
One 9-inch graham cracker piecrust
Chocolate curls

1. Sprinkle gelatin over cold water in a saucepan. Add ⅓ cup of the sugar, salt, and egg yolks. Stir to blend. Cook over low heat, stirring continuously, until gelatin dissolves and mixture thickens. Do not boil.

2. Remove gelatin mixture from heat. Stir in brandy and crème de cacao. Chill until mixture thickens slightly, 5 to 10 minutes.

3. Beat egg whites until stiff. Gradually beat in remaining ⅓ cup sugar. Fold egg whites into chilled mixture. Fold 1 cup of the whipped cream into mixture. Turn filling into piecrust and smooth the top. Chill for 4 hours.

4. Top with remaining whipped cream and garnish with chocolate curls. Makes 8 to 10 servings.

RUTH S. DELP | Trinity Evangelical Lutheran Church, Lansdale, Pennsylvania

Butterscotch Meringue Pie

⅓ cup sifted flour
1 cup brown sugar
¼ teaspoon salt
2 cups milk, scalded
3 egg yolks, beaten slightly
3 tablespoons butter
½ teaspoon vanilla
1 baked 9-inch pie shell

MERINGUE:
3 egg whites
¼ teaspoon salt
6 tablespoons sugar
½ teaspoon vanilla

1. Whisk together flour, sugar, and salt in a saucepan. Set over medium heat. Gradually add milk, stirring constantly, until mixture thickens and boils. Cook 2 minutes. Remove from heat.

2. Stir a small amount of hot milk mixture into egg yolks to temper. Add tempered yolks to mixture in saucepan. Cook, stirring continuously, 1 minute. Add butter and vanilla. Cool slightly. Pour into pastry shell and cool.

3. Preheat oven to 350°F.

4. To make meringue: Whip egg whites and salt until frothy. Beat in sugar, one tablespoon at a time, until meringue is stiff and glossy. Add vanilla and beat just until blended.

5. Spread meringue over pie filling. Bake for 10 to 15 minutes or until meringue is set and lightly browned. Makes 6 to 8 servings.

MARY EVELYN HILL | First Baptist Church, Russell, Kentucky

Caramel Chocolate Pie

2 cups milk
⅓ cup sugar
⅓ cup brown sugar
⅓ cup flour
¼ teaspoon salt
3 egg yolks, beaten
2 tablespoons butter
1 teaspoon vanilla
½ sq. (½ oz.) bitter baking chocolate, shaved
1 baked 9-inch pie shell

MERINGUE:
3 egg whites
¼ cup sugar

1. Combine milk, sugar, brown sugar, flour, and salt in the top half of a double boiler. Cook, stirring frequently, until slightly thickened, 12 to 15 minutes.
2. Stir in egg yolks and cook 5 minutes more. Remove from heat. Add butter and vanilla. Stir until butter is melted. Cool slightly. Stir in shaved chocolate. Cool and pour into baked pie shell.
3. Preheat oven to 325°F.
4. To make meringue: Whip 3 egg whites until stiff peaks form. Gradually beat in sugar.
5. Spread meringue over pie filling. Bake for 10 to 15 minutes or until meringue is set and lightly browned. Makes 6 to 8 servings.

❖ JUNE SPIELMAN | St. John's Guild, St. John's Church, West Bend, Wisconsin

Ann's Kentucky Derby Pie

2 eggs
½ cup sugar
½ cup brown sugar
½ cup flour
½ cup butter, melted
3 tablespoons bourbon

1 package (6 oz.) chocolate chips, melted
1 cup chopped pecans
1 unbaked 9-inch pie shell
½ cup heavy cream, whipped and sweetened
Shaved chocolate or chocolate sprinkles

1. Preheat oven to 350°F.
2. Beat eggs in a mixer bowl until foamy. Gradually add sugar, brown sugar, and flour, beating until smooth.
3. Blend in melted butter. Stir in bourbon, melted chocolate chips, and pecans.
4. Pour filling into pie shell. Bake for 35 minutes or until set. Cool in pie plate. Chill in refrigerator at least 4 hours or overnight. Serve topped with whipped cream and chocolate shavings or sprinkles. Makes 6 to 8 servings.

❖ BETSY LOCKE | Christ Episcopal Church, Charlotte, North Carolina

Eggnog Chiffon Pie

18 graham crackers, crushed
1 tablespoon flour
¼ cup sugar
⅓ cup butter, melted

FILLING:

1 envelope (.25 oz.) unflavored gelatin
4 eggs, separated
¾ cup sugar, divided
½ cup hot water
½ teaspoon salt
2 tablespoons rum
¼ teaspoon nutmeg

1. Preheat oven to 350°F. Lightly grease a 9-inch pie plate.

2. Stir together graham cracker crumbs, flour, sugar, and melted butter. Press mixture into bottom and up sides of pie plate. Bake for 5 minutes. Cool.

3. To make filling: Dissolve gelatin in cold water. Combine egg yolks, ¼ cup of the sugar, hot water, and salt in the top of a double boiler. Cook over boiling water to custard consistency. Stir in gelatin, rum, and nutmeg. Beat egg whites with remaining ½ cup sugar and fold into custard.

4. Pour filling into pie shell. Let stand 5 to 6 hours until firm. Chill until ready to serve. Makes 6 to 8 servings.

MRS. CLARENCE ZIMBRICK | St. John's Guild, St. John's Church, West Bend, Wisconsin

French Chocolate Mint Pie

1¼ cup vanilla wafer crumbs
⅓ cup butter, melted

FILLING:

½ cup butter
1½ cups sifted confectioners' sugar
2 squares (1 oz. each) bitter chocolate, melted
2 eggs, beaten
½ teaspoon vanilla
5 drops oil of peppermint

Whipped cream

1. Preheat oven to 350°F. Lightly grease an 8-inch pie plate.
2. Combine vanilla wafer crumbs and melted butter. Press mixture into bottom and up sides of pie plate. Bake for 10 minutes. Cool.
3. To make filling: Cream butter and confectioners' sugar. Beat in melted chocolate. Add eggs, vanilla, and peppermint oil. Beat until light in color.
4. Pour filling over crumb crust. Chill at least 4 hours or overnight. Serve topped with whipped cream. Makes 6 to 8 servings.

MELISSA BARNES | Christ Church, Frederica, St. Simons Island, Georgia

Chocolate Amaretto Pie

¼ cup butter
½ cup unsweetened cocoa
1 cup butter, room temperature
1½ cups superfine sugar

¼ cup Amaretto liqueur
4 eggs, room temperature
1 baked 9-inch pie shell

1. Melt butter in a small heavy saucepan over medium heat. Remove from heat and stir in cocoa until well blended.
2. Cream butter and sugar in a large mixer bowl. Beat in Amaretto liqueur. Add eggs one at a time, beating 3 minutes after each addition. Continue beating until sugar is dissolved. Add cocoa mixture and stir until smooth.
3. Pour filling into pie shell. Cover and refrigerate at least 4 hours or until firm. Serve chilled. Makes 6 to 8 servings.

CAM CALDWELL | Christ Church, Frederica, St. Simons Island, Georgia

Pecan Pie

1 unbaked 9-inch pie shell
3 eggs, beaten
1 cup light brown sugar
1 cup pecans

½ cup light corn syrup
1 teaspoon vinegar
½ teaspoon vanilla
¼ teaspoon salt

1. Preheat oven to 450°F.

2. Combine eggs, light brown sugar, pecans, light corn syrup, vinegar, vanilla, and salt in a large bowl.

3. Pour into unbaked pie shell. Bake for 10 minutes. Reduce heat to 350°F and bake 55 to 60 minutes more. Cool. Makes 6 to 8 servings.

JULIE ADAMS | Unity Baptist Church, Morgantown, Indiana

French Chocolate Silk Pie

½ cup butter
¾ cup sugar
1 square (1 oz.) dark chocolate, melted
1 teaspoon vanilla

2 eggs
1 baked 9-inch pie shell
Whipped cream

1. Cream butter and sugar until fluffy. Beat in melted chocolate and vanilla until thoroughly blended.

2. Add eggs one at a time, beating 3 minutes after each addition.

3. Pour filling into pie shell. Chill at least 4 hours or overnight. Serve topped with whipped cream. Makes 6 to 8 servings.

MRS. ROBERT W. PETERS | Christ Church, Frederica, St. Simons Island, Georgia

Juanita's Chess Pie

½ cup butter
1 cup sugar
3 eggs

½ cup whole milk or cream
Nutmeg
1 baked 9-inch pie shell

1. Preheat oven to 300°F.

2. Cream butter and sugar.

3. Beat in eggs one at a time. Add milk or cream, sprinkle in nutmeg, and stir to combine. Pour into baked pie shell. Bake 45 to 60 minutes or until firm. Cool on a wire rack. Makes 6 to 8 servings.

BECK and HENRY PARSLEY | Christ Episcopal Church, Charlotte, North Carolina

Dinner for the Adult Confirmands

~ SUGGESTED MENU ~

Roasted Red Pepper and Garlic Dip
PAGE 192

Linguine with Tomatoes and Basil
PAGE 204

Lime Chicken
PAGE 208

Greek-Style Salad
PAGE 219

French Bread

Chocolate Trifle
PAGE 230

CHRIST EPISCOPAL CHURCH
Charlotte, North Carolina

Mile High Raspberry Pie

ALMOND PASTRY CRUST:

¼ cup butter

¼ teaspoon salt

2 tablespoons sugar

1 egg yolk

¾ cup flour

¼ cup almonds, finely chopped

RASPBERRY FILLING:

2 cups fresh or 1 package (10 oz.) frozen raspberries, thawed (reserve a few raspberries for garnish)

1 cup sugar

2 egg whites, room temperature

1 tablespoon lemon juice

Dash of salt

1 cup heavy cream, whipped

½ teaspoon almond extract

1. To make almond pastry crust: Cream butter, salt, and sugar in a mixer bowl until light and fluffy. Add egg yolk and beat well. Stir in flour and almonds to make dough. Press dough into bottom and up sides of a 9-inch pie plate. Refrigerate 30 minutes.

2. Preheat oven to 400°F. Bake pastry crust for 15 minutes. Cool.

3. To make filling: Combine raspberries, sugar, egg whites, lemon juice, and salt in a mixer bowl. Beat until stiff, 15 minutes. Fold in whipped cream and almond extract.

4. Mound filling in pastry shell. Freeze until firm, 2 to 3 hours. Remove from freezer 30 to 45 minutes before serving and garnish with reserved raspberries. Makes 8 servings.

ANNE RITTER | Trinity Evangelical Lutheran Church, Lansdale, Pennsylvania

Lemon Meringue Pie

½ cup plus 1 tablespoon flour

1¼ cups sugar

1¾ cups water

1½ tablespoons butter

3 egg yolks

¼ cup fresh lemon juice

2 teaspoons grated lemon zest

1 baked 9-inch pie shell

MERINGUE:

3 egg whites

6 tablespoons sugar, divided

1. Preheat oven to 375°F.

2. Sift flour and sugar into a large saucepan. Add water and butter, set over low heat, and cook, stirring continuously, until thick. Remove from heat.

3. Beat egg yolks. Spoon a small amount of the hot mixture into egg yolks, stir to temper yolks, and return yolks to pan. Cook, stirring continuously over low heat, for 4 minutes. Remove from heat. Slowly add lemon juice and lemon zest, mixing well. Cool.

4. To make meringue: Beat egg whites until stiff but not dry. Beat in 4 tablespoons of the sugar. Gently fold in remaining 2 tablespoons sugar.

5. Spoon filling into pie shell. Top with meringue. Bake for 10 to 12 minutes or until meringue is lightly browned. Cool. Makes 6 to 8 servings.

CLORIS SAGER | St. John's Guild, St. John's Church, West Bend, Wisconsin

No-Crust German Chocolate Pie

2 squares (1 oz. each) German sweet
   baking chocolate

½ cup butter

1 teaspoon vanilla

3 eggs, beaten

1 cup sugar

3 tablespoons flour

¼ teaspoon salt

1 cup chopped walnuts plus
   more for topping

Whipped cream

1. Preheat oven to 350°F. Lightly grease and flour a 9-inch pie plate.

2. Melt chocolate and butter in a saucepan over low heat. Remove from heat and stir in vanilla. Cool.

3. Combine eggs, sugar, flour, and salt in a mixer bowl. Beat just until blended. Fold in cooled chocolate mixture. Fold in walnuts.

4. Pour filling into pie plate. Bake for 1 hour or until a knife inserted just off center comes out clean. Refrigerate overnight. Serve chilled, topped with whipped cream and chopped walnuts. Makes 6 to 8 servings.

From **ROBERT FRANKLIN**, submitted by **MARY E. DUNN** | Grace on the Hill United Methodist Church, Corbin, Kentucky

Pumpkin Chiffon Pie

¼ cup butter, melted

1¼ cup fine gingersnap crumbs

3 eggs, separated

¼ teaspoon cream of tartar

6 tablespoons sugar

1 tablespoon unflavored gelatin

¼ cup cold water

¾ cup brown sugar

1⅓ cups pumpkin

½ cup milk

½ teaspoon salt

2 teaspoons cinnamon

½ teaspoon ginger

½ teaspoon allspice

1. Preheat oven to 350°F.

2. Combine melted butter and gingersnap crumbs. Press mixture into bottom and up sides of a 9-inch pie plate. Bake for 10 minutes. Cool.

3. Beat egg whites until foamy. Beat in cream of tartar and sugar until stiff peaks form.

4. Dissolve gelatin in cold water.

5. Combine brown sugar, pumpkin, egg yolks, milk, salt, cinnamon, ginger, and allspice in a large saucepan over low heat. Cook, stirring frequently, until mixture comes to a boil. Boil for 1 minute. Stir in gelatin. Fold in egg whites.

6. Transfer mixture into pie shell. Chill for at least 4 hours or overnight. Makes 8 to 10 servings.

SALLY MCCAULEY | Christ Church, Frederica, St. Simons Island, Georgia

Chocolate Chip Walnut Pie

3 eggs

½ cup flour

6 tablespoons butter, melted

1½ cups semisweet chocolate chips

1½ cups chopped walnuts

½ teaspoon salt

½ teaspoon lemon juice

½ cup light corn syrup

1 unbaked 9-inch pie shell

1. Preheat oven to 350°F.

2. Beat eggs in a large mixer bowl.

3. Stir in flour, melted butter, chocolate chips, walnuts, salt, lemon juice, and light corn syrup until well blended.

4. Pour filling into pie shell. Bake uncovered for 45 minutes or until pie shell is dark gold. Filling will be slightly soft in the middle but will harden as it cools. Cool completely. Store in refrigerator but let filling soften before serving. Makes 6 to 8 servings.

NONI HUNTER | Trinity Evangelical Lutheran Church, Lansdale, Pennsylvania

Coconut Cream Pie

⅓ cup flour

¾ cup sugar, divided

2 eggs, separated

2 cups milk

1 cup shredded coconut

1½ teaspoons vanilla, divided

1 baked 9-inch pie shell

1. Preheat oven to 350°F.

2. Whisk together flour and ½ cup of the sugar.

3. Beat egg yolks, add milk, and whisk to combine. Combine egg and flour mixtures in the top of a double boiler. Place over boiling water, stirring continuously until mixture begins to thicken. Cover and cook until well thickened. Stir in coconut and 1 teaspoon of the vanilla. Pour filling into pie shell.

4. Beat egg whites, gradually adding remaining ¼ cup sugar, to form stiff, glossy peaks. Fold in remaining ½ teaspoon vanilla. Spread meringue on top of filling. Bake for 10 to 15 minutes or until meringue is lightly browned. Makes 6 to 8 servings.

❖ **MARY EVELYN COOK** | Christ Church, Frederica, St. Simons Island, Georgia

Peanut Butter Pie

1 cup corn syrup

1 cup sugar

½ teaspoon vanilla

3 eggs, slightly beaten

⅓ cup creamy peanut butter

1 unbaked 9-inch pie shell

1. Preheat oven to 400°F.

2. Combine corn syrup, sugar, vanilla, eggs, and peanut butter in a mixer bowl until thoroughly blended.

3. Pour into unbaked pie shell. Bake for 15 minutes. Reduce heat to 350°F and bake 30 to 35 minutes more. Filling should appear slightly less set in center than around edges. Serve warm or chilled. Makes 6 to 8 servings.

❖ **BETTY JEAN GRIFFIN PORTER** | Pittsboro Baptist Church, Pittsboro, North Carolina

Lemon Chess Pie

2 cups sugar

1 teaspoon flour

1 teaspoon cornmeal

¼ teaspoon salt

¼ cup butter, melted

2 teaspoons grated lemon zest

¼ cup lemon juice

¼ cup milk

4 eggs

1 unbaked 9-inch pie shell

1. Preheat oven to 350°F.

2. Whisk together sugar, flour, cornmeal, and salt. Add butter, lemon zest, lemon juice, and milk. Mix until well combined.

3. Add eggs one at a time, whisking to combine after each addition. Pour into pie shell. Bake for 50 minutes or until firm. Cool on a wire rack. Makes 6 to 8 servings.

TANA BENTZEL | Messiah United Methodist Church, York, Pennsylvania

Key Lime Pie

2¼ cups sweetened condensed milk
Grated zest of 2 limes
3 egg yolks
4½ oz. fresh lime juice

1 baked 9-inch pie shell
Whipped cream

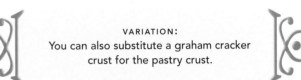

VARIATION:
You can also substitute a graham cracker crust for the pastry crust.

1. Preheat oven to 350°F.

2. Combine condensed milk, lime zest, and egg yolks in a mixer bowl. Mix well. Add lime juice and mix until well blended.

3. Pour filling into pie shell. Bake for 15 minutes or until filling is set. Cool. Top with whipped cream. Makes 6 to 8 servings.

LINDA S. THOMPSON | Oakwood Church of God in Christ, Godfrey, Illinois

Sour Cream Lime Pie

1 cup sugar
3 tablespoons cornstarch
¼ cup butter, room temperature
⅓ cup fresh lime juice
1 tablespoon lime zest
1 cup half-and-half

1 cup heavy cream
1 tablespoon confectioners' sugar
2 cups sour cream, divided
1 baked deep-dish pie shell
Lime zest for garnish

1. Combine sugar, cornstarch, butter, lime juice, lime zest, and half-and-half in a large saucepan over medium heat. Slowly bring to a boil, stirring continuously, until thickened and smooth. Cool.

2. Whip heavy cream in a mixer bowl until soft peaks form. Whip in confectioners' sugar. Fold in 1 cup of the sour cream.

3. Fold remaining cup sour cream into the lime mixture. Pour mixture into pie shell. Top with whipped cream mixture. Garnish with lime zest. Chill until ready to serve. Makes 6 to 8 servings.

KASSIE MINOR | Christ Episcopal Church, Charlotte, North Carolina

Peach Custard Pie

6 cups sliced fresh peaches
1 unbaked 9-inch deep-dish pie shell
½ cup sugar
2 eggs
1 tablespoon flour

2 tablespoons lemon juice
½ teaspoon vanilla
¼ cup butter
Cinnamon

1. Preheat oven to 325°F.

2. Layer sliced peaches into pie shell.

3. Whisk together sugar, eggs, flour, lemon juice, and vanilla. Pour over peaches. Dot with butter and sprinkle with cinnamon. Bake for 1 hour or until set. Cool at least 20 minutes before serving. Serve warm or chilled. Makes 6 to 8 servings.

MEREDITH FORSHAW | Christ Episcopal Church, Charlotte, North Carolina

Golden Ambrosia Pecan Pie

3 large eggs, lightly beaten
¾ cup light corn syrup
½ cup sugar
3 tablespoons brown sugar
2 tablespoons butter, melted
3 tablespoons fresh orange juice

1 teaspoon grated orange zest
⅛ teaspoon salt
1½ cups chopped pecans
⅔ cup shredded coconut
1 unbaked 9-inch deep-dish pie shell

1. Preheat oven to 350°F.

2. Combine eggs, light corn syrup, sugar, brown sugar, melted butter, orange juice, orange zest, and salt in a large bowl. Stir in pecans and coconut.

3. Pour into unbaked pie shell. Bake for 50 to 55 minutes or until center is set. Cool on a wire rack. Serve at room temperature. Makes 6 to 8 servings.

NORA KELLY | Grace on the Hill United Methodist Church, Corbin, Kentucky

Sour Cream Pecan Pie

1 cup sugar
¼ cup flour
3 eggs, separated
1 cup sour cream
¼ teaspoon vanilla

¼ teaspoon salt
1 cup brown sugar
1 cup broken pecans
1 baked 9-inch pie shell

1. Preheat oven to 350°F.

2. Combine sugar, flour, egg yolks, and sour cream in a saucepan over medium heat. Cook, stirring continuously, until thick. Remove from heat. Cool slightly. Stir in vanilla.

3. Beat egg whites and salt to form stiff peaks. Add brown sugar gradually, beating in a little at a time. Fold in pecans.

4. Layer custard into pie shell. Top with meringue. Bake for 15 to 20 minutes or until lightly browned. Makes 6 to 8 servings.

❖ RIT LADNIUK | First Moravian Church, Greensboro, North Carolina

Rose Boston's Pecan Meringue Pie

20 buttery crackers (such as Ritz), crushed
1 cup sugar, divided
1 cup pecans, chopped
3 egg whites

1 teaspoon vanilla
2 cups whipped cream
Chocolate shavings

1. Preheat oven to 300°F. Grease a 9-inch pie plate.

2. Combine crushed crackers, ½ cup of the sugar, and pecans.

3. Whip egg whites until stiff. Whip in remaining ½ cup sugar and vanilla. Fold cracker crumb mixture into egg whites.

4. Spoon mixture into pie plate. Bake for 30 minutes. Cool. Chill at least 4 hours. Just before serving, top with whipped cream and chocolate shavings. Makes 6 to 8 servings.

❖ SUSAN CALHOON | Trinity Presbyterian Church, Little Rock, Arkansas

Sweet Potato and Pecan Pie

2 cups cooked, mashed sweet potatoes
½ cup sugar
½ cup brown sugar
¼ teaspoon salt
⅛ teaspoon ginger

¼ teaspoon cinnamon
¼ teaspoon maple flavoring
4 eggs
1 cup chopped pecans
1 unbaked 9-inch pie shell

1. Preheat oven to 375°F.

2. Combine sweet potatoes, sugar, brown sugar, salt, ginger, cinnamon, and maple flavoring in a mixer bowl. Beat in eggs one at a time until well combined. Stir in pecans.

3. Pour into pie shell. Bake for 45 minutes. Reduce heat and bake 10 minutes more or until set. Makes 6 to 8 servings.

❖ JEANNIE WADE | Christ Church, Frederica, St. Simons Island, Georgia

Foolproof Piecrust (The Best)

4 cups flour, lightly spooned into cup
1 tablespoon sugar
2 teaspoons salt
1¾ cups vegetable shortening
1 large egg
½ cup water
1 tablespoon white vinegar or cider vinegar

No matter how much you handle this dough, it will always be flaky, tender, and delicious. Dough can be left in the refrigerator up to 3 days or frozen. Use it for all kinds of pies, including meat pies.

1. Whisk together flour, sugar, and salt in a large bowl. Cut in shortening with a pastry blender until crumbly.
2. Beat egg, water, and vinegar in a small bowl. Add to flour mixture and stir until all ingredients are moistened.
3. Divide dough into five portions. Use your hands to shape each portion into a flat, round patty ready for rolling. Wrap each patty in plastic or waxed paper and chill at least ½ hour.
4. To prepare a pie shell, lightly flour both sides of a patty and roll it out on a lightly floured board or pastry cloth. Ease the pastry into a 9-inch pie plate, add the pie filling, and top with a second pastry if desired. Bake at 350°F for 40 to 45 minutes. Makes 5 single crusts, 2 double crusts and 1 single crust, or 20 tart shells.

❖ **FAY S. MILLER** | Trinity Evangelical Lutheran Church, Lansdale, Pennsylvania

Pumpkin Pie with Meringue

1 unbaked 9-inch pie shell
1 can (16 oz.) pumpkin
3 eggs, separated
1 can (14 oz.) sweetened condensed milk
½ cup flaked coconut
¼ cup water

1 teaspoon cinnamon
½ teaspoon ginger
½ teaspoon ground nutmeg
Dash of salt
¼ teaspoon cream of tartar
½ cup sugar

1. Preheat oven to 425°F.
2. Prick bottom and sides of pie shell with a fork. Bake on lowest oven rack for 5 minutes.
3. Combine pumpkin, egg yolks, condensed milk, coconut, water, cinnamon, ginger, nutmeg, and salt in a large mixer bowl. Mix until well blended. Pour into pie shell. Shield edges of crust with aluminum foil. Reduce oven temperature to 400°F. Bake on center oven rack for 30 minutes.
4. Beat egg whites and cream of tartar in a mixer bowl until foamy. Gradually add sugar, beating until stiff peaks form and sugar is dissolved. Spread meringue over hot pumpkin filling, sealing to edge of pastry. Reduce oven temperature to 325°F. With crust shielded, bake 25 to 28 minutes more or until meringue is golden brown. Makes 6 to 8 servings.

❖ **LINDA S. THOMPSON** | Oakwood Church of God in Christ, Godfrey, Illinois

Pumpkin Cream Cheese Pie

1 package (8 oz.) cream cheese,
   room temperature
¾ cup sugar, divided
½ teaspoon vanilla
3 eggs, divided, slightly beaten
1 unbaked 9-inch pie shell

1¼ cups pumpkin
1 teaspoon cinnamon
¼ teaspoon ginger
¼ teaspoon nutmeg
Dash of salt
1 cup evaporated milk

1. Preheat oven to 350°F.

2. Beat cream cheese, ¼ cup of the sugar, and vanilla in a mixer bowl. Beat in 1 egg. Spread mixture on bottom of pie shell.

3. Combine pumpkin, remaining ½ cup sugar, cinnamon, ginger, nutmeg, and salt. Blend in remaining 2 eggs and evaporated milk. Pour evenly over cheese mixture. Bake for 65 to 70 minutes or until filling is set. Makes 6 to 8 servings.

TANA BENTZEL | Messiah United Methodist Church, York, Pennsylvania

Fresh Strawberry Pie

1 package (8 oz.) cream cheese,
    room temperature
1 tablespoon milk
1 baked 8-inch pie shell

1 quart strawberries, washed and hulled, divided
1 cup sugar
2 teaspoons cornstarch
Whipped cream

1. Beat cream cheese and milk in a mixer bowl. Spread in bottom of pie shell. Layer half of strawberries into pie shell. Refrigerate.

2. Chop remaining strawberries in a food processor or blender.

3. Combine sugar and cornstarch in a medium saucepan, add the crushed strawberries, and cook over medium-low heat until thickened, 5 to 10 minutes. Remove from heat and let cool.

4. Pour strawberry mixture over strawberries in pie shell. Refrigerate for 4 hours. Top with whipped cream just before serving. Makes 4 to 6 servings.

 MARION BUBECK | Trinity Evangelical Lutheran Church, Lansdale, Pennsylvania

Double-Layer Pumpkin Pie

½ package (4 oz.) cream cheese,
    room temperature
1 tablespoon milk
1 tablespoon sugar
2 cups frozen whipped topping,
    thawed, divided
1 prepared 9-inch graham cracker crust
1 cup cold milk
1 can (16 oz.) pumpkin
2 packages (3.4 oz. each) instant vanilla pudding mix

1 teaspoon cinnamon
½ teaspoon ginger
¼ teaspoon cloves

VARIATION:
Make this dessert with sugar-free pudding mix and fat-free whipped topping.

1. Whisk together cream cheese, milk, and sugar in a large bowl until smooth. Gently stir in 1½ cups of the whipped topping. Spread onto bottom of graham cracker crust.

2. Combine milk, pumpkin, pudding mix, cinnamon, ginger, and cloves. Whisk until well blended and thick. Spread over cream cheese layer. Refrigerate 4 hours or until set. Garnish with remaining whipped topping. Makes 6 to 8 servings.

SHIRLEY ACKERMAN | Unity Baptist Church, Morgantown, Indiana

Queen Charlotte's Tart

2 unbaked 9-inch pie shells
½ cup butter
¾ cup sugar
1 egg

½ cup plus 1 tablespoon rice flour
½ cup sliced almonds
1 teaspoon almond extract
4 to 6 tablespoons raspberry jam

1. Preheat oven to 350°F.

2. Press one piecrust pastry in bottom and ½ inch up sides of an 8 x 2-inch springform pan. Prick all over with a fork. Bake for 10 to 12 minutes or until slightly golden. Cool.

3. Reset oven temperature to 400°F.

4. Melt butter in a saucepan over medium heat. Stir in sugar and cook, stirring continuously, for 1 minute. Add egg, rice flour, almonds, and almond extract and stir to combine. Remove from heat.

5. Spread jam on baked crust. Top with almond filling. Cut second crust into strips and lay across tart for a lattice look. Bake for 30 minutes or until pastry is well risen and golden brown. Cool in pan. Makes 8 to 12 servings.

❖ **EUGENIA ALLDERDICE** | Christ Episcopal Church, Charlotte, North Carolina

Sour Cream Prune Pie

3 egg yolks
1 cup sour cream
1 tablespoon vinegar
1 cup cooked prunes, chopped
⅞ to 1 cup sugar
½ teaspoon cinnamon
½ teaspoon cloves

½ teaspoon nutmeg
½ teaspoon salt
1 unbaked 9-inch pie shell

MERINGUE:
3 egg whites
5 tablespoons sugar

1. Preheat oven to 350°F.

2. Combine egg yolks, sour cream, vinegar, prunes, sugar, cinnamon, cloves, nutmeg, and salt. Pour into pie shell. Bake for 30 minutes. Cool.

3. To make meringue: Reduce oven temperature to 325°F. Beat egg whites until foamy. Beat in sugar until stiff peaks form. Spread meringue on top of prune filling. Return pie to oven for 15 to 25 minutes or until meringue is lightly browned. Cool before serving. Makes 6 to 8 servings.

❖ **MRS. ERWIN GRITZMACHER** | St. John's Guild, St. John's Church, West Bend, Wisconsin

Spiced Wassail

4 cups unsweetened apple juice
3 cups unsweetened pineapple juice
2 cups cranberry juice
¼ teaspoon nutmeg

1 cinnamon stick
3 whole cloves
Lemon and orange slices

1. Combine apple juice, pineapple juice, cranberry juice, nutmeg, cinnamon stick, cloves, lemon slices, and orange slices in a large stockpot. Bring to a boil, reduce heat, and simmer for 10 minutes.
2. Pour into a glass punch bowl. Serve hot. Makes 18 servings.

❖ **MARILYN J. TAYLOR** | Trinity Evangelical Lutheran Church, Lansdale, Pennsylvania

Spice of Christmas Life

¼ cup brown sugar
⅓ cup red cinnamon candies
1 or 2 cinnamon sticks
8 whole cloves

3 cups cranberry juice
3 cups unsweetened pineapple juice
3 to 4 cups water

1. Place brown sugar, cinnamon candies, cinnamon sticks, and cloves into a coffeepot basket.
2. Pour the cranberry juice, pineapple juice, and water into the coffeepot. Percolate and serve. Makes 16 to 20 servings.

❖ **GRACE ON THE HILL UNITED METHODIST CHURCH** | Corbin, Kentucky

Golden Wassail

1 quart unsweetened pineapple juice
1 quart apple cider
1 can (12 oz.) apricot nectar
1 cup orange juice

2 cinnamon sticks
1 teaspoon whole cloves
¼ teaspoon whole cardamom seeds

1. Combine pineapple juice, apple cider, apricot nectar, orange juice, cinnamon sticks, cloves, and cardamom seeds in a large saucepan over medium high heat. Bring to a boil, reduce heat, and simmer for 15 minutes.
2. Strain off cinnamon sticks, cloves, and cardamom seeds. Serve hot with cinnamon sticks and orange slices. Makes 16 to 20 servings.

❖ **ROSEMARY VANDUYN** | Christ Episcopal Church, Charlotte, North Carolina

Cranberry Christmas Tea

1 cup sugar
2 cups water
3 cinnamon sticks
6 to 8 cloves

Juice of 2 oranges
Juice of 2 lemons
1¾ cups ginger ale
4 cups cranberry juice

1. Combine sugar, water, cinnamon sticks, and cloves in a large saucepan over medium heat. Bring to a boil. Boil for 5 minutes or until slightly thickened. Remove cinnamon sticks and cloves.
2. Pour in orange juice, lemon juice, ginger ale, and cranberry juice. Heat and serve. Makes 18 to 20 servings.

KAY CARGILE | Memorial Baptist Church, Tulsa, Oklahoma

Apple Honey Tea

1 can (12 oz.) frozen apple juice concentrate
2 tablespoons instant tea

1 tablespoon honey
½ teaspoon cinnamon

1. Spoon apple juice concentrate into a medium saucepan. Add water, following directions on can, to reconstitute juice.
2. Stir in instant tea, honey, and cinnamon. Simmer over low heat, stirring occasionally, until warmed through, 6 to 8 minutes. Makes 10 to 12 servings.

ESTELLE DEW | Memorial Baptist Church, Tulsa, Oklahoma

Olde Family Eggnog

12 eggs, separated
4 to 6 teaspoons sugar, divided
1 quart milk

2 cups heavy cream
20 to 25 oz. rum
Nutmeg

1. Beat egg yolks with 2 or 3 teaspoons of sugar. Add 1 quart milk and mix until blended. Pour into a punch bowl.
2. Beat egg whites with 2 or 3 teaspoons of sugar. Whip until stiff peaks form. Whip the heavy cream until stiff.
3. Add egg whites and whipped cream to the punch bowl. Stir to combine. Refrigerate overnight.
4. To serve, pour 1 oz. of rum in a mug, pour in eggnog, and stir to blend. Top with nutmeg. Makes 20 to 25 servings.

BOB FREI | First Moravian Church, Greensboro, North Carolina

Hot Mulled Wine

Zest of 1 orange
Zest of 1 lemon
4 cinnamon sticks
5 whole cloves
½ cup sugar

½ cup water
2 bottles (750 ml each) Burgundy
1 orange, sliced into rings
1 lemon, sliced into rings

1. Wrap orange zest, lemon zest, cinnamon sticks, and cloves in cheesecloth and tie into a bundle (or place in a mesh spice ball).

2. Combine sugar and water in a saucepan and drop in spice bundle. Slowly bring to a boil and cook for 5 minutes. Remove from heat.

3. Empty contents of saucepan, including spice bundle, into a stockpot. Pour in wine. Add orange and lemon rings. Simmer on low heat (do not boil) for 40 minutes. Remove spice bundle. Serve warm. Makes 12 to 14 servings.

JULIE PEAK | Trinity Presbyterian Church, Little Rock, Arkansas

House Blessing

The church's occasional liturgy for the blessing of a house reminds us of the sacredness of the homes in which God's people dwell. The service includes carrying a lighted candle and sprinkling water in each room of the house, with a blessing for each according to its unique purpose. It is a lovely occasion for inviting neighbors and friends in to celebrate a new home.

THE REVEREND HENRY NUTT PARSLEY, JR., Rector
Christ Episcopal Church, Charlotte, North Carolina

SUGGESTED MENU

Brie with Chutney, page 118
Chicken Paella, page 139
Christmas Cranberry Salad, page 218
Marinated Green Beans, page 167
Rolls
Pears Baked in Cream, page 183

Sinfully Good Christmas Eggnog

6 eggs, separated
1 cup sugar, divided
1 pint heavy cream, whipped
1 pint half-and-half

1½ cups rye whiskey (such as Canadian Club)
1 oz. Jamaica rum
Nutmeg

1. Beat egg yolks in a large mixer bowl until light yellow. Beat in ½ cup of the sugar.
2. In a separate bowl, beat egg whites until very stiff. Gradually beat in remaining ½ cup sugar.
3. Fold whites into yolks. Add whipped cream, half & half, whiskey, and rum. Stir thoroughly. Chill 2 to 4 hours. To serve, pour into a punch bowl and grate nutmeg over the top. Makes 20 servings.

❖ **BILL BANE** | Trinity Presbyterian Church, Little Rock, Arkansas

Mock Champagne

4 cups sugar
4 cups water
4 cups grape juice or pineapple juice

2 cups orange juice
4 bottles (1 liter each) ginger ale, chilled

1. Combine sugar and water in a large saucepan over medium-high heat. Bring to a boil and cook for 3 minutes, stirring continuously, until sugar is dissolved.
2. Add grape juice or pineapple juice to sugar syrup. Add orange juice. Stir until well blended. Chill for 2 to 4 hours.
3. To serve, pour juice mixture into a punch bowl. Slowly pour in ginger ale. Makes 50 servings.

❖ **DEBRA BURROWS MEANS** | Vincent Memorial United Methodist Church, Nutter Fort, West Virginia

Wedding Punch

1 cup sugar
2 cups water
1 can (12 oz.) frozen lemonade concentrate
3 cans (12 oz. each) frozen orange
   juice concentrate

4 bottles (1 liter each) ginger ale, chilled
Ice cubes
2 pints pineapple sherbet

1. Combine sugar and water in a saucepan over medium-high heat. Bring to a boil and cook for 3 minutes, stirring continuously, until sugar is dissolved.
2. Spoon lemonade concentrate and orange juice concentrate into a punch bowl. Pour in ginger ale. Add ice cubes. Drop in sherbet by the scoopful. Makes 50 servings.

❖ **WOMEN'S MISSIONARY AUXILIARY** | Bay Springs, Mississippi

Great Punch

1 can (12 oz.) frozen lemonade
   concentrate, thawed
1 can (12 oz.) frozen orange juice
   concentrate, thawed
1 quart apple juice, chilled
6 cups cold water

2 bottles (2 liters each) ginger ale, chilled
1 package (16 oz.) frozen whole
   strawberries (not in syrup)

VARIATION:
Substitute champagne for the ginger ale.

1. Spoon lemonade concentrate and orange juice concentrate into a punch bowl.
2. Pour in apple juice and cold water. Stir to dissolve the concentrate.
3. Pour in ginger ale. Float frozen whole strawberries on top. Makes 24 servings.

 CAROL BANE | Trinity Presbyterian Church, Little Rock, Arkansas

Hot Cider

1 gallon unsweetened apple juice
8 whole cloves
1 large cinnamon stick

⅛ teaspoon nutmeg
3 tablespoons lemon juice
¼ cup brown sugar

1. Combine all ingredients in a large stockpot. Bring to a boil, stirring frequently, until brown sugar is dissolved.
2. Cool to room temperature, cover, and refrigerate 2 to 4 hours.
3. Pour through a strainer to remove spices. Reheat slowly. Serve hot in mugs or punch cups. Makes 32 servings.

 CELIA MARSHALL | Christ Episcopal Church, Charlotte, North Carolina

Spiced Cranberry Juice

1 quart water
6 to 8 cloves
1 cinnamon stick
1 tea bag
1 quart cranberry juice cocktail

VARIATION:
Substitute cider or apple juice
for cranberry juice cocktail and add
lemon juice to taste.

1. Combine water, cloves, and cinnamon stick in a stockpot over medium heat. Simmer until water is amber-colored and fragrant.
2. Remove from heat, add tea bag, and steep for 5 minutes.
3. Remove tea bag. Pour in cranberry juice cocktail and stir. Reheat before serving. Makes 10 to 12 servings.

CAROLYN MATTINGLY | Christ Church, Frederica, St. Simons Island, Georgia

Bake Sale Treats & Sweets

Tips for a Successful Bake Sale

Bake sales are excellent fund-raisers for any organization or charity. They also offer the fun and fellowship that come with sharing your very best breads and desserts with others.

However, whenever food is prepared and offered for sale to the public, food safety is very important. Baked goods may be sitting out in the sun for several hours, so don't use any ingredients that require refrigeration. Note that there are acceptable and unacceptable items for bake sales. So while the recipes included in this chapter are all acceptable at bake sales, don't forget that hundreds more of your favorite breads and desserts (which may or may not be recommended for bake sales) can be found in the other chapters in this book.

Whether you are baking a donation in your own kitchen or organizing volunteers for the event, please follow these recommendations.

Acceptable

Fruit pies (those not requiring refrigeration)
Cakes and cupcakes (except cheesecake and cream-filled)
Cookies and brownies
Candy
Bread
Muffins

Unacceptable

Custards and custard pies
Pumpkin pie
Meringue pies
Real cream pies
Cheesecake
Cream-filled cupcakes or doughnuts
Cake frostings and fillings made with cream cheese
Jar or canned bread
Home-canned goods
Flavored oils
Homemade ice cream

Seven-Grain Cereal Bread

½ cup seven-grain cereal

2 cups plus 1 tablespoon water, divided

6 tablespoons butter

¼ cup honey

2 teaspoons salt

5 to 5¼ cups unbleached white flour, divided

2 packages (.25 oz. each) active dry yeast

2 eggs

1 egg yolk

1 tablespoon poppy seeds or sesame seeds

1. Combine seven-grain cereal and 1 cup of the water in a large saucepan over medium heat. Cook, covered, for 20 minutes. Stir in another 1 cup water, butter, honey, and salt. Cool to lukewarm.

2. Combine 2 cups of the flour and the yeast in a large mixer bowl. Stir in cereal mixture and eggs. Beat at low speed for 30 seconds, scraping down sides of bowl constantly. Beat at high speed for 3 minutes. Stir in remaining 3 to 3¼ cups flour by hand or with a dough hook attachment to make soft dough.

3. Turn out onto lightly floured surface and knead until smooth and elastic, 5 to 8 minutes (or knead in mixer with dough hook attachment). Shape dough into a ball. Place in a lightly greased bowl and turn once to coat. Cover and let rise in a warm place until doubled in size, 1 to 1¼ hours.

4. Punch down dough, turn out onto a lightly floured surface, and divide in half. Cover and let rest 10 minutes. Shape into two loaves and place into two greased 9 x 5 x 3-inch loaf pans. Cover and let rise in a warm place until doubled in size, 45 to 60 minutes.

5. Preheat oven to 375°F. Combine egg yolk with remaining tablespoon water. Brush tops of loaves with yolk and sprinkle with poppy seeds or sesame seeds. Bake for 30 for 35 minutes. Cool on wire racks. Makes 2 loaves.

GLORIA STOLARSKI | Church of the Canyons Women's Ministries, Canyon Country, California

Apple Bread

4 cups flour

2 teaspoons baking soda

1 teaspoon salt

2 teaspoons cinnamon

2 cups sugar

1 cup oil

4 eggs

¼ cup sour cream

2 teaspoons vanilla

2 cups chopped apple

1 cup chopped nuts

1. Preheat oven to 350°F. Grease and flour two 8½ x 4½ x 2½-inch loaf pans.

2. Whisk together flour, baking soda, salt, and cinnamon.

3. Combine sugar, oil, eggs, sour cream, and vanilla in a mixer bowl. Beat until well blended. Add flour mixture and beat well. Fold in apples and nuts.

4. Pour batter into pans. Bake for 1 hour or until a tester inserted in center comes out clean. Cool in pans 10 minutes before turning out onto wire racks. Makes 14 to 16 servings.

ENOLA BRIGGS | Messiah United Methodist Church, York, Pennsylvania

Judy's Spiced Applesauce Bread

1¼ cups applesauce
1 cup sugar
½ cup oil
2 eggs
3 tablespoons milk
2 cups flour
½ teaspoon baking powder
1 teaspoon baking soda
½ teaspoon salt

½ teaspoon cinnamon
¼ teaspoon nutmeg
¼ teaspoon allspice
½ cup chopped nuts

TOPPING:
¼ cup chopped nuts
¼ cup brown sugar
½ teaspoon cinnamon

1. Preheat oven to 350°F. Grease and flour a 9 x 5 x 3-inch loaf pan.

2. Combine applesauce, sugar, oil, eggs, and milk in mixer bowl. Beat until well blended.

3. Sift together flour, baking powder, baking soda, salt, cinnamon, nutmeg, and allspice. Stir into batter. Fold in chopped nuts.

4. To make topping: Combine chopped nuts, brown sugar, and cinnamon.

5. Transfer batter to pan. Sprinkle with topping. Bake for 1 hour or until a tester inserted in center comes out clean. Cool in pan 10 minutes before turning out onto a wire rack. Makes 16 to 18 servings.

 COURTNEY OSBORNE | Memorial Baptist Church, Tulsa, Oklahoma

Almond Buttermilk Loaf

2 tablespoons butter
½ cup honey
1 egg
1½ cup whole wheat flour
1 teaspoon baking powder

⅛ teaspoon baking soda
¼ teaspoon salt
½ cup buttermilk or ½ cup plain
    low-fat yogurt
½ to 1 cup chopped almonds

1. Preheat oven to 350°F. Lightly grease an 8½ x 4½ x 2½-inch loaf pan.

2. Cream butter, honey, and egg together in a mixer bowl until light.

3. Sift together whole wheat flour, baking powder, baking soda, and salt. Add to egg mixture alternately with buttermilk or yogurt, beating well after each addition. Stir in almonds.

4. Spread batter in pan. Bake for 40 to 45 minutes or until top is golden brown. Do not overbake. Turn out onto a wire rack to cool. Makes 14 to 16 servings.

This pound cake is light and moist and keeps well. Serve it sliced and topped with fresh fruit.

MARILYN SABOLD | Methow Valley United Methodist Church, Twisp, Washington

Cinnamon Quick Bread

2 cups flour

1 cup sugar

4 teaspoons baking powder

1½ teaspoons cinnamon

1¼ teaspoons salt

1 cup sour milk or buttermilk

⅓ cup oil

2 teaspoons vanilla

2 eggs

STREUSEL:

2 tablespoons sugar

1 teaspoon cinnamon

2 teaspoons butter, room temperature

1. Preheat oven to 350°F. Grease and flour the bottoms only (not sides) of two 8½ x 4½ x 2½-inch loaf pans.

2. Combine flour, sugar, baking powder, cinnamon, salt, sour milk or buttermilk, oil, vanilla, and eggs in a large mixer bowl at medium speed.

3. To make streusel: Combine sugar, cinnamon, and butter until crumbly.

4. Pour batter into pans. Sprinkle streusel over the top. Swirl a knife through the streusel and batter to marble. Bake 45 to 55 minutes or until top is lightly browned. Turn out onto wire racks to cool. Makes 28 to 32 servings.

❖ **TONYA DANIEL** | First Moravian Church, Greensboro, North Carolina

Food Safety Tips

- Keeping food safe starts with clean hands. Wash hands before preparing foods for the bake sale.
- To accommodate those with food allergies, please provide a list of ingredients for each item baked.
- Individually wrap and seal all items to reduce the risk of contamination. Food should not be transported with pets.
- Label your baked goods with your name, address, and phone number.

Recommended further reading: *Cooking for Crowds: A Volunteer's Guide to Safe Food Handling* from the Penn State College of Agricultural Sciences. It is available online and by mail at www.cookingforcrowds.psu.edu.

Apricot Walnut Bread

1 cup dried apricots, cut into small pieces
1½ cups boiling water
1 cup chopped walnuts
1 egg
1 teaspoon vanilla
1 cup sugar

¼ cup vegetable oil
2½ cups flour
1 tablespoon baking powder
½ teaspoon salt
¼ teaspoon cinnamon
¼ teaspoon nutmeg

1. Preheat oven to 350°F. Grease a 9 x 5 x 3-inch loaf pan.

2. Combine apricots and boiling water in a mixer bowl. Let stand until cool.

3. Add walnuts, egg, vanilla, sugar, and salad oil to the apricots. Mix until well blended.

4. Sift together flour, baking powder, salt, cinnamon, and nutmeg. Add to apricot mixture all at once and stir until well combined.

5. Pour batter into pan. Bake for 65 minutes or until browned. Cool in pan 30 minutes before turning out onto a wire rack. Cool completely. Wrap in foil and refrigerate for at least 12 hours before serving. Makes 16 to 18 servings.

 Apricot Walnut Bread makes delicious tea sandwiches. Cut thin slices and spread with cream cheese.

❖ **LUCY VROOMAN** | Christ Church, Frederica, St. Simons Island, Georgia

Orange Bread

2 cups flour
1 teaspoon baking powder
½ teaspoon salt
Juice of 2 oranges plus water to equal 1 cup
1 teaspoon baking soda

1 tablespoon grated orange zest
2 tablespoons butter or vegetable shortening
1 cup sugar
1 egg, beaten
½ cup chopped pecans

1. Preheat oven to 350°F. Grease an 8½ x 4½ x 2½-inch loaf pan.

2. Sift together flour, baking powder, and salt.

3. Combine orange juice, baking soda, and orange zest.

4. Cream butter or shortening and sugar in a mixer bowl. Add egg and beat until well combined. Add flour mixture and orange juice mixture alternately, beating after each addition. Stir in pecans.

5. Pour batter into pan. Bake for 50 minutes or until a tester inserted in center comes out clean. Cool in pan 10 minutes before turning out onto a wire rack. Makes 14 to 16 servings.

❖ **CAROLYN TEMPLE** | Christ Episcopal Church, Charlotte, North Carolina

Hawaiian Banana Nut Bread

3 cups flour

2 cups sugar

1 teaspoon baking soda

1 teaspoon salt

1 teaspoon cinnamon

3 cups chopped nuts

3 eggs, beaten

1½ cups vegetable oil

2 cups mashed ripe banana

1 can (8 oz.) crushed pineapple, drained

2 teaspoons vanilla

1. Preheat oven to 350°F. Grease two 8½ x 4½ x 2½-inch loaf pans.

2. Whisk together flour, sugar, baking soda, salt, and cinnamon. Stir in nuts.

3. Combine eggs, oil, banana, pineapple, and vanilla in a mixer bowl. Beat until well blended. Add flour mixture and blend well.

4. Spoon batter into pans. Bake for 65 minutes or until top is browned. Cool in pans 10 minutes before turning out onto wire racks. Makes 28 to 32 servings.

ELLEN LOWRY | Christ Episcopal Church, Charlotte, North Carolina

VARIATION:
Use muffin pans instead of loaf pans. Bake at 350°F for 15 to 20 minutes.
This recipe will make 12 large muffins or 6 dozen mini muffins.

Blueberry Bread

1 cup sugar

2 eggs

1 tablespoons corn oil

1 cup milk

3 cups flour

4 teaspoons baking powder

1 teaspoon salt

½ cup chopped nuts

1 cup blueberries, fresh or frozen

1. Preheat oven to 350°F. Grease a 9 x 5 x 3-inch loaf pan.

2. Beat sugar, eggs, and corn oil in a large mixer bowl. Blend in milk. With mixer running, gradually add flour, baking powder, and salt. Beat well. Fold in nuts and blueberries.

3. Pour batter into pan. Bake for 50 to 60 minutes or until top is browned and a tester inserted in center comes out clean. Cool in pan 10 minutes before turning out onto a wire rack. Makes 16 to 18 servings.

Adapted from *The Best of the Old Church Cookbooks* by Florence Ekstrand, courtesy of Welcome Press

New England Brown Bread

½ cup flour

2 teaspoons baking soda

1 teaspoon salt

1 cup whole wheat flour

2 cups buttermilk

½ cup dark molasses

1 cup raisins

1. Preheat oven to 350°F. Generously grease two 5¼ x 3¾-inch coffee cans.

2. Combine flour, baking soda, and salt in a large mixer bowl.

3. In a separate bowl, combine whole wheat flour, buttermilk, and molasses. Add to flour in mixer bowl and mix until well combined. Stir in raisins.

4. Pour batter into coffee cans. Bake for 45 to 50 minutes or until a tester inserted in center comes out clean. Cool in cans 20 minutes before turning out onto wire racks. Makes 20 servings.

JOAN KEEFFE | Methow Valley United Methodist Church, Twisp, Washington

Round Cheese Bread

1½ cups Bisquick baking mix

1 cup shredded mozzarella

¼ cup grated Parmesan plus
   more for topping

½ teaspoon dried oregano

½ cup milk

1 egg, beaten

2 teaspoons butter, melted

1. Preheat oven to 400°F. Grease an 8 x 1½-inch round cake pan.

2. Combine baking mix, mozzarella, Parmesan, oregano, milk, and egg in a mixer bowl. Mix to make a thick batter.

3. Spoon batter into pan. Drizzle melted butter and sprinkle Parmesan over the top. Bake for 20 to 25 minutes or until lightly browned. Cool 10 minutes. Cut into wedges. Reheat in microwave to serve warm. Makes 6 to 8 servings.

NORA KELLY | Grace on the Hill United Methodist Church, Corbin, Kentucky

Pecan Corn Sticks

2 eggs, beaten

1 cup buttermilk

2 cups cornmeal

1 cup flour

3 teaspoons baking powder

1 teaspoon baking soda

1 teaspoon salt

¼ cup sugar

¼ cup vegetable shortening or butter, melted

1¾ cups crushed pecans

1. Preheat oven to 450°F. Oil several corn stick pans.

2. Whisk together eggs and buttermilk in a large bowl.

3. Sift together cornmeal, flour, baking powder, baking soda, salt, and sugar. Stir into egg mixture. Add melted shortening or butter and pecans. Mix until well combined.

4. Pour batter into pans. Bake for 12 to 15 minutes or until tops are golden and hot. Makes 3 dozen.

❖ ELIZABETH RHODES MCCARTNEY | Christ Church, Frederica, St. Simons Island, Georgia

Fried Corn Bread

½ cup oil
1 cup self-rising cornmeal
1 egg
1 teaspoon salt
Ice water

 Enjoy this crisp corn bread with soups and vegetables or under a heaping portion of creamed tuna or chipped beef.

1. Heat oil to sizzling in a black cast-iron skillet over medium heat.

2. Combine cornmeal, egg, and salt. Add ice water as needed to thin the batter. Drop batter by the spoonful into hot oil. Cook in batches, turning once, until lightly browned and crisp on both sides, 4 to 6 minutes. Drain on paper towels. Serve hot or reheat in microwave. Makes 2 servings.

❖ CHARLOTTE PARKER HARRIS | Christ Church, Frederica, St. Simons Island, Georgia

Egg-free and Dairy-free Corn Bread

1½ cups plain soy milk
1½ tablespoons vinegar
1 cup cornmeal
1 cup flour
1 teaspoon baking powder

½ teaspoon baking soda
¾ teaspoons salt
2 tablespoons sweetener (sugar, brown sugar, or sugar substitute)
2 tablespoons corn oil

1. Preheat oven to 425°F. Lightly coat a 9 x 9 x 2-inch baking pan with nonstick cooking spray.

2. Combine soy milk and vinegar. Let stand 5 minutes.

3. Whisk together cornmeal, flour, baking powder, baking soda, salt, and sweetener.

4. Stir oil into soy milk mixture. Make a well in center of cornmeal mixture, pour in soy milk mixture, and stir until moistened and blended.

5. Spread batter in baking dish. Bake for 25 minutes or until a tester inserted in center comes out clean. Cool in pan 20 minutes. Cut into squares. Makes 1 loaf.

❖ DEB HENDRICKS | Trinity Evangelical Lutheran Church, Lansdale, Pennsylvania

Irish Soda Bread

2 cups flour
1 teaspoon baking powder
½ teaspoon baking soda
¼ teaspoon salt
3 tablespoons butter

¾ cup low-fat milk
1 tablespoon lemon juice
1 egg white
½ cup raisins

1. Preheat oven to 375°F. Lightly coat a baking sheet with nonstick cooking spray.

2. Whisk together flour, baking powder, baking soda, and salt. Cut in butter with a pastry blender or your fingers until crumbly.

3. Whisk together milk and lemon juice. Whisk in egg white. Make a well in center of flour mixture, add milk mixture, and stir just until moistened. Stir in raisins.

4. Turn out dough onto a lightly floured surface and shape into a 7-inch round loaf. Place loaf on baking sheet. Cut an X on the top of the loaf with a sharp knife. Bake for 30 minutes or until light brown. Serve warm with homemade fruit jam and clotted cream. Makes 6 to 8 servings.

LINDA BATT | Trinity Evangelical Lutheran Church, Lansdale, Pennsylvania

Onion Dill Bread

1 envelope (.25 oz.) active dry yeast
½ cup warm water (105°F to 115°F)
1 cup creamed cottage cheese,
    heated until warm
2 tablespoons sugar
1 tablespoon instant minced onion
2 tablespoons butter, room temperature,
    divided

2 teaspoons dill seed
1 teaspoon salt
¼ teaspoon baking soda
1 egg
2¼ to 2½ cups flour
Coarse salt

1. Soften yeast in warm water (105°F to 115°F). Let stand 10 minutes.

2. Combine warm cottage cheese, sugar, minced onion, 1 tablespoon of the butter, dill seed, salt, baking soda, egg, and yeast in a large mixer bowl. Blend thoroughly. Add flour and mix with dough hook attachment to form a stiff dough. Cover and let rise in warm place until light and doubled in size, 50 to 60 minutes.

3. Stir down dough. Turn out into a well-greased 8-inch round casserole and turn once to coat. Let rise in warm place until light, 30 to 40 minutes.

4. Preheat oven to 350°F. Bake in casserole for 40 to 50 minutes or until golden brown. Cool on a wire rack. Brush remaining tablespoon butter over top of warm loaf and sprinkle with coarse salt. If covered, bread remains fresh for several days. Makes 1 round loaf.

MARILYN J. TAYLOR | Trinity Evangelical Lutheran Church, Lansdale, Pennsylvania

Lemon Poppy Seed Bread

1½ cups flour
1 cup sugar
1 teaspoon baking powder
1 teaspoon salt
1 to 2 tablespoons poppy seeds
Grated zest of 1 lemon
½ cup milk
⅓ cup butter, melted
2 eggs, beaten
½ cup chopped walnuts

TOPPING:
Juice of ½ lemon
¼ cup sugar

VARIATION:
Use muffin pans instead of a loaf pan. Bake at 400°F for 18 to 20 minutes. This recipe will make 12 muffins or 24 mini muffins.

1. Preheat oven to 350°F. Grease a 9 x 5 x 3-inch loaf pan.

2. Stir flour, sugar, baking powder, salt, poppy seeds, and lemon zest in a large mixer bowl. With mixer running, add milk, melted butter, and eggs. Mix until well blended. Stir in nuts.

3. Spoon batter into pan. Bake for 45 to 50 minutes or until a tester inserted in center comes out clean. Set pan on a wire rack.

4. To make topping: Mix lemon juice and sugar. Pour over top of hot loaf. Cool completely in pan. Makes 1 loaf.

BEV MCGUIRE | Trinity Evangelical Lutheran Church, Lansdale, Pennsylvania

Cottage Cheese Dill Bread

2 oz. yeast
½ cup warm water
2 teaspoons sugar
2 cups cottage cheese, small curd
2 tablespoons minced onion
2 tablespoons dill weed

1 teaspoon baking powder
2 teaspoons salt
2 tablespoons sugar
2 eggs
4 to 4½ cups flour
Melted butter

1. Combine yeast, warm water, and sugar. Let stand 10 minutes.

2. Combine cottage cheese, onion, dill weed, baking powder, salt, sugar, and eggs in a mixer bowl. Mix well. Stir in yeast mixture. Add flour 1 cup at a time, mixing well after each addition and changing to the dough hook attachment. Continue kneading until dough is smooth and elastic.

3. Turn out dough into a greased bowl and turn once to coat. Let rise until doubled in size, 1 to 1½ hours.

4. Punch down dough, turn out onto a lightly floured surface, and shape into two loaves. Place each loaf in a greased 8½ x 4½ x 2½-inch loaf pan. Let rise until doubled in size, 45 to 60 minutes.

5. Preheat oven to 350°F. Bake loaves for 30 minutes or until golden brown. Brush tops with melted butter. Cool on wire racks. Makes 2 loaves.

ELAINE KOENIG | St. John's Guild, St. John's Church, West Bend, Wisconsin

Prune Bread

1 box (16 oz.) prunes
2 cups sugar
½ cup butter
1 teaspoon cinnamon
½ teaspoon nutmeg
¼ teaspoon cloves

1 teaspoon salt
4 cups flour
2 tablespoons cocoa
2 teaspoons baking soda
2 eggs

1. Place prunes in a bowl, add water to cover, and soak overnight.
2. Drain prunes, reserving 2 cups of the liquid. Pit and chop prunes.
3. Combine chopped prunes, reserved liquid, sugar, butter, cinnamon, nutmeg, cloves, and salt in a saucepan over medium heat. Bring to a boil and cook for 5 minutes. Cool.
4. Combine flour, cocoa, and baking soda in a mixer bowl. Beat in eggs. Stir in prunes and their liquid.
5. Pour batter into two greased 9 x 5 x 3-inch loaf pans. Let batter rest 30 minutes to 1 hour before baking, to mellow the flavors. Bake in a preheated 350°F oven for 1 hour or until top is browned. Cool in pans 10 minutes before turning out onto wire racks. Makes 2 loaves.

❧ Adapted from *The Best of the Old Church Cookbooks* by Florence Ekstrand, courtesy of Welcome Press

Poppy Seed Bread

3 cups flour
3 eggs
1½ teaspoons salt
1½ cups milk
1½ teaspoons butter flavoring
1½ teaspoons almond extract
2 cups sugar
1½ teaspoons baking powder
1½ tablespoons poppy seeds
¾ cup oil
1½ teaspoons vanilla

GLAZE:
1 cup confectioners' sugar
¼ teaspoon vanilla
¼ teaspoon butter flavoring
2 tablespoons orange juice
¼ teaspoon almond extract

1. Preheat oven to 350°F. Grease and flour a 9 x 5 x 3-inch loaf pan.
2. Combine flour, eggs, salt, milk, butter flavoring, almond extract, sugar, baking powder, poppy seeds, oil, and vanilla in large mixer bowl. Beat for 2 minutes at medium speed.
3. Spoon batter into pan. Bake for 1 hour or until lightly browned. Cool in pan 10 minutes before turning out onto a wire rack.
4. To make glaze: Stir confectioners' sugar, vanilla, butter flavoring, orange juice, and almond extract until smooth. Drizzle over top of loaf. Makes 1 loaf.

❧ **JAYNE MITCHELL** | Memorial Baptist Church, Tulsa, Oklahoma

No-Beat Popovers

2 eggs
1 cup milk

1 cup flour
½ teaspoon salt

1. Preheat oven to 450°F. Grease a 6-cup muffin pan.

2. Break eggs into bowl. Add milk, flour, and salt. Mix with a spoon until well combined but still lumpy.

3. Pour batter into muffin cups until three-quarters full. Bake for 30 minutes without opening oven door. After 30 minutes, carefully poke a fork into each popover to release stem. Continue baking 5 to 10 minutes more or until lightly browned and baked through. Makes 6 popovers.

JEANETTE BESSELS | Christ Church, Frederica, St. Simons Island, Georgia

Raisin Bread

1 loaf frozen bread dough, thawed
¼ cup butter, room temperature
1 teaspoon cinnamon

½ cup sugar
½ cup raisins
Confectioners' sugar icing

1. Preheat oven to 350°F. Lightly grease a baking sheet.

2. Flatten and roll out dough on a lightly floured board. Spread with butter.

3. Combine cinnamon and sugar and sprinkle over the buttered dough. Scatter raisins on top.

4. Roll dough into a round loaf. Bake for 30 minutes or until brown. Cool on a wire rack 20 minutes. Drizzle with confectioners' sugar icing. To serve, cut into slices. Makes 14 to 16 servings.

SHIRLENE HEPLER | Messiah United Methodist Church, York, Pennsylvania

The Flour Mill

Back of the loaf is the snowy flour,
And back of the flour the mill,
And back of the mill is the wheat, and the shower,
And the sun, and the Father's will.

M. D. BABCOCK
Adapted from *The Best of the Old Church Cookbooks* by
Florence Ekstrand, courtesy of Welcome Press

Pumpkin Spice Bread

3 cups sugar

1 cup applesauce

4 eggs or 1 cup imitation eggs

1 can (16 oz.) pumpkin

3½ cups flour

1 teaspoon baking powder

2 teaspoons baking soda

2 teaspoons salt

1 teaspoon nutmeg

1 teaspoon allspice

1 teaspoon cinnamon

½ teaspoon cloves

⅔ cup water

1. Preheat oven to 350°F. Grease and flour two 8½ x 4½ x 2½-inch loaf pans.

2. Combine sugar and applesauce in a mixer bowl. Add eggs and pumpkin and mix until well blended.

3. Sift together flour, baking powder, baking soda, salt, nutmeg, allspice, cinnamon, and cloves. Add flour mixture and water alternately to pumpkin mixture, blending well after each addition.

4. Pour batter into pans. Bake for 1½ hours or until a tester inserted in center comes out clean. Cool in pan 10 minutes before turning out onto a wire rack. Makes 2 loaves.

 **ELIZABETH JONES** | Christ Episcopal Church, Charlotte, North Carolina

Cranberry Loaf

4 cups flour

3 teaspoons baking powder

1 teaspoon baking soda

1 teaspoon salt

2 cups sugar

2 eggs, beaten

4 tablespoons cooking oil

1 cup orange juice

1 cup cranberries, coarsely chopped

1 cup chopped nuts

4 tablespoons hot (not boiling) water

This bread is a "light" version of the sweet holiday fruitcake.

1. Preheat oven to 350°F. Grease two 8½ x 4½ x 2½-inch loaf pans.

2. Sift together flour, baking powder, baking soda, salt, and sugar.

3. Combine eggs, cooking oil, orange juice, cranberries, and nuts in a mixer bowl. Stir until blended. Add flour mixture until well combined. Stir in hot water.

4. Spoon batter into baking pans. Bake for 45 to 60 minutes or until a tester inserted in center comes out clean. Cool in pans 10 minutes before turning out onto wire racks. Makes 2 loaves.

L. WIEMAN | Presbyterian Church of Gonzales, Gonzales, Texas

French Peasant Bread

2 cups lukewarm water
1 package (.25 oz.) rapid-rising dry yeast
1 tablespoon sugar
2 teaspoons salt
4 cups bread flour
1 tablespoon cornmeal
Melted butter

This bread is best right out of the oven. Attach a note to your bake sale loaves instructing to heat in a warm oven before serving.

1. Combine water, yeast, sugar, and salt in a large bowl. Let stand, stirring frequently, until yeast is dissolved, 5 to 10 minutes.

2. Add flour and stir to combine. Cover bowl with a damp cloth and let rise in a warm place for 1 hour.

3. Grease a baking sheet and sprinkle with cornmeal.

4. With floured hands, divide dough in half (do not knead), shape into rounds, and place on baking sheet. Let rise 1 hour.

5. Preheat oven to 425°F. Brush rounds with melted butter. Bake for 10 minutes at 425°F. Reduce temperature to 375°F and bake 20 minutes more. Brush loaves with melted butter. Cool on wire racks. Makes 2 round loaves.

❖ **MARY ANN LAHODNY** | Trinity Presbyterian Church, Little Rock, Arkansas

Rye Bread

½ cake (1 oz.) compressed wet yeast
4¼ cups lukewarm water, divided
1 tablespoon brown sugar
1 tablespoon dark molasses
1 tablespoon salt

½ cup vegetable shortening
3 cups rye flour
8 cups white flour, divided
Melted butter

1. Crumble yeast into ¼ cup of the warm water. Let stand until yeast is soft.

2. Dissolve brown sugar, molasses, salt, and shortening in remaining 4 cups lukewarm water. Add softened yeast, rye flour, and 2 cups of the white flour. Beat until smooth. Cover and let rise until double in bulk, 1 hour.

3. Add remaining 6 cups flour. Knead dough for 20 minutes. Cover and let rise until doubled in bulk, 2 hours. Punch down and let rise again, 1 hour more.

4. Divide dough and shape into four loaves. Place in greased loaf pans. Brush tops with melted butter. Let rise until bread reaches top of pan, ½ to 1 hour. Bake in a preheated 400°F oven for 1 hour. Turn out onto wire racks. Makes 4 loaves.

❖ **MRS. WILLIAM GROTH** | St. John's Guild, St. John's Church, West Bend, Wisconsin

Root Beer Rye Bread

2 packages (.25 oz. each) active dry yeast
½ cup warm water
1 quart root beer
½ cup lard

2 tablespoons salt
⅔ cup dark molasses
3 cups rye flour (do not sift)
7 cups white flour, divided

1. Dissolve yeast in warm water.

2. Heat root beer and lard in a small saucepan over low heat until lard is melted. Add salt and molasses. Stir in yeast mixture. Transfer to a mixer bowl.

3. Mix in rye flour and 3 cups of the white flour. Beat until smooth. Change to the dough hook attachment. With mixer running, gradually add remaining 4 cups white flour and knead until smooth.

4. Turn out dough into a lightly oiled bowl. Turn once to coat. Cover and set aside in a warm place to rise until doubled in size, 2 to 3 hours.

5. Punch down, cover, and set aside to rise again, 1 to 2 hours.

6. Divide dough into four portions, form into loaves, and place in oiled bread pans. Let rise until slightly over top of pan, ½ to 1 hour.

7. Bake in a preheated 325°F for 40 minutes. Turn out onto wire racks to cool. Cooled loaves may be sealed in plastic food storage bags and frozen. Makes 4 loaves.

⁜ Adapted from *The Best of the Old Church Cookbooks* by Florence Ekstrand, courtesy of Welcome Press

Pesto Swirl Bread

1 package (16 oz.) hot roll mix
　(such as Pillsbury)
1 cup hot water (120°F to 130°F)
2 tablespoons butter, room temperature
1 egg

FILLING:
¼ cup olive oil
2 garlic cloves, crushed
½ cup chopped fresh basil or ¼ cup dried basil leaves
½ cup grated Parmesan

TOPPING:
1 egg, slightly beaten
1 tablespoon coarse salt
1 tablespoon chopped fresh basil
　or 1 teaspoon dried basil

1. Combine the contents of the flour packet and yeast packet from the hot roll mix in a large bowl. Whisk to combine. Stir in hot water, butter, and egg. Continue stirring until dough pulls away from sides of bowl.

2. Turn out dough onto a lightly floured surface. With greased or floured hands, shape dough into a ball and knead for 5 minutes until smooth. Invert a large bowl over dough to cover. Let rest 5 minutes.

3. Divide dough in half. Roll each half into 14 x 9-inch rectangle.

4. To make filling: Combine oil and garlic in a small bowl. Brush oil onto each dough rectangle. Combine basil and Parmesan and sprinkle on top.

5. Starting at a long edge, roll up each rectangle and pinch the seam to seal. Place loaves seam side down on a greased baking sheet.

6. To make topping: Lightly brush each loaf with beaten egg. Cover with greased plastic wrap and let rise for 30 minutes. Just before baking, sprinkle with salt and basil.

7. Bake loaves at 350°F for 20 to 30 minutes or until lightly browned and crusty. Cool on wire racks. Flavor improves after 1 day. Makes 2 loaves.

BETTY LINK | Christ Church, Frederica, St. Simons Island, Georgia

Strawberry Bread

3 cups flour
1 teaspoon baking soda
1 teaspoon salt
1 teaspoon cinnamon
2 cups sugar

4 eggs, beaten
1¼ cups oil
1 quart strawberries, hulled and sliced
1¼ cups chopped nuts

1. Preheat oven to 350°F. Grease and flour three 8½ x 4½ x 2½-inch loaf pans.

2. Sift together flour, baking soda, salt, cinnamon, and sugar. Make a well in center, add eggs and oil, and mix until well combined. Stir in strawberries and chopped nuts.

3. Pour batter into pans. Bake for 40 minutes or until a tester inserted in center comes out clean. Slice to serve. Makes 20 to 24 servings.

KATHRYN EYLER | Messiah United Methodist Church, York, Pennsylvania

Date Nut Bread

1 teaspoon baking soda
1 cup boiling water
½ lb. chopped dates
1 cup sugar
1 cup flour

Pinch of salt
1 egg
1 teaspoon vanilla
1 cup chopped walnuts

1. Add baking soda to boiling water, pour over dates, and let stand 30 minutes or until cool.

2. Preheat oven to 350°F. Lightly grease a 9 x 5 x 3-inch loaf pan.

3. Whisk together sugar, flour, and salt in a large bowl.

4. Beat egg and add to dates. Pour dates, vanilla, and nuts into flour mixture. Stir just until moistened.

5. Pour batter into pan. Bake for 45 to 60 minutes or until a tester inserted in center comes out clean. Cool in pan 10 minutes before turning out onto a wire rack. Makes 1 loaf.

THERESA STRAIT | Messiah United Methodist Church, York, Pennsylvania

Peanut Butter Bread

2 cups flour
½ to ¾ cup sugar
1 tablespoon grated orange zest
2 teaspoons baking powder
1 teaspoon salt

¾ cup chunky peanut butter
¼ cup butter, room temperature
1¼ cups milk
1 egg
1 teaspoon vanilla

1. Preheat oven to 375°F. Grease a 9 x 5 x 3-inch loaf pan.

2. Whisk together flour, sugar, orange zest, baking powder, and salt.

3. Combine peanut butter, butter, milk, egg, and vanilla in a mixer bowl. Add flour mixture and stir just until moistened.

4. Pour batter into pan. Bake for 1 hour or until a tester inserted in center comes out clean. Cool in pan 10 minutes before turning out onto a wire rack. Makes 1 loaf.

 **WOMEN'S MISSIONARY AUXILIARY** | Bay Springs, Mississippi

Pear Bread

3 cups flour
1 teaspoon baking soda
¼ teaspoon baking powder
1 teaspoon salt
1 teaspoon cinnamon
1 cup chopped pecans
¾ cup vegetable oil
3 eggs, slightly beaten
2 cups sugar
2 cups pears, peeled and grated
2 teaspoons vanilla

VARIATION:
Use mini loaf pans instead of large loaf pans. Bake at 350°F for 45 to 60 minutes. This recipe will make 5 or 6 mini loaves.

1. Preheat oven to 325°F. Grease and flour two 8½ x 4½ x 2½-inch loaf pans.

2. Combine flour, baking soda, baking powder, salt, cinnamon, pecans, oil, eggs, sugar, pears, and vanilla in a large mixer bowl. Blend on low speed to moisten; then beat until thoroughly combined.

3. Pour batter into pans. Bake for 1 hour 15 minutes or until a tester inserted in center comes out clean. Cool in pan 10 minutes before turning out onto wire racks. Completely cooled bread can be frozen. Makes 2 loaves.

SUE BLEVINS | Trinity Presbyterian Church, Little Rock, Arkansas

Sourdough Bread

1 envelope (.25 oz.) active dry yeast	2 teaspoons sugar
1¼ cups warm water	5½ to 6 cups flour, divided
1 cup Sourdough Starter (recipe follows)	½ teaspoon baking soda
2 teaspoons salt	Melted butter

1. Dissolve yeast in warm water in a large bowl.

2. Blend in sourdough starter, salt, and sugar. Add 4 cups of the flour. Beat for 3 to 4 minutes. Cover and set aside in a warm, draft-free place. Let rise until double in size, about 1½ hours.

3. Sift 1½ cups of the remaining flour with baking soda. Stir into dough. Add up to ½ cup additional flour as needed to make a stiff dough.

4. Turn out dough onto a floured board and knead for 10 minutes. Divide dough in half. Cover and let stand for 10 minutes. Shape into two round or oval loaves. Place on lightly greased baking sheet. With sharp knife, make diagonal gashes across the top. Set aside in warm place and let rise until doubled in size, about 1½ hours.

5. Brush tops of loaves with melted butter. Bake in a preheated 400°F oven for 40 minutes or until browned. Makes 2 loaves.

SOURDOUGH STARTER

1 envelope (.25 oz.) active dry yeast	2 cups flour
½ cup warm water (110°F)	1 teaspoon salt
2 cups lukewarm water	1 tablespoon sugar

1. Dissolve yeast in warm water in a large bowl.

2. Stir in lukewarm water, flour, salt, and sugar. Beat until smooth. Let stand at room temperature, uncovered by day and covered at night, for 3 to 4 days. Stir three times daily.

3. Transfer active starter to a covered container and store in the refrigerator. Take starter as needed for recipes, always reserving at least 1 cup of starter for the next batch. Feed the reserved starter with ½ cup water, ½ cup flour, and 1 teaspoon sugar. Let stand until bubbly and well fermented at least 1 day before using. If it is not used within 10 days, add another teaspoon of sugar.

❖ **PRESBYTERIAN CHURCH OF GONZALES** | Gonzales, Texas

Need a warm, out-of-the-way, draft-free place for dough to rise?
Heat the oven for 1 minute, turn off the heat, and put the bowl of dough inside. Close the oven door and leave undisturbed while the dough rises.

Sopaipillas (Mexican Bread)

1 envelope (.25 oz.) active dry yeast
1 tablespoon warm water (105°F to 115°F)
3 cups flour
½ teaspoon salt

1 tablespoon vegetable shortening
1¼ to 1½ cups buttermilk
Vegetable oil for frying

1. Dissolve yeast in warm water. Let stand 5 minutes.

2. Combine flour and salt in a large bowl. Cut in shortening with a pastry blender. Stir yeast mixture and enough buttermilk into flour mixture to make a soft dough.

3. Turn out dough onto a floured surface and knead 5 to 6 times. Place dough in a well-oiled bowl, turning once so oiled side is on top. Cover and let rise in warm (85°F), draft-free place until doubled in size, about 1 hour.

4. Punch down dough. Turn out onto a floured surface. Roll or pat to a ⅛-inch thickness. Cut into 2½-inch squares with a sharp knife.

5. Pour oil 2 to 3 inches deep in a Dutch oven or deep fryer. Heat to 375°F. Fry dough pieces a few at a time, turning once, until golden brown and crispy. Drain on paper towels. Makes 3 dozen sopaipillas.

❖ SUSAN CALHOON | Trinity Presbyterian Church, Little Rock, Arkansas

Quick Butter Croissants

½ cake (1 oz.) compressed wet yeast
1 cup warm water
¾ cup evaporated milk
1½ teaspoons salt
⅓ cup sugar

1 egg
5¼ to 5½ cups flour, divided
¼ cup butter, melted and cooled
1 cup butter, cold
1 egg beaten with 1 tablespoon water

1. Dissolve yeast in warm water. Add milk, salt, sugar, egg, and 1 cup of the flour. Beat until smooth. Stir in melted butter.

2. Sift 4 cups of the flour into a large bowl. Cut in cold butter with a pastry blender to form pea-size crumbs. Gradually add yeast mixture. Stir gently, blending just until flour is moistened. Cover with plastic wrap. Refrigerate at least 4 hours and up to 4 days.

3. Press dough into a compact ball. Turn out onto a floured surface and knead lightly. Divide into four parts. Work with one portion at a time, covering and refrigerating the rest.

4. Roll out dough into a 17-inch circle. Cut into 8 wedges. Loosely roll the outer edge of each wedge toward the point and bend into a crescent shape. Place 1½ inches apart on an ungreased baking sheet. Cover lightly and let rise at room temperature until doubled in bulk, 2 hours.

5. Brush croissants with egg-water mixture. Bake in a preheated 325°F oven for 35 minutes or until lightly browned. Serve warm or cool on a rack. Makes 32 croissants.

❖ ELAINE KOENIG | St. John's Guild, St. John's Church, West Bend, Wisconsin

Butterhorns

5 cups flour
½ teaspoon salt
½ cup butter
½ cup lard
3 eggs
½ cup sugar
½ cake (1 oz.) compressed wet yeast
¼ cup warm water
1 cup warm milk

NUT FILLING:
2 tablespoons butter
1 cup sugar
1 cup ground almonds
1 egg beaten
Grated zest of ½ lemon
1 teaspoon almond extract

1. Whisk together flour and salt. Cut in butter and lard with a pastry blender until crumbly. Beat eggs, add sugar, and beat again. Stir eggs into flour mixture.

2. Dissolve yeast in warm water. Combine with warm milk and add to flour mixture. Knead until dough is smooth and elastic. Set aside to rise, 1 to 2 hours.

3. To make nut filling: Combine butter and sugar. Add ground almonds and egg to make a paste. Stir in lemon zest and almond extract.

4. Punch down dough, divide into five pieces, and shape each piece into a round patty. Roll out one patty on a lightly floured surface to a ⅛-inch thickness. Spread with one-fifth of nut filling. Cut like pizza into 12 long triangular wedges. Roll up wedges, starting the wide end. Place on lightly greased baking sheets and let rise, ½ to 1 hour. Bake in a 375°F oven for 15 minutes or until lightly browned. Makes 60 butterhorns.

MRS. HEMBEL | St. John's Guild, St. John's Church, West Bend, Wisconsin

Zucchini Nut Bread

3 eggs, beaten
2 cups sugar
2 teaspoons vanilla
1 cup vegetable oil
2 cups grated zucchini, drained
2 cups flour

¼ teaspoon baking powder
2 teaspoons baking soda
1 teaspoon salt
2 teaspoons cinnamon
1 cup chopped pecans

1. Preheat oven to 325°F. Grease and flour two 8½ x 4½ x 2½-inch loaf pans.

2. Combine eggs, sugar, vanilla, and oil until well blended. Stir in zucchini.

3. Sift together flour, baking powder, baking soda, salt, and cinnamon. Toss ½ cup of the flour mixture with chopped pecans. Stir remaining flour mixture into zucchini batter until well blended. Stir in floured pecans. Mix well.

4. Pour batter into pans. Bake for 45 minutes or until a tester inserted comes out clean. Cool in pans 10 minutes before turning out onto wire racks. Slice to serve. Makes 16 to 18 servings.

SHIRLEY HEDGER | Unity Baptist Church, Morgantown, Indiana

Pecan Sticky Buns

3¼ to 3¾ cups flour, divided

1 cup flour

¼ cup sugar

1 envelope (.25 oz.) active dry yeast

½ cup milk

¼ cup water

⅓ cup butter

2 eggs (at room temperature)

½ cup flour

TOPPING:

4 tablespoons butter

1 cup brown sugar

½ cup light corn syrup

1 cup coarsely chopped pecans

FILLING:

4 tablespoons butter, melted

½ cup brown sugar

1. Combine 1 cup of the flour, sugar, and yeast in a mixer bowl.

2. Combine milk, water, and butter in a small saucepan over low heat. Heat until butter melts and temperature measured with a cooking thermometer reaches 120°F to 130°F. Add to flour mixture and beat 2 minutes at medium speed.

3. Add eggs and another ½ cup flour. Beat 2 minutes at high speed. Stir in enough remaining flour to make soft dough. Change to dough hook attachment and knead 8 to 10 minutes. Turn out dough into a greased bowl and turn once to coat. Cover and let rise in a warm, draft-free place until doubled in size, about 1 hour.

4. To make topping: Melt butter in a small saucepan over low heat. Add brown sugar and corn syrup. Continue heating, stirring occasionally, until sugar dissolves. Pour mixture into a greased 13 x 9 x 2-inch baking pan. Sprinkle with pecan pieces.

5. To make filling: Punch down dough, divide in half, and roll each half to 14 x 10 inches. Brush each rectangle with melted butter and sprinkle with brown sugar. Roll up from short edge and seal seams.

6. Cut each roll 10 slices. Place cut side down in pan. Cover and let rise until doubled in size, 45 minutes.

7. Preheat oven to 375°F. Bake for 20 minutes or until golden brown. Cool in pan 5 minutes and then invert onto a serving platter. Makes 20 buns.

✤ **LORRAINE GUARINO** | St. Mark's Lutheran Church, Conshohocken, Pennsylvania

Rhubarb Bread

1⅚ cups sugar, divided

⅔ cup oil

1 teaspoon vanilla

1 egg

2½ cups flour

1 teaspoon baking soda

1 teaspoon salt

1 cup buttermilk

1½ cups cut up rhubarb

½ cup chopped nuts

2 tablespoons melted butter

1. Preheat oven to 350°F. Grease two 8½ x 4½ x 2½-inch loaf pans and line with waxed paper.

2. Combine 1½ cups of the sugar, oil, vanilla, and egg in a mixer bowl.

Bread Blessing

Let God be thanked whene'er is spread
A table with a loaf of bread,
For in each loaf these wonders hide,
And hungering folk are satisfied.
We thank Thee, for our daily bread,
Let also, Lord, our souls be fed;
O Bread of Life, from day to day,
Sustain us on our homeward way. Amen.

Adapted from *The Best of the Old Church Cookbooks*
by Florence Ekstrand, courtesy of Welcome Press

3. Whisk together flour, baking soda, and salt. Add flour mixture and buttermilk alternately to egg mixture, mixing well after each addition. Stir in rhubarb and nuts.

4. Pour batter into pans. Stir remaining ⅓ cup sugar into melted butter. Spread on top of each loaf. Bake for 45 minutes or until top is browned and crusty. Makes 2 loaves.

❖ **GINI WAGNER** | Methow Valley United Methodist Church, Twisp, Washington

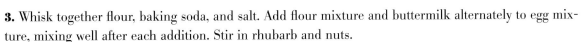

Butterscotch Pecan Rolls

1 tablespoon butter
¼ cup brown sugar
3 tablespoons whole pecans
2 cups biscuit mix
¾ cup milk

FILLING:

2 tablespoons butter, room temperature
¾ cup brown sugar
1½ teaspoons cinnamon
¼ cup coarsely chopped pecans

1. Preheat oven to 375°F. Butter a 12 x 9 x 1-inch jelly roll pan.

2. Combine butter, brown sugar, and pecans. Layer in bottom of pan.

3. Combine biscuit mix and milk to make a dough. Roll out dough into a rectangle to a ¼-inch thickness.

4. To make filling: Spread butter over dough rectangle. Sprinkle with brown sugar, cinnamon, and pecans.

5. Roll dough as for a jelly roll, cut crosswise into 12 slices, and arrange slices in pan. Bake for 20 minutes or until lightly browned. Serve on a plate, spooning the pan mixture on top. Makes 12 servings.

❖ **DOT BRYSON** | First Moravian Church, Greensboro, North Carolina

Sweet Rolls

2 packages (.25 oz. each) active dry yeast
½ cup warm water (110°F to 115°F)
1½ cups lukewarm milk
½ cup sugar
2 teaspoons salt
2 eggs
½ cup vegetable shortening
7 to 7½ cups flour, divided

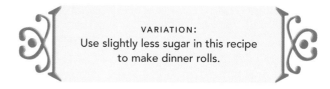

VARIATION:
Use slightly less sugar in this recipe
to make dinner rolls.

1. Dissolve yeast in warm water in a large bowl.

2. Add milk, sugar, salt, eggs, shortening, and 3 cups of the flour. Mix with spoon until smooth. Add enough remaining flour to handle easily.

3. Turn out dough onto a lightly floured board. Knead until smooth, about 5 minutes. Place in a greased bowl and turn once to coat. Cover and let rise in a warm place (85°F) until doubled in size, 1½ hours.

4. Punch down dough. Cover and let rise again until almost double in size, 1½ hours.

5. Punch down dough. Let rise again, 30 minutes.

6. Shape dough into rolls, place on a greased baking sheet, and let rise until almost doubled in size, 30 minutes.

7. Preheat oven to 400°F. Bake rolls for 12 to 15 minutes or until golden brown. Serve hot or at room temperature. Makes 40 rolls.

❖ **GLENDA HORN** | Methow Valley United Methodist Church, Twisp, Washington

Cheddar-Cumin Rolls

1¼ teaspoons active dry yeast
1 teaspoon sugar
1¼ cups warm water
½ lb. cheddar cheese, cubed

3½ cups bread flour, divided
1½ teaspoons salt
1½ teaspoons ground cumin
1½ teaspoons cornmeal

1. Combine yeast, sugar, and water in a glass cup. Set aside until it bubbles, about 10 minutes.

2. Blend cheddar cheese with ½ cup of the flour in a food processor. Add remaining 3 cups flour, salt, and cumin. Pulse to combine.

3. Stir yeast mixture into flour mixture to form a shaggy mass. Turn out dough into a warm bowl, cover, and set aside in a warm place until tripled in size, 3 to 3½ hours.

4. Turn out dough onto a lightly floured board and knead gently. Divide dough in half. Cut each half into six pieces. Shape each piece into a ball and pinch in one spot. Set balls 2 inches apart on a baking sheet that has been sprinkled with cornmeal. Cover with floured cloth and let rise 1½ to 2 hours.

5. Preheat oven to 450°F. Spray rolls with cold water, place on lowest rack of oven, and bake for 20 minutes or until tops are browned and crusty. Makes 12 rolls.

❖ **MARTHA RUSSELL** | Christ Church, Frederica, St. Simons Island, Georgia

Parker House Rolls

1 cake (2 oz.) compressed wet yeast
2 tablespoons lukewarm water
1 cup milk, scalded
3 tablespoons sugar

½ teaspoon salt
1 egg white, stiffly beaten
Flour (enough to knead)
Butter, room temperature

1. Soften yeast cake in lukewarm water.

2. Mix scalded milk, sugar, and salt. Cool to lukewarm.

3. Add yeast to milk mixture. Blend in egg white. Add flour ½ cup at a time and blend thoroughly until dough reaches kneading consistency. Knead thoroughly or until dough is smooth and satiny to the touch, keeps its round shape, and does not stick to the board or hands. Place dough in a oiled bowl, turn once to coat, and cover tightly. Let rise until doubled in bulk, 2 to 2½ hours.

4. Knead down dough, adding just enough flour to prevent sticking. Roll out to a ¼-inch thickness. Cut out dough rounds with a biscuit cutter. Spread butter on each round. Press a knife through the center, creasing the dough. Fold over and press the edges together.

5. Place rolls in a shallow pan 1½ to 2 inches apart. Let rise again, 1 to 1½ hours.

6. Preheat oven to 350°F. Bake rolls for 25 minutes or until lightly browned. Serve while still hot. Makes 18 rolls.

MRS. W. T. MILLER | Presbyterian Church of Gonzales, Gonzales Texas

Graham Rolls

⅔ cup sugar
2 packages (.25 oz. each) active dry yeast
1½ cups warm water
⅔ cup vegetable shortening
2 beaten eggs
1½ teaspoons salt
1 cup warm mashed potatoes
2 cups graham flour
3½ cups bread flour

Graham flour is coarse and flaky. It has a slightly nutty taste.

1. Sprinkle sugar and yeast into warm water. Let stand until bubbly.

2. Combine shortening, eggs, salt, and mashed potatoes in a large bowl. Add graham flour and stir. Add yeast mixture. Mix in bread flour to form a soft dough.

3. Knead dough. Place dough in bowl and cover. Place in refrigerator and let rise overnight.

4. Shape dough into rolls. Place on lightly greased baking sheets. Let rise at room temperature until doubled in size, 1 to 2 hours.

5. Preheat oven to 375°F. Bake rolls for 20 minutes or until lightly browned. Makes 24 rolls.

NANCY ACHESON | Methow Valley United Methodist Church, Twisp, Washington

Spoon Rolls

2 packages (.25 oz.) active dry yeast
2 cups very warm water
½ cup sugar

½ cup oil
1 egg
4 cups self-rising flour

1. Add yeast to warm water.

2. Blend sugar and oil in a large mixer bowl. Beat in egg. Stir in yeast mixture. Stir in flour. Mix until well combined. Gently transfer to a container that has a tight-fitting lid. Cover and refrigerate at least 4 hours and up to 1 week.

3. Preheat oven to 350°F. Grease two 12-cup muffin pans. Drop batter by spoonfuls into muffin cups. Bake for 20 minutes or until lightly browned. Makes 2 dozen.

❖ SALLIE CARGILE | Women's Missionary Auxiliary, Bay Springs, Mississippi

Sugarless Apple Pie

1½ tablespoons tapioca
1 can (6 oz.) frozen apple juice
   concentrate, thawed
Whole Wheat Pie Pastry (recipe follows)

2 to 3 lbs. tart apples, peeled and sliced
Cinnamon
Butter

1. Preheat oven to 450°F.

2. Stir tapioca into apple juice concentrate.

3. Roll out whole wheat pastry for top and bottom crusts. Line a 9-inch pie plate with pastry.

4. Layer apples into pie plate. Top with tapioca mixture. Sprinkle with cinnamon. Dot with butter.

5. Lay pastry for top crust over apples. Trim and crimp the edges. Cut steam slits. Bake for 10 minutes, lower heat to 350°F, and bake 35 to 40 minutes more or until crust is lightly browned. Cool before serving. Makes 6 to 8 servings.

WHOLE WHEAT PIE PASTRY

1 cup flour
1 cup whole wheat flour
¼ teaspoon salt

5 tablespoons water
½ cup oil

1. Combine flour, whole wheat flour, salt, water, and oil in a mixer bowl. Mix until well blended.

2. Gather dough into a ball, divide in half, and form into two patties. Makes pastry for 1 double-crust or 2 single-crust pies.

❖ DORIS MASON | Memorial Baptist Church, Tulsa, Oklahoma

French Apple Pie

SINGLE CRUST:

1 cup flour

½ teaspoon salt

⅓ cup plus 1 tablespoon vegetable shortening

2 tablespoons plus 4 teaspoons water

CRUMB TOPPING:

½ cup butter

½ cup brown sugar

1 cup flour

FILLING:

5 to 7 cups McIntosh apples, peeled and sliced

¾ cup sugar

½ teaspoon cinnamon

½ teaspoon nutmeg

1½ teaspoons butter

1. To make single crust: Mix flour and salt. Cut in shortening until crumbly. Sprinkle with water. Stir just until dough begins to pull together. Gather up into a ball and flatten slightly. Roll out onto a lightly floured surface. Ease into a 9-inch pie plate.

2. To make filling: Toss apples, sugar, cinnamon, and nutmeg until well combined. Heap filling into pie shell. Dot with butter.

3. To make crumb topping: Combine butter, brown sugar, and flour until crumbly. Pat onto top of apples.

4. Place pie in freezer overnight. Place frozen pie in a preheated 325° oven and bake for 1 hour 15 minutes or until crust is lightly browned. Serve warm with whipped cream or ice cream. Makes 6 to 8 servings.

LISA SINN | Trinity Evangelical Lutheran Church, Lansdale, Pennsylvania

Apple Crisp

4 cups sliced apples

Cinnamon

Nutmeg

Sugar

TOPPING:

1 cup flour

1 teaspoon cinnamon

½ cup butter, room temperature

1 cup water

1. Preheat oven to 350°F. Grease a 9 x 9 x 2-inch baking pan.

2. Place apples in a large bowl. Sprinkle with cinnamon, nutmeg, and sugar. Toss to coat. Layer into baking pan.

3. To make topping: Combine flour, cinnamon, and butter until crumbly. Spread evenly on top of apples. Pour water into pan. Bake for 45 minutes or until apples are bubbly. Makes 4 to 6 servings.

BRENDA STAMPLEY | Oakwood Church of God in Christ, Godfrey, Illinois

Apple Cider Pie

¾ cup apple cider
½ cup raisins
1 tablespoon cornstarch
½ teaspoon ginger
½ teaspoon grated lemon zest

1 cup sugar plus more for sprinkling top crust
1 tablespoon flour
5 cups tart apples, peeled, cored,
  and thinly sliced
Pastry for 1 double-crust pie

1. Preheat oven to 375°F.

2. Roll out pastry for top and bottom crusts. Line a 9-inch pie plate with pastry.

3. Combine apple cider, raisins, cornstarch, ginger, and lemon zest in a saucepan over medium heat. Bring to a boil. Cook, stirring continuously, until thickened, 2 minutes. Remove from heat.

4. Stir together sugar and flour in a large bowl. Add apples and toss until coated. Spoon apples into pie shell. Spoon apple cider mixture over apples.

5. Lay pastry for top crust over apples. Trim and crimp the edges. Cut slits in top. Sprinkle with a little sugar. Bake for 40 to 45 minutes or until apples are tender and crust is golden brown. Cool on wire rack for 2 hours before serving. Makes 6 to 8 servings.

❖ GOLDA PACK | First Baptist Church, Russell, Kentucky

My Secret Apple Pie

Pastry for 1 double-crust pie
1¼ cups sugar plus more for
  sprinkling top crust
1¼ teaspoons cinnamon
½ teaspoon nutmeg

½ teaspoon salt
⅓ cup cornstarch
6 to 7 cups sliced apples
¼ cup orange juice
¼ cup honey or maple syrup

1. Preheat oven to 425°F.

2. Roll out pastry for top and bottom crusts. Line a 9-inch pie plate with pastry.

3. Place sugar, cinnamon, nutmeg, salt, and cornstarch into a resealable 1-gallon food storage bag. Add apple slices, shake quickly to coat, and dump immediately into pie shell. Mix orange juice and honey and drizzle over apples.

4. Lay pastry for top crust over apples. Trim and crimp the edges. Cut vent holes. Sprinkle water onto crust and then sprinkle sugar over the wet spots. Cover edges with strips of aluminum foil. Bake for 70 to 75 minutes or until top is lightly browned. Remove foil strips during last 15 minutes of baking. Cool for 20 minutes before serving. Makes 6 to 8 servings.

❖ ERNIE LEVON | Methow Valley United Methodist Church, Twisp, Washington

Cherry Tarts

2 cups flour
1 teaspoon salt
¾ cup lard or 1 cup vegetable shortening
¼ cup cold water

1 can (14.5 oz.) sour cherries
1 cup sugar
3 tablespoons cornstarch
Red food coloring

1. Preheat oven to 475°F. Turn over a 6-cup muffin pan and lightly grease the outside of each muffin cup.

2. Whisk together flour and salt. Cut in lard or shortening with a pastry blender. Add cold water and stir just to pull dough together.

3. Turn out dough onto a lightly floured board. Roll out dough, cut into six squares, and drape each square over the outside of a muffin cup. Gently press the dough around each muffin cup so they hold their shape. Bake for 10 minutes. Cool on the muffin pan.

4. Combine cherries, sugar, and cornstarch in a large saucepan over medium heat. Cook, stirring frequently, until thick and syrupy. Stir in a few drops of red food coloring. Cool slightly.

5. Set each baked tart shell on a plate and spoon in some warm cherry filling. Makes 6 servings.

❖ **ESTHER KLEIN** | St. John's Guild, St. John's Church, West Bend, Wisconsin

Blackberry Pinwheel Cobbler

2 cups sugar
2 cups water
½ cup butter
½ cup vegetable shortening

1½ cups self-rising flour
⅓ cup milk
3 cups fresh blackberries
1 teaspoon cinnamon

1. Combine sugar and water in a saucepan over medium heat. Cook, stirring continuously, until sugar dissolves.

2. Preheat oven to 350°F. Place butter in a 13 x 9 x 2-inch baking dish. Place in oven for 3 minutes or until butter melts. Remove from oven.

3. Cut shortening into flour until mixture resembles coarse meal. Add milk and stir just until moistened.

4. Turn out dough onto a lightly floured surface. Knead lightly 4 or 5 times. Roll dough into a 12 x 9-inch rectangle. Spread blackberries over dough. Sprinkle with cinnamon. Roll up, jelly roll style, starting from a long edge. Cut into twelve 1-inch slices, place cut side down into melted butter, and pour sugar syrup all around. Bake for 55 to 60 minutes or until golden. Makes 8 to 10 servings.

❖ **IRENE GRAVES** | Women's Missionary Auxiliary, Bay Springs, Mississippi

Nellie's Crumb Top Apple Dessert

8 large apples (about 4 lbs.), thinly sliced
½ teaspoon cinnamon
¼ teaspoon nutmeg
⅔ cup sugar
2 tablespoons water

2 tablespoons lemon juice
½ cup butter, room temperature
½ cup brown sugar
1 cup flour

1. Preheat oven to 350°F.

2. Layer apples in a 13 x 9 x 2-inch baking dish.

3. Stir cinnamon and nutmeg into sugar. Sprinkle evenly over apples. Add water and lemon juice.

4. Cream butter and brown sugar until fluffy. Stir in flour until thoroughly mixed. Spread topping over apples. Bake for 50 to 60 minutes or until bubbly. Cool 30 minutes before serving. Makes 6 to 8 servings.

NELLIE GLASSCOCK, submitted by WANDA LORETTE | Grace on the Hill United Methodist Church, Corbin, Kentucky

Mincemeat for Pies

4 lbs. beef
2 tablespoons salt

For every 2 bowls of cooked ground beef, add:
3 bowls ground apples
2 bowls raisins
3 bowls sugar
1 bowl molasses
1 bowl meat stock
1 bowl brandy
1 teaspoon nutmeg
2 tablespoons cinnamon
1 tablespoon cloves

1. Place beef in a stockpot, sprinkle with salt, and add water to cover. Simmer over low heat until very tender, 3 to 4 hours.

2. Drain off and reserve stock. Grind beef in meat grinder. Measure ground beef by the bowlful and return it to the pot.

3. Add apples, raisins, sugar, molasses, reserved beef stock, brandy, nutmeg, cinnamon, and cloves. Simmer for 1 hour. Put up in sterilized canning jars. Makes about 2 quarts. One pint of mincemeat is enough for an 8-inch pie.

MRS. OSCAR KLEIN | St. John's Guild, St. John's Church, West Bend, Wisconsin

Blueberry Cobbler Pie

½ cup brown sugar

½ teaspoon salt

1 tablespoon cornstarch

¾ cup water

1 tablespoon lemon juice

2 tablespoons butter, divided

1½ cups cornflakes

2 cups blueberries

¼ cup chopped nuts

1. Preheat oven to 350°F.

2. Combine brown sugar, salt, and cornstarch in a saucepan over low heat. Gradually add water and cook, stirring continuously, until thickened, 6 to 8 minutes. Stir in lemon juice and 1 tablespoon of the butter. Remove from heat.

3. Melt the remaining tablespoon butter. Pour over cornflakes and toss to combine.

4. Layer blueberries in an 8-inch glass pie plate. Sprinkle with chopped nuts. Pour syrup over all. Top with buttery cornflakes. Bake for 40 minutes or until blueberries are bubbly. Cool slightly before serving. Makes 6 to 8 servings.

MARY RENNINGER | St. Mark's Lutheran Church, Conshohocken, Pennsylvania

Crustless Brownie Pie

1 cup sugar

½ cup flour

¼ cup cocoa

½ cup butter, room temperature

2 eggs

1 teaspoon vanilla

Pinch of salt

½ cup chopped pecans

1. Preheat oven to 325°F. Grease a 9-inch pie plate.

2. Combine sugar, flour, cocoa, butter, eggs, vanilla, and salt in food processor. Blend for 4 minutes.

3. Drop in pecans and spin just until they are mixed in.

4. Spread batter evenly in pie plate. Bake for 35 to 40 minutes or until a tester inserted in center comes out clean. Cool on a wire rack. Makes 6 to 8 servings.

❖ SARA WILLIAMS | First Moravian Church, Greensboro, North Carolina

Peach Blueberry Pie

1 unbaked 9-inch pie shell

4 large ripe peaches, sliced

1 cup fresh blueberries

½ to ¾ cup whipped butter, melted

¼ cup flour

1 egg, beaten

1 cup sugar

1. Preheat oven to 350°F.

2. Layer sliced peaches in pie shell. Pour blueberries over peaches.

3. Whisk together melted butter, flour, egg, and sugar. Spread over blueberries.

4. Bake for 50 minutes or until topping is lightly browned. Cool and serve at room temperature. Refrigerate unused portions. Makes 6 to 8 servings.

❖ ANGIE BURNS | Christ Church, Frederica, St. Simons Island, Georgia

Strawberry Pie

3 tablespoons cornstarch

3 tablespoons strawberry gelatin powder

½ cup sugar

1 cup hot water

1 pint fresh strawberries, sliced

1 baked 9-inch pie shell

Whipped cream

1. Combine cornstarch, gelatin, sugar, and water in a saucepan over medium heat. Bring to a boil, remove from heat, and let cool.

2. Stir strawberries into gelatin mixture. Pour mixture into pie shell. Refrigerate until set, 4 to 6 hours. Serve topped with whipped cream. Makes 6 to 8 servings.

❖ JO RANKIN | Christ Episcopal Church, Charlotte, North Carolina

Peach Cobbler

1 cup flour
½ teaspoon salt
⅓ cup vegetable shortening
4 tablespoons milk
½ cup butter, melted

FILLING:

8 to 10 peaches, peeled and sliced
¼ to ½ cup water
1½ to 1¾ cups sugar
2 tablespoons flour
½ cup butter
1 teaspoon vanilla

1. Preheat oven to 350°F. Lightly grease a 9 x 9 x 2-inch baking pan.

2. Combine flour and salt. Cut in shortening until crumbly. Stir in milk until dough begins to come together. Gather into a ball, wrap in plastic wrap, and chill in refrigerator.

3. To make filling: Place peaches in a saucepan, add ¼ to ½ cup water, and cook over low heat until tender, 8 to 10 minutes. Add more water if necessary to keep pan from running dry. Whisk together sugar and flour and add to peaches. Add butter and vanilla and stir until melted.

4. Spoon peach mixture into baking dish. Roll out pastry and layer on top of peaches. Drizzle melted butter over top of pastry. Bake for 40 to 45 minutes or until lightly browned. Makes 8 to 10 servings.

❖ NELL (FORRESTER) BULLEN | Memorial Baptist Church, Tulsa, Oklahoma

Blueberry Cobbler

6 cups fresh blueberries
¾ cup sugar
2 teaspoons fresh lemon juice
1 teaspoon grated lemon peel
½ teaspoon cinnamon
1 tablespoon quick-cooking tapioca

TOPPING:

1¼ cups flour
⅓ cup cornmeal
⅓ cup sugar
2½ teaspoons baking powder
¼ teaspoon baking soda
¼ teaspoon salt
⅓ cup butter, cut up
1⅓ cups buttermilk
1 tablespoon sugar mixed with a pinch of cinnamon

1. Preheat oven to 350°F. Grease a 2½-quart baking dish.

2. Combine blueberries, sugar, lemon juice and zest, cinnamon, and tapioca in a bowl. Let stand 15 minutes.

3. To make topping: Whisk together flour, cornmeal, sugar, baking powder, baking soda, and salt in a large bowl. Cut in butter with a pastry blender or 2 knives to resemble coarse crumbs. Stir in buttermilk with a rubber spatula just until blended.

4. Transfer blueberry mixture to baking dish. Drop batter by tablespoonful over blueberries. Sprinkle cinnamon-sugar mixture evenly over batter. Bake for 55 to 60 minutes or until topping is golden and filling is bubbly. Cool on a wire rack for 30 minutes. Makes 8 servings.

❖ MEMORIAL BAPTIST CHURCH | Tulsa, Oklahoma

Creamy Pear Pie

4 cups peeled, sliced pears

⅓ cup sugar

2 tablespoons flour

½ teaspoon vanilla

½ teaspoon almond extract

½ teaspoon lemon extract

1 cup (8 oz.) sour cream

1 unbaked 9-inch pie shell

¼ cup flour

2 tablespoons butter, melted

2 tablespoons brown sugar

1. Preheat oven to 400°F.

2. Toss pears with sugar and flour.

3. Stir vanilla, almond extract, and lemon extract into sour cream. Add to pears and mix to combine.

4. Spoon pears into pie shell. Combine flour, melted butter, and brown sugar until crumbly. Sprinkle over pears. Bake for 10 minutes. Reduce heat to 350°F and bake 45 minutes more or until the pears are tender. Cool on a wire rack. Makes 6 to 8 servings.

JUDY TONSETH | Methow Valley United Methodist Church, Twisp, Washington

Mixed Berry Pie

4 cups strawberries

2 cups blueberries

1 cup raspberries or cherries

1½ cups sugar

5 tablespoons quick-cooking tapioca

¼ teaspoon cinnamon

1 unbaked 9-inch deep-dish
   pie shell

TOPPING:

2 cups flour

1 cup brown sugar

2 teaspoons cinnamon

½ teaspoon salt

½ cup butter, melted

1. Preheat oven to 350°F.

2. Combine strawberries, blueberries, raspberries or cherries, sugar, tapioca, and cinnamon. Pour into pie shell.

3. To make topping: Combine flour, brown sugar, cinnamon, and salt. Add melted butter and stir until moistened and crumbly. Sprinkle on top of pie.

4. Bake for 60 minutes or until berries are bubbly. Cool on a wire rack. Makes 6 to 8 servings.

KATE BUCKFELDER | Christ Episcopal Church, Charlotte, North Carolina

Strawberry Crisp

4 cups sliced strawberries

2 tablespoons sugar

¼ to ½ teaspoon cinnamon

1¼ cups whole wheat flour

1¼ cups quick-cooking rolled oats

⅔ cup brown sugar

¼ teaspoon baking soda

⅛ teaspoon salt

⅔ cup cold butter

1. Preheat oven to 350°F. Grease a 9 x 9 x 2-inch baking pan.

2. Place strawberries in a bowl. Combine sugar and cinnamon, sprinkle over the strawberries, and toss gently.

3. Combine whole wheat flour, oats, brown sugar, baking soda, and salt in a large bowl. Cut in butter until mixture resembles coarse crumbs. Reserve 1½ cups of mixture for topping. Pat remaining mixture into bottom of pan.

4. Spoon strawberries into pan and spread evenly. Sprinkle with reserved crumb mixture. Bake for 35 to 40 minutes or until golden brown. Serve warm. Makes 8 to 10 servings.

❖ **FREDA GANTT** | Methow Valley United Methodist Church, Twisp, Washington

Plum Pie

1 double-crust pie pastry

¼ cup brown sugar

¼ cup saltine crumbs

1½ lbs. fresh purple plums,
    pitted and quartered

1 cup sugar

¼ cup flour

1 teaspoon cinnamon

1 tablespoon cold butter

1. Preheat oven to 400°F. Line a 9-inch pie plate with pastry.

2. Combine brown sugar and saltine crumbs. Sprinkle evenly over bottom of pastry and press gently with your fingers.

3. Layer plums into pie shell, starting at outer edge and working in toward the center.

4. Combine sugar, flour, and cinnamon. Cut in butter until crumbly. Sprinkle over plums.

5. Roll out remaining pastry and place over plums. Trim, seal, and flute the edges. Cut slits in the top to allow steam to escape. Bake for 30 minutes. Reduce heat to 350°F and bake 25 minutes more or until golden brown. Makes 6 to 8 servings.

❖ **MARIETTA HENDERSON** | Unity Baptist Church, Morgantown, Indiana

Rhubarb Crunch

3 cups chopped rhubarb

½ cup sugar

1 tablespoon flour

½ teaspoon cinnamon

½ teaspoon salt

TOPPING:

1 cup brown sugar

1 cup rolled oats

¾ cup butter

¾ cup flour

1. Preheat oven to 375°F. Lightly grease an 8 x 8 x 2-inch baking pan.

2. Combine rhubarb, sugar, flour, cinnamon, and salt. Layer evenly in baking dish.

3. To make topping: Mix brown sugar, rolled oats, butter, and flour until crumbly. Sprinkle over top of rhubarb mixture. Bake for 30 or 40 minutes or until topping is lightly browned and rhubarb filling is bubbly. Cool 20 to 30 minutes before serving. Makes 6 to 8 servings.

❖ **LOLA CRAFTON** | Unity Baptist Church, Morgantown, Indiana

Shoo-Fly Pie

2½ cups flour

1 teaspoon baking powder

1½ cups sugar

½ cup butter

2 unbaked 9-inch pie shells

1 cup hot water

½ cup molasses

1 teaspoon baking soda

1. Preheat oven to 350°F.

2. Combine flour, baking powder, sugar, and butter until crumbly. Sprinkle ½ cup of crumb mixture into bottom of each pie shell.

3. Combine hot water, molasses, and baking soda. Stir until molasses is dissolved. Pour half of molasses mixture into each pie shell. Top with remaining crumb mixture. Bake for 45 minutes or until lightly browned. Makes 12 to 16 servings.

❖ **GLADYS REED** | Trinity Evangelical Lutheran Church, Lansdale, Pennsylvania

Lula's Fried Pie Dough

2½ cups flour

1 teaspoon baking powder

½ teaspoon salt

2 tablespoons sugar

½ cup vegetable shortening

Evaporated milk

1 egg, beaten

1. Sift together flour, baking powder, salt, and sugar. Cut in shortening with a pastry blender or your fingers to resemble fine meal.

2. Add evaporated milk to beaten egg to measure 1 cup. Add to flour mixture and stir until dough leaves side of bowl. Knead gently. Wrap tightly in plastic wrap and refrigerate overnight. Use the dough to make deep-fried fruit fritters. Makes enough dough for 6 fritters.

❖ **AUNT LULA BAIN** | Women's Missionary Auxiliary, Bay Springs, Mississippi

One-Bowl Chocolate Pecan Pie

8 squares (1 oz. each) semisweet baking
    chocolate, divided
2 tablespoons butter
1 package (15 oz.) refrigerated
    piecrust pastry

3 eggs, slightly beaten
¼ cup brown sugar
1 cup corn syrup
1 teaspoon vanilla
1½ cups pecan halves

1. Preheat oven to 350°F.

2. Coarsely chop 4 squares of chocolate and set aside. Place remaining 4 squares of chocolate and butter in a large microwavable bowl. Microwave on high setting for 1 to 2 minutes or until butter is melted. Stir to combine.

3. Line a 9-inch pie plate with pastry. Brush bottom of pie shell with a small amount of the beaten egg.

4. Stir eggs, brown sugar, corn syrup, and vanilla into chocolate and butter mixture until well blended. Stir in pecans and chopped chocolate. Pour into pie shell. Bake for 55 minutes or until a knife inserted 2 inches from edge comes out clean. Cool on wire rack. Makes 8 servings.

❖ **ELIZABETH GREEN** | Westside Baptist Church, Antlers, Oklahoma

Piecrust, Hot Water Method

SINGLE-CRUST PASTRY:
½ cup vegetable shortening
⅛ cup boiling water
1 tablespoon sweet milk
1½ cups flour
Pinch of salt

DOUBLE-CRUST PASTRY:
¾ cup vegetable shortening
¼ cup boiling water
1 tablespoon sweet milk
2 cups flour
Pinch of salt

1. Combine shortening, water, and sweet milk in a large bowl.

2. Add flour and salt, mixing until well combined. Press dough into pie plate with your fingers. Dough can be handled as much as necessary but it cannot be rolled. Makes pastry for 1 single-crust or 1 double-crust pie.

❖ **SAM BEARD** | Pittsboro Baptist Church, Pittsboro, North Carolina

Flaky Pastry

2½ cups flour
½ teaspoon salt
1 cup vegetable shortening

1 egg, beaten
Water as needed

1. Whisk together flour and salt. Cut in shortening with a pastry blender or your fingers until crumbly.
2. Add water to beaten egg to measure ½ cup. Stir egg mixture into flour mixture to make a soft pastry.
Makes pastry for 1 single-crust pie or the top pastry for a chicken pie.

AUDNA KEITH | Women's Missionary Auxiliary, Bay Springs, Mississippi

Favorite Piecrust

3 cups flour
1 teaspoon salt
1¼ cups lard

1 beaten egg
2 teaspoons vinegar
5 tablespoons ice water

1. Sift together flour and salt. Cut in shortening with a pastry blender or your fingers.
2. Combine egg, vinegar, and ice water. Add to flour mixture and stir to form a dough. Gather up dough into a ball. Divide dough into four portions and shape into patties. Wrap in plastic wrap and refrigerate. Makes dough for 2 double-crust pies.

Adapted from *The Best of the Old Church Cookbooks* by Florence Ekstrand, courtesy of Welcome Press

Crumb Piecrust

2 cups flour
1 teaspoon salt
2 teaspoons sugar

4 teaspoons milk
⅔ cup vegetable oil

1. Whisk together flour, salt, and sugar.
2. Stir milk into oil, add to flour mixture, and stir until combined. Mixture will be crumbly.
3. Reserve ½ cup of mixture for topping and press remainder into a pie plate. After adding pie filling, sprinkle reserved mixture on top of filling. Bake in a preheated 400°F oven. Makes pastry for 1 single-crust pie with crumb topping.

DEBBIE BRUNER | Unity Baptist Church, Morgantown, Indiana

Piecrust Mix

3 cups flour
1 cup vegetable shortening
1 teaspoon salt

DOUBLE-CRUST PIE:

2 cups mix
¼ cup milk
1 egg, separated
1 tablespoon sugar

1. Combine flour, shortening, and salt. Store in a covered canister at room temperature.

2. To make pastry for a double-crust pie: Combine piecrust mix, milk, egg yolk, and sugar to make a soft dough. Roll out pastry. Brush with beaten egg white.

❖ Adapted from *The Best of the Old Church Cookbooks* by Florence Ekstrand, courtesy of Welcome Press

Piecrust with Honey

4 cups flour
2 teaspoons salt
1¾ cups vegetable shortening
1 tablespoon white or cider vinegar
1 tablespoon honey

1 egg
½ cup water

1. Whisk together flour and salt in a large bowl. Cut in vegetable shortening with a fork until crumbly.

2. Combine vinegar, honey, egg, and water in a small bowl, stirring with a fork. Add to flour mixture and stir until moistened.

3. Divide mixture into 5 portions. Shape each portion into a flat, round patty ready for rolling. Wrap each patty in plastic wrap or waxed paper and refrigerate at least ½ hour and up to 3 days. Dough can also be frozen.

4. To roll out, place patty on a lightly floured board or pastry cloth and dust patty with flour. Roll from the center out to the edges to a ⅛-inch thickness and 2 inches larger than inverted pie pan. Ease pastry into pie plate and press to remove air pockets.

5. To make a single-crust pie: Bake piecrust in a preheated 450°F oven for 12 to 15 minutes or until golden brown. Cool before adding filling.

6. To make a double-crust pie: Assemble pie, cover edge with foil to prevent overbrowning, and bake as directed in the selected recipe. Remove foil during last 15 minutes of baking. Makes piecrust for 2 double-crust and 4 single-crust 9-inch pies or 20 tart shells.

❖ **LORRAINE SHINDLER** | Messiah United Methodist Church, York, Pennsylvania

Raw Apple Cake

1 single-crust refrigerated pie pastry
3 tablespoons butter, room temperature
1 cup sugar
1 egg
1 teaspoon vanilla
3 cups Jonathan apples, peeled and chopped

1 cup flour
1 teaspoon baking soda
½ teaspoon nutmeg
½ teaspoon cinnamon
¼ cup chopped nuts
¼ cup flaked coconut

1. Preheat oven to 350°F. Grease a 9 x 2-inch round cake pan. Ease pie pastry into pan. Trim or fold in the edges.
2. Beat butter, sugar, egg, and vanilla. Stir in apples. Whisk together flour, baking soda, nutmeg, and cinnamon. Add to batter and blend well. Stir in nuts and coconut.
3. Spoon batter into pastry shell. Bake for 45 minutes or until hot and bubbly. Cool on a wire rack. Makes 6 to 8 servings.

Omit or substitute ingredients such as chopped nuts, flaked coconut, chocolate chips, and raisins to accommodate food allergies and personal tastes—or just to experiment!

PASTOR MARC DREYER | Memorial Baptist Church, Tulsa, Oklahoma

Apricot Bundt Cake

1½ cups dried apricots
3 cups flour
2 teaspoons baking powder
½ teaspoon salt
1 cup butter
1 cup sugar
3 eggs

1 teaspoon vanilla
1 cup milk

FILLING:
⅔ cup brown sugar
1 tablespoon flour
3 teaspoons cinnamon, divided

1. Place apricots in a bowl, add hot water to cover, and let stand 30 minutes to soften. Drain well. Coarsely chop.
2. Preheat oven to 350°F. Grease a 10-cup Bundt pan.
3. Sift together flour, baking powder, and salt. Sprinkle a few tablespoons of flour mixture over apricots and toss to lightly coat.
4. Cream butter in a mixer bowl. Beat in sugar, eggs, and vanilla. Add flour mixture and milk alternately, beating well after each addition. Stir in apricots.
5. To make filling: Mix together brown sugar, flour, and 2 teaspoons of the cinnamon.
6. Pour one-third of the batter into pan. Sprinkle filling evenly over batter. Pour in remaining two-thirds batter. Bake for 1 hour or until a tester inserted in center comes out clean. Cool in pan. Invert onto a cake plate and turn out of mold. Sprinkle remaining teaspoon cinnamon over the top. Makes 10 to 12 servings.

BERT ROME | St. Mark's Lutheran Church, Conshohocken, Pennsylvania

Egg-free Blackberry Cake

3 cups flour

1 cup self-rising flour

2 teaspoons cinnamon

1 teaspoon nutmeg

1 teaspoon cloves

1 teaspoon allspice

⅔ cup vegetable shortening

2 cups sugar

2 cups buttermilk

2 teaspoons baking soda

2 cups blackberries

ICING:

¾ cup butter, room temperature

¼ to ½ cup water, divided

1 teaspoon dry vanilla powder

2 lbs. confectioners' sugar

2 tablespoons blackberries

1. Preheat oven to 350°F. Grease a 17 x 12½ x 1-inch sheet pan.

2. Sift together flour, self-rising flour, cinnamon, nutmeg, cloves, and allspice.

3. Cream shortening and sugar in a large mixer bowl. Combine buttermilk and baking soda, add to shortening, and beat to combine. Gradually add 2 cups of the flour mixture, mixing well after each addition. Fold in blackberries. Stir in remaining 2 cups flour mixture.

4. Pour batter into pan. Bake for 30 minutes or until a tester inserted in center comes out clean. Cool in pan on a wire rack.

5. To make icing: Cream butter, ¼ cup of the water, and vanilla powder in a mixer bowl. Gradually beat in confectioners' sugar until smooth. Add more water, up to ¼ cup, if needed to reach spreading consistency. Stir in blackberries. Spread frosting over cake. Makes 16 to 18 servings.

❖ **PHYLLIS HOWARD** | First Baptist Church, Russell, Kentucky

Arkansas Traveler

½ cup butter

1 cup sugar

1 cup flour

1 cup milk

2 teaspoons baking powder

1 to 2 cups blackberries, washed, drained, and sprinkled with sugar

1. Preheat oven to 350°F. Place butter in a 13 x 9 x 2-inch baking dish and put in oven until butter sizzles, 2 to 3 minutes.

2. Whisk together sugar, flour, milk, and baking powder until smooth and free of lumps.

3. Pour batter into hot pan. Pour blackberries into middle of the pan; they will spread out on their own. Bake for 1 hour or until crust is golden brown and berries are bubbling. Serve warm topped with vanilla ice cream. Makes 8 to 10 servings.

VARIATION: Substitute blueberries or sliced peaches for the blackberries.

❖ **CHRISTIE ADDINGTON** | First Baptist Church, Russell, Kentucky

Blackberry Jam Cake

3 cups flour

2 teaspoons baking powder

1 teaspoon baking soda

½ teaspoon salt

2 teaspoons cinnamon

½ teaspoon cloves

½ teaspoon nutmeg

½ teaspoon allspice

1 cup butter

2 cups sugar

3 eggs

1 cup buttermilk

1 cup blackberry jam

ICING:

4 cups confectioners' sugar

3 tablespoons cream

3 tablespoons butter

3 tablespoons blackberry jam

2 teaspoons vanilla

1. Preheat oven to 350°F. Grease three 9 x 2-inch round cake pans and line with waxed paper.

2. Sift flour, measure, and resift with baking powder, baking soda, salt, cinnamon, cloves, nutmeg, and allspice.

3. Cream butter and sugar in mixer bowl until smooth. Add eggs and beat for 2 minutes. Add flour and buttermilk alternately, beating 2 minutes after each addition. Stir in jam until well blended.

4. Pour batter into pans. Bake for 30 minutes or until a tester inserted in center comes out clean. Cool in pans 5 minutes before turning out onto wire racks.

5. To make icing: Combine confectioners' sugar, cream, butter, blackberry jam, and vanilla in a mixer bowl. Beat until smooth.

6. Layer the cakes, spreading icing in between. Ice sides and top of cake. Makes 8 to 10 servings.

ROSE REED | Oakwood Church of God in Christ, Godfrey, Illinois

Orange Layer Cake with Orange Buttercream Frosting

1¼ cup sugar

1 cup buttermilk

1 tablespoon grated orange zest

2½ cups cake flour

2 teaspoons baking powder

½ teaspoon baking soda

½ teaspoon salt

¾ cup butter, room temperature

4 eggs

Orange Buttercream Frosting (recipe follows)

1. Place sugar in a resealable 1-quart freezer food storage bag. Seal bag and place in freezer for 20 minutes. Place large mixer bowl and beaters in freezer for 5 minutes.

2. Adjust oven rack to top of lower third of oven. Preheat oven to 350°F. Grease and flour two 8 x 8 x 2-inch baking pans. Line bottoms with wax paper and grease and flour the paper.

3. Combine buttermilk and grated orange zest.

4. Triple-sift flour, baking powder, baking soda, and salt.

5. Place butter in chilled mixer bowl and reattach beaters. Cream butter until light in color, 3 minutes. With mixer running, add chilled sugar in a steady stream. Beat until fluffy, 3 to 4 minutes. Add eggs one at a time, beating 30 seconds after each addition. Beat until light and airy, 1 to 2 minutes more.

6. Fold in half of flour mixture. Fold in half of buttermilk mixture. Repeat with remaining flour and buttermilk mixtures.

7. Pour batter into pans. Bake for 20 to 25 minutes or until center springs back when pressed with a fingertip. Cool in pans 10 minutes before turning out onto wire racks. Peel off paper. Cool completely.

8. Place one cake layer on a serving plate. Spread half of frosting on top and sides. Top with second cake layer and spread with remaining frosting. Refrigerate 1 hour before serving. Makes 6 to 8 servings.

ORANGE BUTTERCREAM FROSTING

½ cup butter, room temperature

2 tablespoons milk

2 tablespoons orange juice

2 teaspoons grated orange zest

¼ teaspoon salt

4 cups confectioners' sugar

1. Combine butter, milk, orange juice, orange zest, salt, and 1 cup of the confectioners' sugar in a mixer bowl. Beat until smooth and creamy.

2. Gradually add remaining 3 cups confectioners' sugar, beating until smooth and of spreading consistency. Makes 1½ cups frosting.

BRENDA STAMPLEY | Oakwood Church of God in Christ, Godfrey Illinois

Country Blueberry Cake

1 cup flour
½ teaspoon baking powder
⅛ teaspoon salt
¾ cup sugar
⅓ cup butter, melted and cooled

3 eggs
1 teaspoon vanilla
1 cup fresh blueberries or 1 cup frozen
    blueberries, thawed and drained

1. Preheat oven to 350°F. Grease and flour a 9 x 2-inch round cake pan.

2. Whisk together flour, baking powder, and salt.

3. Combine sugar and butter in a mixer bowl. Beat at medium speed until light and fluffy. Add eggs one at a time, beating well after each addition. Add vanilla. Add flour mixture ½ cup at a time, mixing on low speed until blended and smooth.

4. Spread batter evenly in pan. Top with blueberries. Bake for 35 to 40 minutes or until a tester inserted in center comes out clean. Cool in pan 5 minutes. Run a knife or spatula around edge to loosen. Turn out cake onto a wire rack and immediately invert onto another rack so blueberries are on top. Cool completely and transfer to a serving plate. Makes 6 to 8 servings.

KATHY HOAGLAND | Terrace Acres Baptist Church, Fort Worth, Texas

Buttermilk Chocolate Cake

2 cups flour
2 cups sugar
½ cup butter
2 tablespoons cocoa
½ cup vegetable shortening
1 cup water
2 eggs, beaten
½ cup buttermilk
1 teaspoon baking soda
1 teaspoon vanilla
1 teaspoon cinnamon

ICING:
½ cup butter
4 tablespoons cocoa
6 tablespoons buttermilk
1 box (1 lb.) confectioners' sugar
1 teaspoon vanilla
1 cup chopped nuts

1. Preheat oven to 350°F. Grease and flour a 13 x 9 x 2-inch baking pan.

2. Sift together flour and sugar. Combine butter, cocoa, shortening, and water in a saucepan over high heat. Bring to a boil. Pour over flour mixture and mix well.

3. Add eggs, buttermilk, baking soda, vanilla, and cinnamon. Mix until well combined.

4. Pour batter into pan. Bake for 20 to 30 minutes or until a tester inserted in center comes out clean.

5. To make the icing: Combine butter, cocoa, and buttermilk in a saucepan over medium heat. Bring to a boil. Pour mixture over confectioners' sugar, add vanilla and chopped nuts, and beat well. Pour over cake in pan. Cool and slice into bars. Makes 12 to 15 servings.

THELMA NIPPER | Women's Missionary Auxiliary, Bay Springs, Mississippi

Sugar Glaze

Adding confectioners' sugar glaze is an easy way to dress up a coffee cake, tea cake, or one-pan cake such as Country Blueberry Cake. There are many variations on this popular topping, but all involve mixing confectioners' sugar with a liquid such as water, milk, orange juice, or lemon juice. Vanilla and flavored extracts can also be used. A good glaze consistency is thick and syrupy rather than watery. Just pour or drizzle it over the top of the cooled cake.

Carrot Cake with Orange Glaze

1½ cups flour

1½ teaspoons baking powder

¾ teaspoon baking soda

¾ teaspoon cinnamon

¼ teaspoon allspice

¾ cup sugar

¼ cup brown sugar

½ cup coarsely chopped pecans or walnuts

¾ cup liquid egg substitute

½ cup extra light olive oil or canola oil

2 teaspoons finely grated orange zest

1 teaspoon vanilla

1½ cups finely chopped carrots, loosely packed

¾ cup crushed pineapple with juice

ORANGE GLAZE:

1 cup sifted confectioners' sugar

½ teaspoon finely grated orange zest

1 tablespoon freshly squeezed lemon juice

¼ teaspoon water

1. Preheat oven to 350°F. Coat a 9 x 5 x 3-inch loaf pan with nonstick cooking spray.

2. Sift together flour, baking powder, baking soda, cinnamon, allspice, and sugar into a large mixing bowl. Add brown sugar, pressing out all lumps with your fingers. Add pecans or walnuts and toss well to dredge.

3. Combine egg substitute, oil, orange zest, vanilla, carrots, and pineapple in a 1-quart measuring cup. Make a well in dry ingredients, pour in carrot mixture, and stir just to combine. Batter should be thin and lumpy.

4. Pour batter into pan, spreading it into corners and smoothing the top. Bake for 1 to 1¼ hours or cake is springy to the touch and a tester inserted in center comes out clean. Cool in pan 10 minutes before turning out onto a wire rack. Cool to room temperature.

5. To make orange glaze: Combine confectioners' sugar, orange zest, lemon juice, and water until smooth. Spread the glaze over top of cake, letting excess run down the sides. Let glaze harden several hours before cutting the cake. Slice into ½-inch thick pieces. Makes 18 servings.

PRESBYTERIAN CHURCH OF GONZALES | Gonzales, Texas

Chocolate Fudge Cake

½ cup butter
4 squares (1 oz. each) bitter chocolate
1 cup boiling water
2 cups flour
2 cups sugar
2 eggs
1½ teaspoons baking soda
½ teaspoon salt
½ cup sour milk

ICING:

2 cups sugar
2 tablespoons cocoa
½ cup milk
½ cup butter
1 teaspoon vanilla

1. Preheat oven to 350°F. Grease a 13 x 9 x 2-inch baking pan.

2. Combine butter, chocolate, and boiling water in a large saucepan over medium-high heat. Cook, stirring frequently, until mixture becomes thick. Remove from heat.

3. Combine chocolate mixture, flour, sugar, eggs, baking soda, salt, and sour milk in a mixer bowl. Beat until smooth.

4. Transfer batter to pan. Bake for 35 minutes or until a tester inserted in center comes out clean. Do not overbake. Cool in pan on a wire rack.

5. To make icing: Combine sugar, cocoa, milk, and butter in a saucepan over medium heat. Bring to a boil. Boil for 2 minutes without stirring. Remove from heat, add vanilla, and beat until thick. Pour over top of cake in pan. Cool to room temperature. To serve, cut into squares. Makes 8 to 10 servings.

❖ **FLORENCE RILES** | St. Mark's Lutheran Church, Conshohocken, Pennsylvania

Chocolate Cake

2¼ cups flour
½ cup cocoa
2 cups sugar
1 teaspoon salt
2 teaspoons baking soda
2 eggs

1 cup oil
1 teaspoon vanilla
1 cup milk
1 cup hot water
Melted butter

1. Preheat oven to 350°F. Lightly grease an 11 x 7 x 2-inch baking pan.

2. Combine flour, cocoa, sugar, salt, baking soda, eggs, oil, vanilla, milk, and hot water in a mixer bowl. Beat until well blended.

3. Pour batter into pan. Bake for 1 hour or until a tester inserted in center comes out clean. Cut into squares. Serve hot drizzled with melted butter. Makes 10 to 12 servings.

❖ **SHERI L. COOPER** | Memorial Baptist Church, Tulsa, Oklahoma

Chocolate Angel Food Cake

1½ cups sugar, divided
¾ cup cake flour
¼ cup cocoa
1½ cups egg whites (12 egg whites)

¼ teaspoon salt
1½ teaspoons cream of tartar
1 teaspoon vanilla

1. Preheat oven to 375°F.

2. Triple-sift ½ cup of the sugar, flour, and cocoa.

3. Beat egg whites with salt until frothy. Add cream of tartar and beat to a soft peak. Add remaining cup of sugar 2 tablespoons at a time and beat until sugar is dissolved. Blend in vanilla. Gently fold egg whites into flour mixture.

4. Transfer mixture to an ungreased 10 x 4-inch tube pan or angel food cake pan. Bake for 35 to 40 minutes. Invert and cool on a wire rack. Makes 16 servings.

❖ **MRS. WALTER ABEL** | St. John's Guild, St. John's Church, West Bend, Wisconsin

Milky Way Cake

1 cup butter, divided
6 Milky Way candy bars
2 cups sugar
4 eggs
1 teaspoon lemon juice
1⅓ cups evaporated milk
2½ cups flour
½ teaspoon baking soda
2 teaspoons vanilla
1 cup chopped pecans

ICING:

2 tablespoons cocoa
3 tablespoons milk
½ cup butter
½ teaspoon vanilla
½ box (8 oz.) confectioners' sugar
½ cup nuts

1. Preheat oven to 350°F. Grease a 10-cup Bundt pan.

2. Combine ½ cup of the butter and candy bars in a saucepan over low heat until melted.

3. Cream remaining ½ cup butter and sugar. Beat in eggs one at a time.

4. Stir lemon juice into milk. Sift together flour and baking soda. Add flour and milk mixture alternately to batter, beating to combine. Stir in melted candy bar mixture, vanilla, and pecans.

5. Pour batter into pan. Bake for 1 hour. Cool in pan.

6. To make icing: Combine cocoa, milk, and butter in a saucepan over medium-high heat. Bring to a rapid boil. Remove from heat and stir in vanilla. Gradually add confectioners' sugar, beating until smooth. Stir in nuts. Invert cake onto a plate and pour icing over it. Makes 10 to 12 servings.

❖ **TERRY LEE** | Memorial Baptist Church, Tulsa, Oklahoma

One-Bowl Chocolate Cake

6 squares (1 oz. each) semisweet chocolate
¾ cup butter
1½ cups sugar
3 eggs
2 teaspoons vanilla

2½ cups flour, divided
1 teaspoon baking soda
¼ teaspoon salt
1½ cups water

1. Preheat oven to 350°F. Grease and flour two 9 x 2-inch round cake pans.

2. Microwave chocolate and butter in a large microwavable bowl until butter is melted, about 2 minutes on high setting. Stir until chocolate is completely melted. Add sugar and stir until well blended.

3. Add eggs one at a time, beating on low speed with a handheld mixer after each addition. Stir in vanilla. Blend in ½ cup of the flour, baking soda, and salt. Beat in remaining 2 cups of flour alternately with water until well blended and smooth.

4. Pour batter into pans. Bake for 35 minutes or until a toothpick inserted in center comes out clean. Cool in pan 10 minutes before turning out onto wire racks. Cool completely. Frost as desired. Makes 2 chocolate cake layers.

❖ **ANNETTE SLACK** | Oakwood Church of God in Christ, Godfrey, Illinois

Mississippi Mud Cake

1 cup butter, divided
½ cup cocoa
1 cup sugar
4 eggs
1½ cups flour
½ teaspoon salt
1 cup chopped pecans
1 package (16 oz.) mini marshmallows

ICING:
½ cup butter
⅓ cup cocoa
2 cups confectioners' sugar
⅓ cup milk
1 teaspoon vanilla

1. Preheat oven to 350°F. Lightly grease a 12 x 2-inch round cake pan.

2. Melt ½ cup of the butter in a small saucepan over low heat. Stir in cocoa until dissolved.

3. Combine sugar, eggs, flour, salt, and remaining ½ cup butter in a large bowl. Add cocoa mixture and stir well. Stir in pecans.

4. Pour batter into pan. Bake for 25 minutes, turn off oven, and sprinkle marshmallows on top of cake. Keep cake in warm oven until marshmallows are melted.

5. To make icing: Melt butter in a small saucepan over low heat. Stir in cocoa. Mix confectioners' sugar, milk, and vanilla in a bowl. Add cocoa mixture and stir until blended and smooth. Spread over hot cake in pan, swirling icing and marshmallows with a knife. Cool to room temperature. Makes 12 to 14 servings.

❖ **V.P.** | Miracle Deliverance Holiness Church, Columbia, South Carolina

Carrot Chiffon Cake

1½ cups flour
½ teaspoon cinnamon
½ teaspoon cloves
½ teaspoon nutmeg
½ teaspoon allspice
2 level teaspoons baking powder
½ teaspoon baking soda
½ teaspoon salt

1½ cups sugar
1 cup vegetable oil
3 eggs, separated
2½ tablespoons hot water
1 cup grated carrots
1 cup chopped black walnuts
1 teaspoon vanilla

1. Preheat oven to 350°F. Grease a 10-cup Bundt pan.
2. Sift together flour, cinnamon, cloves, nutmeg, allspice, baking powder, baking soda, and salt.
3. Combine sugar, oil, egg yolks, and hot water in mixer bowl until well blended. Beat in carrots. Beat in flour mixture. Stir in black walnuts.
4. Beat egg whites until foamy, add vanilla, and continue beating until stiff. Fold into batter. Pour batter into pan. Bake for 50 to 55 minutes or until a tester inserted in center comes out clean. Cool in pan. Turn out onto a serving plate. Makes 10 to 12 servings.

❖ **LIBBY HULSE** | Memorial Baptist Church, Tulsa, Oklahoma

Cinnamon Toast Cake

2 cups flour
1 cup sugar
2 teaspoons baking powder
1 teaspoon salt
1 cup milk
2 tablespoons butter, melted
1 teaspoon vanilla
½ cup raisins

TOPPING:
½ cup butter, melted
½ cup sugar
1½ teaspoons cinnamon

1. Preheat oven to 350°F. Grease and flour the bottom of a 15 x 10 x 1-inch sheet pan.
2. Sift together flour, sugar, baking powder, and salt into a bowl. Blend in milk, melted butter, vanilla, and raisins.
3. Turn batter into pan and spread evenly. Bake for 20 to 25 minutes or until golden brown. Remove from oven.
4. To make topping: Drizzle melted butter over cake. Combine sugar and cinnamon and sprinkle over cake. Return cake to oven and bake 10 minutes more. Cool in pan 10 minutes. Cut into squares. Serve warm. Makes 20 servings.

LANAE MCCORMICK | Women's Missionary Auxiliary, Bay Springs, Mississippi

Granny Reed's Gingerbread Stack Cake

APPLE FILLING AND TOPPING:

1½ to 2 gallons dried apples
    or 5 to 6 cups cooked, very
    well-drained apples

⅔ cup sugar

1 tablespoon cinnamon

¼ teaspoon ginger

¼ teaspoon allspice

CAKE:

1 cup sugar

1 cup molasses

1 rounded tablespoon butter

2 large or 3 small eggs

3 cups flour

1 teaspoon baking powder

2 teaspoons baking soda

¼ teaspoon salt

½ teaspoon cloves

2 teaspoons ginger

½ teaspoon allspice

1 teaspoon cinnamon

1 cup boiling water

1. To make the apple filling and topping: Begin preparing the apples 1 to 2 days prior to baking the cake. Place dehydrated apples in a stockpot, add 8 to 10 cups water, and cook until apples are soft. Place in a colander and let juice drain off for at least 24 hours.

2. Place apples in a bowl and mash with a potato masher. Add sugar, cinnamon, ginger, and allspice. Mix to a paste consistency. Refrigerate until ready to use.

3. To make cake: Preheat oven to 350°F. Grease five 8 x 1½-inch round cake pans. Combine sugar, molasses, butter, and eggs in a mixer bowl. Whisk together flour, baking powder, baking soda, salt, cloves, ginger, allspice, and cinnamon. Gradually add flour mixture to egg mixture to make a thick batter. Add boiling water and beat until smooth.

4. Place three large serving spoons of batter in each pan. Shake and pat the pans to spread batter evenly. Bake in oven, five pans at a time, watching closely for doneness, 7 to 8 minutes. Cool in pans 5 to 8 minutes before turning out onto a clean white cloth. Cool on cloth 10 minutes, flip over, and cool 10 minutes more.

5. Place one layer of cake on plate. Spread a thin layer of apple mixture over the top. Continue placing layers and thinly spreading with apple mixture until all layers are used up. Spread apple mixture on sides and top of cake. Let set at room temperature for 1 hour. Store in an airtight plastic container in the refrigerator. Makes 8 to 10 servings.

❖ **TOM REED** | First Baptist Church, Russell, Kentucky

Amazing Corn Cake

1 can (17 oz.) cream-style corn
½ cup sugar
3 eggs
1 cup oil
2½ cups flour
1 teaspoon baking powder

1 teaspoon baking soda
1 teaspoon cinnamon
Raisins
Nuts
Caramel or cream cheese frosting

1. Preheat oven to 350°F. Grease and flour a 13 x 9 x 2-inch baking pan.

2. Combine corn and sugar in a mixer bowl. Add eggs and oil and beat until well blended.

3. Whisk together flour, baking powder, baking soda, and cinnamon. Add to batter and mix well. Stir in raisins and nuts.

4. Pour batter into pan. Bake for 30 to 35 minutes. Cool in pan on a wire rack. Frost with caramel or cream cheese frosting. Cut into squares. Makes 12 servings.

❖ MARGARET MATSON | Messiah United Methodist Church, York, Pennsylvania

Date Nut Cake

1 cup chopped dates
1¾ teaspoons baking soda, divided
1½ cups boiling water
½ cup vegetable shortening
1½ cups sugar, divided

2 eggs
1½ cups plus 3 tablespoons flour
¼ teaspoon salt
1 package (6 oz.) chocolate chips
½ cup chopped nuts

1. Preheat oven to 350°F. Grease a 13 x 9 x 2-inch baking pan.

2. Place dates and 1 teaspoon of the baking soda in a large bowl and add boiling water. Let stand until cool.

3. Combine shortening, 1 cup of the sugar, eggs, flour, salt, and remaining ¾ teaspoon baking soda. Mix until well blended. Add to date mixture and stir to combine.

4. Transfer batter to baking pan. Sprinkle chocolate chips, nuts, and remaining ½ cup sugar on top. Bake for 35 to 45 minutes or until a tester inserted in center comes out clean. Cool in pan on wire rack. Cut into squares. Makes 12 servings.

❖ VICKI GILL | Trinity Presbyterian Church, Little Rock, Arkansas

Chocolate Pound Cake

3 cups cake flour

½ cup cocoa

½ teaspoon baking powder

¼ teaspoon salt

½ cup vegetable shortening

½ cup butter, room temperature

3 cups sugar

5 eggs

1 cup milk

1 tablespoon vanilla

1. Preheat oven to 325°F. Grease a 10 x 4-inch tube pan.

2. Whisk together flour, cocoa, baking powder, and salt.

3. Cream shortening and butter in a mixer bowl. Beat in sugar. Add eggs one at a time, beating well after each addition. Add flour mixture alternately with milk and vanilla until well blended.

4. Pour batter into pan. Bake for 1 hour 10 minutes or until a tester inserted in center comes out clean. Cool in pan 10 minutes before turning out onto a wire rack. Makes 16 servings.

MRS. LEDORA SIMMONS | Women's Missionary Auxiliary, Bay Springs, Mississippi

Chocolate Zucchini Cake

½ cup butter

½ cup vegetable oil

1¾ cups sugar

2 eggs

1 teaspoon vanilla

½ cup buttermilk

2½ cups flour

4 tablespoons cocoa

½ teaspoon baking powder

1 teaspoon baking soda

½ teaspoon cinnamon

½ teaspoon cloves

2 cups grated zucchini

¼ cup chocolate chips

1. Preheat oven to 325°F. Grease and flour a 13 x 9 x 2-inch baking pan.

2. Cream butter, oil, and sugar in a mixer bowl. Add eggs, vanilla, and buttermilk. Whisk together flour, cocoa, baking powder, baking soda, cinnamon, and cloves. Beat into creamed mixture. Stir in zucchini.

3. Spoon batter into pan. Sprinkle with chocolate chips. Bake for 40 to 45 minutes or until lightly browned. Cool in pan on a wire rack. Cut into squares or bars. Makes 12 to 15 servings.

ANN ASH | Vincent Memorial United Methodist Church, Nutter Fort, West Virginia

Gingerbread

½ cup butter

½ cup sugar

1 cup molasses

2 eggs

2 cups flour

1 teaspoon baking soda

½ teaspoon salt

1 teaspoon ginger

1 teaspoon cinnamon

½ cup milk

1. Preheat oven to 350°F. Grease and flour two 8 x 8 x 2-inch baking pans.

2. Cream butter and sugar in a mixer bowl. Beat in molasses and eggs.

3. Whisk together flour, baking soda, salt, ginger, and cinnamon. Add flour mixture and milk alternately to batter, mixing well to combine.

4. Pour batter into baking pans. Bake for 30 to 35 minutes or until a tester inserted in center comes out clean. Cool in pans 10 minutes before turning out onto wire racks. Cut into squares. Makes 18 servings.

❖ **MRS. FRED SAGER** | St. John's Guild, St. John's Church, West Bend, Wisconsin

Hot Fudge Cake

1 cup flour	2 tablespoons vegetable oil
¾ cup sugar	1 teaspoon vanilla
6 tablespoons cocoa, divided	1 cup brown sugar
2 teaspoons baking powder	1¾ cups hot water
¼ teaspoon salt	Whipped cream or vanilla ice cream
½ cup milk	

1. Preheat oven to 350°F.

2. Combine flour, sugar, 2 tablespoons of the cocoa, baking powder, and salt in a large bowl. Stir in milk, oil, and vanilla until smooth. Spread batter in an ungreased 9 x 9 x 2-inch baking pan.

3. Combine brown sugar and remaining 4 tablespoons cocoa. Sprinkle over top of batter. Pour hot water over all. Do not stir. Bake for 35 to 40 minutes. Cool in pan 10 minutes and cut into squares. Serve warm topped with whipped cream or ice cream. Makes 9 servings.

❖ **DORIS CHAFFIN** | First Baptist Church, Russell, Kentucky

Lemon Pecan Cake

2 cups butter	1 bottle (1 oz.) lemon extract
2½ cups sugar	4 cups chopped pecans
6 eggs	½ lb. candied cherries
4 cups flour	½ lb. candied pineapple
1 teaspoon baking powder	

1. Preheat oven to 250°F. Grease and flour a large angel food cake pan.

2. Cream butter and sugar in a mixer bowl. Add eggs one at a time, beating well after each addition.

3. Sift together flour and baking powder. Add flour mixture and lemon extract alternately to butter mixture and beat until well blended. Fold in pecans, cherries, and pineapple.

4. Pour batter into pan. Bake for 2 to 2½ hours or until a tester inserted in center comes out clean. Cool in pan 5 minutes before turning out onto a wire rack. Makes 12 to 14 servings.

❖ **NITA HARTER** | Trinity Presbyterian Church, Little Rock, Arkansas

Grandma's Lemon Cake

¾ cup vegetable shortening

1½ cups sugar

2½ cups flour

3 teaspoons baking powder

1 cup milk

1 teaspoon vanilla

4 egg whites

ICING:

2 cups sugar

7 tablespoons cornstarch

2 cups water

¼ teaspoon salt

½ cup fresh lemon juice

4 tablespoons butter

2 egg yolks, beaten

1. Preheat oven to 350°F. Grease and flour three 8 x 8 x 2-inch baking pans.

2. Cream shortening and sugar in a mixer bowl. Sift together flour and baking powder. With mixer running on low speed, add flour mixture and milk alternately to sugar mixture. Beat for 2 minutes. Stir in vanilla.

3. Beat egg whites until stiff. Fold into batter. Gently transfer batter to pans. Bake for 25 minutes or until a tester inserted in center comes out clean. Cool in pans 10 minutes before turning out onto wire racks.

4. To make icing: Combine sugar, cornstarch, water, salt, lemon juice, and butter in a saucepan over low heat. Cook, stirring frequently, until mixture is thick, 10 to 12 minutes. Remove from heat. Beat egg yolks until frothy. Quickly whisk into hot mixture. Cool to room temperature.

5. Layer the cakes, spreading icing in between. Ice sides and top of cake. Makes 10 to 12 servings.

❖ **ROSIE JAHNSEN** | Presbyterian Church of Gonzales, Gonzales, Texas

Double-Maple Cupcakes

½ cup sugar

5 tablespoons butter, room temperature

1 teaspoon vanilla

½ teaspoon imitation maple flavoring

2 large eggs

1¼ cups flour

1¼ teaspoons baking powder

¼ teaspoon salt

¼ cup 1% low-fat milk

¼ cup maple syrup

FROSTING:

3 tablespoons maple syrup

2 tablespoons butter, room temperature

½ teaspoon vanilla

½ teaspoon imitation maple flavoring

⅛ teaspoon salt

1¾ cups confectioners' sugar

1. Preheat oven to 350°F. Lightly grease a 12-cup muffin pan and add paper liners.

2. Combine sugar, butter, vanilla, and maple flavoring in a mixer bowl. Beat at medium speed until well blended, 5 minutes. Add eggs one at a time, beating well after each addition.

3. Whisk together flour, baking powder, and salt. Combine milk and maple syrup. Add flour mixture and milk mixture alternately to batter, beginning and ending with flour and mixing well after each addition.

4. Spoon batter into muffin cups. Bake for 20 minutes or until a tester inserted in center comes out clean. Cool in pan 10 minutes before turning out onto a wire rack. Cool completely.

5. To make frosting: Combine maple syrup, butter, vanilla, maple flavoring, and salt in a mixer bowl at medium speed for 1 minute. Gradually add confectioners' sugar, beating just until blended; do not overbeat. Spread frosting on cupcakes. Makes 12 cupcakes.

❖ LINDA S. THOMPSON | Oakwood Church of God in Christ, Godfrey, Illinois

Fresh Orange Cake

2¼ cups flour

1½ cups sugar

2 teaspoons baking powder

1 teaspoon salt

¼ teaspoon baking soda

½ cup vegetable shortening, room temperature

¼ cup orange juice with pulp

¾ cup milk

2 eggs

Grated zest of 1 orange

1. Preheat oven to 350°F. Grease and flour a 13 x 9 x 2-inch baking pan.

2. Combine flour, sugar, baking powder, salt, baking soda, shortening, orange juice, and milk in a large mixer bowl. Beat on medium speed for 2 minutes.

3. Add the eggs and beat 2 minutes more. Blend in zest.

4. Pour batter into pan. Bake for 30 minutes or until a tester inserted in center comes out clean. Cool in pan 10 minutes. Cut into squares. Serve warm. Makes 12 servings.

❖ BETTE SINN | Trinity Evangelical Lutheran Church, Lansdale, Pennsylvania

Pecan Cake

¾ cup butter, divided

1¼ cups brown sugar, divided

1½ cups cake flour

2 teaspoons baking powder

¼ teaspoon salt

2 eggs, separated

¾ cup chopped pecans

¾ cup milk

1 teaspoon vanilla

1. Preheat oven to 350°F. Place ¼ cup of the butter and ¼ cup of the brown sugar in a 9 x 9 x 2-inch baking pan. Set in oven until melted, about 3 minutes. Remove from oven. Swirl to combine.

2. Sift together flour, baking powder, and salt.

3. Cream remaining ½ cup butter and remaining cup brown sugar until fluffy. Add egg yolks, one at a time, beating well after each addition. Stir in pecans and flour mixture alternately with milk. Stir in vanilla.

4. Beat egg whites until stiff. Fold into batter. Gently transfer batter to pan. Bake for 20 minutes or until lightly browned. Cut into squares and serve warm. Makes 9 servings.

❖ LORAN KELLER | St. John's Guild, St. John's Church, West Bend, Wisconsin

Orange Slice Cake

½ lb. dates, pitted and coarsely chopped
1 lb. candy orange slices, coarsely chopped
2 cups chopped pecans
4 cups flour, divided
1 cup butter
1 cup sugar
4 eggs

2 tablespoons grated orange zest
1 teaspoon baking soda
1½ cups buttermilk

SYRUP:
2 cups sugar
1⅓ cups orange juice

1. Preheat oven to 300°F. Grease and flour a 10 x 4-inch tube pan.

2. Dredge dates, candy, and pecans in ¼ cup of the flour.

3. Cream butter and sugar. Add eggs one at a time, beating well after each addition. Add grated zest. Sift baking soda with remaining 3¾ cups flour. Add flour mixture and buttermilk alternately, beginning and ending with flour. Fold in dates, candy, and pecans.

4. Pour batter into pan. Bake for 1 hour 50 minutes or until a tester inserted in center comes out clean.

5. To make syrup: Combine sugar and orange juice in a saucepan over medium heat, stirring until sugar is dissolved. Pour over hot cake. Let cake cool completely before removing from pan. Makes 16 servings.

❖ **INA RUBENKOENIG** | Terrace Acres Baptist Church, Fort Worth, Texas

White Texas Cake

½ cup vegetable shortening
2 cups sugar
2 egg whites
1¾ cups flour
1 teaspoon baking soda
½ teaspoon salt
1¾ cups buttermilk
1 teaspoon vanilla
½ teaspoon almond extract

ICING:
½ cup butter
1 teaspoon vanilla
1½ cups flaked coconut
⅓ cup buttermilk
1 box confectioners' sugar
1½ cups chopped pecans

1. To make cake: Preheat oven to 350°F. Grease and flour a 17 x 12½ x 1-inch sheet pan.

2. Cream shortening and sugar in the large bowl of an electric mixer. Beat in egg whites.

3. Sift together flour, baking soda, and salt. With mixer running, add flour mixture alternately with buttermilk, vanilla, and almond extract. Pour batter into pan. Bake for 20 minutes. Cool in pan.

4. To make icing: Heat butter in a saucepan over low heat until melted. Remove from heat. Stir in vanilla, coconut, buttermilk, confectioners' sugar, and pecans. Spread icing over top of cake. Cut into squares. Makes 16 servings.

❖ **BARBARA HIGHTOWER** | Oakwood Church of God in Christ, Godfrey, Illinois

Peach Upside-Down Cake

¾ cup brown sugar

1 cup butter, room temperature, divided

1 can (29 oz.) sliced peaches, well drained

2¼ cups flour

1 tablespoon baking powder

2 teaspoons cinnamon

1½ cups sugar

3 large eggs, separated

¾ cup milk

1½ teaspoons vanilla

1. Preheat oven to 350°F. Lightly grease a 9 x 2-inch round cake pan.

2. Melt brown sugar and ¼ cup of the butter in a small saucepan over medium heat. Stir to combine. Pour into bottom of pan and spread evenly.

3. Arrange peaches over brown sugar mixture in concentric circles.

4. Whisk together flour, baking powder, and cinnamon.

5. Cream remaining ¾ cup butter and sugar in a mixer bowl. Beat in egg yolks. Add flour mixture and milk alternately, mixing until well blended. Stir in vanilla.

6. Beat egg whites until stiff. Fold into batter. Spread batter over peach slices. Bake for 55 to 60 minutes or until a tester inserted in center comes out clean. Cool in pan 10 minutes. Invert onto a cake plate. Serve warm or at room temperature. Makes 6 to 8 servings.

VARIATION:
This cake can also be baked in a 9-inch springform pan or an 8 x 8 x 2-inch baking pan.

❖ **LEONA STOTLER** | Church of the Canyons Women's Ministries, Canyon Country, California

Brown Sugar Pound Cake

1 tub (16 oz.) whipped butter

1 box (16 oz.) light brown sugar

1 cup sugar

6 eggs, separated

½ teaspoon baking soda

1 cup buttermilk

3 cups flour

1 teaspoon vanilla

1 cup pecans

1. Preheat oven to 350°F. Grease and flour a 10 x 4-inch tube pan.

2. Beat butter, light brown sugar, sugar, and egg yolks in a large mixer bowl.

3. Stir baking soda into buttermilk. Add flour and buttermilk alternately to egg mixture, beating until combined. Stir in vanilla and pecans.

4. In a separate mixer bowl, beat egg whites until stiff. Fold egg whites into batter. Transfer batter to tube pan. Bake for 2 hours, or until a toothpick inserted in center comes out clean. Cool in pan for 5 minutes and then turn out onto a wire rack. Makes 10 servings.

❖ **MRS. RETHA FOREMAN** | Women's Missionary Auxiliary, Bay Springs, Mississippi

Snow Cake

1 cup egg whites (about 8)
1 cup sugar
Dash of salt
1 teaspoon vanilla

1 cup sifted flour
1 teaspoon baking powder
½ cup butter, melted and cooled
Confectioners' sugar

1. Preheat oven to 350°F. Grease a 10 x 4-inch tube pan and dust with confectioners' sugar.

2. Whip egg whites in a large mixer bowl until frothy. With mixer running at high speed, gradually add sugar. Continue beating until mixture forms stiff, but not dry, peaks. Beat in salt and vanilla.

3. Sift together flour and baking powder. Fold flour mixture into egg whites until well blended. Fold in melted butter.

4. Transfer batter to tube pan. Bake for 1 hour, or until cake springs back when touched lightly. Remove from pan and cool on a wire rack. Dust with confectioners' sugar before serving. Makes 16 servings.

❖ **MOVITA WALKER** | Women's Missionary Auxiliary, Bay Springs, Mississippi

Spicy Chiffon Cake

2 cups flour
1½ cups sugar
3 teaspoons baking powder
1 teaspoon salt
1 teaspoon cinnamon
½ teaspoon nutmeg
½ teaspoon cloves
½ teaspoon allspice
7 eggs, separated
½ cup corn oil
¾ cup cold water
½ teaspoon cream of tartar

ICING:
½ cup butter
2½ tablespoons flour
½ cup milk
½ cup brown sugar
2 cups confectioners' sugar
1 teaspoon vanilla
1 cup chopped pecans

1. Preheat oven to 325°F. Grease and lightly flour a 10 x 4-inch tube pan.

2. In a large bowl, sift together flour, sugar, baking powder, salt, cinnamon, nutmeg, cloves, and allspice. Make a well in the center and add egg yolks, corn oil, and cold water. Stir until smooth.

3. In another bowl, beat egg whites and cream of tartar until very stiff. Fold egg whites into batter. Transfer batter to tube pan. Bake at 325°F for 55 minutes, increase heat to 350°F, and bake 15 minutes more. Cool in pan 10 minutes and then invert onto a plate.

4. To make icing: Melt butter in a saucepan over medium heat. Add flour and stir to combine. Gradually add milk, stirring to combine. Cook for 1 minute and add brown sugar. Remove from heat and stir in confectioners' sugar. Using a handheld mixer, beat until smooth. Stir in vanilla and pecans. Pour over cake. Makes 16 servings.

❖ **PEGGY WINDHAM** | Women's Missionary Auxiliary, Bay Springs, Mississippi

Brown Sugar Pound Cake

1 cup vegetable shortening
½ cup butter
1 box (16 oz.) light brown sugar
½ cup sugar
5 eggs
3 cups flour
½ teaspoon baking powder
½ teaspoon salt
1 cup milk
1 teaspoon maple flavoring
1 teaspoon vanilla
1 cup chopped pecans or walnuts

GLAZE:

1 cup brown sugar
½ cup butter
¼ cup milk
¾ box confectioners' sugar
½ teaspoon maple flavoring

1. Preheat oven to 325°F. Grease and flour a 10 x 4-inch tube pan.

2. Cream shortening and butter. Mix in light brown sugar and sugar. Add eggs one at a time, beating well after each addition.

3. Sift together flour, baking powder, and salt. Add flour mixture and milk alternately to egg mixture, mixing thoroughly with each addition. Stir in maple flavoring, vanilla, and pecans or walnuts.

4. Pour batter into pan. Bake for 1 hour 15 minutes or until a tester inserted near center comes out clean. Cool in pan 10 minutes before turning out onto a wire rack.

5. To make glaze: Combine brown sugar and butter in a saucepan over medium heat. Add milk. Bring to a boil, add confectioners' sugar, and stir until smooth. Remove from heat. Stir in maple flavoring.

6. Spread glaze on top of cake. Cool. Makes 16 servings.

❖ **MIRIAM MCKERN** | Christ Church, Frederica, St. Simons Island, Georgia

Persimmon Cake

2½ cups flour
2 teaspoons baking soda
½ teaspoon allspice
½ teaspoon cinnamon
2½ cups sugar

1 cup vegetable shortening
3 eggs
2 cups coarsely chopped nuts
1 cup raisins
2 cups coarsely chopped persimmons

1. Preheat oven to 300°F. Grease and flour a 10 x 4-inch tube pan.

2. Sift together flour, baking soda, allspice, and cinnamon.

3. Combine sugar, shortening, and eggs in a mixer bowl. Stir in flour mixture and beat until well blended. Fold in nuts and raisins. Stir in persimmons.

4. Transfer batter to pan. Bake for 1¼ hours or until a tester inserted in center comes out clean. Cool in pan 10 to 15 minutes before turning out onto a wire rack. Makes 16 servings.

❖ **JEWELL ICKISON** | First Baptist Church, Russell, Kentucky

Chocolate Chip Orange Pound Cake

½ cup butter, room temperature
½ package (4 oz.) cream cheese,
    room temperature
¾ cup sugar
2 eggs
1 teaspoon vanilla

¼ teaspoon grated orange zest
1 cup flour
1 teaspoon baking powder
1 cup mini chocolate chips
Confectioners' sugar

1. Preheat oven to 325°F. Grease and flour a 9 x 5 x 3-inch loaf pan.

2. Cream butter, cream cheese, and sugar in a mixer bowl. Add eggs, vanilla, and orange zest, mixing just until blended. Mix in flour and baking powder. Stir in chocolate chips.

3. Pour batter into pan. Bake for 45 to 50 minutes or until cake pulls from sides of pan. Cool in pan 10 minutes before turning out onto a wire rack. Cool completely. Sprinkle with confectioners' sugar. Makes 12 to 14 servings.

PATSY GIVIDEN | First Baptist Church, Russell, Kentucky

Cream Cheese Pound Cake

1½ cups chopped pecans, divided
1½ cups butter, room temperature
1 package (8 oz.) cream cheese,
    room temperature
3 cups sugar
6 eggs
3 cups sifted cake flour
Dash of salt
1½ teaspoons vanilla

VARIATION:
Instead of vanilla,
use 1½ teaspoons
lemon extract.

1. Preheat oven to 325°F. Grease and flour a 10 x 4-inch tube pan.

2. Sprinkle ½ cup of the pecans in bottom of pan.

3. Cream butter and cream cheese in a mixer bowl. Gradually add sugar, beating until light and fluffy. Add eggs one at a time, beating well after each addition. Stir in flour and salt. Stir in vanilla and remaining cup pecans.

4. Pour batter into pan. Bake for 1½ hours or until a tester inserted in center comes out clean. Cool in pan 15 minutes before turning out onto a wire rack. Makes 16 servings.

RETA ROMANS | Memorial Baptist Church, Tulsa, Oklahoma

Apricot Brandy Pound Cake

1 cup butter

3 cups sugar

6 eggs

3 cups flour

¼ teaspoon baking soda

½ teaspoon salt

1 cup sour cream

½ teaspoon rum flavoring

1 teaspoon orange flavoring

¼ teaspoon almond extract

½ teaspoon lemon extract

1 teaspoon vanilla

½ cup apricot brandy

1. Preheat oven to 325°F. Grease and flour a 12-cup Bundt pan.

2. Cream butter and sugar in a mixer bowl. Add eggs one at a time, beating well after each addition.

3. Triple-sift flour, baking soda, and salt.

4. Combine sour cream, rum flavoring, orange flavoring, almond extract, lemon extract, vanilla, and apricot brandy. Add flour mixture and sour cream mixture alternately to egg mixture, beginning and ending with flour and mixing until well combined.

5. Pour batter into pan. Bake for 1 hour 10 minutes. Cool in pan 10 minutes before turning out onto a wire rack. This cake freezes well. Makes 12 servings.

EVELYN FRENCH | Christ Church, Frederica, St. Simons Island, Georgia

Million Dollar Pound Cake

2 cups butter

3 cups sugar

6 eggs

4 cups flour

¾ cup milk

1 teaspoon vanilla

1 teaspoon almond extract

1. Preheat oven to 300°F. Grease and flour an angel food cake pan.

2. Cream butter in a mixer bowl until light and fluffy. Gradually beat in sugar at medium speed. Add eggs one at a time, beating well after each addition.

3. With mixer running, add flour 1 cup at a time, alternating with milk added ¼ cup at a time, until well blended. Stir in vanilla and almond extract.

4. Pour batter into pan. Bake 1 hour 40 minutes or until lightly browned. Cool 15 minutes in pan before turning out onto a wire rack. Makes 12 servings.

❖ **SYLVIA FLETCHER** | Memorial Baptist Church, Tulsa, Oklahoma

Brownie Caramel Pecan Bars

½ cup sugar

2 tablespoons butter

2 tablespoons water

2 cups semisweet chocolate chips, divided

2 eggs, lightly beaten

1 teaspoon vanilla

⅔ cup flour

¼ teaspoon baking soda

¼ teaspoon salt

CARAMEL TOPPING:

¼ cup butter

25 caramels, wrappers removed

2 tablespoons milk

1 cup pecan pieces

1. Preheat oven to 350°F. Line a 9 x 9 x 2-inch baking pan with foil. Grease and flour the foil.

2. Combine sugar, butter, and water in a large saucepan over low heat. Cook, stirring continuously, until mixture comes to a boil. Remove from heat, add 1 cup of the chocolate chips, and stir until melted.

3. Add eggs and vanilla to chocolate mixture and beat with a handheld mixer until well blended. Whisk together flour, baking soda, and salt. Stir into chocolate mixture.

4. Spread batter evenly in pan. Bake for 15 to 20 minutes or until brownies pull away from sides of pan.

5. To make caramel topping: Combine butter, caramels, and milk in a microwavable bowl. Microwave for 1 minute on high. Stir. Microwave 1 to 2 minutes more, stirring every 30 seconds or until caramels melt and mixture is smooth.

6. Spread hot caramel topping on hot brownies. Sprinkle with remaining cup chocolate chips and pecans. Cool completely, until chocolate chips on top are hard. Cut into bars. Makes 16 bars.

❖ **STACY L. MORRIS** | Trinity Evangelical Lutheran Church, Lansdale, Pennsylvania

Almond Biscotti

⅓ cup butter, room temperature

2 cups flour, divided

⅔ cup sugar

2 eggs

2 teaspoons baking powder

1 teaspoon vanilla

1½ cups slivered almonds

1 egg yolk

1 tablespoon milk or water

1 cup broken milk chocolate pieces

2 tablespoons vegetable shortening

Brush the surface of the dough with an egg yolk wash to make the baked crust shiny.

1. Preheat oven to 375°F. Lightly grease a baking sheet.

2. Cream butter in a mixer bowl until fluffy, 30 seconds. Add 1 cup of the flour, sugar, eggs, baking powder, and vanilla. Beat until well combined. Stir in remaining cup flour and almonds.

3. Divide dough in half. Shape each portion into a 9 x 2-inch log. Place logs 4 inches apart on baking sheet. Whisk together egg yolk and milk or water. Brush mixture onto each log. Bake for 25 minutes. Cool on baking sheet for 1 hour.

4. Cut each log diagonally into ½-inch slices. Lay slices cut side down on an ungreased baking sheet. Bake at 325°F for 8 minutes. Turn slices over and bake 8 to 10 minutes more or until dry and crisp. Cool on wire rack.

5. Melt chocolate pieces and shortening in a heavy saucepan over low heat. Drizzle over biscotti and let set. Makes 30 biscotti.

COLLEEN HARRIS | Trinity Evangelical Lutheran Church, Lansdale, Pennsylvania

Angel Food Cake

2 cups egg whites

2 teaspoons cream of tartar

2 cups sugar

½ teaspoon salt

1 teaspoon vanilla

1½ teaspoons almond extract

1⅓ to 1½ cups cake flour

1. Preheat oven to 350°F. Set aside a 10 x 4-inch tube pan but do not grease.

2. Beat egg whites and cream of tartar in a large mixer bowl at medium speed until foamy. Beat in sugar 2 tablespoons at a time on high speed. Continue beating until stiff and glossy. Add salt, vanilla, and almond extract with the last addition of sugar. Do not underbeat.

3. Sprinkle flour ¼ cup at a time over meringue and fold in just until flour disappears.

4. Push batter into pan. Run a knife through batter and around the edes to knock out air bubbles. Bake for 55 to 60 minutes or until a tester inserted near center comes out clean. Invert pan onto a funnel and let hang until cake is cold. Remove from pan. Makes 16 servings.

TERRI SISSON | Unity Baptist Church, Morgantown, Indiana

Apple Cheddar Cookies

½ cup butter, room temperature
½ cup sugar
1 egg
1 teaspoon vanilla
1½ cups flour
½ teaspoon baking soda

½ teaspoon cinnamon
½ teaspoon salt
1½ cups shredded cheddar cheese
1½ cups peeled chopped apple
¼ cup chopped nuts

1. Preheat oven to 375°F.
2. Cream butter and sugar in a large mixer bowl until light and fluffy. Stir in egg and vanilla. Add flour, baking soda, cinnamon, and salt and mix until well blended. Stir in cheese, apples, and nuts.
3. Drop by rounded teaspoonfuls onto ungreased baking sheet. Bake for 15 minutes or until lightly browned. Cool on wire racks. Makes 4½ dozen.

❖ **BRENDA KNIGHT** | Terrace Acres Baptist Church, Fort Worth, Texas

Butter Meltaways

½ cup butter
½ cup vegetable oil
½ cup sugar
½ cup confectioners' sugar
1 egg

½ teaspoon vanilla
2¼ cups flour
½ teaspoon baking powder
½ teaspoon cream of tartar

1. Cream butter, oil, sugar, and confectioners' sugar in a mixer bowl until light and fluffy. Beat in egg and vanilla. Whisk together flour, baking powder, and cream of tartar. Add to sugar mixture and mix until well blended. Cover dough and refrigerate overnight.
2. Preheat oven to 350°F.
3. Drop dough by teaspoonful onto ungreased baking sheets. Bake for 15 minutes or until lightly browned. Cool on wire racks. Makes 3 dozen.

❖ **JOY STEWART** | Memorial Baptist Church, Tulsa, Oklahoma

Apricot Cookie Bars

3½ cups flour
2 teaspoons baking powder
½ teaspoon baking soda
1 teaspoon salt
1½ cups sugar

1 cup butter
2 eggs, lightly beaten
2 teaspoons vanilla
8 to 10 canned or fresh apricots,
    pitted and sliced

1. Whisk together flour, baking powder, baking soda, salt, and sugar. Cut in butter with a pastry blender. Stir in eggs and vanilla. Gather up dough into a ball, wrap in plastic wrap, and refrigerate for 24 hours.
2. Preheat oven to 350°F. Press dough into bottom of a 15 x 10-inch jelly roll pan. Arrange sliced apricots on top. Bake for 10 to 20 minutes or until crust browns. Cool in pan. Cut into bars. Makes 20 servings.

❖ **BARBARA MILLER** | Trinity Evangelical Lutheran Church, Lansdale, Pennsylvania

Almond Squares

2 cups flour
1 cup sugar
1 teaspoon baking powder
4 eggs
½ cup whipping cream
1 teaspoon vanilla

FILLING:
½ cup butter, room temperature
¾ cups sugar
4 tablespoons milk
1 teaspoon vanilla
7 oz. sliced almonds

1. Preheat oven to 350°F. Lightly grease a 13 x 9 x 2-inch baking pan.
2. Whisk together flour, sugar, and baking powder.
3. Beat eggs and whipping cream. Stir in vanilla. Stir in flour mixture until well blended. Press dough into pan. Bake for 10 minutes.
4. To make filling: Combine butter, sugar, milk, and vanilla until well blended. Stir in almonds. Spread on top of partially baked dough. Bake 10 minutes more or until filling is set. Cool in pan. Cut into squares. Makes 12 servings.

❖ **BELVA HOFFMAN** | Methow Valley United Methodist Church, Twisp, Washington

Carrot Cookies

¾ cup sugar
1 cup vegetable shortening
1 egg
1 to 1½ cups grated carrots
2 cups flour

2 teaspoons baking powder
½ teaspoon salt
1 teaspoon vanilla
½ teaspoon lemon extract

1. Cream sugar and shortening in a mixer bowl. Blend in egg and carrots.
2. Sift together flour, baking powder, and salt. Add to carrot mixture and mix until well blended. Stir in vanilla and lemon extract. Cover and chill 2 to 3 hours.
3. Preheat oven to 350°F. Grease baking sheets.
4. Drop dough by teaspoonful onto baking sheets. Bake for 12 to 15 minutes or until lightly browned. Cool on wire racks. Makes 3 dozen.

❖ **DORIS MASON** | Memorial Baptist Church, Tulsa, Oklahoma

My Mother's Favorite Lace Cookies

1 cup rolled oats
1 cup sugar
2 tablespoons plus 2 teaspoons flour
¼ teaspoon baking powder

1 teaspoon salt
½ cup butter, melted
1 egg, beaten
2 teaspoons vanilla

1. Preheat oven to 350°F. Line baking sheets with aluminum foil.
2. Whisk together rolled oats, sugar, flour, baking powder, and salt. Add melted butter, egg, and vanilla. Stir until well blended.
3. Drop by the half teaspoonful onto foil, spaced 3 to 4 inches apart. Bake for 8 to 9 minutes or until light and lacy. Cool for 3 to 5 minutes. Push from underneath to release cookies from foil. Makes 4 dozen.

❖ **JOAN MITCHELL** | Trinity Presbyterian Church, Little Rock, Arkansas

White Velvet Cream Cheese Cookies

1 cup vegetable shortening
1 small package (3 oz.) cream cheese,
    room temperature
1 cup sugar

1 egg yolk
½ teaspoon vanilla
2½ cups flour

1. Preheat oven to 350°F. Lightly grease baking sheets.
2. Cream shortening and cream cheese in a mixer bowl. Beat in sugar until fluffy. Beat in egg yolk, vanilla, and flour.
3. Roll out dough on a lightly floured board. Cut with cookie cutters and place on baking sheets. Bake for 15 minutes or until lightly browned. Cool on wire racks. Makes 3 dozen.

❖ **VICKI GILL** | Trinity Presbyterian Church, Little Rock, Arkansas

Blonde Brownies

1 cup butter, melted
1 box (16 oz.) light brown sugar
2 eggs

2 cups flour
1 teaspoon vanilla
1½ cups chopped pecans

1. Preheat oven to 350°F. Grease and flour a 13 x 9 x 2-inch baking pan.
2. Combine melted butter and sugar in a mixer bowl. Beat in eggs, flour, vanilla, and pecans. Mix well.
3. Spread batter evenly in pan. Bake for 30 minutes. Cool in pan. Cut into squares. Makes 12 servings.

❖ **ANNYCE AYCOCK** | Memorial Baptist Church, Tulsa, Oklahoma

Orange Sugar Cookies

1½ cups vegetable shortening

2 cups sugar

2 eggs

2 teaspoons vanilla

2 tablespoons orange juice

1 tablespoon grated orange zest

4½ to 5 cups flour, divided

2 teaspoons baking powder

1 teaspoon salt

FROSTING:

¼ cup vegetable shortening

¼ cup butter

3½ tablespoons flour

¼ teaspoon salt

½ cup orange juice

½ teaspoon grated orange zest

3 cups sifted confectioners' sugar

1. Cream shortening, sugar, and eggs in a mixer bowl. Beat in vanilla, orange juice, and zest.

2. Sift together 1 cup of the flour, baking powder, and salt. Add to creamed mixture and beat until well blended. With mixer running, gradually add remaining 3½ to 4 cups flour until dough is firm but still easily mixed. Chill for 30 minutes.

3. Preheat oven to 350°F.

4. Roll out dough on floured board to a ⅛-inch thickness. Cut with cookie cutters dipped in flour. Place on baking sheets. Bake for 8 minutes or until lightly browned. Cool on wire racks.

5. To make frosting: Melt shortening and butter in a saucepan over low heat. Remove from heat. Blend in flour and salt. Gradually add orange juice and zest. Bring to a boil, stirring continuously, and cool for 1 minute. Remove from heat. Stir in confectioners' sugar. Set pan in ice water to speed cooling and beat to spreading consistency.

6. Spread frosting over tops of cookies. Makes 6 dozen.

❖ GLENDA HORN | Methow Valley United Methodist Church, Twisp, Washington

Peanut Butter Cookies

½ cup vegetable shortening

½ cup butter

1 cup sugar

1 cup brown sugar

1 cup peanut butter

2 eggs, beaten

1 teaspoon vanilla

3 cups flour

1 teaspoon baking soda

½ teaspoon salt

1. Preheat oven to 375°F. Lightly grease baking sheets.

2. Cream shortening, butter, sugar, and brown sugar in a mixer bowl. Add peanut butter and beat well. Gradually mix in eggs, vanilla, flour, baking soda, and salt until well combined.

3. Shape dough into balls. Place 2 inches apart on baking sheet. Press flat with fork. Bake for 10 to 15 minutes or until lightly browned. Makes 4 dozen.

❖ DORIS MASON | Memorial Baptist Church, Tulsa, Oklahoma

White Chocolate Brownies

½ cup butter

1 package (8 oz.) white chocolate chips or coarsely chopped white chocolate, divided

2 large eggs

½ teaspoon plus a pinch of salt

½ cup sugar

½ teaspoon vanilla

½ teaspoon salt

1 cup flour

1 package (6 oz.) semisweet chocolate chips

1. Preheat oven to 350°F. Lightly butter an 8 x 8 x 2-inch baking pan. Line bottom with foil or parchment. Lightly butter foil.

2. Melt butter in a small saucepan over low heat. Remove from heat and add half of white chocolate but do not stir.

3. Combine eggs and a pinch of the salt in a mixer bowl. Beat until frothy. Gradually add sugar, beating until mixture turns pale yellow and forms slowly dissolving ribbons. Add the white chocolate mixture, vanilla, remaining ½ teaspoon salt, and flour. Mix just until combined. Stir in semisweet chocolate chips and remaining white chocolate chips.

4. Spoon batter into pan and smooth top with a spatula. Bake for 30 minutes or until a tester inserted in center comes out almost clean. Cover top with foil during baking to prevent crust from drying out. Cool in pan on a wire rack. Cut into squares. Store in an airtight container at room temperature. Makes 16 servings.

❖ **BECKY ROWELL** | Christ Church, Frederica, St. Simons Island, Georgia

Almond Icebox Cookies

1½ cups butter, room temperature

1 cup sugar

1 cup brown sugar

3 eggs

4 cups flour

1 tablespoon cinnamon

1 teaspoon baking soda

½ cup finely chopped almonds

2 packages (2¼ oz. each) whole unblanched almonds

1. Cream butter, sugar, and brown sugar in a mixer bowl. Add eggs one at a time, beating well after each addition.

2. Whisk together flour, cinnamon, and baking soda. Add gradually to creamed mixture until well combined. Fold in chopped almonds. Shape into two 15-inch rolls and wrap in plastic wrap. Refrigerate for 2 hours or overnight.

3. Preheat oven to 375°F. Slice rolls into ¼-inch rounds. Place 2 inches apart on ungreased baking sheets. Top each with a whole almond. Bake for 8 to 10 minutes or until edges begin to brown. Cool on wire racks. Makes 10 dozen.

❖ **CLEO WILLIAMS** | Memorial Baptist Church, Tulsa, Oklahoma

Gwen Bradford's Ranger Cookies

1¾ cups flour

1 teaspoon baking soda

1½ teaspoons baking powder

¼ teaspoon salt

1 cup butter, room temperature

1 cup sugar

1 cup light brown sugar

2 large eggs

1 teaspoon vanilla

1 cup sweetened flaked coconut

1 cup rolled oats

2 cup cornflakes, coarsely crushed

1. Set oven rack to middle position. Preheat oven to 350°F. Grease baking sheets.

2. Whisk together flour, baking soda, baking powder, and salt.

3. Cream butter, sugar, and light brown sugar in a mixer bowl until light and fluffy. Add eggs one at a time, beating well after each addition. Stir in vanilla. Gradually stir in flour mixture, mixing until well combined. Stir in coconut, oats, and cornflakes.

4. Drop by rounded teaspoonful 2 inches apart onto baking sheets. Bake in middle of oven 10 to 12 minutes or until lightly browned. Transfer with a metal spatula to wire racks to cool. Makes 5 dozen.

MEMORIAL BAPTIST CHURCH | Tulsa, Oklahoma

Sour Cream Brownies

1 cup butter

1 cup water

4 tablespoons cocoa

2 cups flour

2 cups sugar

½ teaspoon salt

2 eggs

½ cup sour cream

1 teaspoon baking soda

ICING:

½ cup butter

4 tablespoons cocoa

6 tablespoons milk

3½ cups confectioners' sugar

1 teaspoon vanilla

1 cup chopped nuts

1. Preheat oven to 375°F. Grease 15½ x 10½ x 1-inch sheet pan.

2. Combine butter, water, and cocoa in a saucepan over medium heat. Bring to a boil.

3. Combine flour, sugar, and salt in a mixer bowl. Add hot cocoa mixture and mix to combine. Beat in eggs, sour cream, and baking soda.

4. Pour batter into pan. Bake for 20 minutes. Remove from oven promptly to prevent cake from drying out.

5. To make icing: Combine butter, cocoa, and milk in a saucepan over medium heat. Bring to a boil, stirring constantly. Reduce heat to low. Sift in confectioners' sugar and stir until smooth. Stir in vanilla and nuts. Spread icing on hot brownies. Cool and cut into squares or bars. Makes 30 servings.

CAROLYN MILLER | Terrace Acres Baptist Church, Fort Worth, Texas

Oatmeal Molasses Drop Cookies

1½ cups flour
1 cup sugar
1 teaspoon baking soda
¼ teaspoon salt
1 teaspoon ginger

¼ teaspoon cloves
½ cup butter, room temperature
1 egg
¼ cup molasses
¾ cup quick-cooking rolled oats

1. Preheat oven to 375°F. Grease baking sheets.
2. Sift together flour, sugar, baking soda, salt, ginger, and cloves into a mixer bowl. Add butter, egg, and molasses. Beat until well combined and smooth, 2 minutes. Stir in oats.
3. Drop by tablespoonful onto baking sheets, spaced 3 inches apart. Bake for 8 to 10 minutes. Cool 1 minute on baking sheets before transferring to wire racks. Makes 3½ dozen.

STEPHANIE MITCHELL | First Baptist Church, Russell, Kentucky

Brown Sugar Icebox Cookies

1¾ cups flour
½ teaspoon baking soda
¼ teaspoon salt
½ cup butter, room temperature

1 cup brown sugar
1 egg
1 teaspoon vanilla
⅔ cup chopped pecans

1. Whisk together flour, baking soda, and salt.
2. Cream butter and brown sugar until well blended. Add egg and vanilla. Mix well. Gradually mix in dry ingredients. Fold in pecans. Shape dough into two rolls and wrap tightly in waxed paper. Chill for 4 hours or overnight.
3. Preheat oven to 375°F. Cut rolls into ¼-inch slices. Place 2 inches apart on ungreased baking sheets. Bake for 7 to 10 minutes or until lightly browned. Makes 4 dozen.

JOY STEWART | Memorial Baptist Church, Tulsa, Oklahoma

Cindy's Crispy Oatmeal Cookies

1 cup butter
1 cup sugar
1 cup brown sugar
1 teaspoon vanilla
2 eggs
1½ cups flour

1 teaspoon baking soda
1 teaspoon salt
2 cups rolled oats
¾ cup raisins
1 cup chopped walnuts

1. Preheat oven to 375°F. Grease baking sheets.

2. Cream butter, sugar, and brown sugar at medium speed in a mixer bowl until light and fluffy. With mixer running, add vanilla, eggs one at a time, flour, baking soda, and salt. Stir in rolled oats, nuts, and raisins by hand or using the slowest mixer speed.

3. Drop by teaspoonful 3 inches apart onto baking sheets. Bake for 10 minutes or until lightly browned. Cool on wire racks. Makes 5 dozen.

❖ **SARAH MIGEOT** | Trinity Presbyterian Church, Little Rock, Arkansas

Texas Cookies

1 cup butter

1 cup brown sugar

1 cup oil

1 egg

1 cup flaked coconut

1 cup rolled oats

1 cup crispy rice cereal (such as Rice Krispies)

1 cup chocolate chips

2 teaspoons vanilla

1 teaspoon salt

1 teaspoon baking soda

1 teaspoon cream of tartar

3½ cups flour

1. Preheat oven to 350°F. Lightly grease baking sheets.

2. Cream butter and brown sugar in a mixer bowl. Blend in oil and egg. Stir in coconut, oats, cereal, chocolate chips, vanilla, salt, baking soda, cream of tartar, and flour.

3. Drop by teaspoonful onto baking sheet, 3 inches apart. Press down with a fork. Bake for 10 to 12 minutes. Cool on a wire rack. Makes 6 dozen.

❖ **ANNETTE SLACK** | Oakwood Church of God in Christ, Godfrey, Illinois

Walnut Squares

½ cup flour

⅛ teaspoon baking soda

½ teaspoon salt

1 egg

1 cup brown sugar

½ teaspoon vanilla

1 cup chopped walnuts

1. Preheat oven to 325°F. Grease an 8 x 8 x 2-inch baking pan.

2. Sift together flour, baking soda, and salt.

3. Beat egg in a mixer bowl until foamy. Beat in brown sugar and vanilla until well blended. Stir in flour mixture. Stir in walnuts.

4. Spread batter into pan. Bake for 25 to 30 minutes or until top has a dull crust. Cut into 2-inch squares while still warm. Cool completely before removing from pan. Makes 16 servings.

❖ **JEAN THOMAS** | Oakwood Church of God in Christ Godfrey, Illinois

Orange Crisps

1½ cups flour
¼ teaspoon baking soda
¼ teaspoon salt
1 cup butter
½ cup sugar

½ cup light brown sugar
1 egg
1 tablespoon grated orange zest
2 tablespoons orange juice
½ cup chopped pecans

1. Whisk together flour, baking soda, and salt.

2. Cream butter, sugar, and light brown sugar in a mixer bowl. Beat in egg and orange zest. Stir in flour mixture and orange juice until well blended. Stir in pecans. Cover dough and chill for 30 to 60 minutes.

3. Preheat oven to 375°F.

4. Drop dough by half teaspoonful 2 inches apart onto ungreased baking sheets. Bake for 6 to 8 minutes or until brown around edges. Cool on wire racks. Makes 3 dozen.

❖ MRS. WILLIAM R. SCHILLINGER | Pittsboro Baptist Church, Pittsboro, North Carolina

Pumpkin Cookies

1¼ cups flour
2 teaspoons baking powder
¼ cup vegetable shortening
½ cup sugar
1 egg, beaten
½ cup pumpkin
½ teaspoon vanilla
½ cup chopped nuts
½ teaspoon lemon extract
½ cup raisins

GLAZE:
¼ cup butter
1 cup brown sugar
Confectioners' sugar

1. Preheat oven to 350°F.

2. Sift together flour and baking powder.

3. Cream shortening and sugar in a mixer bowl. Stir in flour mixture until moistened. Stir in egg, pumpkin, vanilla, nuts, lemon extract, and raisins.

4. Drop by teaspoonful onto ungreased baking sheets. Bake for 15 minutes or until lightly browned. Cool on wire racks.

5. To make glaze: Melt butter and brown sugar in a large saucepan over medium heat. Remove from heat. Stir in confectioners' sugar ¼ cup at a time until desired consistency is reached. Cool to room temperature. Drizzle glaze over cookies. Makes 3 dozen.

❖ NANCY LITTERAL | First Baptist Church, Russell, Kentucky

Toffee Nut Bars

½ cup butter
½ cup brown sugar
1 cup flour

FILLING:

2 eggs
¼ cup corn syrup
¾ cup brown sugar
1 teaspoon vanilla
2 tablespoons flour
1 teaspoon baking powder
½ teaspoon salt
1 cup flaked coconut
1 cup chopped nuts

1. Preheat oven to 350°F. Lightly grease a 15 x 10½ x 2-inch baking pan.

2. Combine butter, brown sugar, and flour until crumbly. Press into bottom of pan. Bake for 10 to 15 minutes or just until starting to brown.

3. To make filling: Beat eggs in a mixer bowl until frothy. Stir in corn syrup, brown sugar, and vanilla. Sift flour, baking powder, and salt into egg mixture. Stir until well blended. Stir in coconut and nuts.

4. Turn filling mixture into pan and spread evenly over crust. Bake for 25 minutes or until top is browned. Cool in pan for 10 minutes. Cut into bars. Makes 48 bars.

RUTH FREYTAG | Church of the Canyons Women's Ministries, Canyon Country, California

Brownies

1 cup butter

3 squares (1 oz. each) unsweetened chocolate

4 eggs

2 cups sugar

1½ cups flour

2 teaspoons vanilla

Confectioners' sugar

1. Preheat oven to 350°F. Grease and flour a 15 x 10½ x 2-inch baking pan.

2. Melt butter and chocolate in a microwave, 1 minute on high.

3. Beat eggs in a mixer bowl. Beat in sugar. Add melted chocolate and butter and blend well. Stir in flour and vanilla.

4. Pour batter into pan and spread evenly. Bake for 15 minutes. Cool in pan 5 minutes. Sift confectioners' sugar over the top. Cool completely. Cut into squares. Makes 15 servings.

MARY LOUISE WILSON | Trinity Presbyterian Church, Little Rock, Arkansas

7-Layer Cookies

½ cup butter, melted

1 cup graham cracker crumbs

1 cup flaked coconut

1 cup chopped pecans

1 package (6 oz.) chocolate chips

1 package (6 oz.) butterscotch morsels

1 can (14 oz.) sweetened condensed milk

1. Preheat oven to 350°F.

2. Pour melted butter into a 13 x 9 x 2-inch baking pan. Tilt pan to evenly coat.

3. Layer graham cracker crumbs, coconut, pecans, chocolate chips, and butterscotch chips into pan. Pour sweetened condensed milk over all. Bake for 30 minutes. Cut into bars while still warm. Makes 36 bars.

SANDY HENRY | First Baptist Church, Russell, Kentucky

Raisin Oatmeal Bars in a Jar

½ cup rolled oats

½ cup raisins

1 cup brown sugar, divided

2 cups Bisquick baking mix, divided

1 teaspoon cinnamon

½ cup chocolate chips or butterscotch chips

1. Sterilize a wide-mouth, 1-quart canning jar and lid. Dry thoroughly.

2. Layer ingredients into jar in this order: oats, raisins, ½ cup of the brown sugar, 1 cup of the baking mix, cinnamon (sprinkle it in), remaining ½ cup brown sugar, and remaining baking mix. If there is space left, add more raisins or add chocolate chips or butterscotch chips. Close jar.

3. Enclose a gift card with this recipe:

Empty this jar of goodies into a bowl. Stir in ½ cup butter (room temperature), 1 egg, and 1 teaspoon vanilla. Generously coat an 8 x 8 x 2-inch baking pan with cooking spray. Press mixture into pan. Bake at 350°F for 20 to 22 minutes or until golden brown. Cut into squares. Makes 16 squares.

❖ SANDY FARRIS | Terrace Acres Baptist Church, Fort Worth, Texas

Peanut Butter Brownies

6 eggs

3 cups sugar

1½ cups brown sugar

1 cup creamy or chunky peanut butter

½ cup vegetable shortening

1 tablespoon vanilla

4 cups flour

1½ tablespoons baking powder

1½ teaspoons salt

½ cup chopped peanuts

1. Preheat oven to 350°F. Lightly grease three 13 x 9 x 2-inch baking pans.

2. Combine eggs, sugar, brown sugar, peanut butter, shortening, and vanilla in a mixer bowl until thoroughly blended. Add flour, baking powder, and salt. Mix just until smooth.

3. Spread batter into pans. Sprinkle with peanuts. Bake for 20 to 25 minutes or until cooked through but still moist. Cut into bars and cool in pans. Makes 4 dozen.

❖ JUDY URICH | Trinity Presbyterian Church, Little Rock, Arkansas

Chocolate Pecan Brownies

¾ cup flour

¼ teaspoon baking soda

¾ cup sugar

⅓ cup butter

2 tablespoons water

1 package (12 oz.) semisweet chocolate

  chips, divided

1 teaspoon vanilla

2 large eggs

½ cup chopped pecans

1. Preheat oven to 325°F. Grease a 9 x 9 x 2-inch baking pan.

2. Whisk together flour and baking soda.

3. Combine sugar, butter, and water in a small saucepan over medium heat. Bring to a boil. Remove from heat. Stir in 1 cup of the chocolate chips and vanilla until chocolate is melted and mixture is smooth. Transfer mixture to a medium bowl. Cool to room temperature.

4. Stir in eggs one at a time, beating well after each addition. Gradually stir in flour mixture until smooth. Stir in remaining chocolate chips and pecans.

5. Pour batter into pan. Bake for 30 to 35 minutes or until a toothpick inserted in center comes out clean. Cool in pan on wire rack. Cut into squares. Makes 16 servings.

❖ JENNIFER FREY | Sorento Assembly of God Church, Sorento, Illinois

Louisiana Brownies

¾ cup cocoa

1½ cups flour

3 cups sugar

1½ cups cooking oil

1½ tablespoons vanilla

1½ teaspoons salt

4 eggs

1 cup chopped pecans

ICING:

1 box confectioners' sugar

4 tablespoons cocoa

1½ teaspoons vanilla

6 to 8 tablespoons milk

1 cup chopped pecans

1. Preheat oven to 350°F. Coat a 15½ x 10½ x 1-inch sheet pan with nonstick cooking spray.

2. Combine cocoa, flour, sugar, oil, vanilla, salt, eggs, and pecans in a mixer bowl. Beat on medium speed just until combined, 2 minutes.

3. Pour batter into pan. Bake for 30 to 40 minutes or until set.

4. To make icing: Combine confectioners' sugar, cocoa, vanilla, and milk in a mixer bowl. Mix until smooth and of spreading consistency. Stir in pecans.

5. Spread icing on hot brownies. Cool in pan. Cut into bars. Makes 30 servings.

L. WIEMAN | Presbyterian Church of Gonzales, Gonzales, Texas

Chocolate Peanut Butter Brownies

½ cup flour

½ teaspoon baking soda

¼ teaspoon salt

¼ cup butter, melted

¼ cup peanut butter

2 squares (1 oz. each) unsweetened chocolate

1 egg, beaten

1 cup brown sugar

1 teaspoon vanilla

½ cup chopped peanuts or pecans

1. Preheat oven to 350°F. Grease an 8 x 8 x 2-inch baking pan.

2. Sift together flour, baking soda, and salt.

3. Combine melted butter, peanut butter, chocolate, and egg in a mixer bowl. Gradually add brown sugar and beat until well blended. Stir in vanilla. Add flour mixture and peanuts or pecans.

Omit the salt from this recipe if you use salted peanuts.

4. Pour batter into pan. Bake for 30 minutes or until brownies spring back when pressed. Cool in pan on a wire rack. Cut into squares. Makes 16 servings.

SAM BEARD | Pittsboro Baptist Church, Pittsboro, North Carolina

Dream Bars

CRUST:

½ cup butter

1 cup flour

½ cup brown sugar

FILLING:

2 eggs, beaten

2 tablespoons flour

1½ cups cocoa

½ cup nuts

1 cup brown sugar

½ teaspoon baking powder

1 teaspoon vanilla

Dash of salt

1. Preheat oven to 350°F. Grease a 9 x 9 x 2-inch baking pan.

2. To make crust: Combine butter, flour, and brown sugar until crumbly. Press mixture into bottom of pan. Bake for 10 minutes.

3. To make filling: Combine eggs, flour, cocoa, nuts, brown sugar, baking powder, vanilla, and salt in a mixer bowl. Beat until well blended. Spread over crust. Return to oven and bake 15 minutes more. Cool in pan. Cut into bars. Makes 16 servings.

❖ **ANNETTE SLACK** | Oakwood Church of God in Christ, Godfrey, Illinois

Buffalo Chips

2 cups butter, melted

2 cups sugar

2 cups light brown sugar

4 eggs

2 teaspoons vanilla

2 cups quick-cooking rolled oats

2 cups cornflakes (such as Post Toasties)

4 cups flour

1 teaspoon baking soda

2 teaspoons baking powder

1 package (6 oz.) chocolate chips

2 cups pecan halves

1. Preheat oven to 350°F. Lightly grease baking sheets.

2. Combine melted butter, sugar, and light brown sugar in a mixer bowl. Add eggs, vanilla, rolled oats, and cereal.

3. Sift together flour, baking soda, and baking powder. Add to dough and mix to combine. Stir in chocolate chips and pecans.

4. Use an ice cream scoop to put portions of dough onto baking sheet, 6 cookies per sheet. Bake for 18 minutes. Cool on wire racks. Makes 18 cookies.

❖ **LYNDA MCKEE** | Presbyterian Church of Gonzales, Gonzales, Texas

Butterscotch Brownies

1 package (6 oz.) butterscotch chips
⅔ cup butter
2 cups brown sugar
4 eggs
2 teaspoons vanilla

2 cups flour
1 teaspoon baking powder
1 teaspoon salt
1 cup chopped nuts

1. Preheat oven to 350°F. Lightly grease a 13 x 9 x 2-inch baking pan.

2. Melt butterscotch chips and butter in a saucepan over medium heat. Stir in brown sugar. Add eggs one at a time, beating well after each addition. Stir in vanilla. Gradually beat in flour, baking powder, and salt. Fold in nuts.

3. Spread batter evenly in pan. Bake for 30 to 35 minutes. Cool in pan. Cut into squares. Makes 12 servings.

❖ **L. WIEMAN** | Presbyterian Church of Gonzales, Gonzales, Texas

Chocolate Almond Biscotti

1½ cups almonds, divided
4 cups flour
¾ cup mini semisweet chocolate chips
2 teaspoons baking powder
2 teaspoons cinnamon
5 large eggs
2 cups sugar
½ cup butter, melted
1½ tablespoons grated orange zest
Semisweet chocolate, melted

A two-step baking process makes biscotti extra crisp— just right for dunking in hot coffee or cocoa.

1. Preheat oven to 350°F. Coat two baking sheets with nonstick cooking spray.

2. Chop ½ cup of the almonds in a food processor until finely ground.

3. Coarsely chop remaining cup almonds and place in a bowl. Add flour, chocolate chips, baking powder, and cinnamon.

4. Beat eggs in a mixer bowl at medium speed until fluffy. Add finely ground almonds, sugar, melted butter, and orange zest. Beat until well blended. Gradually blend in flour mixture to form a sticky dough.

5. Turn out dough onto a floured work surface. Shape each piece into a 12 x 2-inch log. Place two logs on each baking sheet and pat down slightly. Bake for 25 to 30 minutes or until firm in center. Let cool slightly.

6. Using a serrated knife, cut each partially baked log diagonally into ½-inch thick slices. Place slices cut side up on baking sheets. Return to oven and bake, turning once, until lightly browned on both sides, 10 to 14 minutes more. Cool on a wire rack. Drizzle with melted chocolate. Makes 8 dozen.

❖ **GINNY SAWYER** | First Presbyterian Church, Du Quoin, Illinois

Coconut Macaroons

2 egg whites
½ cup sugar
½ teaspoon salt

1½ teaspoons vanilla
4 tablespoons flour
2½ cups flaked coconut

1. Preheat oven to 300°F. Line baking sheets with parchment.

2. Beat egg whites until stiff. Add sugar, salt, and vanilla. Fold in flour and coconut.

3. Drop by teaspoonful onto baking sheets. Bake for 30 minutes. Remove from paper while hot. Cool on wire racks. Makes 2 dozen.

❖ **NITA HARTER** | Trinity Presbyterian Church, Little Rock, Arkansas

Peanut Butter Scotchies

1 cup sugar
1 cup corn syrup
1 cup peanut butter

6 cups crispy rice cereal (such as Rice Krispies)
1 cup chocolate chips
1 cup butterscotch chips

1. Grease a 13 x 9 x 2-inch baking dish.

2. Combine sugar and corn syrup in a saucepan over low heat. Cook until sugar is dissolved. Do not boil. Add peanut butter and mix well.

3. Pour mixture over cereal. Stir until well blended. Press mixture firmly into pan.

4. Melt chocolate chips and butterscotch chips in a saucepan over medium heat. Spread over mixture in pan. Cool to room temperature. Cut into bars. Makes 36 bars.

❖ **DARLA S. REED** | First Baptist Church, Russell, Kentucky

Date Nut Kisses

3 egg whites
1 cup sugar
½ lb. dates, finely chopped

1 tablespoon flour
2 cups pecans, finely chopped

1. Preheat oven to 300°F. Grease baking sheets.

2. Beat egg whites and sugar in a mixer bowl until very stiff, 15 to 20 minutes.

3. Toss dates with flour to coat. Gently fold dates and pecans into egg whites.

4. Drop mixture by teaspoonful onto baking sheets. Bake for 20 to 30 minutes or until lightly browned. Cool on wire racks. Makes 3 dozen.

❖ **PRESBYTERIAN CHURCH OF GONZALES** | Gonzales, Texas

Secret Recipe Chocolate Chip Cookies

2¼ cups flour
½ cup rolled oats
1½ teaspoons baking soda
½ teaspoon salt
¼ teaspoon cinnamon
2 teaspoons vanilla
1 cup butter

¾ cup sugar
¾ cup brown sugar
1 teaspoon lemon juice
1 egg
2 cups semisweet chocolate chips
1 to 1½ cups chopped pecans or walnuts

1. Preheat oven to 350°F. Line two baking sheets with parchment paper.
2. Combine flour, oats, baking soda, salt, and cinnamon. Sprinkle vanilla over the top.
3. Cream butter, sugar, brown sugar, and lemon juice in a mixer bowl. Add egg and beat until fluffy. Stir in flour mixture until well blended. Stir in chocolate chips and pecans or walnuts.
4. Drop dough by tablespoonful onto baking sheets. Bake for 14 to 15 minutes or until lightly brown. Cool on wire racks. When completely cool, store at room temperature in an airtight container. Makes 3 dozen.

❖ **PAT SHREWSBURY** | First Baptist Church, Russell, Kentucky

Chocolate Newtons

½ cup butter
1 cup sugar plus more for topping
2 egg yolks
1½ squares (1.5 oz.) chocolate, melted
3 cups flour
1 teaspoon baking soda
½ teaspoon salt

½ cup buttermilk
1 teaspoon vanilla

FILLING:
2 egg whites
½ cup sugar
¾ cup flaked coconut

1. Preheat oven to 375°F. Grease baking sheets.
2. Cream butter and sugar in a mixer bowl. Beat in egg yolks. Add melted chocolate.
3. Sift together flour, baking soda, and salt. Add flour mixture and buttermilk alternately to chocolate mixture until well blended. Stir in vanilla.
4. To make filling: Beat egg whites until stiff. Gradually beat in sugar. Continue beating until very stiff.
5. Roll out dough to a ⅛-inch thickness. Cut with a 3-inch round cookie cutter or biscuit cutter. Place half of rounds on baking sheet. Top each with a scant teaspoon of filling. Top with a second round and press edges together. Sprinkle lightly with sugar. Bake for 8 to 10 minutes or until lightly browned. Cool on wire racks. Makes 2 dozen.

❖ **JOANN MCQUADE** | Trinity Presbyterian Church, Little Rock, Arkansas

Jumbo Raisin Cookies

2 cups raisins

1 cup water

1 cup vegetable shortening

1 cup sugar

1 cup brown sugar

3 eggs

1 teaspoon vanilla

4 cups flour

1½ teaspoons cinnamon

1 teaspoon baking soda

1 teaspoon baking powder

2 teaspoons salt

1 teaspoon nutmeg

1 teaspoon allspice

1 cup nuts

1. Preheat oven to 400°F. Grease baking sheets.

2. Combine raisins and water in a saucepan over medium heat. Simmer until raisins are plump and moist, 8 to 10 minutes. Remove from heat and cool to room temperature. Do not drain.

3. Cream shortening, sugar, and brown sugar in a large mixer bowl. Beat in eggs and vanilla. Sift together flour, cinnamon, baking soda, baking powder, salt, nutmeg, and allspice. Slowly blend flour mixture into sugar mixture. Stir in cooked raisins with their liquid and nuts.

4. Form dough into balls and place on baking sheets. Bake for 12 to 15 minutes or until lightly browned. Cool on wire racks. Makes 6 dozen.

❖ **ROBERTA SMITH** | Vincent Memorial United Methodist Church, Nutter Fort, West Virginia

Chocolate Oatmeal Cookies

1½ cups flour

½ cup cocoa

½ teaspoon baking soda

¾ teaspoon salt

1¼ cups brown sugar

1½ cups quick-cooking rolled oats

½ cup vegetable shortening

1 teaspoon vanilla

5 tablespoons hot water

1 egg

1 to 2 teaspoons hot water

1. Preheat oven to 375°F. Grease baking sheets.

2. Sift together flour, cocoa, baking soda, and salt. Add brown sugar and oats, stirring to combine.

3. Combine shortening, vanilla, and hot water in a mixer bowl. Add half of flour mixture and beat until smooth. Beat in egg. Gradually add remaining flour mixture and mix well. Add hot water to make dough less stiff.

4. Shape dough into 1-inch balls. Place 3 inches apart on baking sheet. Press flat with the bottom of a glass that has been greased and sugared to prevent sticking. Bake for 6 to 8 minutes or until lightly browned. Cool on wire racks. Makes 3 dozen.

❖ **DORIS MASON** | Memorial Baptist Church, Tulsa, Oklahoma

Preacher Cookies

4 cups sugar
1 cup milk
½ cup butter
6 tablespoons cocoa

1 cup peanut butter
2 teaspoons vanilla
5 cups quick-cooking rolled oats

1. Line two baking sheets with waxed paper.

2. Combine sugar, milk, butter, and cocoa in a saucepan over medium heat. Bring to a boil and cook, stirring continuously, for 1½ minutes.

3. Remove from heat. Add peanut butter and vanilla. Stir until peanut butter melts.

4. Add oatmeal and stir to coat. Drop by spoonful onto waxed paper. Refrigerate for 30 minutes or until firm. Makes 3 dozen.

❖ **MARY BURROWS JACKSON** | Vincent Memorial United Methodist Church, Nutter Fort, West Virginia

Pecan Wafers

⅔ cup flour
¼ teaspoon baking powder
¼ teaspoon salt
2 eggs

1 cup brown sugar
1 teaspoon vanilla
1 cup chopped nuts

1. Preheat oven to 400°F. Grease baking sheets.

2. Sift together flour, baking powder, and salt.

3. Beat eggs in a mixer bowl until thick. With mixer running, gradually add brown sugar and flour mixture. Stir in vanilla and nuts.

4. Drop by teaspoonful 2 inches apart on baking sheets. Bake for 6 to 7 minutes or until lightly browned. Transfer immediately to wire racks for cooling. Makes 5 dozen.

❖ **LOTTA M. HUNT** | Christ Church, Frederica, St. Simons Island, Georgia

Chocolate Chip Cookies

2⅔ cups butter
2 cups sugar
2 cups brown sugar
4 eggs
4 teaspoons vanilla

6 cups flour
2 teaspoons baking soda
2 teaspoons salt
1 package (12 oz.) semisweet chocolate chips
½ cup nuts

1. Preheat oven to 375°. Set aside two ungreased baking sheets.
2. Combine butter, sugar, brown sugar, eggs, and vanilla in a mixer bowl. Gradually mix in flour, baking soda, and salt. Stir in chocolate chips and nuts.
3. Drop by rounded teaspoonful 2 inches apart on baking sheets. Bake for 8 to 10 minutes or until lightly brown. Makes 15 dozen.

❖ LEE MINOR | Memorial Baptist Church, Tulsa, Oklahoma

Peanut Blossoms

1¾ cups flour
½ cup sugar plus more for coating
½ cup brown sugar
1 teaspoon baking soda
½ teaspoon salt
½ cup vegetable shortening

½ cup peanut butter
2 teaspoons milk
1 teaspoon vanilla
1 egg
48 Hershey's chocolate kisses

1. Preheat oven to 375°F. Set aside baking sheets but do not grease.
2. Combine flour, sugar, brown sugar, baking soda, salt, shortening, peanut butter, milk, vanilla, and egg in a large mixer bowl. Mix at low speed until dough forms.
3. Shape rounded teaspoonfuls of dough into balls. Roll balls in sugar to coat. Place on ungreased baking sheets. Bake for 10 to 12 minutes or until golden brown. Top each hot cookie with a candy kiss, pressing down so cookie cracks around edges. Cool on wire racks. Makes 4 dozen.

❖ LYN ALEXANDER and DEBBIE SCHROEDER | Unity Baptist Church, Morgantown, Indiana

Chocolate Macaroons

6 egg whites
4½ cups confectioners' sugar
4 squares (1 oz. each) baker's
   unsweetened chocolate, cut into pieces,
   melted, and cooled

2 tablespoons cold water
1 teaspoon vanilla
1 lb. whole unblanched almonds,
   grated or finely chopped
¼ teaspoon salt

1. Beat egg whites in a mixer bowl until stiff. Gradually sift in confectioners' sugar and beat until smooth. Beat in chocolate, cold water, and vanilla. Stir in almonds and salt. Chill for 30 minutes.
2. Preheat oven to 350°F. Grease baking sheets.
3. Drop mixture by teaspoonful onto baking sheets. Bake for 15 minutes. Cool on wire racks. Makes 12 dozen.

❖ FRIEDA LAUGE | St. John's Guild, St. John's Church, West Bend, Wisconsin

Macadamia Nut Cookies

2¼ cups flour

1 teaspoon baking soda

1 teaspoon salt

1 cup butter, room temperature

½ cup sugar

½ cup brown sugar

2 eggs

1 teaspoon vanilla

1¼ cups macadamia nuts, coarsely chopped

½ cup flaked coconut

1½ packages (9 oz.) butterscotch chips

1. Preheat oven to 350°F. Set aside ungreased baking sheets.

2. Sift together flour, baking soda, and salt.

3. Cream butter, sugar, and brown sugar until fluffy. Beat in eggs and vanilla. Stir in dry ingredients until thoroughly blended. Fold in nuts, coconut, and butterscotch chips.

4. Drop by rounded tablespoon onto baking sheet. Bake for 12 minutes or until lightly browned. Cool on wire racks. Store at room temperature in a covered tin. Makes 40 cookies.

MRS. ROBERT ALLEN | Christ Church, Frederica, St. Simons Island, Georgia

Molasses Spice Cookies

2 cups flour

2 teaspoons baking soda

2 teaspoons cloves

2 teaspoons ginger

2 teaspoons cinnamon

Pinch of salt

¾ cup butter

1 cup sugar

1 egg

4 tablespoons molasses

1. Sift together flour, baking soda, cloves, ginger, cinnamon, and salt.

2. Cream butter and sugar in a mixer bowl. Beat in egg. Add flour mixture and blend until well combined. Stir in molasses. Cover and chill for 2 to 4 hours.

3. Roll dough into walnut-size balls. Place on an ungreased baking sheet. Bake at 350°F for 10 minutes. Cool on a wire rack. Makes 3 dozen.

RUTH STEWART | Christ Church, Frederica, St. Simons Island, Georgia

Filbert Cookies

3 eggs, separated, divided

1 cup plus 5 tablespoons sugar, divided

1 cup flour

½ lb. filberts, ground

Maraschinos, cut in half

1. Beat egg yolks in a mixer bowl. Beat in 1⅛ cups of the sugar. Whisk 2 of the egg whites until frothy, add to yolk mixture, and beat well. Fold in flour and filberts. Shape dough into a roll, wrap in plastic wrap, and refrigerate overnight.

2. Cut dough roll into ¼-inch slices. Place on a baking sheet. Beat remaining egg white until stiff. Beat in remaining 3 tablespoons sugar. Frost each dough round with egg white mixture. Top with half a cherry. Bake at 350°F for 30 minutes or until lightly browned. Makes 3 dozen.

❖ **LEONA WILKENS** | St. John's Guild, St. John's Church, West Bend, Wisconsin

Scotch Shortbread

2 cups flour	Pinch of salt
½ cup sugar	1 cup butter

1. Preheat oven to 325°F. Lightly grease three baking sheets.

2. Sift together flour, sugar, and salt. Cut in butter with a pastry blender. Knead by hand until dough comes together.

3. Divide dough in thirds. Roll out each piece into an 8-inch-diameter circle. Score with a knife into 8 wedges but do not separate. Place on baking sheets. Bake for 30 to 45 minutes or until brown around the edges. Serve warm or at room temperature. Makes 24 servings.

❖ **ELWOOD "BUS" HANNINGS, JR.** | Trinity Evangelical Lutheran Church, Lansdale, Pennsylvania

Persimmon Cookies

1 cup persimmon pulp	½ teaspoon salt
1 teaspoon baking soda	½ teaspoon nutmeg
½ cup butter	½ teaspoon cinnamon
2 cups sugar	
1 egg	CINNAMON SUGAR:
1 teaspoon baking soda	½ cup sugar
2½ cups flour	1 teaspoon cinnamon

1. Stir together persimmon pulp and baking soda.

2. Combine butter, sugar, egg, baking soda, flour, salt, nutmeg, cinnamon, and persimmon pulp in a mixer bowl. Beat until well blended. Cover and chill for 2 hours.

3. To make cinnamon sugar: Stir together sugar and cinnamon.

4. Preheat oven to 375°F. Roll dough into 1-inch balls. Roll balls in cinnamon sugar to coat. Place on ungreased baking sheets. Bake for 12 minutes or until lightly browned. Makes 4 dozen.

❖ **DEBBIE BRUNER** | United Baptist Church, Morgantown, Indiana

Marmalade Bars

½ cup pitted chopped dates
¾ cup orange marmalade
½ cup butter
1 cup brown sugar
1 teaspoon vanilla

2 eggs
1¾ cups flour
1 teaspoon baking soda
½ teaspoon salt
1 cup chopped nuts

1. Preheat oven to 350°F. Set aside a 13 x 9 x 2-inch baking pan but do not grease.
2. Combine dates and marmalade.
3. Cream butter, brown sugar, and vanilla in a mixer bowl until fluffy. Beat in eggs. Whisk together flour, baking soda, and salt. Add to butter mixture, beating until well combined. Stir in nuts.
4. Spread two-thirds of dough evenly into bottom of pan. Top with date mixture. Drop remaining dough by tablespoonful evenly over date layer. Bake for 20 to 25 minutes. Cut into bars. Cool in pan. Makes 24 bars.

❖ PEG HERDMAN | St. Mark's Lutheran Church, Conshohocken, Pennsylvania

Anise Platzen

6 medium eggs
2¼ cups sugar
1 teaspoon anise oil

2½ cups sifted flour
½ teaspoon salt

1. Beat eggs in a mixer bowl until light and frothy. Add sugar and beat for ½ hour. Stir in anise oil. Sift together flour and salt. With mixer running on low speed, gradually add flour mixture. Continue mixing until well blended.
2. Drop dough by teaspoonful onto well-greased baking sheets. Dough should be round and about 1¼ inches in diameter. Let stand overnight.
3. Bake at 350°F for 10 to 15 minutes or until golden brown. Makes 3 dozen.

❖ ESTHER KLEIN | St. John's Guild, St. John's Church, West Bend, Wisconsin

Lemon Bars

1 cup butter, room temperature
¼ teaspoon salt
½ cup confectioners' sugar plus
    more for topping
2¼ cups flour, divided

4 eggs, lightly beaten
1 tablespoon grated lemon zest
5 tablespoons fresh lemon juice
2 cups sugar
¼ cup flour

1. Preheat oven to 350°F. Set aside a 13 x 9 x 2-inch baking pan but do not grease.

2. Combine butter, salt, ½ cup of the confectioners' sugar, and 2 cups of the flour in a mixer bowl, beating to make a soft dough. Press evenly into pan. Bake for 15 to 20 minutes or until golden.

3. Reduce heat to 325°F. Combine eggs, lemon zest, lemon juice, sugar, and remaining ¼ cup flour. Blend until smooth. Pour mixture over crust. Bake for 25 minutes or until firm. Cool in pan. Dust with confectioners' sugar and slice into bars. Makes 32 bars.

JEAN BARNETT | Presbyterian Church of Gonzales, Gonzales, Texas

Colossal Cookies

½ cup butter

1½ cups sugar

1½ cups brown sugar

4 eggs

1 teaspoon vanilla

2 cups chunky peanut butter

6 cups rolled oats

2½ teaspoons baking soda

1 cup chocolate chips

1. Cream butter, sugar, and brown sugar in a large mixer bowl until well blended. Beat in eggs and vanilla. Add peanut butter and mix well. Stir in oats, baking soda, and chocolate chips. Cover and let stand so that oats can soften, 1 hour.

2. Drop by teaspoonful onto greased baking sheet. Flatten with fork. Bake at 350°F for 10 minutes or until lightly browned. Makes 6 dozen.

AUNT IRENE GRAVES | Women's Missionary Auxiliary, Bay Springs, Mississippi

Ginger Cookies

2½ cups sugar, divided

1⅓ cups oil

2 eggs

½ cup molasses

4 cups flour

1 tablespoon plus 1 teaspoon baking soda

1 teaspoon salt

2 teaspoons cinnamon

2 teaspoons ginger

1. Preheat oven to 350°F. Set aside baking sheets but do not grease.

2. Mix 2 cups of the sugar and oil in a mixer bowl until well blended. Add eggs and beat well. Stir in molasses.

3. Add flour, baking soda, salt, cinnamon, and ginger. Mix well.

4. Drop by teaspoonful into remaining ½ cup sugar to partially coat. Place on baking sheets. Bake for 10 to 12 minutes or until lightly browned. Do not overbake. Cool on wire racks. Makes 5 dozen.

❖ LEE MINOR | Memorial Baptist Church, Tulsa, Oklahoma

Suzy's Cinnamon Sticks

1 cup butter

¾ cup sugar

2 cups flour

1 egg, separated

4 teaspoons cinnamon

1 teaspoon vanilla

1 cup chopped pecans

1. Preheat oven to 350°F. Butter a rimmed baking sheet.

2. Cream butter and sugar. Gradually add flour, egg yolk, cinnamon, and vanilla. Beat until smooth

3. Turn out dough onto baking sheet and pat down to a ¼-inch thickness. Brush unbeaten egg white over entire surface. Sprinkle pecans over the top and press down into dough. Bake for 30 minutes. Cool on baking sheet on a wire rack. Cut into bars. Makes 4 dozen.

❖ JEAN REESE | Presbyterian Church of Gonzales, Gonzales, Texas

Date Pinwheel Cookies

2½ cups chopped dates

1 cup sugar

1 cup water

1 cup chopped nuts

1 cup vegetable shortening

2 cups brown sugar

3 eggs, beaten

4 cups flour

1 teaspoon baking soda

½ teaspoon salt

1. Combine dates, sugar, and water in a saucepan over low heat. Cook until thick. Stir in nuts.
2. Cream shortening and brown sugar. Add eggs and beat well. Add flour, baking soda, and salt. Mix until well combined. Cover and chill at least 30 minutes.
3. Divide dough in half. Roll out each portion to a ¼-inch thickness. Spread half of date mixture on each piece. Roll up into a log, wrap in waxed paper, and refrigerate overnight.
4. Cut log into ¼-inch thick slices. Place on a greased baking sheet. Bake at 400°F for 10 to 12 minutes or until lightly browned. Makes 4 dozen.

❖ **MRS. PURLE WHITE** | Women's Missionary Auxiliary, Bay Springs, Mississippi

Raspberry Tea Thins

1¼ cups butter	**2½ cups flour**
⅔ cup sugar	**½ teaspoon salt**
1 egg	**Raspberry jam or preserves**
1 teaspoon vanilla or almond extract	**Confectioners' sugar**

1. Cream butter and sugar in a mixer bowl. Beat in egg and vanilla. Sift together flour and salt. Add to butter mixture and stir until well combined. Gather up dough, wrap in plastic wrap, and chill for 3 to 4 hours.
2. Roll out dough on a lightly floured surface or a marble pastry slab to a ⅛-inch thickness. Cut into rounds using a 2-inch diameter cookie cutter. Spoon about 1 teaspoon of jam onto one round, cover with another round, and pinch the edges together to seal. Place on baking sheets.
3. Bake at 350°F for 8 to 10 minutes or until lightly golden. For tender cookies, do not overbake. Press warm cookies into confectioners' sugar to coat. Cool on wire racks. Makes 3 dozen.

❖ **ADELE AHLUM** | Trinity Evangelical Lutheran Church, Lansdale, Pennsylvania

Daisy Creams

3 lbs. sugar	**2⅛ cups water**
1 cup butter	**1 teaspoon vanilla**

1. Butter a cold marble slab.
2. Combine sugar, butter, and water in a saucepan over medium-high heat. Bring to a boil and cook until mixture registers 262°F on a candy thermometer. Do not stir the mixture while it is boiling.
3. Remove from heat. Stir in vanilla.
4. Pour mixture on marble slab. Fold in edges until cool enough to handle. Pull candy until it turns white. Pull into long strings 1½-inch wide. Cut into pieces before candy turns hard. Let set overnight. Store in a cool place. Makes about 3½ lbs.

❖ **VERNA HESS** | St. John's Guild, St. John's Church, West Bend, Wisconsin

Chewy Chocolate Cookies

1¼ cups butter
2 cups sugar
2 eggs
2 teaspoons vanilla
2 cups flour

¾ cup cocoa
1 teaspoon baking soda
½ teaspoon salt
1 cup chopped nuts
1 package (6 oz.) peanut butter chips

1. Preheat oven to 350°F. Set aside baking sheets but do not grease.
2. Cream butter and sugar in a large mixer bowl. Blend in eggs and vanilla.
3. Whisk together flour, cocoa, baking soda, and salt. Gradually blend into butter mixture. Stir in nuts and peanut butter chips.
4. Drop by teaspoonful onto baking sheets. Bake for 8 to 9 minutes or until puffy. Do not overbake. Cool on baking sheet until set, about 1 minute, and transfer to a wire rack. Makes 3 dozen.

✤ WOMEN'S MISSIONARY AUXILIARY | Bay Springs, Mississippi

Cinnamon Cookies

6 eggs
3 cups sugar
4 cups flour
4 teaspoons baking powder

1½ cups coarsely chopped pecans
1 teaspoon cinnamon
1 teaspoon vanilla or lemon extract

1. Preheat oven to 350°F. Grease baking sheets.
2. Combine eggs and sugar in a mixer bowl. Beat for 5 minutes.
3. Sift flour and baking powder over pecans. Add to egg mixture and blend well. Stir in cinnamon and vanilla or lemon extract.
4. Drop by teaspoonful onto baking sheets. Bake for 10 to 12 minutes or until lightly browned. Cool on wire racks. Makes 5 dozen.

✤ MRS. GUSSIE DUBOSE | Adapted from *Presbyterian Cookbook*, 2nd Edition, 1924 | Presbyterian Church of Gonzales, Gonzales, Texas

Butterscotch Sticks

¼ cup butter
1 cup brown sugar
1 egg
1 cup flour

1 teaspoon baking powder
¼ teaspoon salt
¼ cup broken nutmeats
1 teaspoon vanilla

1. Preheat oven to 400°F. Line an 11 x 7 x 2-inch baking pan with parchment paper and grease the parchment.

2. Melt butter in a small saucepan over medium heat. Add sugar and stir until dissolved. Remove from heat. Cool to lukewarm.

3. Transfer sugar mixture to a mixer bowl. Add egg and beat well. Whisk together flour, baking powder, and salt. Stir into batter. Stir in nutmeats and vanilla.

4. Spread batter in pan. Bake for 10 to 15 minutes or until firm. Cut into strips about 4 x 1 inches while still hot. Transfer to a wire rack. Makes 2 dozen.

❖ Adapted from *The Best of the Old Church Cookbooks* by Florence Ekstrand, courtesy of Welcome Press

Hawaiian Drop Cookies

2 cups flour
2 teaspoons baking powder
½ teaspoon salt
⅔ cup vegetable shortening
1¼ cups sugar

½ teaspoon vanilla
½ teaspoon almond extract
1 egg
¾ cup crushed pineapple, drained
½ cup finely chopped coconut

1. Preheat oven to 325°F. Set aside baking sheets but do not grease.

2. Sift together flour, baking powder, and salt.

3. Cream shortening, sugar, vanilla, and almond extract. Beat in egg until fluffy. Blend in pineapple and flour mixture.

4. Drop dough by teaspoonful into coconut to coat one side. Set 3 inches apart on baking sheet. Bake for 20 minutes. Cool on wire racks. Makes 4½ dozen.

❖ **HEATHER MCLEAN NICHOLS** | Methow Valley United Methodist Church, Twisp, Washington

Ricotta Cookies

1 cup butter
2 cups sugar
3 eggs
1 container (16 oz.) ricotta
4 cups flour

1 teaspoon baking soda
1 teaspoon salt
2 teaspoons vanilla
2 teaspoons lemon juice or coconut extract
White icing

1. Cream butter and sugar in a mixer bowl. Add eggs and mix well. Add ricotta, flour, baking soda, salt, vanilla, and lemon juice or coconut extract. Cover and chill for 1 hour.

2. Preheat oven to 425°F. Grease baking sheets.

3. Drop by teaspoonful onto baking sheets. Bake for 8 to 10 minutes or until lightly browned. Cool on wire racks. Frost with white icing. Makes 6 dozen.

❖ **BONNIE GALLOWAY** | Messiah United Methodist Church, York, Pennsylvania

Pumpkin Spice Bars

2 cups flour
2 teaspoons baking powder
1 teaspoon baking soda
½ teaspoon salt
2 cups sugar
2 teaspoons cinnamon
½ teaspoon pumpkin pie spice
4 eggs, beaten
1 cup vegetable oil
1 can (16 oz.) pumpkin
1 cup chopped nuts and/or raisins

FROSTING:

1 small package (3 oz.) cream cheese,
    room temperature
6 tablespoons butter, room temperature
1 teaspoon vanilla
1 teaspoon milk
2 cups confectioners' sugar
Chopped nuts

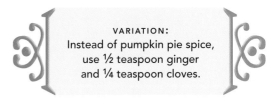

VARIATION:
Instead of pumpkin pie spice,
use ½ teaspoon ginger
and ¼ teaspoon cloves.

1. Preheat oven to 350°F. Grease a 12 x 9 x 1-inch jelly roll pan.

2. Combine flour, baking powder, baking soda, salt, sugar, cinnamon, and pumpkin pie spice in a mixer bowl. Blend in eggs, oil, pumpkin, nuts and/or raisins.

3. Pour batter into pan. Bake for 25 to 30 minutes or until a tester inserted in center comes out clean. Cool in pan.

4. To make frosting: Combine cream cheese, butter, vanilla, milk, and confectioners' sugar in a mixer bowl. Beat until smooth. Spread frosting over cake. Sprinkle with chopped nuts. Cut into bars. Makes 3 dozen.

❖ **JEANNE KUTROW** | Christ Episcopal Church, Charlotte, North Carolina

Martha Washington Candy

2 boxes (1 lb. each) confectioners' sugar
2 cups chopped nuts
1 can (14 oz.) sweetened condensed milk
2 packages (14 oz. each) flaked coconut

½ cup butter
1 package (12 oz.) chocolate chips
½ lb. paraffin

1. Combine confectioners' sugar, nuts, sweetened condensed milk, coconut, and butter in a mixer bowl. Mix until well combined.

2. Roll mixture into walnut-size balls. Chill.

3. Melt chocolate chips and paraffin in the top half of a double boiler. Drop candies into chocolate sauce to coat. Remove with tongs and set on waxed paper. Cool to room temperature. Store in a covered container in the refrigerator. Makes 6 dozen.

❖ **MELBA KITCHENS** | Terrace Acres Baptist Church, Fort Worth, Texas

Sand Tarts

1 cup butter
1½ cups sugar
2 eggs
3 cups flour
1 teaspoon baking powder
1 teaspoon vanilla
Pecan halves

CINNAMON SUGAR:

1 tablespoon sugar
1 teaspoon cinnamon

1. Combine butter, sugar, eggs, flour, baking powder, and vanilla in a mixer bowl. Beat until well blended. Cover and refrigerate overnight.

2. To make cinnamon sugar: Stir sugar and cinnamon together until well blended.

3. Roll out dough to a ⅛-inch thickness. Cut into rounds with a cookie cutter and place on ungreased baking sheets. Top each cookie with a pecan half and sprinkle with cinnamon sugar.

4. Bake at 375°F for 8 to 10 minutes or until lightly browned. Cool on wire racks. Makes 4 dozen.

JOANN GARRAUX | Unity Baptist Church, Morgantown, Indiana

Mocha Fudge

1 package (12 oz.) semisweet chocolate chips
1 cup milk chocolate chips
2 tablespoons milk
1 can (14 oz.) sweetened condensed milk

4 teaspoons instant coffee dissolved in
1 tablespoon warm water
1 teaspoon vanilla
1 cup chopped nuts

1. Line an 8 x 8 x 2-inch baking pan with aluminum foil.

2. Combine semisweet chocolate chips, milk chocolate chips, milk, sweetened condensed milk, coffee mixture, and vanilla in a heavy saucepan over low heat. Cook, stirring occasionally, until chocolate is melted. Remove from heat. Stir in nuts.

3. Spread mixture evenly in pan. Chill until firm, 3 hours.

4. Turn out fudge onto a cutting board. Peel off foil. Cut into squares. Store in a covered container in the refrigerator. Makes about 2 lbs.

LINDA S. THOMPSON | Oakwood Church of God in Christ, Godfrey, Illinois

Orange Fudge

2 cups sugar
¼ teaspoon cream of tartar
2 tablespoons grated orange zest
2 tablespoons orange juice
½ cup evaporated milk

¼ cup water
1 teaspoon lemon juice
1 cup chopped pecans
1 tablespoon butter

1. Grease an 8 x 8 x 2-inch baking pan.

2. Mix sugar and cream of tartar in a large saucepan. Add orange zest and orange juice and mix well. Stir in evaporated milk and water. Cook over medium-low heat to the soft ball stage (234°F to 240°F on a candy thermometer).

3. Add lemon juice, pecans, and butter. Beat until creamy.

4. Transfer mixture to pan and spread evenly. Refrigerate 2 hours or until firm. Cut into squares. Store in a covered container in the refrigerator. Makes 4 dozen.

❖ **KAY CARGILE** | Memorial Baptist Church, Tulsa, Oklahoma

No-Cook Fudge

1 box (1 lb.) confectioners' sugar
¼ cup cocoa
1 cup butter, melted

¼ cup peanut butter
1 teaspoon vanilla

1. Butter an 8 x 8 x 2-inch baking pan.

2. Sift confectioners' sugar and cocoa into a large bowl.

3. Add melted butter, peanut butter, and vanilla. Mix until well blended.

4. Spread mixture in pan. Chill until set, 3 to 4 hours. Cut into small squares. Store in a covered container in the refrigerator. Makes 4 dozen.

❖ **DAWN SECHRIST** | Messiah United Methodist Church, York, Pennsylvania

Divinity

2 cups sugar
½ cup water
½ cup light corn syrup

2 egg whites
½ teaspoon vanilla
½ cup chopped nuts

1. Combine sugar, water, and corn syrup in a heavy saucepan over medium-high heat. Cook until sugar is dissolved (248°F on a candy thermometer).

2. Beat egg whites until stiff. Pour hot syrup in a long, thin thread onto egg whites. Beat until very stiff. Stir in vanilla and nuts.

3. Drop by teaspoonful onto waxed paper or a buttered pan. Cool to room temperature. Store in a covered container. Makes about 24 candies.

MRS. FRED SAGER | St. John's Guild, St. John's Church, West Bend, Wisconsin

Million Dollar Fudge

4½ cups sugar

1 can (12 oz.) evaporated milk

1 teaspoon vanilla

½ cup butter

1 package (10 oz.) marshmallows

1 package (12 oz.) chocolate chips

1½ cups chopped nuts

1. Lightly butter an 8 x 8 x 2-inch baking pan.

2. Combine sugar and evaporated milk in a large saucepan over medium-high heat. Bring to a boil and cook for 8 minutes.

3. Remove from heat. Add vanilla, butter, marshmallows, chocolate chips, and nuts. Mix until well combined.

4. Spread mixture evenly in pan. Refrigerate overnight. Cut into squares. Store in refrigerator. Makes 4 dozen.

NANCY MONTGOMERY | Trinity Presbyterian Church, Little Rock, Arkansas

Peanut Patties

2 cups sugar

½ cup water

½ cup light corn syrup

2 cups roasted peanuts

2 tablespoons butter

½ teaspoon baking soda

Red food coloring

1 teaspoon vanilla

1. Combine sugar, water, and corn syrup in saucepan over medium heat. Cook without stirring until mixture boils. Continue cooking until mixture will spin a short thread (230°F to 234°F on a candy thermometer). Remove from heat.

2. Add peanuts, butter, baking soda, a few drops of red food coloring, and vanilla. Beat until creamy.

3. Drop quickly by tablespoonful onto waxed paper or a lightly greased baking sheet. Cool. Store in a covered container. Makes 3 dozen.

AUNT IRENE GRAVES | Women's Missionary Auxiliary, Bay Springs, Mississippi

Peanut Butter Fudge

1 lb. white almond bark, melted
1 cup creamy peanut butter
½ cup milk chocolate chips, melted

1. Butter an 8 x 8 x 2-inch pan.
2. Combine melted almond bark and peanut butter. Stir until smooth.
3. Spread mixture into pan. Pour melted chocolate chips over mixture. Swirl through both layers with a knife to make a marbled pattern. Chill until firm, 3 to 4 hours. Cut into squares. Makes about 4 dozen.

❖ **JOY STEWART** | Memorial Baptist Church, Tulsa, Oklahoma

Peanut Butter Cups

1 cup butter, melted
1 cup crunchy peanut butter
1 box (1 lb.) confectioners' sugar

1½ cups graham cracker crumbs
1 package (6 oz.) chocolate chips, melted

1. Combine melted butter, peanut butter, confectioners' sugar, and graham cracker crumbs. Press mixture into a 13 x 9 x 2-inch baking pan.
2. Spread melted chocolate chips on top. Cool. Cut into small squares. Makes about 7 dozen.

❖ **WOMEN'S MISSIONARY AUXILIARY** | Bay Springs, Mississippi

Microwave Toffee

¾ cup finely chopped pecans, divided
½ cup butter
1 cup sugar

1 teaspoon salt
¼ cup water
¾ cup semisweet chocolate chips

1. Sprinkle ½ cup of the pecans in a 9-inch circle on a greased baking sheet.
2. Coat the top 2 inches of a 2½-quart glass bowl with butter. Place remaining butter in bowl. Add sugar, salt, and water but do not stir. Microwave just until mixture begins to turn light brown, 8 to 11 minutes on high.
3. Pour mixture over pecans. Let stand 1 minute. Sprinkle with chocolate chips and remaining ¼ cup pecans. Chill until firm, 3 to 4 hours. Break into bite-size pieces. Makes 1 lb.

❖ **DOT MILLS** | Vincent Memorial United Methodist Church, Nutter Fort, West Virginia

Kids' Favorites

ANNUAL VALENTINE
DINNER AND DANCE

For the last ten years, the youth of Crescent Hill Presbyterian Church in Louisville, Kentucky, have made Valentine's Day a special treat for church members and friends. The annual Valentine dinner and dance is held in the church fellowship hall, which is specially decorated for the occasion (think "middle school prom"). One of the adult members of the youth team, chef Elias Sahiouny, assembles a "dream team" of cooks to prepare the meal. Being a Lebanese American, he often chooses a menu with a Middle Eastern flair. The young people wear their dressiest clothes to greet the guests, serve the meal, and spin the tunes for the after-dinner dance.

Crescent Hill church members share a commitment to inclusiveness, so this is not a traditional "couples" event. Everyone, in couples or alone, straight and gay, is encouraged to attend. The meal is served around large tables so that everyone enjoys good company as they eat. The dance is very much an intergenerational affair. You will see mothers and sons dancing together, and teenage girls line up to dance with the physician who is an accomplished ballroom dancer.

The event also serves as a fund-raiser for youth activities, usually raising $1,000 to support summer mission trips.

CRESCENT HILL PRESBYTERIAN CHURCH
Louisville, Kentucky

Crowd Pleaser

1 cup butter
2½ teaspoons garlic salt
3 tablespoons Worcestershire sauce
5 cups honeycomb cereal
5 cups crunchy corn cereal
    (such as Corn Chex)

1 cup melba rounds
1 cup cashews
5 cups mini cheese crackers
2 cups tiny pretzels
1 cup peanuts

1. Preheat oven to 250°F. Place butter in a roasting pan and set pan in oven just until butter is melted, 1 to 2 minutes.

2. Remove pan from oven. Stir garlic salt and Worcestershire sauce into melted butter. Add honeycomb cereal, Chex, melba rounds, cashews, cheese crackers, pretzels, and peanuts. Stir until well combined.

3. Return pan to oven and bake for 1 hour, stirring every 15 minutes to prevent mixture at edges of pan from overbrowning. Transfer to a large bowl and allow to cool. Store in airtight containers at room temperature or in resealable bags in the freezer. Makes 20 cups.

❖ **NAN ALLISON** | Christ Episcopal Church, Charlotte, North Carolina

Fruit Pizza

½ cup butter
1½ cups sugar, divided
1 teaspoon baking soda
1 teaspoon cream of tartar
½ teaspoon oil
1 egg
2 teaspoons vanilla, divided
¼ teaspoon salt
2½ cups flour

1 package (8 oz.) cream cheese,
    room temperature
1 can (20 oz.) crushed pineapple,
    drained, juice reserved
Assorted fresh fruits, such as bananas,
    kiwifruit, grapes, strawberries, cherries,
    and raspberries, sliced
1 to 2 tablespoons cornstarch

1. Preheat oven to 350°F.

2. Combine butter, 1 cup of the sugar, baking soda, cream of tartar, oil, egg, 1 teaspoon of the vanilla, salt, and flour in a mixer bowl. Mix until well blended.

3. Pat dough into bottom and up sides of a rimmed baking sheet. Bake for 10 minutes. Cool completely.

4. Beat cream cheese, remaining teaspoon vanilla, and remaining ½ cup sugar in a mixer bowl until fluffy. Fold in pineapple. Spread mixture on crust.

5. Arrange fresh fruits on top of cheese mixture.

6. Combine reserved pineapple juice and cornstarch in a saucepan over medium heat. Cook, stirring continuously, until thickened. Cool slightly. Drizzle over fruit. Chill until ready to serve. Cut into squares. Makes 24 servings.

❖ **LINDA HOGUE** | Vincent Memorial United Methodist Church, Nutter Fort, West Virginia

Party Pizza Appetizers

1 lb. hot sausage, cooked, drained,
   and crumbled
1 cup chopped onion
½ cup grated sharp cheese
½ cup grated Parmesan

1½ teaspoons oregano
1 teaspoon garlic salt
1 can (8 oz.) tomato sauce
1 can (6 oz.) tomato paste
3 tubes (16.3 oz. each) refrigerated flaky biscuits

1. Combine sausage, onion, cheese, Parmesan, oregano, garlic, salt, tomato sauce, and tomato paste in a large bowl.
2. Separate each biscuit into three rounds. Place rounds on baking sheets and flatten slightly. Spoon tomato mixture onto each round and spread almost to edges.
3. Place baking sheets in freezer. Freeze just until dough and sauce turn hard, 1 to 2 hours. Transfer pizzas to resealable freezer storage bags. Bake frozen pizzas in a 425°F oven for 10 minutes. Makes 90 servings.

❖ GRACE ON THE HILL UNITED METHODIST CHURCH | Corbin, Kentucky

Hot Dog Bites

20 saltine crackers
2 hot dogs
3 tablespoons mustard

3 tablespoons ketchup
3 tablespoons pickle relish
5 slices American cheese, quartered

1. Preheat oven to 350°F. Lightly grease a baking sheet and place crackers on it in a single layer.
2. Cut each hot dog into ten pieces.
3. Combine mustard, ketchup, and pickle relish in a small bowl to make a sauce.
4. Add some cheese, a piece of hot dog, and some sauce to each cracker. Bake for 10 minutes. Makes 20 appetizers.

❖ WINIFRED KUNKEL | Church of the Canyons Women's Ministries, Canyon Country, California

Caramel Popcorn

6 quarts air-popped popcorn
   (do not add butter or oil)
1 cup salted cocktail peanuts
1 cup butter
2 cups brown sugar

½ cup corn syrup
1 teaspoon salt
½ teaspoon baking soda
1 teaspoon vanilla

1. Preheat oven to 250°F. Put popcorn and peanuts in a roasting pan.

2. Combine butter, brown sugar, corn syrup, and salt in a medium saucepan over medium-high heat. Bring mixture to a boil and continue boiling for 5 minutes, stirring constantly. Remove from heat and immediately stir in baking soda and vanilla (syrup will bubble).

3. Pour syrup over popcorn and peanuts and mix to combine. Bake, uncovered, for 1 hour, stirring every 15 minutes. Transfer caramel corn mixture to waxed paper and allow to cool. Makes 6¼ quarts.

GINNY HAWKINS | Trinity Evangelical Lutheran Church, Lansdale, Pennsylvania

Butter Pecan Popcorn

Nonstick cooking spray
½ cup popcorn kernels
½ cup chopped pecans
2 tablespoons butter

⅓ cup light corn syrup
¼ cup instant butter pecan pudding mix
¾ teaspoon vanilla

1. Preheat oven to 300°F. Apply nonstick cooking spray to a 17 x 12 x 2-inch roasting pan.

2. Pop the popcorn and discard any unpopped kernels. Place popcorn and pecans in roasting pan. Set pan in oven to keep warm.

3. Melt butter in a small saucepan over medium heat. Remove from heat and stir in corn syrup, pudding mix, and vanilla.

4. Remove pan from oven. Pour syrup over popcorn and toss gently with a large spoon to coat. Makes 8½ cups.

LINDA S. THOMPSON | Oakwood Church of God in Christ, Godfrey, Illinois

Herbed Pretzels

1 box (13.5 oz.) unsalted hard pretzels,
    broken into bite-size pieces
½ cup butter-flavored popcorn oil or
    garlic-flavored olive oil

½ teaspoon dill weed
¼ to ½ teaspoon lemon pepper
½ teaspoon garlic powder
1 envelope (1 oz.) dry ranch dressing mix

1. Preheat oven to 250°F.

2. Combine pretzels, popcorn or olive oil, dill weed, lemon pepper, garlic powder, and ranch dressing mix in a large bowl.

3. Transfer mixture to a large roasting pan. Bake, uncovered, for 25 minutes, stirring several times to prevent overbrowning near the edges of the pan. Allow to cool. Store in a covered container at room temperature. Makes 16 oz.

LIZ NICHOLAS | Trinity Evangelical Lutheran Church, Lansdale, Pennsylvania

Hush Puppies

8 cups oil for frying
3 cups cornmeal
2 teaspoons baking powder
1½ teaspoons salt
1½ cups milk

½ cup water
1 egg, beaten
1 small onion, minced
2 or 3 garlic cloves, minced

1. Pour oil 2 to 3 inches deep into a deep fryer and heat to 365°F.

2. Combine cornmeal, baking powder, salt, milk, water, egg, onion, and garlic in a large mixing bowl. Shape the batter into small balls, using about 1 tablespoon for each.

3. Gently slide the balls into the hot oil with a long-handled spoon. Cook in batches, 8 to 10 at a time, until they are nicely browned, 6 to 8 minutes. Remove with a slotted spoon and roll on paper towels to drain. Serve hot. Makes 2 dozen.

KATHY HOAGLAND | Terrace Acres Baptist Church, Fort Worth, Texas

Quesadillas

1½ cups (6 oz.) shredded Monterey Jack
¾ cup (3 oz.) shredded sharp
   cheddar cheese
4 Flour Tortillas (recipe follows)

1 can (4 oz.) whole green chilies, drained,
   cut in half, and seeds removed
3 tablespoons sliced green onions with tops
2 small tomatoes, chopped

1. Combine Monterey Jack and cheddar cheese. Place ½ cup of cheese on each tortilla. Top with a piece of chilie. Fold in half. Secure with wooden toothpicks.

2. Cook quesadillas on an ungreased griddle over medium heat until cheese melts. Remove toothpicks. Top with onions and tomatoes. Makes 4 servings.

FLOUR TORTILLAS

1¼ cups flour
½ teaspoon salt

3 tablespoons vegetable shortening
⅓ cup lukewarm water

1. Mix flour and salt. Cut in shortening until particles are fine. Gradually stir in water with a fork until dough begins to come together.

2. Turn out dough onto a lightly floured surface. Knead about 50 times. Divide dough into four parts. Roll each piece into a ball. Cover with damp cloth. Let rest 15 minutes.

3. Roll each ball into an 8-inch circle. Cook, turning once, on an ungreased griddle or in a skillet over moderate heat until browned, 4 to 6 minutes. Cool. Makes 4 tortillas.

JUDY TONSETH | Methow Valley United Methodist Church, Twisp, Washington

Zesty Submarine

1 loaf French bread

Butter, room temperature

1 tablespoon vinegar

1 tablespoon olive oil

¼ teaspoon garlic salt

4 or 5 crisp lettuce leaves

½ lb. sliced salami or bologna

1 large tomato, sliced

Salt and pepper

½ lb. sliced American or Swiss cheese

½ lb. sliced ham

6 to 10 pickle slices

½ cucumber, thinly sliced

1 large onion, diced

1 green pepper, cut into rings

1 yellow pepper, cut into rings

1 hot pepper, cut into rings

1 can (2.25 oz.) sliced black olives

1. Slice bread horizontally in half with a large serrated knife. Spread bottom half with butter.

2. Stir together vinegar, olive oil, and garlic salt. Dip lettuce leaves into mixture. Layer lettuce, salami, and tomato on buttered half of bread. Sprinkle with salt and pepper.

3. Layer cheese, ham, pickles, cucumbers, onions, pepper rings, hot pepper rings, and black olives over tomatoes. Place top half of bread to complete sandwich and secure with toothpicks. Cut crosswise on the diagonal into wedges. Makes 6 servings.

RUBY L. CARR | Miracle Deliverance Holiness Church, Columbia, South Carolina

Youth Gathering Supper

⌘ SUGGESTED MENU ⌘

Sloppy Joes from Mom on No-Knead Never-Fail Bread
PAGE 370 AND PAGE 377

Baked Beans from Mom
PAGE 374

Seven-Layer Salad
PAGE 372

Baked German Potato Salad
PAGE 96

Tandy Cake Dessert
PAGE 382

Iced Tea
PAGE 389

Fruit Punch and Lemonade

TRINITY EVANGELICAL LUTHERAN CHURCH
Lansdale, Pennsylvania

Corn Dogs

1 cup cornmeal

1 cup flour

2 tablespoons sugar

2 teaspoons baking powder

½ teaspoon salt

1 egg, lightly beaten

1 cup milk

2 tablespoons vegetable shortening, melted

1 package (16 oz.) wieners

1. Heat oil in a deep fryer or a deep saucepan to 365°F.

2. Combine cornmeal, flour, sugar, baking powder, and salt in a medium bowl. Add egg and milk and blend well. Stir in melted shortening.

3. Dip wieners in batter and fry in deep fat. Remove with slotted spoon and drain on paper towels. Serve hot. Makes 8 corn dogs.

Cut the wieners in half to make miniature corn dogs. They're good for smaller fingers.

❖ **SOCIAL COMMITTEE** | Terrace Acres Baptist Church, Fort Worth, Texas

Sloppy Joes from Mom

1½ lbs. ground beef or turkey

1 medium onion, chopped

4 tablespoons brown sugar

3 tablespoon yellow mustard

3 tablespoons white vinegar

¾ cup ketchup

8 hamburger buns

1. Brown ground beef or turkey in a skillet over medium heat. Drain off fat.

2. Add onion and cook, stirring occasionally, until onion is limp and golden, 4 to 6 minutes.

3. Stir in brown sugar, mustard, vinegar, and ketchup. Cover and simmer until heated through, 20 minutes. Serve on hamburger buns. Makes 8 servings.

❖ **GRACE WALZ** | Trinity Evangelical Lutheran Church, Lansdale, Pennsylvania

Chicken Enchiladas

¼ cup butter

1 cup chopped onion

¼ cup flour

3 cups water

3 chicken bouillon cubes

1 cup sour cream or plain low-fat yogurt

3 cups cooked chicken, cut into dice

2 cups grated cheddar cheese, divided

1 can (4 oz.) chopped mild green chilies

1 jar (2 oz.) sliced pimientos

½ teaspoon chili powder

Ten 8-inch flour tortillas

1. Preheat oven to 350°F. Lightly grease a 13 x 9 x 2-inch baking dish.

2. Melt butter in a large skillet over medium heat. Add onions and sauté until soft but not browned, 4 to 6 minutes.

3. Add flour, water, and bouillon cubes to onions. Cook, stirring continuously, until bouillon cubes dissolve and mixture thickens. Remove from heat. Stir in sour cream or plain yogurt.

4. Combine 1 cup of the hot sour cream mixture, chicken, 1 cup of the cheese, chilies, pimiento, and chili powder in a large bowl. Stir until well blended.

5. Dip each tortilla in remaining sour cream mixture to soften. Spoon one-tenth of chicken mixture onto each tortilla, roll up, and place seam side down in baking dish. Spoon remaining sauce over enchiladas. Top with remaining cheese. Bake uncovered for 25 minutes. Makes 5 servings.

❖ **KAREN MATTISON** | Trinity Evangelical Lutheran Church, Lansdale, Pennsylvania

Pigs in Blanket

1 lb. round steak, pounded thin and
   cut into 4-inch squares
3 tablespoons minced onion

3 slices of bacon, cut into dice
Bacon drippings
Salt and pepper

1. Spoon some onion and bacon onto the center of each steak square. Sprinkle with salt and pepper. Roll up and secure with toothpicks or tie with butcher's string.

2. Heat bacon drippings in a skillet over medium heat until sizzling. Add meat bundles and cook, turning evenly, until browned on all sides.

3. Pour water into skillet to reach 1 inch up side of skillet. Reduce heat to a simmer. Cover and simmer for 1 hour. Serve hot, seasoned with salt and pepper. Makes 4 to 6 servings.

❖ **LYDIA SPIELMAN** | St. John's Guild, St. John's Church, West Bend, Wisconsin

Cheese Enchiladas

1 large onion, chopped
1 can (4 oz.) peeled green chilies, chopped
½ lb. grated cheddar cheese
½ lb. grated Monterey Jack

2 hard-boiled eggs, chopped
6 to 8 frozen corn tortillas, thawed
2 cans (10 oz. each) enchilada sauce

1. Preheat oven to 350°F. Grease a 13 x 9 x 2-inch baking dish.

2. Toss onion, chilies, cheddar cheese, Monterey Jack, and eggs until combined.

3. Pour half of enchilada sauce into a wide, shallow bowl. Warm in microwave. Dip a tortilla into sauce until softened. Place 2 to 3 tablespoons of the cheese mixture in center of tortilla. Roll up and place seam side down in baking dish. Repeat to soften, fill, and roll each tortilla.

4. Pour remaining sauce on top of enchiladas. Bake for 25 to 30 minutes or until cheeses melt. Serve hot. Makes 6 to 8 servings.

❖ **JEAN BARNETT** | Presbyterian Church of Gonzales, Gonzales, Texas

Quick Taco Bake

1 lb. ground beef

½ cup chopped onion

1 package (1 oz.) taco seasoning mix

1 can (15¼ oz.) corn

1 can (15 oz.) tomato sauce

2 cups shredded cheese

2 cups Bisquick baking mix

1 cup milk

2 large eggs

1. Preheat oven to 350°F.

2. Brown ground beef and onion in a large skillet over medium-high heat. Drain off fat. Stir in taco seasoning, corn, and tomato sauce. Spoon mixture into a 13 x 9 x 2-inch baking dish. Top with cheese.

3. Combine baking mix, milk, and egg. Pour over cheese. Bake for 35 minutes or until top is browned and cheese is melted. Serve hot. Makes 4 to 6 servings.

JOY SANDERS | Methow Valley United Methodist Church, Twisp, Washington

Seven-Layer Salad

1 head iceberg lettuce, torn into
   bite-size pieces

½ cup chopped green or red onion

1 cup mayonnaise, divided

½ cup chopped celery

1 package (10 oz.) frozen peas,
   thawed and drained

2 tablespoons sugar

2 cups shredded cheddar cheese

10 slices of bacon, cooked until crisp,
   drained, and crumbled

1 can (8 oz.) water chestnuts, drained and sliced

1. Layer lettuce and onion in a large bowl. Spoon ½ cup of the mayonnaise evenly over top.

2. Layer celery and peas. Spoon remaining mayonnaise on top.

3. Sprinkle sugar, cheese, and bacon over mayonnaise. Cover with plastic wrap and refrigerate at least 8 hours before serving. To serve, add water chestnuts and toss all ingredients until well combined. Makes 4 to 6 servings.

TERRY L. SCOTT | Trinity Evangelical Lutheran Church, Lansdale, Pennsylvania

VARIATIONS:
Layer in 1 cup of sliced carrots and 2 large sliced tomatoes for color.
Add sliced hard cooked eggs with bacon layer and use Swiss cheese instead of cheddar.
Use fresh spinach leaves instead of or in addition to iceberg lettuce.
Add 1/2 cup chopped green pepper for color and flavor.

Mexican Dip

1 lb. ground beef
½ cup chopped onion
1 garlic clove, mashed
½ teaspoon salt
1 can (8 oz.) tomato sauce
¼ cup ketchup

½ teaspoon dried oregano
1 teaspoon sugar
1 package (8 oz.) cream cheese
⅓ cup Parmesan
1 green chili pepper or 1 small jalapeño

1. Combine ground beef, onion, garlic, and salt in a large skillet over medium heat. Cook until beef is browned. Drain off fat.

2. Add tomato sauce, ketchup, oregano, sugar, cream cheese, Parmesan, and chili pepper or jalapeño. Stir to combine.

3. Transfer mixture to an electric slow cooker. Cook on high for 4 to 6 hours. Serve with chips, crackers, or bread. Makes 3½ cups.

GRACE ON THE HILL UNITED METHODIST CHURCH | Corbin, Kentucky

Chicken Tortilla Rolls

6 to 8 boneless skinless chicken thighs
⅓ cup olive oil
¼ cup lime juice
1 large garlic clove, peeled and minced
1 teaspoon oregano
¾ teaspoon ground cumin
½ teaspoon salt

¼ teaspoon chili powder
Dash of hot pepper sauce
6 to 8 small flour tortillas
Guacamole
Salsa
Sour cream

1. Place chicken in a glass or ceramic bowl. Whisk together oil, lime juice, garlic, oregano, cumin, salt, chili powder, and hot pepper sauce. Pour over chicken, turning chicken to coat evenly. Cover with plastic wrap and marinate overnight in refrigerator.

2. Grill or broil chicken until browned, 10 to 15 minutes.

3. Wrap tortillas in foil and place on grill or in a 325°F oven until warm.

4. Cut cooked chicken into strips. Place strips on warm tortillas and top with guacamole, salsa, and sour cream. Fold tortillas to enclose ingredients. Serve immediately. Makes 6 to 8 servings.

DEBRA O'STEEN | Oakwood Church of God in Christ, Godfrey, Illinois

Deluxe Macaroni and Cheese

2 cups small-curd cottage cheese
1 cup (8 oz.) sour cream
1 egg, lightly beaten
¾ teaspoon salt
Garlic salt

Pepper
2 cups grated sharp cheddar cheese
1 package (7 oz.) elbow macaroni,
    cooked and drained
Paprika

1. Preheat oven to 350°F. Grease 2½-quart casserole.
2. Combine cottage cheese, sour cream, egg, salt, garlic salt, and pepper in a large bowl. Add cheddar cheese and toss to combine. Stir in macaroni.
3. Transfer mixture to casserole. Bake uncovered for 25 to 30 minutes or until heated through. Sprinkle with paprika. Makes 8 to 10 servings.

TERRI SISSON | Unity Baptist Church, Morgantown, Indiana

Baked Beans from Mom

2 cups dried lima beans, soaked overnight
    and drained
½ cup ketchup
4 tablespoons brown sugar

1 teaspoon dry mustard
Salt and pepper
½ cup bean juice, reserved from cooking liquid
5 slices of bacon, cooked and drained

1. Place beans in a stockpot over medium-high heat. Bring to a boil. Reduce heat and simmer uncovered for 1 hour. Drain, reserving ½ cup of the cooking liquid.
2. Preheat oven to 350°F. Grease a 2-quart casserole.
3. Place beans in casserole. Combine ketchup, brown sugar, mustard, salt, pepper, and bean juice. Mix well and pour over beans. Top with bacon. Cover and bake for 1½ hours or until hot and bubbly. Makes 6 to 8 servings.

LISA SINN | Trinity Evangelical Lutheran Church, Lansdale, Pennsylvania

Party Yam Bake

1 can (40 oz.) yams, drained
1 can (8 oz.) crushed pineapple,
    drained, juice reserved
2 tablespoons light brown sugar

2 tablespoons butter, melted
3 tablespoons chopped pecans
¾ cup mini marshmallows

1. Preheat oven to 350°F. Coat a 1½-quart casserole with nonstick cooking spray.

2. Mash yams in a mixer bowl. Add pineapple juice, light brown sugar, and melted butter. Beat until well combined. Stir in pineapple and pecans.

3. Transfer mixture to casserole. Bake for 20 minutes. Add mini marshmallows on top and bake 10 minutes more. Let stand 10 minutes before serving. Makes 8 servings.

✤ **MARGARET DE MEO** | Methow Valley United Methodist Church, Twisp, Washington

Jeff's Snickerdoodles

2¾ cups flour
1 teaspoon baking soda
2 teaspoons cream of tartar
½ teaspoon salt

1 cup butter, room temperature
2 eggs
1½ cups plus 1 tablespoon sugar, divided
1 teaspoon cinnamon

1. Sift together flour, baking soda, cream of tartar, and salt.

2. Cream butter, eggs, and 1½ cups of the sugar in a mixer bowl. Add flour mixture and beat until well combined. Chill dough for 30 minutes.

3. Preheat oven to 375°F.

4. Stir cinnamon into remaining tablespoon sugar. Shape dough into 1-inch balls, roll in cinnamon sugar, and place 2 inches apart on an ungreased baking sheet. Bake for 8 to 10 minutes or until lightly browned but still soft. Cool on wire racks. Makes 5 dozen.

✤ **DIANE GROVE** | Church of the Canyons Women's Ministries, Canyon Country, California

Microwave Peanut Brittle

1 cup sugar
½ cup white corn syrup
1 cup roasted salted peanuts

1 teaspoon butter
1 teaspoon vanilla
1 teaspoon baking soda

1. Lightly grease a baking sheet.

2. Combine sugar and white corn syrup in a 1½-quart casserole. Microwave on high setting for 4 minutes.

3. Stir in peanuts. Microwave for 3 to 5 minutes until light brown.

4. Add butter and vanilla to mixture, blending well. Microwave on high 1 to 2 minutes more or until peanuts are lightly browned and mixture is very hot. Add baking soda and gently stir until light and foamy.

VARIATION: Instead of peanuts, use 2 cups of salted cashews.

5. Pour mixture onto a baking sheet. Allow to cool. Break into small pieces. Store at room temperature in an airtight container. Makes 1 lb.

✤ **DOROTHY R. MYERS** | Trinity Evangelical Lutheran Church, Lansdale, Pennsylvania

Chocolate Scotcharoos

½ cup sugar
1 cup light corn syrup
1 cup peanut butter

6 cups crispy rice cereal (such as Rice Krispies)
6 oz. chocolate chips, melted in microwave
6 oz. butterscotch chips, melted in microwave

1. Lightly grease a 13 x 9 x 2-inch baking pan.
2. Combine sugar and corn syrup in a 3-quart saucepan over moderate heat. Bring to a boil. Remove from heat. Stir in peanut butter and crispy rice cereal.
3. Press mixture into pan. Let stand until cool. Drizzle with melted chocolate and melted butterscotch. Let cool. Cut into squares. Refrigerate for 1 hour before serving. Makes 12 servings.

MARIAN BOLL | Church of the Canyons Women's Ministries, Canyon Country, California

Caramel Dip with Apples

1 package (8 oz.) cream cheese,
    room temperature
¾ cup brown sugar

1 teaspoon vanilla
4 or 5 apples, cored and cut into wedges

Beat cream cheese, brown sugar, and vanilla in a mixer bowl until smooth and creamy. Transfer to a serving bowl or party dip set. Serve with apple wedges for dipping. Makes 8 servings.

JOY HEDGER | Unity Baptist Church, Morgantown, Indiana

Homemade Doughnuts

Cooking oil
1 tube (7.5 oz.) refrigerated biscuits

CINNAMON SUGAR:
2 tablespoons sugar
1 teaspoon cinnamon

GLAZE:
2 tablespoons confectioners' sugar
1 teaspoon milk
Almond extract

> Fry the doughnut holes, too. The kids will think you are so smart!

1. Pour cooking oil into a skillet to a ½-inch depth. Heat until sizzling.

2. Flatten each piece of biscuit dough to ½ inch. Use a knife or a small biscuit cutter to cut a hole out of the middle.

3. Place doughnuts in hot oil and fry, turning once, until puffed up and golden brown, 4 to 6 minutes. Drain on paper towels.

4. To make glaze: Stir together confectioners' sugar, milk, and a drop or two of almond extract. Drizzle over half of hot doughnuts.

5. To make cinnamon sugar: Stir together sugar and cinnamon. Sprinkle over remaining doughnuts.

6. Serve warm or at room temperature. Makes 12 servings.

❖ **SARAH MIGEOT** | Trinity Presbyterian Church, Little Rock, Arkansas

No-Knead Never-Fail Bread

2 cups flour
2⅓ cups whole wheat flour
1¾ cups warm water (105°F to 115°F), divided
2 packages (.25 oz.) active dry yeast

2 tablespoons honey
⅓ cup vegetable oil
1½ teaspoons salt
⅓ cup wheat germ

1. Grease a 9 x 5 x 3-inch loaf pan.

2. Put flour and whole wheat flour in a bowl. Place in a warm oven (180°F) for 15 minutes.

3. Combine ¾ cup of the warm water in a large bowl. Stir in yeast and honey and let stand until foamy, about 10 minutes.

4. Add remaining cup warm water, oil, salt, and wheat germ to yeast mixture. Add flour 1 cup at a time, mixing well after each addition. Turn out onto a floured surface and shape into loaf. Place in pan and cover with lightly greased plastic wrap. Let rise until 1 inch over side of pan, 35 minutes.

5. Preheat oven to 400°F. Bake for 35 minutes or until top is golden brown and bread sounds hollow when tapped. Cool in pan 10 minutes before turning out onto a wire rack. Cool completely before slicing. Makes 1 loaf.

❖ **CAROL BALCH** | Trinity Evangelical Lutheran Church, Lansdale, Pennsylvania

Chocolate-Covered Granola Bars

4 cups rolled oats

½ cup sugar

1 cup brown sugar

1 cup butter, melted

1 cup chocolate chips

1 cup smooth peanut butter

1. Preheat oven to 350°F. Grease a 15 x 10-inch jelly roll pan.

2. Combine rolled oats, sugar, brown sugar, and melted butter. Mix until well blended. Press mixture evenly into pan. Bake for 12 minutes. Remove from oven and let stand for 3 to 5 minutes.

3. Melt chocolate chips and peanut butter in a small saucepan over low heat. Stir until thoroughly blended. Smooth mixture over oats while both are still very warm. Refrigerate until set, 2 to 4 hours. Cut into bars. Makes 20 servings.

❖ **PAT HELENBROOK** | Northbrook United Methodist Church, Roswell, Georgia

White Chocolate-Covered Popcorn

1 packet (3 oz.) microwave popcorn

4 oz. white almond bark, broken into pieces

> A little almond bark goes a long way in this recipe. Don't add too much.

1. Pop popcorn following package directions. Turn out into a large glass bowl.

2. Melt almond bark in a small bowl in the microwave. Pour melted bark over popcorn and toss to coat evenly. Turn out popcorn onto waxed paper to cool.

❖ **KERRY SEAVER** | Terrace Acres Baptist Church, Fort Worth, Texas

Cutest Mice in Town

Slivered almonds

16 Hershey's chocolate kisses, unwrapped

1 cup chocolate chips, melted in microwave

16 Maraschinos with long stems

Red decorating gel

1. Arrange slivered almonds in pairs on a piece of wax paper for the mice ears.

2. Dip the bottom of a Hershey's kiss in melted chocolate. Set the kiss onto a pair of almonds at the base and press gently to join all three pieces. The kiss is the mouse head.

3. Dip a long-stemmed cherry completely in melted chocolate. Place on waxed paper with stem up and attach it to the head. Let cool. The chocolate-covered cherry is the body and the stem is the tail.

4. Dot the eyes and nose (tip of the kiss) with red decorating gel. Makes 16 servings.

❖ **SARAH MIGEOT,** courtesy of **DEBBIE MURPHY** | Trinity Presbyterian Church, Little Rock, Arkansas

Chocolate Peanut Squares

1 cup butter, divided

6 squares (1 oz. each) semisweet chocolate, divided

1½ cups graham cracker crumbs

1 cup flaked coconut

½ cup chopped unsalted peanuts

2 packages (8 oz. each) cream cheese, room temperature

1 cup sugar

1 teaspoon vanilla

1. Melt ¾ cup of the butter and 2 squares of the chocolate in microwave, stirring every 30 seconds, 1 to 2 minutes on high.

2. Stir in graham cracker crumbs, coconut, and peanuts. Press mixture onto bottom of 13 x 9 x 2-inch baking pan. Chill for 30 minutes.

3. Combine cream cheese, sugar, and vanilla until well blended. Spread over crust. Chill 30 minutes.

4. Melt remaining ¼ cup butter and remaining 4 squares of chocolate in microwave. Spread over cream cheese layer. Chill 30 minutes. Cut into squares. Makes 4 dozen.

❖ **MARSHA FOX** | Memorial Baptist Church, Tulsa, Oklahoma

Coca-Cola Cake

1 cup butter, room temperature

2 cups flour

1¾ cups sugar

3 tablespoons cocoa

1 teaspoon salt

1 teaspoon baking soda

½ teaspoon vanilla

½ cup buttermilk

2 eggs

1 cup Coca-Cola

1½ cups mini marshmallows

ICING:

½ cup butter

⅓ cup Coca-Cola

3 tablespoons cocoa

4 cups confectioners' sugar

1 cup nuts

1. Preheat oven to 350°F. Grease and flour two 8 x 1½-inch round cake pans.

2. Combine butter, flour, sugar, cocoa, salt, baking soda, vanilla, buttermilk, eggs, Coca-Cola, and marshmallows in a mixer bowl. Beat until well combined.

3. Pour batter into pans. Bake for 40 to 45 minutes or until a tester inserted in center comes out clean. Cool in pans 10 minutes before turning out onto wire racks. Cool completely before icing.

4. To make icing: Cream butter, Coca-Cola, cocoa, and confectioners' sugar until smooth and of a spreading consistency. Stir in nuts.

5. Assemble cake layers, spreading icing as a filling and on sides and top of cake. Makes 6 to 8 servings.

❖ **INA RUBENKOENIG** | Terrace Acres Baptist Church, Fort Worth, Texas

Mama Goose's No-Peek Cookies

2 egg whites
⅔ cup sugar
Dash of salt

½ teaspoon vanilla
1 package (6 oz.) chocolate chips
1 cup chopped nuts

1. Preheat oven to 350°F. Line a baking sheet with aluminum foil.
2. Beat egg whites until stiff. Gradually beat in sugar, salt, and vanilla. Fold in chocolate chips and nuts.
3. Drop by teaspoonful on baking sheet. Put in oven, turn off heat, and leave undisturbed overnight. Do not peek! Makes 2 dozen.

❖ CAROLYN HOWELL | Memorial Baptist Church, Tulsa, Oklahoma

Shoo-Fly Cake

4 cups flour
2 cups brown sugar
1 cup butter

1 cup corn syrup
2 teaspoons baking soda
2 cups boiling water

1. Preheat oven to 350°F. Grease and flour two 8 x 1½-inch round cake pans.
2. Combine flour, brown sugar, and butter until crumbly. Set aside 1½ cups of crumb mixture for topping.
3. Combine remaining crumb mixture, syrup, baking soda, and boiling water in a large bowl. Mix well to make a thin batter.
4. Pour batter into pans. Top with reserved crumb mixture. Bake for 45 to 60 minutes or until browned. Cool in pan on a wire rack. Serve warm or at room temperature. Makes 12 to 16 servings.

❖ GINNY SHANK | Trinity Evangelical Lutheran Church, Lansdale, Pennsylvania

Chocolate Chip Bars

½ cup butter
2 cups sugar
4 eggs
3 cups Bisquick baking mix

6 oz. chocolate chips
½ cup chopped nuts
½ teaspoon vanilla

1. Preheat oven to 350°F. Grease a 13 x 9 x 2-inch baking pan.
2. Cream butter and sugar in a mixer bowl. Beat in eggs and baking mix until well blended. Stir in chocolate chips, nuts, and vanilla.
3. Spread batter in pan. Bake for 45 minutes or until lightly browned. Cut into bars while still warm. Makes 12 or 16 servings.

❖ DEBRA STALEY | Church of the Canyons Women's Ministries, Canyon Country, California

Chocolate Waffles from Mother

½ cup shortening

1 cup sugar

2 squares (1 oz. each) unsweetened
    chocolate, melted

2 eggs

½ teaspoon salt

1¼ cups flour

½ teaspoon cinnamon

Vanilla ice cream

1. Preheat waffle iron following manufacturer's instructions.

2. Cream shortening and sugar in a mixer bowl. Add chocolate, eggs, salt, flour, and cinnamon. Beat until smooth.

3. Place 2 heaping tablespoons of batter on iron, close cover, and bake until done. Serve hot with vanilla ice cream. Makes 4 to 6 servings.

❖ **GRACE FARRELL** | Trinity Evangelical Lutheran Church, Lansdale, Pennsylvania

VARIATION:
Instead of melting unsweetened chocolate, stir 6 tablespoons unsweetened cocoa into 2 tablespoons melted butter.

Snickers Cake

1 box (18.25 oz.) German chocolate cake mix

Water, oil, and eggs to prepare cake mix

1 package (14 oz.) caramels, unwrapped

½ cup butter

⅓ cup milk

¾ cup chocolate chips

1 cup chopped nuts

1. Preheat oven to 350°F. Grease a 13 x 9 x 2-inch baking pan.

2. Prepare cake mix following package directions.

3. Refrigerate half of the batter. Pour remaining batter into pan. Bake for 20 minutes. Remove pan from oven. Reduce oven temperature to 250°F.

4. Combine caramels, butter, and milk in the top half of a double boiler over medium heat. Cook, stirring occasionally, until caramels are melted.

5. Pour caramel sauce over hot cake and spread evenly. Top with chocolate chips and nuts. Spoon remaining batter over top. Return pan to oven (250°F) and bake for 20 minutes. Increase temperature to 350°F (without removing cake from oven) and bake 10 minutes more. Cool in pan on wire racks to room temperature, about 2 hours. Cut into squares. Refrigerate until ready to serve. Makes 4 dozen.

❖ **JAN DESALVO** | Northbrook United Methodist Church, Roswell, Georgia

Chocoroon Pie

3 squares (1 oz. each) unsweetened chocolate
½ cup butter
3 eggs, lightly beaten
¾ cup sugar

½ cup flour
1 teaspoon vanilla
⅔ cup sweetened condensed milk
2¾ cups flaked coconut

1. Preheat oven to 350°F. Grease a 9-inch pie plate.

2. Melt chocolate and butter in large saucepan over low heat. Remove from heat. Stir in eggs, sugar, flour, and vanilla. Pour into pie plate.

3. Combine sweetened condensed milk and coconut. Spoon over chocolate filling, leaving a ½- to 1-inch border of chocolate showing. Bake for 30 minutes. Cool on a wire rack. Chill for 4 hours before serving. Makes 6 to 8 servings.

❖ **ELYDA KESSLER** | Trinity Evangelical Lutheran Church, Lansdale, Pennsylvania

Mystery Bars

2 eggs
1 box (1 lb.) dark brown sugar
1½ cups flour
2 teaspoons baking powder
Dash of salt

1 teaspoon vanilla
1 cup butter, melted
1 cup chopped pecans
Confectioners' sugar

1. Preheat oven to 325°F. Grease a 13 x 9 x 2-inch baking pan.

2. Beat eggs until frothy. Add brown sugar and beat until well combined.

3. Sift together flour, baking powder, and salt. Add to egg mixture and blend to combine. Blend in melted butter and vanilla. Stir in pecans.

4. Pour mixture into pan. Bake for 45 minutes. Cool in pan and cut into bars. Roll bars in confectioners' sugar. Makes 12 or 16 servings.

❖ **ZAIDEE CLARK** | Northbrook United Methodist Church, Roswell, Georgia

Tandy Cake Dessert

4 eggs
1 cup milk
2 cups sugar
½ teaspoon salt

2 teaspoons baking powder
2 cups flour
1 cup peanut butter
1 package (12 oz.) chocolate chips

1. Preheat oven to 350°F. Grease a 15 x 10-inch jelly roll pan.

2. Whisk together eggs, milk, sugar, and salt. Whisk in baking powder and flour.

3. Spread mixture in pan. Bake for 20 minutes. Remove from oven, spread peanut butter over top, and let cool.

4. Melt chocolate chips in microwave. Spread melted chocolate over peanut butter. Refrigerate until set. Cut into squares. Makes 35 servings.

❖ **HOLLY A. COE** | Trinity Evangelical Lutheran Church, Lansdale, Pennsylvania

Popcorn Candy Cake

1 package (16 oz.) mini marshmallows

¾ cup vegetable oil

½ cup butter

5 quarts popped popcorn

1 package (24 oz.) spiced gumdrops

1 cup salted peanuts

1. Grease a 10 x 4-inch tube pan.

2. Combine marshmallows, oil, and butter in a large saucepan over medium heat. Cook, stirring continuously, until melted and smooth.

3. Combine popcorn, gumdrops, and peanuts in a large bowl. Add marshmallow mixture and toss until well combined. Press mixture into pan. Cover and refrigerate for 5 hours or overnight. Dip pan in hot water for 5 to 10 seconds to unmold. Slice with an electric knife or a serrated knife. Makes 16 servings.

VARIATION:
Instead of gumdrops, use M&M's candies.

❖ **REED STANBERY** | Methow Valley United Methodist Church, Twisp, Washington

Cracker Jacks (Caramel Corn)

2 cups brown sugar

1 cup butter

½ cup corn syrup

1 teaspoon salt

2 teaspoons vanilla

½ tablespoon baking soda

8 quarts popped corn

1 cup peanuts

1. Preheat oven to 225°F. Lightly grease several shallow pans.

2. Combine sugar, butter, corn syrup, and salt in a saucepan over medium-high heat. Bring to a boil and cook for 5 minutes. Stir in vanilla and baking soda.

3. Pour mixture over popcorn and peanuts. Toss to combine. Transfer to shallow pans and bake, stirring occasionally, for 30 to 40 minutes. Test after 30 minutes to see if coating hardens when cool. Delicious and fattening! Makes 8¼ quarts.

❖ **LOIS M. MCLEAN** | Methow Valley United Methodist Church, Twisp, Washington

Peanut Butter Balls

½ cup peanut butter
½ cup honey, corn syrup, or jelly
1 cup instant dry milk
1 cup ready-to-eat cereal
   (such as Grape-Nuts or Cheerios)
½ cup raisins

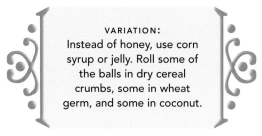

VARIATION:
Instead of honey, use corn syrup or jelly. Roll some of the balls in dry cereal crumbs, some in wheat germ, and some in coconut.

1. Combine peanut butter, honey, dry milk, cereal, and raisins in bowl. Mix until well blended. Roll into 1-inch balls. Store in a covered container in the refrigerator. Makes 2 dozen.

❖ **LAURA HESS** | Church of the Canyons Women's Ministries, Canyon Country, California

Peanut Butter Cup Cookies

1 cup sugar
1 cup creamy peanut butter
1 egg
1 package (12 oz.) Reese's miniature peanut butter cups

1. Preheat oven to 375°F.
2. Combine sugar, peanut butter, and egg until well blended.
3. Drop 1 tablespoon of mixture into each cup of a 24-cup mini muffin pan. Bake for 10 minutes.
4. Remove from oven. Push a peanut butter cup into the middle of each cookie. Place in refrigerator for a few minutes to harden the chocolate. Makes 24 servings.

❖ **SHARON ZIEGLER** | Church of the Canyons Women's Ministries, Canyon Country, California

Kiwifruit Popsicles

6 kiwifruit, peeled
1 can (8 oz.) crushed pineapple
½ cup water

⅓ cup sugar
¼ teaspoon grated ginger

1. Chop kiwifruit in a food processor or blender. Add pineapple, water, sugar, and ginger. Blend until smooth.
2. Pour mixture into popsicle molds. Freeze until firm, at least 6 hours or overnight. Makes 10 servings.

❖ **VERA BIEREND** | Church of the Canyons Women's Ministries, Canyon Country, California

Feeding the Little Ones

Many churches, like many families, have discovered that there are plenty of wholesome, easy-to-prepare foods that children find tasty and fun to eat.

Here are a few ideas:

Apple wedges and cubes of cheese
Fresh fruit juices and smoothies
Fresh fruit sections—banana, orange, pineapple, melon, peach, strawberry
Chopped raw vegetables and dip
Pretzels, popcorn, bread sticks, pita chips, whole wheat crackers
Mini rice cakes with peanut butter
Nuts and dried fruits, especially raisins
Cheerios, granola, or other cereals
Homemade muffins or corn bread
Fresh soybeans (edamame)
Frozen fruits bars with chunks of real fruit

PLEASE NOTE that snacks containing honey, nuts, or popcorn are not recommended for children under 2 years of age.

Gumdrop Cookies

½ cup butter
½ cup white sugar
½ cup brown sugar
1 egg
1 teaspoon vanilla
1 cup flour

½ teaspoon baking powder
½ teaspoon baking soda
¼ teaspoon salt
½ cup gumdrops, cut into small pieces
¾ cup rolled oats
½ cup flaked coconut or nuts

1. Preheat oven to 375°F. Lightly grease baking sheets.

2. Cream butter, sugar, and brown sugar in a mixer bowl. Beat in egg and vanilla. Whisk together flour, baking powder, baking soda, and salt. Add to dough and mix well. Stir in gumdrop pieces, oats, and coconut or nuts.

3. Drop dough by teaspoonful onto baking sheets. Bake for 8 to 10 minutes. Cool on wire racks. Makes 4 dozen.

CINDY SMOOT | Unity Baptist Church, Morgantown, Indiana

M&M's Candies Oatmeal Cookies

½ cup butter, melted
6 tablespoons light brown sugar
6 tablespoons sugar
¾ teaspoon vanilla
1 egg

¾ cup flour
½ teaspoon baking soda
¼ teaspoon salt
1 cup quick-cooking rolled oats
½ lb. M&M's candies

1. Preheat oven to 375°F.

2. Combine melted butter, light brown sugar, sugar, vanilla, and egg in the large bowl of an electric mixer. Mix until well blended.

3. Sift together flour, baking soda, and salt. Add to egg mixture and mix to combine. Gradually stir in rolled oats and M&M's candies.

4. Drop by tablespoonful onto baking sheet (5 or 6 candies per cookie). Bake for 8 to 12 minutes, until lightly browned. Makes 3 dozen.

❖ JANET BUCHANAN | First Moravian Church, Greensboro, North Carolina

Tutti-Frutti Smoothie

1 cup chopped strawberries
1 cup fresh blueberries
½ cup sliced bananas

1¼ cups pineapple
½ cup firm tofu
1 cup ice cubes

Combine strawberries, blueberries, bananas, and pineapple in a blender until smooth. Add tofu and ice cubes and liquefy. Serve immediately. Makes 6 servings.

❖ EDEN PURDY | Northbrook United Methodist Church, Roswell, Georgia

Banana Blueberry Yogurt Shake

1 container (8 oz.) strawberry-flavored yogurt
1 medium banana
½ cup frozen blueberries
1 cup milk

Combine yogurt, banana, blueberries, and milk in a blender until smooth. Serve immediately or refrigerate until ready to serve. Makes 1 serving.

❖ KAYANNE FORNEY | Trinity Evangelical Lutheran Church, Lansdale, Pennsylvania

Cranberry Floats

2 cups cranberry juice, chilled, divided
1 cup orange juice, chilled, divided
1 can (6 oz.) frozen lemonade concentrate,
    thawed, divided

2 cans (12 oz. each) ginger ale, chilled
1 pint vanilla ice cream

Combine cranberry juice, orange juice, and lemonade concentrate. Stir until concentrate is dissolved. Divide evenly among 6 tall glasses. Pour ginger ale in each glass and top with a scoop of vanilla ice cream. Makes 6 servings.

❖ **MELISSA HARRIS** | Trinity Evangelical Lutheran Church, Lansdale, Pennsylvania

Orange Sherbet Punch

2 bottles (1 liter each) lemon-lime
    soft drink (such as 7-Up), chilled
2 trays of ice cubes

1 can (6 oz.) frozen orange juice concentrate
½ gallon orange sherbet
Orange slices

1. Pour 1 bottle of soft drink into a large punch bowl. Add ice cubes.
2. Scoop in frozen orange juice concentrate. Stir until concentrate is mostly dissolved. Scoop in orange sherbet.
3. Pour remaining bottle of soft drink into punch bowl. Punch will foam. Float orange slices in the punch. Makes 64 servings.

❖ **ANDREA LEACH** | Trinity Evangelical Lutheran Church, Lansdale, Pennsylvania

Watermelonade Slush

2 cups seeded watermelon cubes
2 cups frozen strawberries
1 can (6 oz.) frozen lemonade or
    limeade concentrate

2 cups ice cubes (about 10 cubes)
4 to 6 fresh strawberries

Combine watermelon, frozen strawberries, and lemonade or limeade concentrate in a blender. Gradually add ice cubes, blending until smooth. Pour into serving glasses. Float a fresh strawberry in each glass. Makes 4 to 6 servings.

❖ **VANESSA DRAPER** | Oakwood Church of God in Christ, Godfrey, Illinois

Purple Cow

½ cup grape juice, chilled
Vanilla ice cream
Club soda, chilled

Pour grape juice in a large glass. Add 1 small scoop ice cream and mix gently with a long spoon. Add 2 more small scoops ice cream. Slowly pour in chilled club soda, swirling gently with spoon. Serve immediately. Makes 1 serving.

❖ **VANESSA DRAPER** | Oakwood Church of God in Christ, Godfrey, Illinois

Fruit Smoothie

1 cup low-fat vanilla-flavored yogurt
1 cup fresh peaches, sliced
1 ripe banana, sliced
¼ cup wheat germ plus more for topping

½ cup orange juice
1 cup ice cubes
Peach and banana slices for garnish

Combine yogurt, peaches, banana, wheat germ, orange juice, and ice cubes in a blender or food processor. Blend until smooth, about 1 minute. Pour into tall glasses. Garnish with reserved fruit and sprinkle with wheat germ. Makes 2 servings.

❖ **YVONNE M. HAYWOOD** | Oakwood Church of God in Christ, Godfrey, Illinois

Cantaloupe Cooler

1 cantaloupe, honeydew, or crenshaw
   melon, peeled, seeded, cut into
   large chunks, and chilled
½ cup ice water

¼ cup tightly packed mint leaves
8 ice cubes
2 tablespoons freshly squeezed lime juice
⅛ teaspoon fine sea salt

Combine melon, ice water, mint leaves, ice, lime juice, and salt in a blender. Process until smooth. Serve immediately as this cooler will separate upon standing. Makes 2 to 4 servings.

❖ **YVONNE M. HAYWOOD** | Oakwood Church of God in Christ, Godfrey, Illinois

Iced Tea

10 tea bags
1 cup sugar

Juice, rind, and pulp of 1 lemon
2 cups boiling water

1. Place tea bags, sugar, and lemon juice, rind, and pulp in a 4-cup Pyrex measuring cup. Add boiling water. Stir, holding on to tea bag strings, until sugar is dissolved. Let stand for 1 hour.
2. Remove tea bags. Pour tea through a strainer to remove lemon seeds, pulp, and rind. Pour into a 1-gallon beverage container. Add cold water and ice cubes to fill.

❖ **MARILYN WILLIAMS** | Trinity Evangelical Lutheran Church, Lansdale, Pennsylvania

Peanut Butter Bananarama Shake

1 very ripe banana, sliced
2 tablespoons peanut butter
1 cup milk

2 ice cubes
1 teaspoon honey

Combine banana, peanut butter, milk, ice cubes, and honey in a blender. Mix until smooth. Add more milk if too thick. Serve immediately before banana begins to darken. Makes 1 serving.

❖ **LOUISE DUNLAP** | First Presbyterian Church, Du Quoin, Illinois

Hot Chocolate Mix

3 cups dry milk powder
½ cup cocoa

1 cup sugar
Dash of salt

Combine milk powder, cocoa, sugar, and salt until well blended. Store at room temperature in an airtight container. For each serving, stir 3 heaping teaspoonfuls of mix into ½ cup hot water and stir to dissolve. Makes 40 to 50 servings.

❖ **PAT WALKER** | Women's Missionary Auxiliary, Bay Springs, Mississippi

Cooking for a Crowd

Whether you've agreed to bring a dish for 12 or 24 people to a potluck supper or are organizing volunteers to cook for a holiday event for 50 or more, one of these days you will probably have a need for large-quantity recipes. In *Church Socials*, you'll find plenty of recipes that can be supersized for a crowd, a party, or for a very large family.

SAFETY FIRST

Obviously the most important consideration when feeding a crowd is proper food safety measures. Cleanliness is paramount. When cooking large batches, it's important that the foods are cooked *thoroughly*. If you are transporting food, you must think ahead to keep hot foods hot and cold foods cold for the duration of the trip and during the serving period as well.

Electric slow cookers are perfect for keeping foods warm. Plan on borrowing an extra one for a large party. To keep foods cold, nestle the serving dish in a bowl or tray of ice. An ice chest can also come in handy.

TO DOUBLE OR NOT TO DOUBLE?

Most recipes can be successfully supersized (prepared in one batch) up to four times the serving amount of the original recipe. If you need more than four times the recipe amount, it is advisable to prepare the recipe in several batches.

Many recipes can be multiplied to feed larger crowds. However, not all ingredients need to be multiplied. Never double (or triple, etc.) the amount of salt and fat in a recipe. If fat is required to coat the pan, only use enough to cover the bottom of the pan. With salt, if you're doubling the recipe, only add 1.5 times the amount of salt originally called for and then season to taste. In general, always taste cooked foods for seasoning before adding salt and pepper.

Cooking times may not necessarily need to be multiplied by the same factor as the recipe ingredients. Some dishes may take less than double time and some may take even more, depending on the size of the dish. Use an instant-read thermometer to be sure foods are cooked thoroughly.

If you're cooking two or more items together in the oven, rotate and switch the pans halfway through the cooking time. No oven has a uniform temperature.

Be very careful when supersizing any baked goods. Generally, the amount of salt and leavening (baking powder, baking soda, etc.) is not doubled when the recipe is doubled. With larger pan sizes, less leavening is required to achieve the same rise. It is advisable to make the basic recipe several times rather than try to bake a supersized recipe. However, for those of you who really want to make larger baked goods, especially cakes, there is a good resource. Rose Levy Berenbaum's *The Cake Bible* has a chapter that has calculated the baker's percent for many items. She includes a specific chart for supersized butter cakes, cheesecakes, pound cakes, and icing.

If you're making lots of cookie dough at once, keep the dough that is not being baked in the refrigerator. If cookie dough becomes warm, the cookies will spread too much in the oven.

HOW TO FEED A CROWD

Here's some helpful information on the quantities of food needed for parties of various sizes.

FOOD ITEM	SERVING SIZE	FOR 12	FOR 24	FOR 48
Meat & shellfish, bone-in & unshelled	¾ lb.	9 lbs.	18 lbs.	36 lbs.
Meats & fish, boneless	¼ lb.	3 lbs.	6 lbs.	12 lbs.
Meat, cold cuts	2½ oz.	1 lb.	4 lbs.	8 lbs.
Cheese, sliced	1 oz.	¾ lb.	1½ lbs.	3 lbs.
Chicken salad	1 cup	3 qts.	½ gal.	3 gals.
Pasta salad	½ cup	1½ qts.	3 qts.	1½ gals.
Potato salad, baked beans, coleslaw	½ cup	1½ qts.	3 qts.	1½ gals.
Rolls	1 roll	1 doz.	2 doz.	4 doz.
Crackers	4	8 oz.	1 lb.	2 lbs.
Tossed salad	1½ cups	4½ qts.	9 qts.	4½ gals.
Salad dressing	2 tbsp.	1½ cups	3 cups	6 cups
Dip	2 tbsp.	1½ cups	3 cups	6 cups
Chips	1 oz.	12 oz.	1½ lbs.	3 lbs.
Fruit/vegetable dippers	4 pcs.	4 doz.	8 doz.	16 doz.
Cakes	1⁄16 cake	1 cake	2 cakes	3 cakes
Cookies	2	2 doz.	4 doz.	8 doz.
Ice cream	½ cup	1½ qts.	3 qts.	1½ gals.
Coffee, brewed	¾ cup	9 cups	18 cups	36 cups
Coffee, ground	-	1½ cups	3 cups	5 cups
Tea, brewed	¾ cup	9 cups	18 cups	36 cups
Tea, loose	-	¼ c.	½ c.	1 c.
Tea bags	-	12	24	48
Tea, iced	1 cup	3 qts.	1½ gals.	3 gals.
Punch	½ cup	1½ qts.	3 qts.	1½ gals.
Mineral water	8 oz.	3 qts.	6 qts.	12 qts.
Milk	1 cup	3 qts.	1½ gals.	3 gals.
Ice	¼ lb.	3 lbs.	6 lbs.	12 lbs.

Here are suggested guidelines for the amounts needed to feed a group of approximately 100 people. Remember, serving sizes vary depending on the type of crowd and meal served.

ENTRÉES

Beef roast: 50 lbs.
Chicken: 55 to 60 lbs.
Fish: 25 lbs.
Ground beef: 20 to 25 lbs.
Ham (with bone): 35 to 40 lbs.
Pork roast: 35 lbs.
Spare ribs: 75 lbs.
Stewing beef: 25 lbs.
Turkey: 75 to 100 lbs.
Spaghetti: 15 to 20 lbs.
Spaghetti sauce: 5 gallons
Hot dogs: 20 lbs.
Sandwich filling: 16 to 18 cups
Gravy: 1 to 2 gallons

SIDE DISHES

Baked beans: 12 lbs.
Potatoes (for mashed): 35 lbs.
Potatoes (for scalloped): 35 to 40 lbs.
Sweet potatoes: 25 lbs.
String beans: 20 to 25 lbs.
Squash: 50 lbs.
Carrots: 25 to 30 lbs.
Cranberry sauce: 6 lbs.

SALADS

Coleslaw: 24 lbs.
Lettuce: 12 to 15 heads
Tomatoes: 25 to 38 lbs.
Celery: 12 to 15 bunches
Canned fruit: 20 to 25 cans
Apples: 25 lbs.
Melon balls: 30 melons
Oranges: 4 dozen
Peaches: 37 lbs.
Strawberries: 20 quarts
Salad dressing: 2 quarts

BREAKFAST FOODS

Eggs: 20 to 22 dozen
Bacon: 20 to 25 lbs.
Sausage patties: 16 to 18 dozen
Biscuits: 12 dozen
Sausage gravy: 1 to 2 gallons
Pancakes: 30 to 32 dozen
Cereal: 30 to 35 small packets
Fruit juices: 4 to 5 gallons

STAPLES

Bread (sandwiches): 12 to 15 loaves
Bread with meal: 6 loaves
Rolls: 12 dozen
Butter: 3 lbs.
Potato chips: 5 lbs.
Pickles: 1 gallon
Olives: 1 gallon

BEVERAGES

Soda: 16 to 20 liters
Milk: 6 to 7 gallons
Juice concentrate: 18 6-oz. cans
Coffee: 2 lbs.
Cream: ½ gallon
Sugar: 1 pound

DESSERTS

Pie (9-inch): 12 to 15 pies
Cake (13 x 9-inch pan): 7 cakes
Cake (15 x 10-inch pan): 4 cakes
Ice cream: 4 to 5 gallons
Whipping cream: 2 quarts

Charts reprinted courtesy of Carol Stevens, Shaboom's Kitchen, http://www.shaboomskitchen.com

FOR FURTHER INFORMATION:

Cooking for Crowds: A Volunteer's Guide to Safe Food Handling, a publication of Penn State College of Agricultural Sciences, is available online or by mail order at www.cookingforcrowds.psu.edu

Cooking for a Crowd, A Food Safety Program for Quantity Cooks, is a workshop offered by the University of Maine Cooperative Extension. For information, call Louise Kirkland, 207-942-7396 or check http://www.umext.maine.edu/foodsafety/HTMdocuments/Cookforcrowd.htm

Index